Sustainable Work in Europe

Labour, Education & Society

Edited by György Széll,
Heinz Sünker, Anne Inga Hilsen
and Francesco Garibaldo

Volume 38

PL ACADEMIC RESEARCH

Kenneth Abrahamsson / Richard Ennals (eds.)

Sustainable Work in Europe

Concepts, Conditions, Challenges

PL ACADEMIC RESEARCH

Bibliographic Information published by the Deutsche Nationalbibliothek
The Deutsche Nationalbibliothek lists this publication in the Deutsche Nationalbibliografie; detailed bibliographic data is available in the internet at http://dnb.d-nb.de.

Library of Congress Cataloging-in-Publication Data
A CIP catalog record for this book has been applied for at the Library of Congress.

ISSN 1861-647X
ISBN 978-3-631-87350-2 (Print)
E-ISBN 978-3-631-86872-0 (E-Book)
E-ISBN 978-3-631-87621-3 (E-PUB)
DOI 10.3726/b19658

Peter Lang – Berlin · Bruxelles · Lausanne · New York · Oxford

This publication has been peer reviewed.

www.peterlang.com

Contents

Figures

Tables

Allan Larsson

Preface: What you will learn from reading this book

Never in modern times has Working Europe been faced with such a fundamental and far-reaching transition pressure. We are at the beginning of two powerful transition processes, innovation-driven digital transformation, and policy-driven climate transition. On top of these processes, we are now facing a pandemic-driven restructuring of important sectors of our economies and the way we are working.

That is what this book is about. I am proud to introduce this new thinking to you. It has been a privilege for me to work with a great team of academics and experts, to better understand these perspectives and the potential of new policies and initiatives. This book offers a new intellectual framework for thinking and planning for the future of work in Europe

It highlights research, current policies, and innovative ways to support more sustainable work in Europe. It places job-quality in a new context of labour market transformation, driven not only by international competition and full employment policies. It takes a deeper look at mechanisms of change, and driving forces caused by digitalisation, climate change and the erratic pandemic. It also looks at sustainable work in a life-course perspective, followed by senior employment. Successful sustainable work presupposes social protection, and gender-based welfare systems, including pension rights. Finally, policies for equality and equity over the life span are good both for the individual, and for society, and for the world of work.

By combining knowledge about the ongoing transformation processes and the policy process, represented by UN Sustainable Development Goals and the European Pillar of Social Rights, this book provides a joint arena for new thinking and planning for the future.

I hope this book will inspire you to take research and policies forward in new and innovative ways.

Richard Ennals

Foreword

Over recent years, European workplaces have been subject to a high level of turbulence and pressure, due to digitalisation and green transformation. The ongoing Covid pandemic has reshaped working conditions, and led to hybrid work for some groups, and increasing health stress for those who cannot work from home. Various strategies to meet the new challenges have been developed by countries, social partners, and companies. All countries in Europe, whether or not they are members of the European Union, are struggling with the new uncertainty, and with social and labour market challenges. The European Union has launched the major recovery programme "Next Generation EU". The policy dialogue on basic income at European level, and in various member countries, has been confronted by the Nordic model, highlighting collective agreements, and giving the social partners a major role. The European Road to Sustainable Work must build on two perspectives: healthy and productive working conditions over the life-course, and the policies and measures to achieve a low carbon and non-fossil-based society and working life.

The Nordic tradition of Working Life Research, underpinned by a set of core values which have been shared across political divides over several decades, provides an important alternative to the dominant model of liberal capitalism which has been favoured in the United States and the United Kingdom.

This book seeks to present this Swedish approach, together with developments in the European Union. Theory is linked to practice and to policy. Furthermore, this project is undertaken at a time of tumultuous change in technology, economics, and society. This book builds on a special double issue 6.1-2, March 2021, of the *European Journal of Workplace Innovation*, of which I am editor in chief. Most chapters have been revised for this book, and some completely new chapters have been added. As a result, the book offers a broader European perspective on Sustainable Work.

The Preface was contributed by Allan Larsson, who has had a distinguished career as Swedish Minister of Finance, Director-General of Employment and Social Affairs in the European Commission, and continues as personal adviser to several senior national and international figures; not to mention his efforts to facilitate and co-ordinate the major policy dialogue leading to the European Pillar of Social Rights.

The lead editor is Kenneth Abrahamsson, who is a veteran manager and funder of Swedish Working Life Research, and adjunct professor in Human Work Science, Luleå University of Technology. He has led the collaborative process which resulted in both the journal special double issue and this book.

Contributors include Lennart Levi, international doyen of Psychosocial Medicine, who served as a member of the Swedish Parliament for ten years. Swedish authors are from several disciplines and institutions. Their chapters are complemented by perspectives from the European Union, from Occupational Safety and Health (EU-OSHA and Perosh), and from the European Workplace Innovation Network (EUWIN).

I have taken the role of honorary co-editor, because I believe that it is very important to have a clear presentation of the future of Sustainable Work, as seen in Sweden and the European Union. At present the government in my own country, the UK, has preferred to follow different policies, following departure from the European Union. We can learn from the experience of colleagues in Sweden and other Nordic countries, as well as from the European Union. One day we may have the opportunity to put such alternative ideas into practice in the UK.

We gratefully acknowledge the invaluable support of many colleagues during the stages of the collaborative project which has resulted in this book, including Maria Albin, Elisabeth Lagerlöf and Chris Mathieu, who co-edited the earlier double special issue of the *European Journal of Workplace Innovation*, and Hans Christian Garmann Johnsen, Hildegunn Aslaksen and Clare Hildebrandt, members of the journal editorial team.

January 2022

I Sustainable work, job quality and equality

Kenneth Abrahamsson

Sustainable work in Europe: Introductory remarks

Much is changing. Globalisation, digitalisation, international competition, new demographic, and technological transformations are having fundamental impacts on working conditions, working hours and the location of work. The development towards work without boundaries, a platform economy and labour market polarisation have significant repercussions for employment relations, social protection, and the role of social partners. Temporary jobs and precarious working conditions are increasing in the service sector, while high-performance jobs are becoming more common in the advanced manufacturing sector. More knowledge is needed on how to accomplish secure and adaptable employment, health and safety at work, proper work life balance, a good social dialogue and effective participation of workers. New workplace innovations for job quality, productivity and growth are increasingly necessary on the road to future work. Equality, social protection, and improvement of living and working conditions are major visions, both in the ILO's 2019 centenary mission, and in the UN Sustainable Development Goals to be attained by 2030.

Scenarios and projections of the future of work is a policy field in its own. In 1995 the American futurist and policy thinker Jeremy Rifkin presented his book *The End of Work. The Decline of the Global Labour Force and the Dawn of the Post Market Era.* Rifkin's ideas and contributions have been subject to criticism and discussion over the years (Rifkin, 1995). It has also strengthened scientific interest in the concepts of jobless growth and technological disruptions. Over the years, employment rates and the number of full-time employees has shifted. Back in the mid-1990s there were deep concerns over growth and employment. In the public debate, there were various explanations for the weak performance of EU Member States: trade and technology. Today, more than 25 years later, we know more about the interaction between technology, trade, and employment

Employment rate in EU countries vary substantially. In 2020, the share of the population aged 20–64 in work was, on average 72.3 %. Sweden, the Netherlands and Germany had on employment rate over 80 %, while many countries in the other end range less than 70.0 %; e.g. Croatia, Spain, Italy and Greece from 66,9 % to 61.1 % in that order (Eurostat, 2021). One of the explanations is lower levels of women employment in some European countries. There have also been major fluctuations in unemployment level and employment rate the last two decades, mainly caused by the repercussions of the financial crises 2008 and the current impact of the pandemic. There is no current evidence that we are approach the end of work, rather there has been an increase in the service sector and in various forms of self-employment.[1]

A report written by Michel Servoz, a former DG of DG Employment in the EU-Commission, points at that 90 % of jobs now require IT-skills and that sixty-one million people in the EU have insufficient basic skills (Servoz 2019). The major focus of this policy study is to highlight and analyse the impact of the digital revolution, AI, new technology and robotics on labour markets, job structures but also the continous change in skills required, job destruction, job creation and job retention.[2]

> As this report has shown, a major shift in the economy is taking place. All the major components of automation are increasingly taking over various tasks traditionally carried out by people or performing tasks that were beyond reach until now. This transformation seems to be taking place silently, effortlessly, but in fact creates insecurity and anxiety for many workers, citizens, consumers and patients as to the place of humans in society.

Today the digital challenge operates together with the green transition and non-fossil future policies, and followed by the pandemic shock and its impact on society, public health and working life.

The aim of this book is to highlight European approaches to sustainable work, digitalisation, and job-related transitions, in the context of the implementation of the European Pillar of Social Rights and the European Social models. A starting point for this research initiative was a Swedish project, headed by Maria Albin, of the Karolinska Institute, Sweden and financed by the Swedish Innovation Agency, Vinnova. Its purpose was to strengthen research on sustainable work in the European Framework Programme Horizon 2020, and later Horizon Europe.

During this project journey, we have broadened the connotation of sustainable work, to comprise both healthy and productive working conditions in a life-course perspective and facing sustainable work in the context of the green transformation and necessary adaptions to climate change and low carbon

---

1 https://ec.europa.eu/eurostat/documents/7870049/12843519/KS-FT-21-003-EN-N.pdf/0de7faf6-43e0-4bfd-99f0-f92777b86a28. Downloaded 26 January 2022.

2 European Commission, European Political Strategy Centre, Servoz, M., *AI, the future of work?: work of the future!: on how artificial intelligence, robotics and automation are transforming jobs and the economy in* Europe, Publications Office, 2019, https://data.europa.eu/doi/10.2872/913422. Downloaded 26 January 2022.

policies. Before the pandemic, the policy discussion and research on the future of work was extremely intense. The ILO, OECD, the EU Commission, as well as many policy producing institutions, were actively involved in framing futures of work in times of digitalisation, climate change and just transition.

In 2020, many future ideas collapsed as an effect of the Covid-19 pandemic, with its fundamental and far-reaching Europe-wide shock impacting the economy, labour market and working life. It has also had severe repercussions on public and occupational health, family and living conditions, following on various organisational, social, and mental lockdowns. The policy process has not, however, been caught in a revolving door, with sustainable work out, and Covid-19 in. On the contrary, the need for an in-depth discussion of sustainable work in Europe and the global context, is even stronger in this new situation.

The Nordic countries have a strong tradition in occupational health and safety research, as well as in research on sustainable work systems. The strategic importance of sustainable work, as a resource for health, innovation, and growth, is emphasised in the European innovation strategy, and by the social partners. Therefore, workplace innovation and workers' health and wellbeing need to be a more visible and coherent theme in the EU's research programme Horizon Europe.

Sustainable work and sustainable work systems have been used as a policy concept and buzzword in working life and research for the last two decades, but the relation between work and environmental aspects has a much longer history in occupational health research. Sustainable work aims to illuminate and support a process to cope with present and future challenges at the workplace: it is not a product nor an end goal. A sustainable workplace reflects the reconciliation between health, the development of work environment for the employees, and a productive and value-creating mission for the enterprise or production organisation.

The book is divided into three slightly overlapping sections. The first section focuses on the concept of sustainable work, its policy background and relation to job quality, inequalities, gender perspectives, older workers, and senior employment. The second section highlights sustainable workplace innovations, digitalisation, and the green transformation. The final section covers implementation and the channels and methods to connect research, policies, and good practices. That is done by highlighting the role of workplace innovations, social partners and the social dialogue, OSH research collaboration and dissemination and the importance of higher education to implement the SDGs.

The chapter by Kenneth Abrahamsson illuminates and describes various understandings and aspects of the concept of sustainable work. The shifting character of the European workplace will also have repercussions for the concept of sustainable work as such, and its relation to workplace innovations, job quality, precarious work. Sustainable work is also a response to climate change and the greening of European enterprises, production systems and workplaces.

In his chapter, Franz F. Eiffe introduces the Eurofound reference framework of sustainable work, and its components are discussed. Furthermore, sustainable work outcome indicators on the societal and the individual level are presented, and how sustainable work can be implemented in practice. Attention is also paid to the impact of the green transition for sustainable work. The chapter closes with some conclusions and a policy outlook.

The next chapter by Maria Albin, Theo Bodin and Eskil Wadensjö highlights the tension between two trends: increased expectations on career longevity and increasing socioeconomic inequalities in health. This is further explored as a gap between job demands and the individual capacity, and the risk of being "locked-in" or forced out when facing this scenario. Attention is on which, macro- and micro-level measures are needed to decrease the vulnerability for mainly manual and low-skilled workers.

Policymakers often talk about good and decent work but tend to forget that one in five European workers are carrying out repetitive tasks, not taking more than one minute. Frank Pot's chapter analyses the opposite to good and sustainable work, namely monotonous and repetitive work. When researchers emphasise the importance of job quality, they say nobody should be left behind in these times of transition. Let us not forget this special category of workers with monotonous and repetitive work.

Sustainable work, career longevity and senior employment can also be seen from a gender perspective. Susan Reh, Shruti Raghuraman, Åsa Lundqvist, Victoria Tischler, Emma Jeanes and Laura Trigg's chapter presents a research review on current conditions for older female workers in Europe. The authors identify issues including work and domestic conflicts, menopause, stress, and income disparities that have a negative impact on older female workers. Attention is also paid to research gaps as multiple, interaction factors that constrain their working life, and novel supporting interventions.

The employment of older workers is high and rising in the Nordic countries, and most seniors have flexible access to employment or retirement from their early sixties on. However, there is still potential for further improvements, even in the Nordic countries. The chapter by Bjørn Einar Halvørsen describes and analyses this development, and the main policies and reforms behind it in the Nordic countries over the last 20 years.

In his reflections over the first section, Russell Lansbury points to the interplay between employment, retirement, leisure, and post-work involvements. As being an expert on industrial relations, he also analyses the role of employers, and the need for a social contract to promote sustainable work.

The second section illuminates the need for workplace innovations and new ways of work as a recurrent theme in the book. Chris Mathieu and Susanne Boethius make some basic definitional statements regarding innovation, job quality, sustainability, work, and sustainable work in their chapter. In their analyses of the relationship between innovation and job quality, they identify the role of activating and pacifying innovations in work life changes.

The aim with Lena Abrahamsson and Jan Johansson's chapter is to identify obstacles, and find pathways for sustainable work, in a digital future. We are all concerned about how our work will be in the future: will we be able to handle the new technology, or will technology control us?

Green transformation and institutional adaption to climate change have fundamental impacts on working life. The chapter by Ulrika Harlin, Martina Berglund, Katrin Skagert, Andreas Wallo, and Mattias Elg illustrates industrial approaches addressing sustainability dimensions from a start-up firm's major greenfield project to establish a large-scale production of battery cells and solutions for energy storage in Europe, with Sweden as the starting point. Key elements for green transformation, competitiveness, and development of socially sustainable industry are addressed, with a focus on organisational resilience, supply of competences, sustainable work, and enablers for sustainable change processes in organisations.

Against the background of an EU policy shift towards more environmentally sustainable practices, several policy initiatives are driving efforts in the circular economy arena. The chapter from EU-OSHA by Cornelia Daheim, Jessica Prendergast, Jörg Rampacher, Annick Starren, Emmanuellle Brun and Ioanna Anyfantis. emanates from a research-based foresight on the impact of the circular economy on sustainable work. It is a policy initiative caused by the European Commission's European Green Deal initiative, which has the overarching aim of making Europe climate neutral by 2050. Presented here are the results and insights generated to date from EU-OSHA's ongoing foresight project: four scenarios with a 2040 horizon which look at possible alternative futures of the circular economy in Europe and how they would impact on work and OSH.

The third section focusses on various channels to promote better workplaces in Europe. Peter Totterdill and Rosemary Exton share experiences as co-leaders of Workplace Innovation Europe CLG, a not-for-profit organisation created to promote the concept and practice of workplace innovation through research, consultancy, workforce development and policy advocacy. It also reflects the authors' close involvement in EUWIN (the European Workplace Innovation Network) since its creation in 2013 as a community of researchers, policymakers, social partners and enterprises.

The social partners play a core function on workplace change in Europe. Anders Kjellberg looks at the shifting role of trade unions in the social dialogue by using models, institutional settings, and statistics to track developments both in a Swedish and European perspective. His chapter reflects over the Swedish labour market model in a European context by looking at variations in union density, role of social partners and power relations in working life in a more general context.

The work of the European network for national work environment research institutes, PEROSH is presented by Mary Trainor, Louis Laurent, Jan Michiel Meeuwsen and Paulien Bongers from the PEROSH scientific committee. The PEROSH partnership acts collectively to strengthen co-operation on OSH research and accelerate the generation of knowledge in key areas of OSH; and disseminate and exchange knowledge and information on OSH issues. It also summarises PEROSH outreach and networking activities at national, European, and global level.

Finally, Lennart Levi, one of the pioneers in Swedish occupational health research, presents a global survival perspective on Stressors at Work and Elsewhere, by focusing the challenges of Agenda 2030 for the world of work. Lennart Levi is strongly arguing that higher education needs to take a leadership in the implementation of the SDGs and SDG 8 on Decent Work and Economic Growth.

So, what is the next step for policy development and research on sustainable work in Europe? In some concluding remarks, Kenneth Abrahamsson, reflects on policies, institutional factors and research needed in the effort to foresee and form the future of work in Europe up to 2030. Finally, Richard Ennals, co-editor makes some reflections in his Postscript.

References

European Commission, 2019. European Political Strategy Centre, Servoz, M., *AI, the future of work?:Work of the future!: On how artificial intelligence, robotics and automation are transforming jobs and the economy in Europe*, Publications Office.

Eurostat. 2021Quality report of the European Union Labour Force Survey 2019. 2021 edition. Luxembourg: Publications Office of the European Union,

Rifkin, J. (1995) *The end of work. The decline of the global labour force and the dawn of the post market era.* New York: A Tarcher/Putnam Book.

Kenneth Abrahamsson

Sustainable work, climate change and job quality

Abstract: The future of work is today discussed at global level in Agenda 2030 and SDG 8, by ILO and in the Global Deal, which is a multi-stakeholder initiative for social dialogue and inclusive growth. Future of work, social innovations and inclusive growth are also central policy missions for the OECD, the European Commission, and its agencies Cedefop, EU-OSHA and Eurofound. The European Pillar of Social Rights highlights the need for a European social model, promoting a progressive interplay between economic development, good working conditions and social protection. Climate change, the green deal, digitalisation, and labour market dynamics are reflected in most future of work dialogues. This chapter analyses concepts of quality of work, decent work, and sustainable work. Its purpose is to build bridges between sustainable work for healthy and productive work over the life-course, and sustainable production models needed to meet the challenges of climate change. Finally, digitalisation, labour market transformations and increasing career longevity make job shifts and skills upgrading more common, and sustainable work must be seen in a life-course and lifelong perspective. The purpose of this chapter is to reflect on sustainable work systems and sustainable work in the context of climate change, digitalisation, and the pandemic.

Keywords: good work, job quality, employment relations, green deal, workplace innovations, the precariat, future of work

Introductory comment on sustainable development

The concept of sustainable development was launched by the Brundtland Commission in *Report of the World Commission on Environment and Development: Our Common Future* in 1988 (UN 1988). The Commission focused on environmental sustainability: the survival of our planet, but also gave priority to social sustainability. In her foreword to Our Common Future, Gro Harlem Brundtland underlined the need for a new era of economic growth that is both socially and environmentally sustainable, as well as socially responsible.[1]

1 https://sustainabledevelopment.un.org/content/documents/5987our-common-future.pdf.Downloaded. Quote from chairwoman's foreword.

> Many critical survival issues are related to uneven development, poverty, and population growth. They all place unprecedented pressures on the planet's land, waters, forests, and other natural resources, not least in developing countries.

The EU adopted its first Sustainable Development Strategy at the European Council in Gothenburg 2001 (EU 2001). This was followed by the renewed Sustainable Development Strategy for the enlarged EU in June 2006, defining sustainable development in the following terms: "Sustainable development means that the needs of the present generation should be met without compromising the ability of future generations to meet their own needs." The strategy's key objectives cover environmental protection, social equity and cohesion, prosperity, and the EU's international obligations (European Council 2006).

The European Council set out seven key challenges, with targets and policies to meet them, i.e., climate change, transport systems, sustainable consumption and production patterns, management of natural resources, public health equity, socially inclusive societies and quality of life, and finally support for global sustainable development. Sustainable work and sustainable work systems were only mentioned indirectly in the EU Sustainable Development Strategy, but it is evident that health promotion and quality of life have central roles in the strategy.

In 2015, the United Nations launched the Sustainable Development Goals comprising 17 general goals and 169 sub-targets. SDG number 8 concerns decent work and economic growth. The SDGs also contain a strong social concern.[2]

> The Sustainable Development Goals (SDGs) aim to encourage sustained economic growth by achieving higher levels of productivity and through technological innovation. Promoting policies that encourage entrepreneurship and job creation are key to this, as are effective measures to eradicate forced labour, slavery, and human trafficking. With these targets in mind, the goal is to achieve full and productive employment, and decent work, for all women and men by 2030.

The purpose of Goal 8 Decent work and economic growth is to promote inclusive and sustainable economic growth, employment, and decent work for all. The UN SDG's focus corresponds to ILO policies for decent work (UN SDG 8).

> Decent work means opportunities for everyone to get work that is productive and delivers a fair income, security in the workplace and social protection for families, better prospects for personal development and social integration. It is also important that all women and men are given equal opportunities in the workplace. A continued lack of decent work opportunities, insufficient investments and underconsumption lead to an

2 https://www.sdgfund.org/goal-8-decent-work-and-economic-growth. Downloaded 20 October 2022.

> erosion of the basic social contract underlying democratic societies: that all must share in progress.

The Global Deal for decent work and inclusive growth was launched 2016 by Swedish Prime Minister Stefan Löfven as a concrete input to the UN 2030 Agenda for Sustainable Development. Its purpose is to bring together various stakeholders to promote joint solutions, while still representing their different interests. Effective social dialogue requires mutual respect and trust, to create favourable conditions for collaboration between employers, workers, and governments.[3] This mission is now organised and managed in collaboration with the OECD (ILO and OECD 2020).

In November 2017 the European Pillar of Social Rights was launched at an EU summit meeting in Gothenburg, Sweden. The vision of the pillar is to find a balance between economic development and growth, good working condition and social protection.[4]

> The aim of the European Pillar of Social Rights is to serve as a guide towards efficient employment and social outcomes when responding to current and future challenges which are directly aimed at fulfilling people's essential needs, and towards ensuring better enactment and implementation of social rights.

The European Pillar focusses on three policy dimensions concerning future of work in the EU. They are equal opportunities and access to the labour market, fair working conditions and social protection and inclusion. The European Pillar of Social Rights is related to some of the SDGs, but not all of them. SDG 8 Decent Work and Inclusive Growth directly shares the same field of action as EPSR. Of particular interest are also SDG 1 No poverty, SDG 3 Health and Well-being, SDG 4 Quality Education and SDG 5 Gender Equality, SDG 9 Industry, Innovation and infrastructure and SDG 10 Reduced inequalities and finally SDG 17 Partnership for the Goal. It constitutes a major challenge for policies, research and, direct actions to analyse the intersection between Sustainable Development Goals and the European Pillar of Social Rights. The vision of the pillar underlines quality of work, workplace innovations and employment security (EU 2017, p. 5).

> Innovative forms of work that ensure quality working conditions shall be fostered. Entrepreneurship and self-employment shall be encouraged. Occupational mobility shall be facilitated.

3 https://www.theglobaldeal.com/about/. Downloaded 08 October 2020.

4 https://ec.europa.eu/commission/sites/beta-political/files/social-summit-european-pillar-social-rights-booklet_en.pdf. Downloaded 15 October 2020.

> Employment relationships that lead to precarious working conditions shall be prevented, including by prohibiting abuse of atypical contracts. Any probation period should be of reasonable duration.

The need for good and constructive partnerships is also highlighted, with special focus on the social dialogue and the role of social partners.

> Social dialogue plays a central role in reinforcing social rights and enhancing sustainable and inclusive growth. Social partners at all levels have a crucial role to play in pursuing and implementing the European Pillar of Social Rights, in accordance with their autonomy in negotiating and concluding agreements, and the right to collective bargaining and collective action.

The concept of sustainable work has been developed over recent decades. It took several years, however, before workplace sustainability was adopted as a member of the sustainable development family. Today, social partners are actively involved in the policy discourse on the future of the Green Deal as a mission for Europe.[5] Its main purpose is to make EU's economy sustainable, by meeting climate and environmental challenges with powerful policy missions to create new opportunities together with a just and inclusive transitions. The Green Deal calls for comprehensive and long-term policies, and is also a future mission of the European Social Dialogue.

Thus, the dynamic policy concept of sustainability is embedded in several policy circles with the biosphere and global survival as the broadest perspective, followed by climate change and environmental challenges, as well as sustainable energy systems. Social sustainability comprises welfare systems, health and living conditions. In a labour market context, it is crucial to talk about sustainable work life providing good conditions for job entrants, people at work, as well as individuals in the transition to retirement.

Climate change, green deal, and sustainable work

There are growing needs for stronger measures to bridge the gap between climate policies and new energy systems and the efforts for occupational health and safety, the crucial role of social partners and the value of employee driven innovations. New forms of work and the dissolution of the traditional workplace and standard employment relations call for a widened use of the content of sustainable work. The Green Deal, low carbon omissions and new energy systems

---

5 https://ec.europa.eu/info/strategy/priorities-2019-2024/european-green-deal_en. Downloaded 08 October 2020.

will have substantial impacts on work organisation and production systems. European trade unions share support for urgent policies in this field.[6]

> Reducing rapidly EU's greenhouse gas emissions is a top priority for European Trade Unions, since there are no jobs on a dead planet. The increasing frequency and intensity of extreme weather events, such as the floods that affected Europe this summer, reminds us of the urgent need to act. The Sixth IPCC Assessment Report published in Aug ust 2021, also constitutes a serious warning, telling us that now is the time to adopt ambitious measures, or it will be too late.

Global warming has fundamental impact nature, the biodiversity, water and land and the topography of various geographical regions. The trend towards overheating also has severe repercussions on social systems, on public health and welfare, and finally on working contexts. Further, it has direct impact on inequalities in society. The 2021 report of the *Lancet Countdown on health and climate change: code red for a healthy future* illuminates these new risks and presents an in-depth overview of public health impact of global warming.

> The 2021 report of the Lancet Countdown finds a world overwhelmed by an ongoing global health crisis, which has made little progress to protect its population from the simultaneously aggravated health impacts of climate change. The inequities of these impacts and the response, including those of gender, are brought into sharp focus within each of the indicators presented.

In a European context, the employment impact of overheating is difficult to calculate. Job loss is anticipated to be stronger in countries with large agricultural sectors, and tourism. Other and often more industrialised countries might not be affected in the same way. On the other hand, the green transformation will also create new jobs. The process of job destruction, job retention and job creation, is however, not a new process in industrial history, but the twin challenges of climate change and digitalisation, will, together with the pandemic, speed up the labour market dynamics and job transitions both at the labour market level and for the individual employee. EU has a positive view on job creation in the green economy and anticipated one million new jobs in EU by 2030, under the condition the right supporting policies.[7]

OECD has presented a forward look on labour market transformations up to the year 2030 caused by the green transition. Decreasing sectors are gas, coal,

---

6 https://www.etuc.org/en/document/etuc-position-just-transition-legal-framework-complement-fit-55-package

7 European Commission, Directorate-General for Communication, *A socially fair transition*, Publications Office, 2021, https://data.europa.eu/doi/10.2775/835138

fossil-based electricity, crude oil and petroleum and coal products, while solar and wind electricity, renewals and waste electricity nuclear power and hydro and geothermal electricity will expand. The employment shift from declining to growing firms will increasingly characterise the green labour market transformation.[8]

The European policy response is the Green Deal, the Next Generation EU Recovery and facility programme and the fit for 55 initiatives. President of the European Commission, Ursula von der Leyen recently stated.[9]

> The fossil fuel economy has reached its limits. We want to leave the next generation a healthy planet as well as good jobs and growth that does not hurt our nature. The European Green Deal is our growth strategy that is moving towards a decarbonised economy. Europe was the first continent to declare a commitment to be climate neutral in 2050, and now we are the very first ones to put a concrete roadmap on the table. Europe walks the talk on climate policies through innovation, investment and social compensation.

To meet the triple challenge of digitalisation, green transition and the pandemic, the *Recovery and Resilience Facility* has been implemented. Its purpose is to make European economies and societies "more sustainable, resilient and better prepared for the challenges and opportunities of the green and digital transitions."

The Facility is structured around six pillars: green transition; digital transformation; economic cohesion, productivity, and competitiveness; social and territorial cohesion; health, economic, social, and institutional resilience; policies for the next generation. Another major initiative by the EU Commission with focus on climate, energy and transport is the so-called "*Fit for 55 package*" with the purpose to adapt current laws with the EU's climate goals for 2030 and 2050. As part of a low carbon society and zero fossil omissions, one of the focusses is to develop renewable energy and energy efficiency directives and, in the long run, regulate CO_2 emissions of cars and vans and in addition, prioritise regulation land use and forestry regulation.[10]

The Green Deal is also connected to and interacting with European industrial policies by launching *Industry 5.0*. Its aim is to bridge the need for wellbeing of workers, new production models, new technologies and the respect for the

8 https://www.oecd.org/employment/greeningjobsandskills.htm

9 https://ec.europa.eu/commission/presscorner/detail/en/IP_21_3541. Downloaded 07 January 2022.

10 https://www.consilium.europa.eu/en/policies/climate-change/eu-climate-action/

production limits of the planet. In short, it takes a further step from Industry 4.0 by "putting research and innovation at the service of the transition to a sustainable, human-centric and resilient European industry".[11] The EU investment in the Digital Decade until 2030 must also be mentioned in this context.[12] These initiatives comprise a policy focus on digital skills, secure and sustainable infrastructure and supporting digitalisation in business and public sector.

The current transformation of the world of work, industry, and society in the context of digitalisation and green deal call for new skills initiatives. The European Skills Agenda is a five-year plan to help individuals and businesses develop more and better skills and to put them to use. To support the green transition, the Commission will develop a European competence framework on education for climate change and sustainable development, similarly to frameworks for entrepreneurial and digital skills.[13] EU Agency for the development of vocational training, Cedefop, has green skills as one of the prioritised themes.[14]

> Environmental change is an increasingly important driver of labour demand and skills supply across all sectors. Therefore, the positive impacts of the transition to a greener economy can be maximised by simultaneously developing the skills, knowledge and competences required by resource-efficient processes and technologies; and integrating these into businesses and communities.

Cedefop (2021) has recently launched a new forecast on green skills on the future labour market in the report *The green employment and skills transformation: insights from a European Green Deal skills forecast scenario.*" Becoming "greener" will bring about such profound changes in technology, design, production, services, consumption and investment that it is impossible to achieve without sufficiently skilled people."[15]

Climate change and just transition

Current EU policies also underline the role of a socially fair transition to meet the needs of vulnerable households, micro-enterprises, and transport users. One of the new instruments launched a new *Social Climate Fund* to help citizens

---

11 https://ec.europa.eu/info/research-and-innovation/research-area/industrial-research-and-innovation/industry-50_en
12 https://ec.europa.eu/info/strategy/priorities-2019-2024/europe-fit-digital-age/europes-digital-decade-digital-targets-2030_en
13 https://ec.europa.eu/social/main.jsp?catId=1223&langId=en
14 https://www.cedefop.europa.eu/en/projects/skills-green-economy
15 https://www.cedefop.europa.eu/files/4206_en.pdf

finance investments in energy efficiency, new heating and cooling systems, and cleaner mobility. Another policy initiative is the *Just Transition Fund,* focussed on coal and carbon-intensive regions and with these priority fields; investments in Small and Medium-sized Enterprises. creation of new firms, research and innovation, environmental rehabilitation, clean energy, up- and reskilling of workers, job-search assistance, and transformation of existing carbon-intensive installations. The policy concept of just transition has many connotations but is to a large extent focusses on regions and not specific type of jobs. European trade unions want to extent the content of the Just transition concepts in a workplace orientation.[16]

> ETUC calls for the adoption of policy measures to operationalise the ILO Guidelines for a Just Transition, adopted in 2015. Concretely, European trade unions are calling for the adoption of a Just Transition legal framework as part of the European Green Deal, to accompany the Fit for 55 package.

Policies and measures to deal with climate change has a global occurrence. A report by Mertins-Kirkwood and Duncalfe (2021) highlights the challenges of just transition in a Canadian context.[17]

> As a concept, just transition refers to a framework for minimising the potential harm to workers and communities caused by the shift away from fossil fuels while maximising the potential benefits that decarbonization entails.

Canada's Task Force for Just Transition has presented seven principles for a just transition as seen from a work life and social perspective.[18]

---

16 https://www.etuc.org/en/document/etuc-position-just-transition-legal-framework-complement-fit-55-package

17 Roadmap to a Canadian Just Transition Act A path to a clean and inclusive economy Hadrian Mertins-Kirkwood and Clay Duncalfe.

18 Source: https://www.policyalternatives.ca/sites/default/files/uploads/publications/National%20Office/2021/04/Roadmap%20to%20a%20Canadian%20just%20transition%20act.pdf. Downloaded 07 January 2022.

Box 1: Seven principles for a just transition from Canada's Task Force on Just Transition

1. Respect for workers, unions, communities, and families;
2. Worker participation at every stage of transition;
3. Transitioning to good jobs;
4. Sustainable and healthy communities;
5. Planning for the future, grounded in today's reality;
6. Nationally coherent, regionally driven, locally delivered actions; and,
7. Immediate yet durable support.

Sustainable work and climate change: A revolving door?

We can approach the subject of sustainable work from various doors. One door might have the label of healthy and inclusive workplaces. A similar door goes to good work in a lifelong perspective. Employee driven innovations and workers co-determination is another door, however, not so often open. Then there are several doors of various sizes and obstacles that prevent access from various groups as migrants, persons with disabilities, groups with short education, or doors with special gender-based locking devices.

If we approach the workplace through a climate change and low carbon omission set of doors, we add a new dimension to the sustainable workplace. Traditionally, climate issues in an OSH perspective have been focussing on indoor and outdoor temperature, ventilation, lighting, and access to sunlight. With the current development of the overheated planet, we can anticipate job losses due to high outdoor temperature. In the long run, climate change will both contribute to job destruction and job creation. The green transition has mobilised a set of policies and tools to slow down global heating by using and developing fossil free energy systems in society, transport and working life. The adaption to a low fossil society and working life will create new form of labour market dynamic with further education, skills upgrading and investment in new green skills (ILO 2013).

So, which are the central policy fields from a working life and social partners perspective? In a Swedish policy-oriented review of research on green transition, the following dimensions were highlighted.[19]

19 https://forte.se/app/uploads/2021/03/fort-0041-rapport-gron-omstallning-web-ta-1.pdf. Downloaded 07 January 2022.

- The fossil-free transition primarily comprises technical analysis of how the transition towards a fossil-free or climate-neutral society can be brought about, focusing on challenges and opportunities within different sectors.
- Green growth is a stated political strategy which aims for ecological sustainability as well as economic growth, green jobs, and investment.
- Circular economy focuses on the use of materials and resources and is often regarded as a central part of the green transition, also being important with respect to society's impact on the climate.
- Finally, the socio-ecological transition largely stems from criticism of the more established realpolitik strategies for the green transition and, among other things, questions whether economic growth should be the objective of the national economy, placing more focus on social aspects and fairness.

EU-OSHA has recently monitored a foresight on the circular economy which pointed at four scenarios. Its purpose has been to illuminate future developments related to the circular economy, their impact on the nature and organisation, of work, work environment a new risks and challenges to be met. This foresight is presented in Section II of this book.[20]

Strategic framework for OSH: Urgent synergy needs

As been shown above, the European Commission has launched several powerful policy initiatives in the context of climate change, digitalisation, and the pandemic. Many initiatives are on the structural and institutional level and contains new regulations and economic support to reach a more fair and just transition. The European Pillar of Social Rights provides a general policy framework for industrial and social change in Europe. To bridge the gap between policies and practice is much more complicated and surrounded by obstacles, if you at the same time will create the synergies between various policy fields. And in the end of the day, looking at working conditions,

The European Commission's *Strategic Framework on Health and Safety at Work 2021–2027* is another policy measure and it defines the key priorities and actions for improving workers' health and safety, addressing rapid changes in the economy, demography and work patterns.[21]

---

20 https://osha.europa.eu/en/emerging-risks/circular-economy

21 https://eur-lex.europa.eu/legal-content/EN/TXT/?uri=CELEX%3A52021DC0323&qid=1626089672913#PP1Contents

> EU occupational safety and health (OSH) legislation is essential to protect the health and safety of the almost 170 million workers in the EU.[22] Protecting people from health and safety hazards on the job is a key element of achieving sustained decent working conditions for all workers. It has allowed the reduction of health risks at work, and improvements in OSH standards across the EU and across sectors. However, challenges remain, and the Covid-19 pandemic has exacerbated risks that need to be addressed.

The strategic framework was announced in the European Pillar of Social Rights action plan.[23] It focusses the key priorities and actions necessary for improving workers' health and safety, with particular attention to the post-pandemic world, green and digital transitions, and other determinants of the future of the European workplace.

"The Strategic Framework takes a tripartite approach: involving EU institutions, Member States, social partners and other stakeholders, and focuses on three key priorities:

1. anticipating and managing change in the context of green, digital, and demographic transitions.
2. improving the prevention of work-related accidents and diseases and striving towards a Vision Zero approach to work-related deaths.
3. increasing preparedness to respond to current and future health crises."

EU-OSHA and its future foresight, policy development and data collection play a central role in the strategic framework.[24]

Searching for definitions of sustainable work

The concept of sustainable work has been increasingly used in policy quarters and research over the last two decades (Hvid & Lund 2002) and (Fischer & Zink 2012). There are numerous definitions that sometimes overlap and in other contexts comprise a specific part of the concept. The Swedish Vinnova-supported *Platform for* Sustainable Work in Horizon 2020 used this broad definition:[25]

---

22 Eurostat, lfsa_eegan2, employees only (excluding family workers)

23 https://ec.europa.eu/info/strategy/priorities-2019-2024/economy-works-people/jobs-growth-and-investment/european-pillar-social-rights/european-pillar-social-rights-action-plan_en

24 https://osha.europa.eu/en/safety-and-health-legislation/eu-strategic-framework-health-and-safety-work-2021-2027

25 http://sustainablework2020.se/. Downloaded 15 October 2022.

> Sustainable work highlights the dynamic fit between employees and working conditions and is a generic policy concept. Sustainable work promotes health, wellbeing, learning and influence, as well as productivity, innovation, and growth. The goal is to promote continual growth and regeneration of human, social, economic, and ecological resources. The strategic importance of sustainable work, as a resource for health, innovation, and growth, is emphasised in the European innovation strategy, and also by the social partners. Therefore, sustainable work needs to be a more visible and coherent theme in Horizon 2020.

Docherty et al. (2009) highlighted balanced development of various resources operating in a work system. Sustainability is primarily identified with ecological and environmental issues, nowadays quite often connected with climate crisis and striving for a low-carbon society. They focused on human and social sustainability at work, but also point to human, social, economic, and ecological dimensions where business goals, social goals and job quality come together (FAS 2009).[26]

Eurofound has inspired the European discourse on job qualities and has chosen to highlight a life-course perspective on sustainable work (Eurofound 2015a, p. 2).

> Eurofound's working definition of "sustainable work over the life course" means that working and living conditions are such that they support people in engaging and remaining in work throughout an extended working life. These conditions enable a fit between work and the characteristics or circumstances of the individual throughout their changing life, and they must be developed through policies and practices at work and outside of work.

The life-course perspective on sustainable work differs from an age-management perspective, focusing on adjusted workplaces for older workers. In a lifespan and career longevity approach, work environment for young workers could have negative impact on working conditions in middle-age or for older worker. The Eurofound's perspective is described by Eiffe in this book.

One of many challenges in this context is to bridge the gap between sustainable work and the notion of workplace innovation. Sustainable working life, or sustainable work systems, are so far open concepts that need further specification. Common policy concepts in Sweden have been "good work" or "developing work", while the concepts of sustainable work and healthy workplaces are now

---

26 Docherty et al. (2009) Creating Sustainable Work Systems. Developing social sustainability and Docherty in Håkansta, C. & Abrahamsson, K. (eds) (2008) Workplaces of the Future. Work-In-Net Foresight Seminar held in Stockholm, Sweden.

being used more often. Thus, sustainable work has more and more been used in addition to social and environmental sustainability; and they all have high policy popularity both among agencies, social partners, and other actors.

Conceptual framework for quality of work

Working realities differ between countries, in various types of jobs and for different groups. Preventive initiatives in occupational health have roots in the late 19th century. Standards were not set to reach the highest levels of good work, but to avoid the most dangerous workplaces, to counteract risks and fatal injuries, to hinder dangerous exposure of chemicals, noise, and too heavy tasks. Good work, in a historic sense, tends to start from the bottom-line, and define what is not acceptable and humane. Early legislation also focused on child-labour and women's nightwork.

Today, there are many concepts or models to describe job qualities. One strand is to look at attractive jobs from a life-course perspective, i.e., attractive jobs for young people or work ability and healthy for older workers. Gardner et al. (2001) have illuminated good work as good deeds, productive contribution or what in Sweden is labelled as "ett gott dagsverke": a good day of work. Biggs (2015) follows the Studs Terkel (1972) tradition of shaping the life and character of various occupations and work communities. "We may love our work, hate our work, find meaning in our work or none, but it's what we do all day long, and it shapes us" (Biggs, 2017, p. 11). A common model is to describe good or bad jobs is the *Demand-Control, DC model* and its focus on job strain, control, and stress (Theorell & Karasek, 1996). The DC model has been broadened to Demand Control, Resource model, the DCR model. They have inspired various streams on research on occupational health and safety in a work organisation perspective. Karasek (2017) discusses another variation of the model as the ADC model or the *Associationalist Demand Control* model, by including a wider societal context.

Work and identity are reflected in the concept of *coherence and meaning of work* promoted by Antonovsky (1996). *Work communities* and the social context of work are investigated and conceptualised in many different research approaches, e.g., work as communities of practice (Wenger, 1998), *working cultures* (Terkel, 1972) or *workers' collective* by Lysgaard (Axelsson et al., 2019) Paid and unpaid work: gender challenge and issues of work life balance is a field with increasing interest during last decades. Another metaphor is *healthy corporations* and *healthy workplaces*, often used for corporate branding. *High road workplaces* (Parent-Thirion et al., 2017) in knowledge intensive and technology dominated environment is another sector of the field of good workplaces. Finally, we can once more point to the concept of sustainable work systems (Zink 2014).

Eurofound and ILO (2019) share a definition of job quality in their joint report *Working conditions in a global perspective* (Eurofound and ILO, 2019, p. 1).[27]

> Job quality is increasingly recognised as a major policy concern. It is central to the ILO's Decent Work Agenda and to the European Union's Quality of Work policies. For workers, for the enterprises and organisations that employ them, and for societies, there are benefits associated with high-quality jobs, and costs associated with poor-quality jobs.

The EU conception of good work and inclusive work environments also focused on the mission of job-creation and diversity in working life.[28]

> Regaining full employment not only involves focusing on more jobs, but also on better jobs. Increased efforts should be made to promote a good working environment for all including equal opportunities for the disabled, gender equality, good and flexible work organisation permitting better reconciliation of working and personal life, lifelong learning, health and safety at work, employee involvement and diversity in working life.

Job quality can be assessed in various ways. In policies and in public debate it is common to talk about good jobs and bad jobs (Green, 2006). But what is a good job and what constitutes good work? The report *Indicators of Job Quality in the* European Union (2009) published by the European Parliament, underlines that job quality is a multidimensional concept that can be approached with different methods and various theoretical approaches. That report was launched when the slogan "more and better jobs" was an integral part of the European Employment Strategy and the Lisbon Strategy. It was also presented at a time when policy attention to good jobs indicators was at a higher level. There is, however, no one single way to understand and measure job quality (OECD 2014).

The multidimensional nature of job quality makes the development of a single indicator or a system of indicators more difficult as, prior to such development, it is necessary to define what aspects should be taken into consideration and their

27 https://www.eurofound.europa.eu/sites/default/files/ef_publication/field_ef_document/ef18066en.pdf Eurofound and International Labour Organization (2019), Working conditions in a global perspective, Publications Office of the European Union, Luxembourg, and International Labour Organization, Geneva. Downloaded 1 February 2021.

28 European council (2001). Presidency conclusions. Stockholm meeting 23 and 24 March 2001.par. 26. Source: https://www.consilium.europa.eu/ueDocs/cms_Data/docs/pressData/en/ec/00100-r1.%20ann-r1.en1.html. Downloaded 1 February 2021.

overall impact on job quality. Job quality can be approached in three ways according to the report. The first method is to look at job satisfaction as "an overall indicator of job quality". The second approach is to ask workers what makes a good job, and finally defining job quality from theories and models of social and medical sciences. The third way comprises several scientific roads. Economists and sometime sociologists could use wages and labour compensation as an indicator of good jobs. Sociologists, psychologists, and political scientists, as well as scholars from management science, could look at power relations and industrial democracy, and participatory options.

The OECD has developed a framework to measure the quality of jobs, with reference to three objective dimensions (Cazes, et.al. 2015). They constitute, according to OECD a comprehensive assessment of job quality.[29] This model differs from the labelling of job quality, work quality and employment quality.

- *Earnings quality* captures the extent to which earnings contribute to workers' well-being in terms of *average earnings* and their *distribution* across the workforce.
- *Labour market security* captures those aspects of economic security related to the risks of job loss and its economic cost for workers. It is defined by the risks of unemployment and benefits received in case of unemployment.
- *Quality of the working environment* captures non-economic aspects of jobs including the nature and content of the work performed, working-time arrangements and workplace relationships. These are measured as incidence of job strain characterised as *high job demands* with *low job resources.*

Job quality is, however, not a static phenomenon. The Eurofound and ILO report on working conditions in a global perspective has a positive view on improving job quality by reducing excessive demands on workers, limit their risk-exposure and developing good work practices (Eurofound and ILO, 2019, p. 2).[30]

Workplace innovation and sustainable work: Similar and different

Workplace innovation has received growing attention and interest both in research and European policy formation(Lorenz&Potter 2019). A valuable

---

29 http://www.oecd.org/statistics/job-quality.htm and http://www.oecd.org/sdd/labour-stats/Job-quality-OECD.pdf

30 https://www.ilo.org/wcmsp5/groups/public/---dgreports/---dcomm/---publ/documents/publication/wcms_696174.pdf. Downloaded 26 September 2020.

overview of this development has been presented by Oeij, Rus, and Pot (2017) in the book *Workplace Innovation. Theory, Research and Practice*. It aims to clarify concepts, theories, models, experimenting and policy development (Oeij & Dondt 2017). It also reflects shifting European policies from DG Employment and DG Grow (Oeij et al. 2017).

Sustainable work and workplace innovations are conceptual siblings with an overlapping DNA-structure. Sustainable work belongs to the larger family of job quality, which can be divided into job quality, work quality and employment quality. Thus, sustainable work reflects the goals and visions of good work and a healthy and safe work environment, while workplace innovation strives for a productive balance between organisational determinants and development on the one hand, and good and healthy working conditions on the other (Kira & Eijnatten 2009) and (Kira & Eijnatten 2013). With some simplification, one might say that sustainable work, so far has a stronger focus on job quality and work environment over a life-course, while workplace innovation is more strongly allied with work organisation research and innovative forms of work. An innovative work-organisation does not by definition become healthy and beneficial for the worker i.e., the theoretical discourse on the uberisation of work, and negative impact of platform work, could be good examples (Warhurst, Mathieu & Wright, 2017).

DG Grow presents a broader definition of workplace innovations covering various dimensions and levels of enterprises, economy, and labour market.[31]

> To stay at the competitive edge, companies need to invest not only in technological innovation but also in non-technological practices. Workplace innovation can mean many things: such as a change in business structure, human resources management, relationships with clients and suppliers, or in the work environment itself. It improves motivation and working conditions for employees, which leads to increased labour productivity, innovation capability, market resilience and overall business competitiveness. All enterprises, no matter their size, can benefit from workplace innovation.

The concept of workplace innovation exists in a cluster of ideas, models and driving forces. The approach represented by the EUWIN community underlines the role of employee-supported workplace innovation that also highlights the role of social partners and the workplace dialogues as a method (Alasoini et al., 2017). In the efforts to find a working definition, Oeij and Dhondt (2017) take an integral approach highlighting the combined role of improved organisational

31 https://ec.europa.eu/growth/industry/policy/innovation/workplace_en. Downloaded 19 September 2020.

performance and quality of working life. Furthermore, they stress the interactive and participatory role for employees, organisational design, leadership and quality and performance indicators. The importance of framework agreements between social partners and governments for sectoral or local workplace innovation initiatives has been underlined (Pot et al., 2017, p. 107).

From standard employment to atypical and precarious jobs

Employment relations have a strong impact on work environment and workers' health. When Guy Standing (2011) presented his study *The precariat. A new and dangerous class*, he also highlighted the dynamic relations between employment relations and quality of work. Traditionally, research into OSH-dimensions and quality of work analysed working conditions in large enterprises, or SMEs with employees following the pattern of standard employment.

Today, both standard employment relations and the workplace are much more flexible. Modern working life can increasingly be described as *Work without boundaries* (Allvin et al., 2011). There are various ways and categories to describe jobs with or without employment relations. On each end of the scale, you have standard employment and unemployment. Between these categories exist temporary and precarious jobs, portfolio jobs and self-employment (Lewchuk 2017).

Eurofound (2015b) has identified several new forms of work, in which employment relations tend to be more complex; employee sharing, job sharing, interim management, casual work, ICT-based mobile work, portfolio work, crowd employment and collaborative employment. Many of these forms of work are not connected with traditional employment relations, but represent various forms for an employer to hire competence or skills for specific task. Another concept used in a comparative European context is employment vulnerability, which is a multidimensional phenomenon including employment contract, employment relations, type of firm and occupation (Baziellier et.al.,2016).

Eurostat (2018) reports that self-employment could vary between 6 and 8 % in Norway, Denmark, and Sweden up to 30 % in Greece. Individuals being account-owners in small firms are often more vulnerable than individual being employed, and can rely on labour laws, social protection, and sometimes union rights (Conen & Schippers, 2019).

Kalleberg and Vallas define precarious work as work that is *uncertain, unstable* and *insecure,* and in which *employees bear the risks* of work (as opposed to businesses or the government) and *receive limited social benefits and statutory entitlements* (Kalleberg & Vallas, 2017, p. 1).

Rodgers (1989), in Conen & Schippers (2019), has identified four dimensions of precariousness; income adequacy for a decent standard of living, social protection by unions or the law, degree of certainty in long term employment conditions, and influence and control over the labour process. An additional dimension of precarious working conditions is the factor of multiple job holders (Bouwhuis, et.al. 2019). There are also relations between precarious work and social conditions, and labour market position and social conditions of individuals are important health determinants (Van Aerden et al., 2017) and (Ojala&Pyöria 2019). A study in the US from 1995 – 2017 showed that women, and especially women with children, are overrepresented in precarious jobs in comparison with men (Albelda et al., 2020). A study of a Canadian population showed that immigrants: both males and females, more commonly work in-voluntary part-time work (Hira-Friesen, 2018).

A recent Swedish review on research of future work environment and employment relations pointed to the dynamic relation between forms of employment relations and quality of work and that non-standard employment relations are often associated with risk of illness, weak social protection, and lack of work life balance (Sawee, 2020).

Good jobs, bad jobs, or new jobs? Concluding remarks on future of sustainable work

Job quality, employment conditions and skills requirements are significant dimensions of the European workplace. Are European jobs good or bad in an international comparative sense (Holzer et. al 2012)? It is, of course, not possible to give a clear and evidence-based response to such a broad question (Hvid&Falkum 2018). One hypothesis could be that there are larger variations in job quality between Europe, and some other continents or countries with insufficient job protection, restricted or forbidden unions. lower wage and worse work environment. The book *Are bad jobs inevitable? Trends, Determinants and Responses to Job Quality in the Twenty-First Century* (Warhurst et al., 2012) highlights driving forces and institutional mechanisms behind bad jobs and opportunities of good jobs in an international context. The introductory chapter raises seven major questions on good and bad jobs' discourse in the form of scenarios. The first scenario *Jobs are getting better* reflects the idea of upward convergence. Its opposite side is labelled in the second scenario *Jobs are getting worse,* in line with Braverman's (1974) argument on degradation of work. Increasing stress and job strain at work, falling occupational health or more precarious jobs and uncertain employment conditions are taking that direction.

The third scenario focuses on the *Polarisation of Job quality*, a perspective being subject to an in-depth discussion among scholars on various ways to assess job quality, e.g., wages, working hours, employment conditions or job security. Scenarios four and five are illustrations of the polarisation idea and comprise *Good jobs are getting better* and *Bad jobs are getting worse*, a development often signified by growing income gaps. Finally, the authors presented a twisted development in scenarios six and seven where *Good jobs go bad* and *Bad jobs are getting better*. These seven scenarios illuminate the complexity in the development of job qualities in countries and regions with various labour market regimes and different institutional context, different positions of social partners.

So, what about new jobs? In recent years the discussion on job destruction, job creation or job retention has been quite hot, and shifted character when analyses and studies were deepened (Frey & Osborne, 2013). From the alarming signals that half of current jobs would be abolished or lost in cyberspace within the next two decades, due to digitalisation and technological disruption, today's predictions move in an interval between 6 and 12 % depending on type of work organisation, skill levels of the workforce and the number of low qualified jobs (Arntz et al., 2016). One possible development is that the gig economy and digitalisation can increase polarisation between good and bad jobs. The shifting character of the standard employment model to new employment contracts, increasing levels of temporary jobs, or patterns of self-employment, bogus self-employment included, will also contribute to shape the job quality of new jobs.

The European Agency for Safety and Health at Work has published a future study on OSH risks and hazards *Foresight on new and emerging occupational safety and health risks associated with digitalisation by 2025 European Risk Observatory Report.* It was before the Covid-19 pandemic, and some of the risks might have been accelerated, due to the current threats to public and occupational health. The rapid digital transformation of the world of work has had a fundamental impact on organisation of work and working conditions (European Agency for Safety and Health at Work, EU-OSHA 2018).[32]

Another policy study on scenarios of the future of work from an occupational risk and health hazard perspective has been published by NIOSH (2020). It is also looking into new forms of work, the role of AI and Industry4.0 in the new digital context of work (NIOSH, 2020).[33] This review comprises peer-reviewed

32 https://osha.europa.eu/en/publications/foresight-new-and-emerging-occupational-safety-and-health-risks-associated. Downloaded 08 October 2020.

33 NIOSH (2020) Potential Scenarios and Hazards in the Work of the Future: A Systematic Review of the Peer-Reviewed and Grey Literatures.

literature, work scenarios from the grey literature, and themes in published literature. One special concern is the fragmentation of the traditional workplace, i.e., the distributed workplace, remote work, and hoffices. This scenario has been sharply illuminated and speeded up as an adaption to the Covid-19 pandemic, and it also comprises social dissolution at work. A more profound development is that increasing inequalities seem to be an underlying factor in the scenario. "The concept of unequal distribution of wealth, income, opportunity, gender, race, and access to information underlays many of the scenarios in the grey and supplemental literature" (NIOSH, 2020, p. 20).

In the final conclusions, the authors investigate new OSH-risks and hazards in the context of increasing career longevity in times of expanding new technology, AI, and automation. Will they be able to embark on the new skill market or forced to leave the labour market after displacement? There is not a yes or no answer to this question. The answer depends on the provision of support service, adaptation of workplaces, and a continuous social dialogue at national and global levels.

Towards greener and more sustainable jobs in Europe

Table 1 is an effort to summarise various perspectives on good work ideas and work improvement programmes, in the context of four dimensions of quality; job quality with good work environment and healthy and safe jobs, employment quality and job security, flexible work organisation and, finally recognising climate and energy aspects. Two other crucial aspects are the roles of work improvement programmes for precarious jobs, and workers participation, co-determination, and employee friendly models for change. Surrounding factors and determinants on macro-level are the pace of labour market transformation, technology disruptions and the creation of new jobs. Covid-19, digitalisation, and the promotion of green and climate friendly jobs will speed up labour market mobility, and job shift for individual workers. Thus, sustainable work also needs to consider and develop sustainable employment systems that can manage the growing numbers of job shifts, career re-orientations and transitions.

The social concern about the jobs of the future is expressed in SDG 8 and in the European Pillar of social rights. In the article *Redefining working conditions in Europe*, Vendramin and Parent-Thirion (2019) analysed data and values on what constitutes job quality from the employees' point of view. They reflect on ideas and concepts of job quality, flexicurity and sustainable work. The Lisbon strategy launched the vision of more and better jobs, a vision that was distorted during the global financial crisis of 2008. Looking ahead, they argue for the idea of sustainable work.

"Recently, the notion of sustainable work seems to have prevailed. It offers a more convincing response to an ageing population, to the desire to increase the proportion of older workers in the labour force, and to the marked increase in musculoskeletal and psychosocial problems among workers of all ages" (Vendramin & Parent-Thirion, 2019, p. 274).

By shifting from decent work to sustainable work, they underlined the necessity of finding a good work concept that functions both in our times and in the future. Sustainable work does not only focus on career longevity, but it also stresses the need to consider and concern climate change, new energy systems and the road to green work. Stressing sustainable work in a life-course, and not only sustainable jobs, illuminates the crucial role of job transition, career development and the adaption to new work system as well as gender structures and work-life balance.

Tab. 1. Overview of work improvement programmes and quality focus with reference to sustainable work and green jobs.

Work improvement programme/Job quality focus	Job quality/ OSH, Good DCR match	Employment quality – job security/ working hours/skills	Flexible work organisation – Employeefriendly or firm-friendly	Climate, energy& SDGs – Low-carbon/ transformation
Decent jobs: Healthy & safe work conditions ILO/Global Deal	High OSH priority	Job security, union rights, freedom of expression	Inclusive growth, social inclusive workplaces	New focus in SDG perspective
Good work 1: Dignity & ethics Gardner et al. (2001)	Values and deeds: subjective job satisfaction	–	–	–
Good work 2: Power balance Swed. Metal Fed/ LO Sweden	High OSH priority	Job security, union rights, freedom of expression	Social dialogue and workers' co-determination	Green Deal policies not so visible from start
Human Sustainable work 1: Life- course work/Docherty/ Eurofound	OSH over the life course/	Job security and job shift support crucial in a life-course view	New forms of work, work-life balance, social partner dialogue	New synergies of sustainable work and the green deal

(*Continued*)

Tab. 1. Continued

Ecological Sustainable work 2: Green low-carbon jobs EU/OECD/ILO	OSH priority for green jobs in agriculture, forestry etc	Job security and union rights also part of Global deal-decent jobs	New workplace innovations for low-carbon jobs-employee involv.	The major future challenge – Next Generation EU/ Global Deal
Workplace innovations 1: Dialogues for development EUWIN	High OSH-priority and job quality	Flexible employment relations	Strong focus on employee driven WP innovations – strong links with industry	Workplace innovations crucial to manage green deal
Workplace innovations 2: Sustainable production systems EU Green Deal	Resilient energy system and new environmentally friendly material. OSH one aspect of many	Sustainable production systems–flexible employment forms in use	Sustainable and lean production models in high international competition	Global drive for green deal and low-carbon enterprises – need for just transition

The major challenge is how the vision and concept of sustainable work can be used to create good working conditions in a transformative labour market characterised by job destruction, job creation and job retention (World Economic Forum 2016). Individual working lives cannot not be characterised as a linear development in a context of lifelong employment at the same factory, office, or service arena. Life is changing, jobs are disappearing, and others arise, the workers' individual job transitions can sometimes be explained in the form of a free choice, but more often caused by social, economic, technological determinants. A societal vision and model of sustainable work from comprehensive school to senior or post-work positions, presupposes a lifelong learning system integrating youth education, adult education and vocational education, higher education, and a broad range of staff-development and on-the-job learning (Vendramin & Parent–Thirion, 2019, p. 294):

> Sustainable work is a desirable horizon for Europe, insofar as it is likely to underlie a multidimensional approach to quality of work that will consider working individuals as a whole, with their characteristics, their constraints and their trajectories. The ILO could also choose this direction, which is already reflected in the many points raised during the national dialogues on the future of work (ILO, 2017). Moreover, since the concept of sustainable work initially brought together two issues: that is to say, sustainable development and working systems, it could probably be used to combine the priorities of sustainable development and decent work.

The triple challenges of digitalisation, green transition and the pandemic call for more sustainable workplace innovations. Each of these mega trends are applying enormous pressures on the European workplace, on governments and the social dialogue and on individual employees. Taken together, they are speeding up the process of labour market transformation from declining brown sectors to expanding green fields. A good basic education, higher education and lifelong learning and competence development at work are necessary preconditions for this fundamental transformation of the world of work. And, in the context of the new demography with ageing and migration as driving forces, lifelong learning might also be transformed into long life learning. So sustainable work can be a desirable horizon, not only for Europe, but for quality of work in a global sense.

References

Alasoini, T., Ramstad, E., & Totterdill, P. (2017) National and regional policies to promote and sustain workplace innovation. In Oeij, P., Rus, D., and Pot, F. (eds), *Workplace Innovation. Theory, Research and Practice.* Cham: Springer.

Albelda, R., Bell-Pasht, A., & Konstantinidis, C. (2020) Gender and precarious work in the United States: Evidence from the contingent work supplement 1995–2017. *Review of Radical Political Economics*, 52 (3), pp. 542–563.

Allvin, M., Aronsson, G., Hagström, T., Johansson, G., & Lundberg, U. (2011) *Work without Boundaries. Psychological Perspectives on the New Working Life.* Chichester: Wiley-Blackwell.

Antonovsky, A. (1996) The sense of coherence – An historical and future perspective. *Israel Journal of Medical Sciences*, 32 (3–4), pp. 170–178.

Arntz, M., Gregory, T., & Zierahn, U. (2016) The risk of automation for jobs in OECD countries: A comparative analysis. *OECD Social, Employment and Migration Working. Papers*, No. 189, Paris: OECD Publishing.

Axelsson, J., Karlsson, J.Ch., & Skorstad, E. (2019) *Collective Mobilization in Changing Conditions: Worker Collectivity in a Turbulent Age.* Basingstoke: Palgrave Macmillan,

Bazillier, R., Boboc, C., Calavrezo, O. (2016) Measuring employment vulnerability in Europe. *International Labour Review*, 155 (2), pp. 265–280.

Biggs, J. (2015) *All Day Long. A Portrait of Britain at Work.* London: Serpent's Tail.

Bouwhuis, S., Geuskens, G.A., Boot, C.R.L., Van Der Beek, A.J., & Bongers, P.M. (2019) Health differences between multiple and single job holders in precarious employment in the Netherlands: A cross-sectional study among Dutch workers. *PLoS One*, 14 (9).

Braverman, H. (1974) *Labor and Monopoly Capital. The Degradation of Work in the Twentieth Century.* New York and London: Monthly Review Press.

Cazes, S., Hijzen, A., & Saint-Martin, A. (2015) Measuring and assessing job quality: The OECD job quality framework. *OECD Social, Employment and Migration Working Papers*, No. 174, Paris: OECD Publishing.

Cedefop (2021). *The Green Employment and Skills Transformation: Insights from a European Green Deal Skills Forecast Scenario*. Luxembourg: Publications Office. http://data.europa.eu/doi/10.2801/112540

Conen, W. & Schippers, J. (eds) (2019) *Self-Employment as Precarious Work: A European Perspective*. Cheltenham: Edward Elgar Publishing.

Docherty, P., Kira, M., & Rami Shani (2009) *Creating Sustainable Work Systems. Developing Social Sustainability*. 2nd ed. London: Routledge.

EU (2001) A Sustainable Europe for a Better World: A European Union Strategy for Sustainable Development. EU Commission's proposal to the Gothenburg European Council. Luxembourg: Office for Official Publications of the European Communities.

EU (2017) European Pillar of Social Rights. EU Publication Office.

EU-OSHA (2018) Foresight on new and emerging occupational safety and health risks associated with digitalisation by 2025 European Risk Observatory Report. Bilbao.

Eurofound (2015a) *Sustainable Work over the Life Course: Concept Paper*. Luxembourg: Publications Office of the European Union.

Eurofound (2015b) *New Forms of Employment*. Luxembourg: Publications Office of the European Union.

Eurofound (2019) *Sustainable Work over the Life Course: Concept Paper*. Dublin: Eurofound.

Eurofound and ILO (2019) *Working Conditions in a Global Perspective*. Publications Office of the European Union, Luxembourg, and International Labour Organization, Geneva.

European Council (2006) Renewed EU Sustainable Development Strategy as adopted by the European Council on 15/16 June 2006. Document No:10917/06

European Parliament (2009) Indicators of job quality in the European Union. Directorate general for internal policies policy department A: Economic and scientific policy employment and social affairs. Brussels: European Parliament.

Eurostat (2018) Labour Force Survey (LFS) ad-hoc module 2017 on the self-employed persons Assessment Report 2018 edition. *Statistical Reports Eurostat*. Luxembourg: EU Publication Office.

FAS (2009) Sustainable work – a challenge in times of economic crises. Conference in connection with the Swedish EU Presidency, Stockholm October 2009. Conference report.

Fischer, K. & Zink, K.J. (2012) Defining elements of sustainable work systems – A system-oriented approach. *Work 41:* 3900–3905.

Frey, C. B. & Osborne, M. A. (2013) *The Future of Employment: Ho Susceptible are Jobs to Computerisation?* Oxford: Oxford Martin School, Oxford University.

Gardner, H., Csikszentmihaly, M.& Damon, W. (2001) *Good Work. When Excellence and Ethics Meet.* New York: Basic Books.

Green, F. (2006) *Demanding Work: The Paradox of Job Quality in the Affluent Economy.* Oxford: Princeton University Press.

Hira-Friesen, P. (2018) Immigrants and Precarious Work in Canada: Trends, 2006–2012. *Journal of International Migration and Integration*, 19 (1), pp. 35–57.

Holzer, H., Lane, J, Rosenblum, D., & Anderson, F. (2011). *Where Are All the Good Jobs Going? What National and Local Job Quality and Dynamics Mean for U.S. Workers.* New York: Russel Sage Foundation.

Hvid, H.S. & Lund, H.L. (2002) Sustainable work: concepts and elements of practice. *Journal for Transdisciplinary Environmental Studies, 1* (2), 20 s.

Hvid, H. & Falkum, E. (eds) (2018) *Work and Wellbeing in the Nordic Countries. Critical Perspectives on the World's Best Working Life.* London: Routledge.

Håkansta, C. & Abrahamsson, K. (eds) (2008) Workplaces of the Future. Work-in-Net Foresight Seminar held in Stockholm, Sweden, September 2008.

ILO (2013) *Sustainable Development, Decent Work, and Green Jobs*. Geneva: ILO.

ILO (2017) *Synthesis Report of the National Dialogues on the Future of Work.* Geneva: ILO.

ILO (2019) *Work for a Brighter Future. Global Commission on the Future of Work.* Geneva: ILO.

ILO and OECD (2020) *Social dialogue, Skills, and Covid-19. The Global Deal for Decent Work and Inclusive Growth Flagship Report*. Geneva: ILO.

Kalleberg, A.L. (2011) *Good Jobs, Bad Jobs: The Rise of Polarized and Precarious Employment Systems in the United States, 1970s to 2000s.* New York: Russel Sage Foundation.

Kalleberg, A.L. & Vallas, S.P. (2017) Probing precarious work: Theory, research, and politics. *Research in the Sociology of Work*, 31, pp. 1–30.

Karasek, R. (2017) Science and Research. Psychological Value in Work and Political Economy. Foreword to Oeij, P., Rus, D., and Pot, F. (eds), *Workplace Innovation. Theory, Research and Practice.* Cham: Springer.

Kira, M. & Eijnatten, F. M. van (2009). Socially sustainable work organizations: A chaordic systems approach. *Systems Research and Behavioral Science,* 25 (6), 743–756

Kira, M. & Eijnatten, F.M. van (2013). Socially sustainable work organizations: A debate. *Systems Research & Behavioral Science*, 30 (4), 506–509.

Lewchuk, W. (2017) Precarious jobs: Where are they, and how do they affect well-being? *Economic and Labour Relations Review*, 28 (3), pp. 402–419.

Lorenz, E. & Potter, J. (2019), Workplace organisation and innovation in small and medium-sized enterprises, *OECD SME and Entrepreneurship Papers*, No. 17, Paris: OECD Publishing,.

NIOSH (2020) Potential scenarios and hazards in the work of the future: A systematic review of the peer-reviewed and gray literatures. Schulte, et al. *Annals of Work Exposures and Health*, 2020, 1–31

OECD (2014) "How good is your job? Measuring and assessing job quality", Chapter 3, *OECD Employment Outlook* 2014. Paris: OECD Publishing.

Ojala, S. & Pyöriä, P. (2019) Precarious work and the risk of receiving a disability pension *Scandinavian Journal of Public Health*, 47 (3), pp. 293–300.

Oeij, P. & Dondt, S. (2017) Theoretical Approaches Supporting Workplace Innovation. Pages 63–78 in Oeij, P., Rus, D., Pot, F. (eds). *Workplace Innovation. Theory, Research and Practice*. Cham: Springer.

Oeij,P., Rus, D., Pot, F. (eds) (2017) *Workplace Innovation. Theory, Research and Practice*. Cham: Springer.

Oeij, P.R.A., et al. (2017) Implementing workplace innovation across europe: Why, how and what? Oeij, P., Rus, D., & Pot, F. (eds). *Workplace Innovation. Theory, Research and Practice*. Cham: Springer, pp. 149–169.

Parent-Thirion, A., Vermeylen, G., Wilken, M., Biletta, I., & Pot, F.D. (2017) Towards the high road of workplace innovation in Europe? An illustration of the usefulness of the dataset of the European Working Conditions Survey. In Oeij, P., Rus, D., Pot, F. (eds). *Workplace Innovation. Theory, Research and Practice*. Cham: Springer

Perry, J.A., Berlingieri, A., & Mirchandani, K. (2019) Precarious work, harassment, and the erosion of employment standards. *Qualitative Research in Organizations and Management: An International Journal*, 15 (3), pp. 331–348.

Pot, F. D., Rus, D., & Oeij, P.R.A. (2017) Introduction: The need to uncover the field of workplace innovation. Pages 1–8 in Oeij, P., Rus, D., Pot, F. (eds). *Workplace Innovation. Theory, Research and Practice*. Cham: Springer.

Rodgers, G. (1989). Precarious work in Western Europe: the state of the debate. Pages 1-16 in Rodgers, G. and Rodgers, J. (eds), *Precarious Jobs in Labour Market Regulation: The Growth of Atypical Employment in Western Europe*. Geneva: International Institute for Labour Studies.

Servoz, M. (2019) The future of work? Work of the future! On how artificial intelligence, robotics and automation are transforming jobs and the economy in Europe. AI report. European Commission.

Standing, G. (2011) *The Precariat. The New Dangerous Class.* New York: Bloomsbury Academic.

Sustainable Work in Horizon 2020 (2014, February) Research Agenda for Sustainable Work as a Resource for Health, Innovation and Growth in Horizon 2020 reflections from an international workshop. Lund University

Swedish Agency for Work Environment Expertise (2020) *Work Environment of the Future – Trends, Digitalization, and Employment Forms: Three Systematic Reviews*. Gävle: Sawee.

Terkel, S. (1972) *Working: People Talk about What They Do All Day and How They Feel about What They Do*. New York: New Press.

Theorell, T. & Karasek, R. A. (1996) Current issues relating to psychosocial job strain and cardiovascular disease research. *Journal of Occupational Health Psychology*, 1(1), pp. 9–26.

Van Aerden, K., Gadeyne, S., & Vanroelen, C. (2017) Is any job better than no job at all? Studying the relations between employment types, unemployment, and subjective health in Belgium. *Archives of Public Health*, 75 (1), art. no. 55.

Van Horn, C.E. & Heidkamp, M. (2019) Older workers, precarious jobs, and unemployment: Challenges and policy recommendations. *Generations*, 43 (3), pp. 21–28.

Vendramin, P. & Parent-Thirion, A. (2019) Redefining working conditions in Europe. *International Development Policy*, Vol. The ILO @ 100, no.11, pp. 273–294

Warhurst, C., Carré, F., Findlay, P., &Tilly, C. (2012) *Are Bad Jobs Inevitable? Trends, Determinants and Responses to Job Quality in the Twenty-First Century.* New York: Palgrave.

Warhurst, C., Mathieu, C., & Wright, S. (2017) Workplace innovation and the quality of working life in an age of uberisation. In Oeij, P., Rus, D., and Pot, F. (eds). *Workplace Innovation. Theory, Research and Practice.* Cham: Springer.

Wenger, E. (1998) *Communities of Practice: Learning, Meaning, and Identity.* Cambridge: Cambridge University Press.

World Economic Forum (2016) *The Future of Jobs. Employment, Skills and Workforce Strategy for the Fourth Industrial Revolution.* Geneva: World Economic Forum.

UN (1988) *Our Common Future. Report of the World Commission on Environment and Development.* New York: United Nation.

Zink, K.J. (2014) Designing sustainable work systems: The need for a systems approach. *Applied Ergonomics* 45 (2014), pp. 126–132.

Franz Ferdinand Eiffe

Eurofound's reference framework: Sustainable work over the life course in the EU

Abstract: In this chapter, the Eurofound reference framework of sustainable work is introduced, and its components are discussed. Section 2 presents sustainable work outcome indicators on the societal and the individual level, and provides some reflections of how those can be used jointly to map overall beneficial work environments for sustainable work. Section 3 investigates contextual factors such as infrastructures, workplace practices and job quality. The specific role of motivation is highlighted in Section 4, based on empirical analysis. The chapter closes with some conclusions and a policy outlook.

About Eurofound

Founded in 1975 and located in Dublin, Ireland, the European Foundation for the Improvement of Living and Working Conditions (Eurofound) is a tripartite European Union Agency, whose role is to provide information, advice and expertise on working conditions and sustainable work, industrial relations, labour market change and quality of life and public services, to support the EU Institutions and bodies, Member States and Social Partners in shaping and implementing social and employment policies, as well as promoting social dialogue on the basis of comparative information, research and analysis.

Keywords: Eurofound, job quality, sustainable work, work environment, work life balance, employment levels, green transition

Introduction

Demographic change has triggered policy debates and responses across Europe. The need to keep workers in employment longer is a consequence that requires rethinking of new solutions for working conditions, and career paths helping workers to retain their physical and mental health: as well as motivation and productivity, throughout an extended working life. Given the pressures of demographic change, a work environment needs to be created that satisfies the needs of different groups of workers; not only older workers, but also those with care responsibilities, for example, or people with physical disabilities or mental health problems, to allow for the participation of the largest possible numbers in the labour force.

With a focus on climate change and the transition towards a low carbon economy as a main priority of the European Commission (2021), further challenges arise for sustainable work. The key question in this regard is how to ensure that most affected regions and occupations in Europe (such as coal mining regions and others) get full support, by facilitating employment opportunities in new sectors and those in transition, and offering reskilling opportunities.

Eurofound has entitled the broad goal set out by this statement as "*making work sustainable over the life course*". Identifying and analysing the factors and actions underpinning sustainable work throughout working life has been a research priority for Eurofound since 2013. In a first step, the rather expansive concept of sustainable work was illuminated by a framework that explains our approach, and that has been used as reference point for a range of Eurofound research projects examining different aspects of sustainable work (e.g. Eurofound 2015, 2016a, 2017a, 2017b).

The Eurofound framework of sustainable work over the life course

Eurofound first published a conceptual paper on *Sustainable Work over the Life Course* in 2015. There, sustainable work is defined as the interplay of working and living conditions being such that "*they support people in engaging and remaining in work throughout an extended working life*" (Eurofound, 2015, p. 5). Eurofound hence takes the perspective of the working individual being in a concrete job situation (job quality) that interacts with its private life domain. Key features are around job quality, work-life balance, developing skills and employability, having enough earnings etc. The issue of addressing critical life events and being supported through transitions is a further crucial element in our approach. In addition, the framework opens a societal perspective, by emphasising the central role of policies, infrastructures, regulations and practices in shaping both the individual and work context to unfold within institutional settings and socioeconomic developments

With the objective to bring this concept a step further, Eurofound commissioned a feasibility study (Virtanen et al. 2018) with the guiding research question of how and to what extent the conceptual framework can be operationalised, in order to measure outcomes of sustainable work and associated determinants. Based on extensive literature research and the consultation of leading experts in the field, the authors of this study developed: together with Eurofound, an analytical reference framework mapping out the main constituents of sustainable work and their interrelations as illustrated in Fig. 1. Consequently, the single components of the reference framework were operationalised, and key measures selected, composing a final dashboard of indicators.

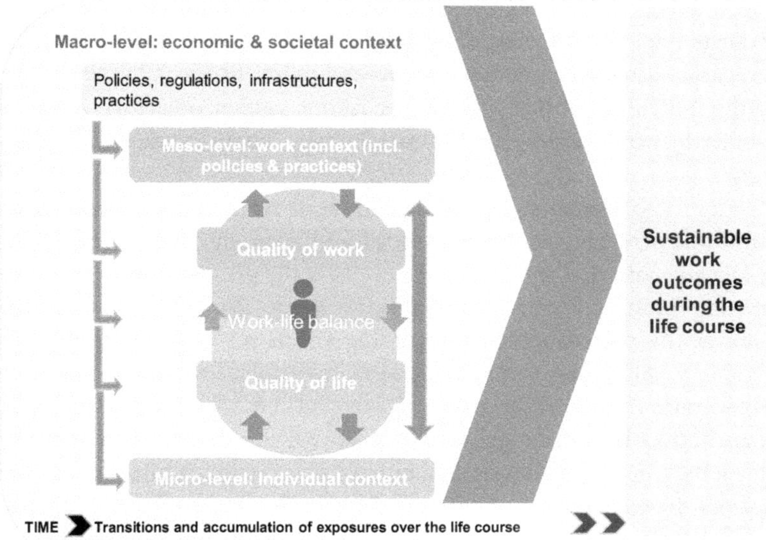

Fig. 1. Eurofound Sustainable Work Framework.
Source: Virtanen et al. 2018.

What are sustainable work outcomes?

Can sustainable work be measured? Yes and no. No, because there is no single indicator which captures the whole nature of the phenomenon as outlined above; and yes, because as the literature demonstrates, there are various indicators that summarise outcomes, reflecting a sustainable work environment. However, there are many ways of measuring one or the other aspect of sustainable work, and previous research has shown various efforts of how to do it (e.g. Fleuren 2019). Eurofound's approach adds a new angle to this debate in bringing both the macro- and micro-perspective together, arguing that both essentially contribute to understanding the full scope of the phenomenon.

Sustainable work outcome indicators were proposed by Eurofound in order to operationalise the framework`s underlying definition as quoted above ("*engaging and remaining in work throughout an extended working life*"). They refer to increased labour market participation across the life cycle. The indicators hence quantify objectives related to sustainable work or results of sustainable work environments on various levels (individual, macro). First, they capture the societal and economic objective of keeping workers longer in the labour market due to population ageing, demographic change and financial constraints (e.g. as regards sustainable pension systems and public finance). Secondly, they refer to the individual worker and his/her labour market trajectory (fulfilling work; ability to work until/beyond retirement age; labour market history and transitions).

The definition of sustainability in the context of work implies simultaneous efforts towards achieving individual, social and economic work- and labour market-related goals, that will enable the needs of the present worker to be met without compromising his/her ability of future work. This requires sustainable conditions at the current job (e.g. regarding effects on workers' health), the worker's ability, willingness and motivation to do this job (or a similar one) now and in the future (health, skills, work engagement) (see e.g. Eurofound 2018a) and the institutional preconditions for workers to participate in the labour market (available jobs, employment levels, labour market services). While the selection of indicators depends on various factors such as the scope of the study, data availability and data quality, Eurofound suggests a couple of specific indicators on two levels that are comparable across EU Member States:

Macro-level

The indicators proposed at societal level illuminate various aspects of what the OECD (2006) once called "Live longer, Work longer". While the outcome indicators deliver snapshots of the situation of Member States at a certain time, they also feed into policy debates of giving people better choices, and incentives to continue working at an older age. They allow for evaluating whether *work systems* are sustainable from a macro-economic policy angle and deliver useful evidence for policy makers to design policies encouraging greater labour market participation at an older age, by "fostering employability, job mobility and labour market demand" (ebd.). The following indicators were suggested:

Senior employment rate of workers aged 55 plus: This indicator was included in the final list for two reasons: First, the employment rate of older workers (and especially its development over the years) gives evidence of a country's capability/capacity to keep the ageing workforce in the labour market. Besides the general employment level and labour market structure, the indicator also highlights how well the interplay of institutional and economic incentives (negative or positive) works in encouraging a later transition from work to retirement. Secondly, senior employment levels also imply labour opportunities for this age group and available jobs. Senior employment levels in themselves, however, say little about the overall sustainability of work in a broader understanding. Factors that impact on senior employment at the company and/or local levels would also include age management programmes, and initiatives with the focus of a smooth transitioning from work to retirement, with benefits for companies as regards knowledge retention. While there is a longer tradition of such practices in some countries like Sweden or the Netherlands (e.g. Wikström et al., 2018), it requires a cultural shift and change in HR management in other, particularly Eastern European, countries (e.g. Joniaková and Blštáková, 2015).

The duration of working life provides a measure of the average number of years for a given country and year. It complements the employment rate of older workers, by exploring how many years today's young people are expected to be active in the labour market throughout their life course (under the currently prevailing age-specific participation rates). This information adds the life course perspective to the mere quantitative level of employment ,and can be used to monitor developments in relation to early retirement. The average is computed over all adults in a specific country, and is hence strongly influenced by the proportion of the inactive population outside the labour force. Therefore, no conclusions can be derived about the number of years that people who are currently employed work. The indicator instead emphases the combined effect of the proportion of the active labour force and life expectancy. Variations of the measure are mainly explained by the general participation rate. The measure relates to the discussion of sustainable work as it accounts for systemic career interruptions (e.g. shorter duration of women due to childcare responsibilities) and differences in pension ages (between men and women / between workers of different countries).

The final indicator proposed at the macro-level is the measure of *healthy life years (HLY) at age 65:* The life expectancy of the population beyond retirement age indicates the general health of a population. Whether extra years of life gained through increased longevity are spent in good or bad health is a crucial question, introducing the concept of quality of life (years enjoyed free from the limitation of illness or disability), and highlighting the well-functioning/ wellbeing of a society and its institutions. The indicator hence complements the other two, by estimating average health prospects when reaching retirement age /leaving the labour market. HLY also monitors health as a productive factor, as it not only improves the situation of individuals, but would also relieve public healthcare expenditure, and further boost the likelihood that people continue to work later into life (Eurostat, 2020).

Figure 2 jointly explores the development of all three indicators over a time span of 18 years (2002–2020) for the EU27. Overall, the indicators provide evidence that people work longer today, and that higher proportions of men and women aged 55–64 are active labour market participants than back in 2002. The average duration of working life has increased, as has the number of healthy life years at age 65. The main driver of these developments was the continuous growth of female labour market participation, with substantially shrinking gender gaps in all employment-related indicators. This increase went on even during the years of the economic and financial crisis and the subsequent recession (2008–2013).

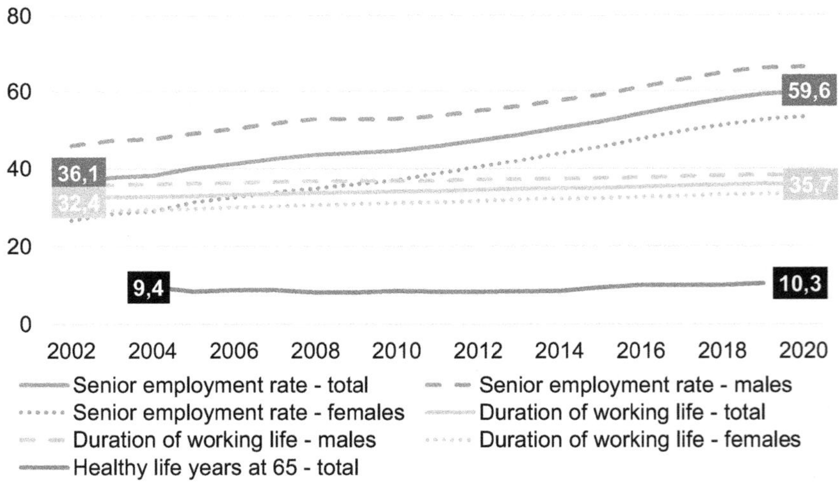

Fig. 2. Macro-level sustainable work outcomes, EU27.
Source: Eurostat.

However, the figure looks at the EU as one single labour market, while both developments and levels differ largely across Member States. Senior employment rates, for instance, range from 77.6 % in Sweden to 44.1 % in Luxembourg. Similarly, the duration of working life is highest in Sweden, Denmark and the Netherlands, with 40 years or more and lowest in Italy, Croatia and Greece with figures of 33 years or less. Healthy life years at 65 range from 16.2 in Sweden to 4.7 in Latvia and Slovakia. This highlights that both health- and labour market-related sustainable work outcomes vary hugely among Member States, and makes a case for country-level analysis and monitoring.

Micro-level (individual)

The outcome indicators at individual level explore work engagement, work ability and health outcomes. They are a crucial complement to the macro-level measures as they introduce individual work outcomes. Data availability at the micro-level lags well behind the long time series and well-established data basis of the macro indicators. Some are only available for a single year, and the concepts behind (such as work engagement) are relatively new. Still, we believe that a first step is achieved with these indicators being part of the EWCS programme. Inclusion into the LFS, and further conceptual development would be desirable for future monitoring.

Work engagement (tot. / 55+) has been defined as a "positive, fulfilling, work related state of mind that is characterised by vigour, dedication and absorption" (Schaufeli et al. 2003). The concept describes the relationship of the worker with his or her work and the organisation (Green et al. 2017; Van Dam et al. 2017). Engagement has emerged in the last years as the concept that meets both the interest of workers and employers. It was proposed as a sustainable work outcome, as it is positively associated with well-being, high levels of job performance and hence sets the conditions for the worker being able to enjoy and stay at work. Engagement at work is an incentive to keep on working. Social partners and public authorities can set the conditions under which engagement flourishes, such as favourable workplace practices, staff involvement, etc.

Self-perceived health status of workers (overall/aged 55 plus) is the second micro-level indicator suggested. The proportion of workers reporting very good or good health is based on EU-SILC, and available since 2008. It has been extensively tested in terms of validity and reliability. Workers` health is both the precondition, but also to a certain extent the outcome, of labour market participation. Sustainable work is inextricably linked to health, and previous research has shown strong links between population`s health and work ability (Eurofound, 2019b, Söderbacker et al., 2020).

The *attitude towards the sustainability of the current job* can be captured via the EWCS, where respondents are specifically asked: "Do you think you will be able to do your current job or a similar one until you are 60 years old?". For respondents aged 56 or older, the question was changed to: "Do you think you will be able to do your current job or a similar one in five years' time?". The fact that the proportion of respondents that were unable to answer the question is similar for older and younger workers might indicate that the question is no more difficult to answer for younger people than it is for those who are older. Nevertheless, the answers to these questions reflect the perception of employees towards the sustainability of their current job. Analyses of which aspects of the job contribute answering "Yes" to this question shed light on what workers think is important for them to be able to remain in work. From a data quality perspective, the item is however far from being perfect, and further cognitive testing and other data quality measures would be needed.

Overall assessment: Taking a joint perspective

Table 2 gives an overview of all sustainable work outcome indicators proposed by Eurofound, and illustrates the width band in each of them across EU27 Member States. The table illustrates the wide range of outcomes among various countries, and highlights that there is room for improvement within the European Union in making work overall more sustainable. It emphasises the point that monitoring should take place at Member State level.

	Work engagement* (all workers) Scale 0-100	Work engagement* (55+) Scale 0-100	Very good or good self-perceived health status (all workers), %	Very good or good self-perceived health status (55-64), %	Able to do your current job until the age of 60* / in 5 yrs. time if >56, %	Employment rate (55-64), %	Expected duration of working life, years	HLY at age 65**
Lowest value	69	64	59.4	33.8	47.4	44.1	31.2	4.7
Highest value	80	84	93.6	88.1	79.0	77.6	42.0	16.2

Tab. 2. Overview of sustainable work outcome indicators (micro- and macro-level), 2020.
Source: Eurofound, Eurostat, *2015 data, **2019 data.

A monitoring tool could take a joint perspective, categorising the sustainable work environment as per a country`s overall performance in the outcome indicators, both at the micro and macro-level. For both analytical and illustrative purposes, composite indicators on both levels could be developed, based on normalised sustainable work outcome indicators. On this basis, a sustainable work scale could be developed, mapping countries of different categories: Countries with comparatively (i) high outcomes in both societal and individual level outcomes, (ii) low outcomes in both, (iii) a combination of either high macro-level and low micro-level outcomes or (iv) the other way around. However, such an exercise would require in-depth debates among policy makers, experts and civil society, in selecting a final dashboard of outcome indicators, and on weights assigned to them.

The context of sustainable work

In the Eurofound conceptual framework, sustainable work requires a match between the job and availability for work. At certain points during the life course, difficulties may arise in one or both domains. During these transitions, external support might be needed. Transitions take place, not only between jobs, but also between employment and unemployment, periods of learning or caring, or when returning to work after a period of illness. Eurofound emphasises two levers that can be used to increase the chances of achieving a match between work and the individual: the improvement of job quality (to better match a person's availability for work) and improving availability for work (to better match the demands of the labour market). Finally, attention should also be paid to policies and practices that support not only those who are employed but also those who are currently outside the labour market, due to, for example sickness absence or unemployment, taking into account the work-life balance, health, work ability, and skills. It is obvious that, from a labour market perspective, some groups face pronounced disadvantages as for instance those with functional impairments, disabilities or chronic diseases. As previous research has shown (e.g. Eurofound, 2018b, 2019c), their options for sustainable work need hence to be boosted by courageous policy responses. These range from social and labour market policy mixes to social partner agreements, the design of the workplace, and company-level action (such as applied return-to-work schemes, flexible work arrangements and generally better recognition).

The core context: Job quality

The most direct and obvious determinant of the sustainability of work is the characteristics of the job. Eurofound's job quality framework (2012, 2017) assesses working conditions along seven key dimensions measured at the workplace level based on data from the EWCS. Job quality is defined as an objective measure of the potential impact of the characteristics of jobs on the well-being of workers:

- *Skills and discretion*: the opportunities for workers to exercise autonomy, apply their skills, participate in the organisation, and develop professionally
- *Social environment*: the extent to which workers experience both supportive social relationships and adverse social behaviour
- *Physical environment*: the degree to which workers are exposed to physical and environmental risks at work
- *Work intensity*: the level of time, workload and emotional demands that put pressure on workers

- *Prospects*: the degree of job security and opportunities to progress in one's career
- *Working time quality*: the duration, scheduling and flexibility of working time arrangements
- *Earnings*: the income from work

How do these seven dimensions affect the sustainability of work over the life course? Although this is basically an empirical question that has to be answered by research (see preliminary analysis in Eurofound 2019a; Eurofound 2019b), three features of job quality have to be taken into account, particularly in order to understand its relationship to the sustainability of work: firstly, each of the dimensions affects the well-being of workers; secondly, although they are often empirically correlated, the relative importance of the different dimensions can vary across jobs; and finally, high quality in one dimension may compensate for lower quality in another. For instance, higher earnings can help to compensate for certain working time quality or work intensity issues. However, one dimension can never perfectly substitute for another, and it is questionable whether certain elements of a job can really be compensated for. Certain physical demands, for instance, cannot be compensated by earnings, as they can have an irreversible negative impact on health. In practice, workers may combine either negative or positive scores on all or several dimensions

Employability and skills

Individual skills and competencies are crucial to entering the labour market ,and to remaining at work. Lack of skills can result from initial low-level qualifications, changing requirements, obsolescence of skills over time or simply structural changes in the demand for labour. Keeping skills updated throughout the life course in a changing labour market is challenging. Continuous development of competencies and acquisition of qualifications depends both on lifelong learning opportunities, and a person's life and work circumstances. However, a high level of employability is: besides the supply of jobs, one prerequisite for achieving employment security. Conversely, low levels of employability put individuals in danger of losing attachment to a labour market where job security cannot be guaranteed.

Company practices and workplace social dialogue

Company-level policies are the crucial place for the proper implementation of practices related to sustainable work. The job climate in this regard is shaped by the way in which government regulation and collective agreements are applied in practice, the workers' voice is heard (or not) and worker participation evolves. Company and workplace practices provide the "meso-context" in keeping people being engaged and healthy at the workplace. Companies implement measures affecting job quality, but also as regards achieving a better fit between the needs and abilities of the individual and the requirements of the job, and to improving the overall work environment.

Workplace practices and the approach to workplace social dialogue touch upon the core of the work experience. How do companies organise their day-to-day business, and what is the role of employees in the organisation? Inclusive HRM practices and strong employee involvement in decision-making are associated with beneficial performance outcomes as regards innovation, productivity or workplace wellbeing (Eurofound, 2016a; Eurofound 2016b; Eurofound, 2017a; Eurofound 2017b). Work engagement is positively associated with organisational justice, and other motivational features linked to an active role for the employee at the workplace (Eiffe. 2018). High-involvement workplaces better manage to assign active roles to staff and increase employee commitment and work engagement, with positive impacts on performance and productivity. Many workplace practices such as regular staff meetings, employee involvement in decision making or official employee representatives at the workplace are all positively associated with sustainable work outcomes (Eurofound, 2016a; Eurofound 2020a; Eurofound 2020b).

However, an active approach to making work sustainable can help to achieve overarching social objectives. Practices contributing to such goal include, for instance, age management in companies, to prevent the premature exit of workers. Apart from adapting the job and the workplace, a possible revision of the role of older workers can be helpful. As the strength of the productive characteristics of the old and the young may differ considerably, there is great potential for diversity management to exploit the complementarities of these characteristics, and to widen the scope for mutual learning between generations.

Work-life balance

The reconciliation of working and private life is an important element in the sustainable work framework, as it marks the intersection between job quality and quality of life. The framework ultimately regards a lack of work–life balance as a barrier to employment. The perspective is broader, in the sense that it also takes into account more than just the work-family balance, explicitly taking a life-course perspective, and acknowledging that work and life demands, and resources differ across the life-cycle. Striking a balance between work and other aspects of life is increasingly fundamental for workers, and especially so for those with care responsibilities. A balance between employer-friendly and employee-friendly flexibility is also struck at the workplace level. This does not mean that there is a strict trade-off. Many companies in the EU already promote workplace policies that are conducive to work-life balance, to attract and retain workers. Modernised work practices such as teleworking, part-time work and flexible working time must be considered as instruments to improve the work-life balance, so that reconciliation becomes feasible (Eurofound, 2018b).

Social partners

Although the institutional arrangements and levels of inter-institutional co-operation differ across countries, in most Member States social partners have a role to play alongside the public authorities. Case studies indicated that the social partners have been instrumental in promoting sustainable work in many Member States (Eurofound, 2016a). Social partners often raise awareness, initiate discussions, provide support and campaign on a number of questions related to low pay, lifelong learning, health and safety, gender equality, and sustainable work as a whole. They need to be heard in the processes of legislation drafting. In some cases, the social partners may use tripartite negotiations to give advice or put proposals to the government, on several issues related to sustainable work, which may have some concrete outcomes. For example, the National Labour Council and the Labour Foundation in Belgium, as well as the Social and Economic Council in the Netherlands, have played a major role in developing advice, which has often been adopted subsequently in key legislation.

For this to work best, however, the social partners need to have an incentive to co-operate and find a compromise. If this happens, it often leads to a better-supported agreement, which can be defended to the workers and employers more easily. Apart from institutionalised tripartite co-operation, various policy frameworks, information campaigns, committees and network projects (usually government-led) may also boost partnership efforts between relevant social partners and policymakers.

Overall, a strong role taken by the social partners is significant in successfully pursuing strategies contributing to sustainable work, and creating a favourable working environment. In general, their contributions can have a wide impact on comprehensive approaches and relevant sectoral policies. Nevertheless, much depends on the institutional and legal frameworks in which the social partners operate, and the extent of inclusion such frameworks provide.

Legislation, policies, infrastructures

Legislation and public policies intervene at points outside of the workplace across a life course. Social protection systems assist with critical life events (providing, for instance, income support for transition periods, sickness insurance, child benefits, unemployment benefits and pensions). Quality services, for example a comprehensive care infrastructure, provide support, ideally in a coordinated and integrated way. Through legislation, rights to certain working time and leave options (such as part-time work and parental leave) are guaranteed. A range of policies are aimed at creating inclusive labour markets through labour market activation, tackling labour market segregation, and improving access to employment for the disadvantaged. Legislation establishes rights to non-discrimination, including the adaptation of workplaces to workers with special needs, and to life-long learning. Social partners are involved in the shaping and implementation of these policies and legislative initiatives.

A just transition towards a low carbon economy[1]

A Green Deal and sustainable work

With the European Green Deal (European Commission, 2021), the EU is setting in motion a set of policies and measures aimed at preventing and alleviating the effects of climate change. The main objective is to embark on the transition to a climate-neutral economy. These much-needed climate policies, however, may have undesirable distributional effects on individuals, work and companies. As well as their intended effects, some measures, such as carbon taxes, can have associated regressive effects, negatively impacting on people with lower income levels, and hence lowering their acceptability. Based on the most recent national experiences, Eurofound (2021) identifies those climate policies having significant distributional effects, and explores how these are being addressed in the various Member States.

The transition to a carbon-neutral economy, including the circular economy and the implementation of the EU's recovery instrument Next Generation EU will have an impact on the sustainability of work in general, and on those who are most affected in particular. The socioeconomic effects include employment shifts, and the transformation of jobs and working conditions, as well as the distributional impact of climate change policies. Eurofound is set to engage in research

1 This chapter builds on Eurofound 2021.

on these topics with its 2021–2024 Programming Document. Eurofound will co-operate with various international organisations and EU agencies, for example with the European Environment Agency (EEA) in the area of social impacts of climate change policies. Further partnership with the International Labour Organization (ILO) is also foreseen on the subject of the changing world of work.

Social dialogue towards a just transition

In general, examples of initiatives by social partners, including collective agreements, addressing the potential undesirable consequences of the transition to a climate-neutral economy, are still relatively scarce. The few cases identified in Eurofound (2021), however, illustrate how social partners, sometimes in bipartite or tripartite settings (for example, in the Polish mining sector and the Spanish electricity sector), and at all levels (from EU level to company level) are working together in the context of the transition to a climate-neutral economy.

The information collected through Eurofound's Network of Correspondents shows that business or employer representative organisations' main concerns are ensuring that climate policies do not reduce competitiveness or become a competitive disadvantage. The Malta Employers' Association may be an exception, as it explicitly highlights that it is important to consider the socioeconomic impacts of climate policies, and makes specific suggestions for the design of climate policies. For example, the association contends that such policies should ensure education for all, by promoting lifelong learning and capacity building; ensure fair wages by favouring licensed suppliers; provide support to suppliers engaged in environmental campaigns; and encourage involvement in corporate social responsibility initiatives.

Workers' representatives have addressed the issue in several countries. They consider it vital to ensure a just transition to a climate-neutral economy for the workforce. Trade unions in Finland and Portugal are concerned with the reskilling of workers and their need for further education. Trade unions in Austria, Hungary and Luxembourg also worry about the financial consequences of the transition in terms of purchasing power and distribution of income. Austria's Chamber of Labour (AK), for instance, maintains that a just transition means shaping climate and energy policies, in such a way that the requirements of climate policy and workers' interests are taken equally seriously. The GSEE's Environmental Secretariat appeals for a just transition to a low-carbon economy, through the creation of high-quality jobs and the involvement of the trade unions in the policy process.

In Sweden, the Swedish Trade Union Confederation (LO) wrote its own LTS in 2018. According to it, climate- and sustainability-oriented investments will provide both old and new companies with a wide range of new business opportunities. The unions demand that the new jobs are "green decent jobs", meaning that they should be ecologically, socially and economically sustainable. The jobs must be resource efficient, with a low environmental impact, have a good working environment under decent working conditions and a reasonable salary. The best way of ensuring this is through collective agreements. LO's LTS also emphasises that the best way to avoid unemployment resulting from climate policies is investment in lifelong learning and further education of employees.

These examples and initiatives show the interlinkage of environmental sustainability with sustainable work, but also highlight the need for actors to intervene in order to design the transition as fairly as possible. They also emphasise that sustainable work cannot only be considered from an individual point of view, but needs to be reflected against the background of social and environmental necessities.

The role of work motivation for sustainable work

Motivational factors are a key in the decision-taking towards transitioning from work to retirement (Zeidler et al. 2015). Labour market participation in general, and staying in the labour market until or beyond reaching eligibility for a pension, require some degree of individual motivation. Particularly, as regards older workers, their motivation of remaining or re-entering the labour market is key for the overall employment rate of this group. Evidence has shown that motivation shifts, from extrinsic factors such as income or reward, to intrinsic sources (such as perceiving the job as meaningful) with increasing age (e.g. Barnes-Farell and Matthews, 2007). The meaningfulness of the job is hence a core factor to keep people in the labour market at older ages.

Eurofound research (Eiffe, 2019) has highlighted the link between motivation and a couple of sustainable work outcomes on the micro-level. The results show that motivation at work: either intrinsically driven by the content of the job, or by organisational factors such as recognition of work well done, appropriate payment, career prospect or fairness, is important for employees in various regards. Motivated employees have higher levels of work engagement, a lower likelihood of their work negatively affecting health, less days of sick leave, and are generally more likely to perceive their job as sustainable. The results also emphasise that motivational categories are linked to varying extents to sustainable work outcomes in all age groups.

Conclusions and policy discussion

Eurofound's concept of sustainable work acknowledges the need of welfare states to extend working lives, and to adapt to new risks (in terms of social protection), by emphasising the necessity to keep a balance between policy measures at the macro-level, favourable work environments and workplace measures and improved job quality. A further essential element is the life-course perspective underpinning the need to focus on workers of all age groups. This makes sustainable work a complex policy area, for which a holistic approach is desirable.

In turn a focus on extending the statutory retirement or other labour-market related measures is not enough to make work sustainable over the life course. Policy makers need to be aware that the workplace itself, and related practices resulting in the perception of justice, recognition, fair payment, career opportunities and motivating environments, matter to achieve this goal (Bakker and Demerouti, 2014). The systematic measurement of motivation and wellbeing at the workplace can help to develop alert systems for intervention. Consequently, the sustainability of work also needs to be addressed at the workplace. Companies must be prepared and willing to keep and invest in older employees. Governments can support good workplace practices with workplace innovation funds, and other instruments to provide consultancy and training. Other more global policy measures can build upon such practices.

Eurofound has provided empirical evidence supporting hypotheses on pathways, as outlined in the analytical framework of sustainable work (Fig. 1): Obvious relationships were for instance found between favourable socioeconomic developments, well-functioning welfare-state institutions, and overall positive sustainable work outcomes. Previous research also highlighted correlations between high-involvement workplace measures such as workplace social dialogue and employee involvement, and sustainable work outcomes. Most importantly: Job quality matters, and must be considered the core determinant of sustainable work outcomes.

For monitoring purposes, indicator dashboards can be useful to keep track of developments across various aspects of sustainable work. It was shown in this chapter that various indicators capture different phenomena and distinct aspects of sustainable work on micro-, macro- and potentially also on meso-level. Selections of specific indicators are normative choices, and are furthermore based on statistical criteria such as data availability and data quality. While these aspects do not impose problems in themselves, it is essential to properly justify these choices (for instance via broad policy debates involving the civil society,) and make them explicit. Synthetic measures of sustainable work to illustrate overall desirable outcomes are useful complements, supporting the holistic perspective.

However, more research is clearly needed to explore the effectiveness of sustainable work policy mixes. This regards the implementation in various sectors of the labour market (particularly against the backdrop of the growing service sector), assessments of big industries vs. SMEs, and the relevance of the concept for various types of workers such as self-employed, platform workers and many others.

Policies addressing sustainable work

Making work individually sustainable means, from a policy point of view, creating a fit between structural characteristics of a job (job quality) and the characteristics of an individual in relation to work (abilities, needs, health, skills, etc.), so that they can interact complementarily at the workplace. From a macroeconomic point of view, policy makers need to react to developments, with growing numbers of retirees straining public budgets and slowing economic growth. Interventions should take place at all levels: government level (legislation, regulation, public services, infrastructure, public funding), sectoral and company level (collective agreements, social dialogue) and individual level (lifelong learning, new learning, upskilling, employability, etc.). In the following a few areas will be highlighted (without being exhaustive), where all actors have a stake:

Following up on the OECD council recommendation on ageing and employment

In 2015, the OECD put forward an age-friendly agenda in three broad policy areas, with the main objective to promote employment at an older age. These included (i) improving incentives to work at an older age, (ii) encouraging employers to retain and hire older workers and (iii) improving employability of older workers by adopting a life-cycle approach (OECD 2019). This is very much in line with the Eurofound sustainable work agenda, and needs to be implemented as part of a new EU 2030 strategy. All areas are crucial for achieving better sustainable work outcomes, and need to be addressed by policy makers at national and EU level.

Activation policies for young and old (life-course perspective)

While the share of the economically inactive population has substantially declined over the past 15 years (from 27.7 % in 2000 to 21.7 % in 2019 in the EU27), there is still a lot of potential to further integrate inactive people of all age groups into the labour market. A focus must be put on young people not in education, employment or training (NEETs), with the objective to prevent scarring effects for further career paths. Further enforcement of youth guarantees is needed at Member State levels. Customised active labour market policies are key to re-skill and up-skill people at risk of or in unemployment. Policy makers and social partners need to align forces to keep older workers employable and productive, to prevent skill obsolescence. A strong focus should lie on closing the age gap in digital literacy.

Work-life balance policies

The reconciliation of work and private life or work and personal responsibilities is a crucial element in the sustainable work framework, and is key for starting employment, remaining in or returning to work, work engagement and productivity at work (see Eurofound, 2018a; Eurofound 2018b). Work-life balance needs hence to be put at the core of employment policies at EU and national level: This includes family leave entitlements and flexible work arrangements for parents and carers, as set out in the Directive for work-life balance (adopted in June 2015).

Gender equality and gender mainstreaming

Though it was not the focal point of this chapter, it is well known from previous research that there are substantial differences in sustainable work outcomes between men and women. Gender mainstreaming and a focus on gender equality is hence indispensable in designing sustainable work policies. Occupational inequalities in sustainable work are also to be assessed from a gender perspective. Female-dominated occupations, such as for instance health and care, fare relatively poorly regarding many dimensions of job quality, and are over-proportionally exposed to emotionally demanding work (Eurofound, 2020a, 2020b), with serious repercussions on health and well-being.

High involvement workplaces

Previous research has shown that involving workplaces and well-functioning workplace social dialogue are likely to produce more motivated, more engaged and more productive and healthier workers (e.g. Eiffe, 2018; Eurofound, 2016a; Eurofound 2016b, 2017b; Kornelakis et al., 2018). Such evidence should encourage employers and social partners to implement inclusive measures in companies, and to increase employees' voice and active participation in organisational decisions at the workplace.

Return-to-work schemes

Return-to-work schemes can help to facilitate the re-entry into the labour market after spells of long-term sick leave, for instance of cancer survivors. Multidisciplinary interventions of physical training, psychological and vocational elements can improve return-to-work. Some authors suggest rehabilitation outpatient services in communities or reintegration teams at large workplaces and/or multinational corporations (de Boer et al., 2015). Important shifts in the policy making process are required, to guarantee the provision of equitable and supportive legal frameworks for ill-workers. To this end, employment, health and social security systems must co-operate, in order to set up coherent return-to-work pathways (Mbengi et al. 2018).

Addressing job quality

The key message of the Eurofound Sustainable Work Framework is that job quality and working conditions are at the core of keeping people engaged and working longer at a better health. Past EU strategies and initiatives (such as the Lisbon Strategy or Europe 2020) have incorporated the view that the conditions under which work is performed need to be looked at. The OECD has agreed in its job strategy that the quality of working environment will be closely monitored. The Joint Assessment Framework (JAF) of the European Commission tracks job quality as a non-recommendation semester objective, and Eurostat provides information on quality of employment on its website. The European Pillar of Social Rights stresses the importance of fair working conditions. However, this proclamation needs to be further filled with substance at all levels. A coherent system of regularly monitoring working conditions with key indicators in each dimension could be the backbone of a future Europe 2030 strategy on Employment and Job Quality.

Social dialogue towards a just transition to a low-carbon economy

Social dialogue can be an important tool to deal with (some) side effects of climate policies. There is evidence that the undesired effects of some climate policies, especially if they affect firms and workers in certain sectors and regions, can be addressed by social partners and that solutions can be achieved through social dialogue and joint initiatives. As of early 2021, there are few examples of social dialogue and collective bargaining initiatives in this area across Europe. Social partners need not only to engage in dealing with current problems, but also pro-actively anticipate potential effects on sectors, companies, etc.

References

Bakker, A.B. and Demerouti, E., 2014. Job demands–resources theory. Wellbeing: A complete reference guide, pp. 1–28.

Barnes-Farrell, J. and Matthews, R.A., 2007. Age and work attitudes. In Aging and work in the 21st century (pp. 163–186). Psychology Press.

de Boer, A.G., Taskila, T.K., Tamminga, S.J., Feuerstein, M., Frings-Dresen, M.H. and Verbeek, J.H., 2015. Interventions to enhance return-to-work for cancer patients. *Cochrane Database of Systematic Reviews*, (9).

Eiffe, F., 2018. Sustainable work – The role of motivation for sustainable work. Eurofound Working Paper Series WPEF18010, Dublin: https://www.eurofound.europa.eu/sites/default/files/wpef18010.pdf

Eiffe, F., 2019. Working conditions and sustainable work – Context of sustainable work: Analysing status quo and progress, Eurofound Working Paper Series WPEF19010, https://www.eurofound.europa.eu/sites/default/files/wpef19010.pdf

Eurofound, 2015. Sustainable work over the life course: Concept paper. Publications Office of the European Union, Luxembourg.

Eurofound, 2016a. Sustainable work throughout the life course: National policies and strategies, Publications Office of the European Union, Luxembourg.

Eurofound, 2016b. Win–win arrangements: Innovative measures through social dialogue at company level, Publications Office of the European Union, Luxembourg.

Eurofound, 2017a. Sixth European Working Conditions Survey – Overview report (2017 update), Publications Office of the European Union, Luxembourg.

Eurofound, 2017b, Working time patterns for sustainable work. Publications Office of the European Union, Luxembourg.

Eurofound, 2017c. Innovative changes in European companies: Evidence from the European Company Survey, Publications Office of the European Union, Luxembourg.

Eurofound, 2017d. Working conditions of workers of different ages: European Working Conditions Survey 2015. Publications Office of the European Union, Luxembourg.

Eurofound, 2018a. Striking a balance: Reconciling work and life in the EU. Publications Office of the European Union, Luxembourg.

Eurofound, 2018b. The social and employment situation of people with disabilities. Publications Office of the European Union, Luxembourg.

Eurofound, 2019a. Working conditions and workers' health. Publications Office of the European Union, Luxembourg.

Eurofound, 2019b. Working conditions and workers' health. Publications Office of the European Union, Luxembourg.

Eurofound, 2019c. How to respond to chronic health problems in the workplace? Publications Office of the European Union, Luxembourg.

Eurofound, 2020a. Gender equality at work. European Working Conditions Survey 2015 series. Publications Office of the European Union, Luxembourg. Eurostat, 2020.

Eurofound, 2020b. At your service: Working conditions of interactive service workers. European Working Conditions Survey 2015 series, Publications Office of the European Union, Luxembourg.

Eurofound, 2021. Distributional impacts of climate policies in Europe. Publications Office of the European Union, Luxembourg.

European Commission, 2021. A European Green Deal – Striving to be the first climate-neutral continent, https://ec.europa.eu/info/strategy/priorities-2019-2024/european-green-deal_en

Fleuren, B.P., 2019. Caught somewhere in time: Conceptualizing, measuring, and predicting sustainable employability (Doctoral dissertation, Maastricht University).

Green, A., & Livanos, I. (2017). Involuntary non-standard employment in Europe. European Urban and Regional Studies, 24(2), 175-192.

Joniaková, Z. and Blštáková, J., 2015. Age management as contemporary challenge to human resources management in Slovak companies. Procedia Economics and Finance, 34, pp. 202–209. Kiasuwa Mbengia, R., Tiraboschi, M., Bouland, C. and de Brouwer, C., 2018. How do social security schemes and labor market policies support the return-to-work of cancer survivors? A review article on challenges and opportunities in the European Union.

Kornelakis, A., Veliziotis, M. and Voskeritsian, H., 2018. Improving productivity: the case for employee voice and inclusive workplace practices. ETUI Research Paper-Policy Brief, 1.

Mbengi, R. K., Tiraboschi, M., De Brouwer, C., & Bouland, C. (2018). How do social security schemes and labor market policies support the return-to-work of cancer survivors? A review article. Journal of cancer policy, 15, 128–133.

OECD, 2006. Live longer, work longer. Ageing and employment policies. OECD, Paris, France.

OECD, 2019. Working better with age. Ageing and employment policies, OECD Publishing, Paris, France. https://doi.org/10.1787/c4d4f66a-en. Virtanen, M., Ervasti., J, Ropponen, A., 2018. Working conditions – Measuring sustainable work over the life course – feasibility study, Eurofound Working Paper Series

WPEF18063, Dublin: https://www.eurofound.europa.eu/sites/default/files/wpef18063.pdf

Schaufeli, W. B., Bakker, A. B., & Salanova, M. (2003). Utrecht work engagement scale-9. Educational and Psychological Measurement.

Söderbacka, T., Nyholm, L. and Fagerström, L., 2020. Workplace interventions that support older employees' health and work ability – a scoping review. *BMC Health Services Research*, 20, pp. 1–9.

Virtanen, M., Ervasti, J. and Ropponen, A., 2018. Measuring sustainable work over the life course - feasibility study, Eurofound Working Paper WPEF18063, https://www.eurofound.europa.eu/sites/default/files/wpef18063.pdf

Zeidler, R., Burr, H., Pohrt, A., & Hasselhorn, H. M. (2015). Arbeit und Gesundheit. Zentralblatt für Arbeitsmedizin, Arbeitsschutz und Ergonomie, 65(3), 149–160.

Frank Pot

Monotonous and repetitive work: Some people are more unequal than others

Abstract: Monotonous and repetitive work is an affront to human dignity. It also carries risks of stress and RSI (repetitive strain injury). Over the years more than 20 % of the working population in Europe carries out tasks of less than one minute. However, in the last decade there has been very little in-depth research into this kind of work. It is time to place repetitive work prominently on the agendas again. We can learn from programmes that were executed in Denmark and Belgium in the past. We can better enforce existing legislation. Criteria for "good work" are available, as well as appropriate design theories. Policymakers and researchers emphasise the importance of job quality. They say nobody should be left behind in these times of transition. Let us not forget this special category of workers with monotonous and repetitive work.

Keywords: monotonous work, repetitive work, work organisation, job quality, good work

Repetitive work mostly undisputed

There are inequalities in the labour market, but people who do repetitive work are a special category. They are more unequal than others. The aim of this chapter is to contribute to initiating a discussion about the acceptability of monotonous and repetitive work, and about measures to alleviate and reduce it. Repetitive work last received public attention In the EU in the late 1980s and early 1990s when legislation, research and development programmes were introduced. We think this kind of work is less common now because of robotisation, but it probably is not. We think there is no other way, given the global competition, but there are examples of better alternatives. We talk a lot about sustainable employability, but apparently that does not apply to people who do repetitive work. We talk about meaningful work and purpose-led organisations, but monotonous and repetitive work is an affront to human dignity. It also carries risks of stress and RSI. It is time to place repetitive work prominently on the agenda again.

Butcher shops and slaughterhouses are well-known examples of repetitive work, but it occurs in many sectors. Think of cleaning work, agriculture and horticulture, production work (cars, bicycles, food, clothing, etc.), distribution centres, fish processing, construction and packaging work in all sectors.

During the Covid-19 pandemic, we noticed that many of these jobs were labelled by the authorities as "essential jobs" for society. The general public also became aware that people who do this work are extra vulnerable to contamination. They often have bad and/or temporary employment contracts, and, in the case of migrant workers, poor housing. All of this has been put on the social partners' agenda with greater attention, unfortunately without considering the organisation of work as a problem (Erol & Schulten, 2021). This also goes for the European trade unions in the meat industry (EFFAT, 2020). The same holds for UNI Global Union (2021) in its guide for workers, organisers and policymakers regarding Amazon. The main topics of criticism are unreasonable rhythms of work that contribute to injury rates, which are much higher than the industry average, with too few breaks and close monitoring and surveillance.

Royal Gazelle bicycle company

Let me give a more extensive example from the Netherlands. In 2015, I visited the new bicycle factory of the more than 100-year-old Royal Gazelle in Dieren, which had been opened by the King shortly before. People were proud of the new building, which looked bright and clean. However, the assembly tasks were 90 seconds. This was called "world class manufacturing". Working conditions were significantly better (5S Method, less dangerous chemicals) than 100 years ago, but the job content was not. Management still followed the principles of Scientific Management, although with a modern-style.

The HR director told me that the employees were content with their work. Well, at least not the people I spoke to privately later. Moreover, we know from social psychology that people cannot live with the cognitive dissonance that they are actually doing inhumane work day after day. In their experience and in their expressions, they adjust to a positive interpretation, especially if they think they cannot change it after all. The works council at Gazelle does not dare to say anything, because the management threatens to leave for low-wage countries. In addition, the management brings in migrant workers from Poland during busy times. This is done by supposedly outsourcing the work to Otto Workforce, and having some production lines supposedly leased by the same company. This type of contracting is a bogus construction intended to circumvent the higher wages and other benefits in the collective labour agreements of Gazelle (metal sector) and of the temporary employment sector.

Producing bicycles can also be done in a different way. In the Koga bicycle factory in Heerenveen there is no assembly line, but there are production cells. Every operator assembles an entire bicycle and discusses the layout of his workplace. During busy times, temporary workers are engaged in accordance with the collective agreement for temporary agency work. Sustainable employability is guaranteed.

What's new?

Of course we should keep in mind that this way of organising work has a long tradition, and cannot easily be changed. Adam Smith (1767, p. 603) described how machines and division of labour made higher productivity and wealth of nations possible, but at the expense of the intellectual, social and martial virtues of the labouring poor. In his view, this could be partly compensated by the provision of elementary education by the government. Taylor further developed this approach in his Scientific Management. However, that did not deliver on the promises of easy performance and reasonable wages, and led to deskilling, exhaustion and industrial action.

Successive counter-movements (Human Relations, Sociotechnical Systems Design, Total Quality Management, Sustainable Work, Lean, Workplace Innovation) could not change that on a large scale, although its representatives emphasised that the knowledge of the workers should be used and developed.

Serious effects

Monotonous and repetitive work is inhumane from a values perspective: it also involves several risks. The most well-known and most frequently researched risk is repetitive strain injury (RSI) due to repetitive movements (Houtman et al., 1994; Leclerc et al., 2001). Monotonous work contributes to work disability as well (Sterud, 2013). So far, this has been the focus of most attention. In addition, research has shown that an imbalance of job demands and decision latitude increases the risk of mental health, coronary heart disease and even mortality (Hansen et al., 2003; Niedhammer et al., 2021). Furthermore, people with poor job content are less active in the neighbourhood and in politics than people with a good quality of work. They are also more receptive to populist ideas (Pot, 2021).

This reminds me of the study of Robert Blauner of 1964, "Alienation and freedom", in which he describes four types of alienation often experienced by manual workers in industry: powerlessness, meaninglessness, isolation (instead of belonging and membership) and self-estrangement. "When work is self-estranging, occupation does not contribute in an affirmative manner to personal identity and selfhood, but instead is damaging to self-esteem" (Blauner, 1973, pp. 32–33). Finally there are the missed opportunities: skills and competences are not used and not developed, which is detrimental for both the employees and the organisation. Implicitly, images of people play a role here. An approach related to Taylorism sees humans as a potentially disruptive factor that must be directed and controlled. Approaches such as sustainable work, innovative work organisation and workplace innovation emphasise the creative potential of people.

Why are these forms of work organisation accepted?

Why do people not care, and accept repetitive work as a kind of normal despite these serious effects? Is it global competition that drives us this way, although there are alternative models available? Do we really think that this kind of work is good for this kind of people, neglecting behavioural theories that explain why workers seem to be happy? Do we legitimise it with the ideology of meritocracy, denying the unequal start (Sandel, 2020)? Do we not care because many of the employees are migrant workers, who should be happy with the opportunity to do this work? Looking at the meat industry, even the general public seem to have more concerns about animal wellbeing than about the wellbeing of the workers. Do consumers prefer low prices to employee well-being? I am afraid many people will answer "yes" to all of these questions.

Criteria for quality of job content

The reason for acceptance cannot be insufficient knowledge, as we have well founded theories.

The Job Demands-Control (JDC) model provides two predictions. High job demand as well as low job control represent risk factors such as stress and low skill discretion that are detrimental to health outcomes such as coronary heart disease, mental ill health etc. The model also predicts that high job demand, as well as high job control foster motivation and learning. Central features of the JDC-model are also the strain and learning hypotheses, referring to two interaction hypotheses on the balance between job demands and job control. Jobs with high demands and low control can be called "high strain jobs" which are a risk for work-related stress. Moreover, stress inhibits learning. Jobs with high demands and high control are called "active jobs" which offer opportunities for learning and coping with stressors (1979). Later, this model was extended with the social support dimension and with innovative and productive work behaviour (Karasek & Theorell, 1990). Recently, the Job Demands-Control-Support model was extended to the organisational level (Karasek, 2020).

In the action regulation theory – which was developed by Hacker (1986, 2003) – "complete jobs" is the central concept. Hacker distinguishes three stages of action regulation: action preparation, task execution and evaluation. Complete jobs cover all these stages. "Activities can be considered to be sequentially complete when they do not merely allow people to execute the task, but also allow them to do the required preparatory cognitive operations (in particular goal setting and deciding on the measures to be taken). These cognitive operations are particularly necessary when people participate in organising the work, and checking the results of one's work. Moreover a task is considered to be hierarchically complete, when the mental regulation is not limited to automated processes, but also requires controlled, i.e., knowledge-based and, moreover, intellectual control processes. Sequentially and hierarchically complete activities offer the crucial option of learning, as opposed to deterioration of skills and abilities in simple and limited routine activities" (Hacker, 2003, p. 112).

In 1981 De Sitter integrated the "job demands-control-model" (Karasek, 1979) into his theory of modern sociotechnical design. "It is not the problems and disturbances in the work that cause stress, but the hindrances to solving them" (De Sitter, 1981, p. 155). In order to maintain this balance, control capacity is required at individual job level (called internal control capacity or job autonomy) as well as regarding the work organisation, in particular the reduction of organisational complexity at production group and plant level (called external control capacity or shop floor consultancy/participation). This has been summarised by De Sitter et al. (1997) in the title of their paper "From complex organisations with simple jobs to simple organisations with complex jobs".

A common misconception is that applying these job quality criteria leads to jobs that require more education. As a result, there would be too few jobs for people with low education. However, this is not the consequence of the design theories discussed above. Jobs at any level of education can have the balance between job demands and job control, as well as be complete with not only executive tasks.

Based on these theories, questions for surveys: including questions on repetitive work, have been developed such as the European Working Conditions Survey of Eurofound. In the Netherlands the methodology for well-being at work (assessment and redesign) was developed, commissioned by the Ministry of Social Affairs and Employment (Pot et al., 1994).

What do we know in figures?

Little is known about the extent of repetitive work, in which sectors it occurs and how it develops. Only the figures from Eurofound's European Working Conditions Surveys (EWCS 2005–2015)[1] provide an indication (Tab. 3). EWCS 2020 is delayed due to the Covid-19 pandemic. The questions are: "Does your work involve short and repetitive tasks shorter than 1minute? Shorter than 10 minutes?" The explanation is that repetitive movements such as a mouse click are not intended. That is a different question.

1 European Working Conditions Surveys (EWCS) | Eurofound (europa.eu).

Tab. 3. Does your job involve short repetitive tasks of less than 1 minute? Does your job involve short repetitive tasks of less than 10 minutes?

European working conditions surveys	No short repetitive tasks	Between 1 and 10 minutes	Less than 1 minute	Total
2005	54.4 %	25.3 %	20.2 %	100.0 %
2010	51.2 %	25.5 %	23.4 %	100.0 %
2015	53.8 %	24.6 %	21.6 %	100.0 %

In Europe as a whole, the figures remain roughly the same over time, 45–48 % of the employees do repetitive work of less than 10 minutes, over 20 % do repetitive work of less than one minute. That is remarkable, because we know that a lot of repetitive work has disappeared. After all, mail is no longer sorted by hand. Welding of bodies in the automobile industry is no longer done by people but by robots. In addition, repetitive work has gone to low-wage countries. Is there always new repetitive work added?

Another question in the EWCS regarding negative aspects of job content is "Does your job involve monotonous tasks?" This question is not very specific, and may also reflect personal feelings. Nevertheless, the EU score in 2015 of 46 % is almost the same as repetitive work (24,6 + 21,6 = 46,2). Countries with the lowest scores (between 25 and 30 %) are Germany, Malta, the Netherlands, Sweden and Norway.

Immigrant workers is an extra vulnerable category, as research in Sweden shows. They generally do not participate at the labour market under the same conditions as native-born. They more often tend to be employed in low-skilled jobs, generally have lower occupational status, are more often in temporary employment, are more frequently working part-time and are overrepresented in jobs where they work long hours for low pay (Aslan Akay & Ahmadi, under revision).

Very little research has been done in this field and the results are difficult to interpret.

In the 2018 BIBB / BAuA employment survey in Germany, 37 % of employees in logistics professions were employed in the simple work category. Among all employees this was 19 %. In addition, there was a decrease in simple work of 8 percentage points between 2018 and 2012 for the logistics professions (BAuA, 2020, p. 129). This percentage may be lower because of automation, but alternatively because more people have started working in logistics, especially in non-repetitive work. Ittermann and Virgillito (2019) do not see a decrease in numbers. The opposite seems true for the meat industry. Because preparatory and support tasks have been automated, it has become more difficult to realise job enlargement and task enrichment, and the percentage of repetitive work is increasing.

The scope of repetitive work has also increased recently, due to further division of labour. The craftsmanship to cut easily saleable pieces from large pieces of slaughtered cattle has virtually disappeared. The large pieces pass several people, and each makes his own prescribed cuts in the piece, 5 to 6 seconds on what are called somewhat misleadingly "vario lines". That work can be done by cheaper unskilled workers and the craftsmen, who could sometimes make a fist when it came to pay or working conditions, have disappeared. That you can look at "vario lines" differently, says Jan van Westreenen, director of Ameco in Apeldoorn, NL. He emphasises that it is about easing the work. You no longer have to work with 75 kg bolts. "Everyone makes a number of slices and is responsible for his own piece. Nor is there any bloody work".

Now that the work is lighter, many women also work in the meat processing company. One might appreciate the good intentions of the management, but light repetitive work is also an affront to human dignity and entails RSI and stress risks.

The Swedish trade union LO observed in 2011, that the proportion of workers and lower-ranking employees who state that they have too simple tasks has increased significantly. The largest increase is among female workers. There the proportion with too simple tasks increased from 18 % in 1991 to 27 % in 2009. The proportion who constantly repeat the same work step many times per hour increased by 10 % among both workers and salaried employees during the period 1991 to 2009. The report was based on data from Statistics Sweden's Labour Force Surveys, and on descriptions of how typical LO jobs have changed over the past 20 years. For many members of LO's unions, it was no surprise that there have been more impoverished jobs. The return to the assembly line has led to fragmented tasks. In the private service sector, there are significantly more impoverished and tightly controlled jobs, for example in transport, property management, security, and warehousing. (Gellerstedt, 2011).

What can we expect?

It is not certain what we can expect, an increase or decrease of repetitive work. A recent report of Wageningen University expects a lot of repetitive work and bad working conditions (little space, unpleasant temperatures) in greenhouse horticulture to last for a long time to come, despite automation, robotisation and digitalisation (Pekkeriet & Splinter, 2020). It is remarkable that although the European Commission (2021a) raises the issue of poor working and living conditions in agriculture and horticulture, it does not bring the task content under discussion. At Audi in Germany, experiments are being held with production cells instead of assembly lines. On many lines a 60-second cycle is run. On the assembly island, however, with tasks of a couple of minutes, old and disabled employees can also keep up: no one has to worry about holding up the others or even causing the line to stop, according to Hubert Waltl, Audi's production manager.[2] However, at Audi we are still talking of tasks of a couple of minutes. Lager (2019) shows that technological innovation and repetitive work remain dominant in the lighting industry in Germany.

"Human-oriented working conditions, such as those associated with empowerment and innovative work organisation, are by no means a sure-fire success in this context" (p. 281). In warehouses new technologies and ergonomics do not seem to improve job quality either. "All in all, the presented cases seem to suggest, that all the talk about ergonomic approaches seems to be more of a fig leaf than a wide-spread strategy to solve one of most pressing problems in logistics in Germany today: labour shortage. Most solutions presented here aim to raise the number of picks per shift, lower error-rates, diminish training time, and eliminate idle times. The foremost solutions to this are various assistance systems and advanced software systems in the background. These solutions typically cut away tasks like getting a new order list to pick, and planning a route through the warehouse. These tasks get replaced with more picks. The consequences are a higher work intensity and progressing taylorisation of tasks, leading to the desired results: More picks per shift, without the need to increase the number of employees, and a further simplification of work tasks, thereby reducing the needed training time. Hence, we see a mostly digital Taylorism scenario in order picking" (Lager et al., 2021, p. 49).

Of course most employees doing monotonous and repetitive work could do more interesting and challenging work. Cedefop's "European skills and jobs survey" (ESJS) shows that in 2014 about 39 % of EU employees had skills that were not being fully used in their jobs, and so did not have potential to develop their skills further. The jobs of overskilled workers typically entailed a low level of task complexity and lacked adequate learning opportunities (Cedefop, 2018). Recent German research shows that new technologies do not change this situation. In Germany, research into simple work in industry and logistics shows that new technologies hardly replace this work. The task content also changes very

2 Montageinseln statt Fließband: Audi plant Revolution der Produktion | Automobilwoche

little. The (low) decision latitude for people with simple work remains the same for most employees (62.1 %), for some slightly less (19.8 %) and for some slightly more (18.1 %) (Ittermann & Virgillito, 2019, p. 85). The European Commission concludes that overqualification is on the rise, and underqualification is declining (European Commission, 2019c).

Forecasting has always proved very difficult. This also applies to the future of work. We can try to make representations of it. In a recent German project, artists were asked to do this. That produces interesting SF scenarios. Will new technologies and new modes of production liberate humanity from labour, or can we expect an AI technocracy (Schmeink & Schneider, 2021)? Journalist Emily Guendelsberger (2019) is describing an already existing and expanding brave new world in the USA, in which people work in low-wage cyborg jobs, while suppressing their humanity, dignity, family and other non-work priorities. She worked at an Amazon warehouse, McDonalds and a call centre.

Previous policies

Alleviating monotonous and repetitive work through job rotation, ergonomic aids and breaks has become quite common, but these measures do not address the heart of the matter, the organisation of work.

Of course, we have had the famous examples of semi-autonomous teams at Volvo and Saab in Sweden in the past, applying sociotechnical systems design. But new foreign owners returned to their familiar Taylorism, albeit in the new guise of lean (Boglind, 2013; Blomquist et al., 2013).

A company that does actively strive to reduce repetitive work is the Danish company Coloplast (medical devices: catheters, stomas). In 2008 it was decided to do this and to monitor it. The Corporate Social Responsibility (CSR) report 2012/2013 showed that the percentage of workplaces with "very short-cycle work" had fallen from 6.5 % in 2009 via 2.2 % in 2010 and 1.5 % in 2011 to 0. 5 % in 2012. The remaining workplaces were always ergonomically optimised (Coloplast, 2013, pp. 18–19).

In Denmark, a programme was set up in the 1990s to reduce "dangerous repetitive work", including research (Hansen et al., 2003). Quantitative targets were even set in 1992: a 50 % reduction before the year 2000. Evaluations show that these targets have not been fully achieved, but that quite a few companies in the meat sector, food, metal and other manufacturing industries have been able to significantly reduce the repetitive work (Hasle et al., 2004).

In a more recent example of a joint approach in Flanders, Vermeerbergen et al. (2018) examined eighteen companies in industry and services that had participated in a sociotechnical redesign programme within the framework of the Flemish initiative Flanders Synergy, in collaboration with VOKA, the East Flanders Chamber of Commerce. The results show that the introduction of production cells (a work unit is responsible for a complete product or service), or semi-autonomous teams, leads to a decrease in the number of repetitive tasks. Task rotation was not a sufficient condition for reducing repetitive work. In some organisations the number of repetitive tasks decreased due to task rotation, in others the number increased. The authors emphasise that improving individual tasks or workplaces did not help. Real improvements are only possible by redesigning the organisation and the process, in their case using sociotechnical redesign. Based on the projects in the food industry, Flanders Synergy: recently the name was changed to Workitects, produced (in Dutch) a brochure and a book that describe for companies which measures they can take to alleviate and reduce repetitive work (De Craecker & Eeckelaert, 2021).

Legislation

World-wide the reference is the 8th Sustainable Development Goal (SDG8) of the UN which aims at: among other things, "decent and productive work for all". The ILO defines decent work as "productive work for women and men in conditions of freedom, equity, security and human dignity".[3]

As said before, repetitive work can be harmful to workers' health. There is enough scientific evidence for that. It is therefore in principle contrary to all OSH legislation. After all, this legislation says that work should not be harmful to workers' health. In addition, there are laws and regulations that specifically concern repetitive and monotonous work. In Europe, this is primarily the Council Directive of 12 June 1989 on the introduction of measures to encourage improvements in the safety and health of workers at work (89/391/EEC). Article 6 (d) is about "adapting the work to the individual, especially as regards the design of work places, the choice of work equipment and the choice of working and production methods, with a view, in particular, to alleviating monotonous work and work at a predetermined work-rate and to reducing their effect on health."

Several countries have adopted this, sometimes with their own accents, in national legislation. Binding provisions in Sweden say about repetitive work: "The employer shall ensure that there is normally no work that is repetitive, closely

3 Decent work (ilo.org).

controlled or restricted. If, nevertheless, an employee must perform such work on account of particular circumstances, the employer shall prevent the risks of ill-health or accidents as a consequence of health-endangering or unnecessarily fatiguing loads. This preventive work must lead to increased variation in the work, for example, through job rotation, job diversification or breaks." And about job decision latitude: "The employer shall ensure that the employees have possibilities of influencing the arrangement and conduct of their work, so that they obtain adequate variation of movement and recovery (Swedish Work Environment Authority, 2012, pp. 9–10)." The Dutch Working Conditions Act of 1999 says in article 3 (c): "Where this can reasonably be required, the design of the workstations, the working methods, tools, and the actual work required shall be adapted to employees' individual characteristics" and in 3 (d): "Monotonous work, and work that needs to be carried out at a particular speed, shall be avoided, where this can reasonably be required, and if not, shall be limited."[4]

Swedish and Dutch legislation is about avoiding and reducing repetitive and monotonous work. This therefore goes further than alleviating repetitive and monotonous work in European regulations. However, phrases like "normally no work that is repetitive" and "as can be reasonably required" are subject to interpretation. Application and enforcement is difficult. An evaluation of the European Commission (2004, p. 31) says: "In conclusion, the feeling of the working population indicates that much still needs to be done as regards work control, and work organisation preventing high cadences and repetitive work and also psychosocial risks".

This suggests an insufficient application of some of the general principles of prevention foreseen in the Framework Directive 89/391. In Sweden, the limited compliance to these fundamental provisions was evaluated in a large research review in 2013. It appeared that Inspection and employers pay attention to technical issues such as risks for accidents, noise, chemicals, vibrations and also micro-ergonomics (eg. adequate lifting equipment), but far less to organisational issues and provisions (Frick, 2014). My impression is that the same holds for the Netherlands. I noticed that even union officials did not know that the law says anything about repetitive and monotonous work.

---

4 Arbeidsomstandighedenwet (ilo.org).

Non-binding standards

An international standard is the Psychosocial Risk Management Excellent Framework (PRIMA-EF) (Leka & Cox, 2008). It refers to the Council Directive of 1989, and stresses the importance of primary risk prevention. This means that psychosocial risks in the workplace: one of them being monotonous work, should be addressed in the first place. Primary prevention approaches seek to combat work-related stress, by changing elements in the way work is organised and managed. Secondary prevention approaches aim to combat work-related stress, by developing individual skills in stress management through training. Recently voluntary standards were published by ISO (2021). In the list for hazard identification related to psychosocial risks, ISO mentions aspects of how work is organised such as: performing work of little value or purpose; low levels of influence and independence (e.g. not being able to influence the speed, order or schedule of work tasks and workload); underuse of skills; lack of task variety or performing highly repetitive tasks; fragmented or meaningless work and machine pacing (par. 6.1.2.1.2).

The recommended measures are quite general, for example "increasing workers' control over the way they do their work, e.g. by introducing flexible working, job-sharing, more consultation about working practices or enabling workers to control the pace of work tasks." The interesting thing is that the importance of measures at the level of the organisation of work is emphasised: "In many cases, this requires redesign of work processes, not only adjustment of tasks (par. 8.1.2.2)."

New policies

To start with, policymakers need much more knowledge about the extent of repetitive work, where it occurs, and what factors determine that it stays and does not change for the better. The discussion about this can lead us to goals that can be achieved in a shorter term, or can help to change unintended effects. For instance, it seems more sensible to use AI to support human labour than to replace it (Acemoglu & Restrepo, 2019). Innovations should not only lead to higher productivity, but also contribute to solving social problems. Industry 5.0 should be human-centric and socio-centric, according to DG Research and Innovation. Robots could take over a number of repetitive and simpler tasks. "Putting core human needs and interests at the heart of the production process (…) also means making sure the use of new technologies does not impinge on workers' fundamental rights, such as the right to privacy, autonomy and human dignity" (European Commission, 2021c, p. 14). It is encouraging that the

European Social Partners (2020, p. 11) agreed that the "The control of humans over machines and artificial intelligence should be guaranteed in the workplace."

DG EMPL also emphasised the importance of human capital: "Robust economic expansion in the EU cannot be sustained without higher total factor productivity growth, which relies more on the efficient use of productive factors, rather than just expanding their use. Total factor productivity thrives in Member States and regions with strong labour market institutions and in firms that invest in workers" training and innovative capital and processes. Policies that help to develop human capital and facilitate workplace innovation are most effective in increasing productivity in the long term, provided labour markets do not discriminate and firms can access the necessary capital' (European Commission, 2019a, p. 28).

Workplace innovation could be easily integrated in EU policy agendas such as innovation, new skills, "more and better jobs" and "social dialogue". On its innovation web page DG GROW refers to "key enabling technologies, such as workplace innovation" (DG GROW, 2021).

In a recent Discussion Paper EU-OSHA uses the concept of "social innovation in the workplace", meaning non-technical innovations that emphasise good quality jobs and employee participation. The argument is that the fourth industrial revolution should go together with social innovation in the workplace (EU-OSHA, 2019).

Organisational choice

Another critical challenge is to understand the reluctance of business leaders and managers to implement workplace innovation or sustainable work systems, despite the advantages demonstrated by a vast and growing body of research. The programmes discussed above required considerable effort to overcome barriers including lack of knowledge and competence, fear of loss of power, a desire to stick to traditions, adversarial industrial relations, and indifference to the fate of people who do repetitive work. Even in cases where the argument of greater productivity and global competition seems valid, there must still be the moral consideration of whether we want it. "Organisational choice" does exist and moral values matter.

Sometimes management takes the easy route by choosing job rotation or customisation of individual tasks (job crafting). The Flemish example already showed that this does not help. Research into repetitive work in the logistics sector also points to this (Blazejewski & Walker, 2018). An approach to work organisation and management system at organisational level is needed (Oeij et al., 2017; Parker & Grote, 2019; Parding et al., 2020).

Soft but firm regulation needed

We have seen that the existing legislation is not very hard ('normally no work that is repetitive' and "as can be reasonably required"). I am not sure whether stricter regulation would make a difference in practice. The most common national and regional interventions are based on "soft regulation" in its various forms, including programmes that provide general policy frameworks and recommendations, information on good practices, the training and education of managers and employees, advisory and consulting services, benchmarking tools, grants and subsidies to companies, and research. An important lesson from the analysis of these measures is that programmes should promote "collaborative innovation" in learning networks, clusters or regional innovation systems that extend beyond the borders of individual organisations (Alasoini, 2016). Such collaborative approaches strengthen the innovation momentum through peer-to-peer interaction and shared learning. Focused on repetitive work, these programmes will have to emphasise that this type of work is inhumane and poses a risk to the physical and mental health of the workers.

Recently several scientists from the USA emphasised the importance of the socioeconomic system. The "massive market failure", as Rodrik and Sabel (2019) call it, to create a "good jobs economy", should be compensated by a better coordinated policy and more action by governments, social partners and research institutes.

Osterman (2018, p. 27) argued that, to support a "good jobs economy", the development of "countervailing power, or, to put it bluntly, coercion" is needed if creating a supportive environment that helps sustain stakeholder behaviour (soft regulation) is not enough. Trade unions, shareholders with broader goals for their investments, governments and the general public (values) could play their part in both strategies.

The emphasis on job quality is also supported by the MIT Task Force on the Future of Work: "We must first understand that today's challenge, and likely tomorrow's, is *not* too few jobs. Instead, it is the quality and accessibility of the jobs that will exist and the career trajectories they will offer to workers, particularly to those with less education. Addressing this challenge means channeling technological progress and accompanying productivity growth into a strong labour market that delivers broadly distributed income growth and economic security, as occurred in the decades after World War II" (Autor et al., 2019, p. 46). The importance of job quality is also underlined in the conclusions of the evaluation of the Europe 2020 Strategy: the employment policy was rather successful but "cannot encompass all the aspects of the changing workplace, in which the quality of jobs matters as much as their availability. In the future, greater attention should be given to the aspect of the quality of work" (European Commission, 2019b, p. 7).

Although the situation in Europe is slightly better than in the USA, due to the social economy that dominates in Europe, the debate on proper policies continues. In Europe workplace innovation is considered not appropriate for hard/direct regulation. The market failure is also visible in EU countries.

Workplace innovation is still not widespread, and the number of precarious and non-standard jobs has been increasing, due to the economic crisis and new technologies. This is why the European Commission, in its Action Plan European Pillar of Social Rights (2021b), encourages national authorities and social partners to foster workplace innovation. EU and national authorities have shown that they can successfully stimulate social dialogue, and develop campaigns for knowledge dissemination and capacity building. However persistent endeavours are needed, and it is a challenge to focus part of these programmes to monotonous and repetitive work, and to involve social partners, government, labour inspectorate and researchers. Additionally much more applied research is needed to develop alternative processes and forms of work organisation. A recent study of Eurofound and Cedefop (2021) shows again that forms of work organisation that provide high levels of autonomy to employees, as well as direct employee participation in decision making, are positively related to innovation performance. Apart from a better economic performance, this will also create sustainable work and a good jobs economy. Even in those cases of repetitive work where the argument of greater productivity and global competition seems valid, we will have to emphasise that this type of work is an affront to human dignity, and poses a risk to the physical and mental health of the workers. This argument fits into the wider context of the debate on GDP: economic growth must be balanced against the effects on collective wellbeing.

References

Acemoglu, D., & Restrepo, P. (2019). *The Wrong Kind of AI? Artificial Intelligence and the Future of Labor Demand.* National Bureau of Economic Research. The Wrong Kind of AI? Artificial Intelligence and the Future of Labor Demand | NBER.

Alasoini, T. (2016). *Workplace Development Programmes as Institutional Entrepreneurs: Why They Produce Change and Why They Do Not.* Aalto University (dissertation).

Aslan Akay, P. & Ahmadi, N. (in progerss. The work environment of immigrant employees in Sweden – A systematic review. Paper submitted to *Journal of International Migration and Integration.*

Autor, D., Mindell, D. A., & Reynolds, E. B. (2019). *The Work of the Future: Shaping Technology and Institutions.* Massachusetts Institute of Technology.

BAuA (Bundesanstalt für Arbeitsschutz und Arbeitsmedizin) (2020). *Stressreport Deutschland 2019: Psychische Anforde-rungen, Ressourcen und Befinden.* Bönen: Druck & Verlag Kettler GmbH.

Blauner, R. (1973) *Alienation and Freedom: The Factory Worker and his Industry.* University of Chicago Press (6th impression).

Blazejewski, S., & Walker, E.-M. (2018). Digitalization in Retail Work: Coping With Stress Through Job Crafting, *Management Revue – Socio-Economic Studies, 29* (1), 79–100.

Blomquist, B., Engström, T., Jonsson, D., & Medbo, L. (2013). Assembly systems and work in the Swedish automotive industry. In A. Sandberg (Ed.) (2013). *Nordic Lights. Work, Management and Welfare in Scandinavia* (pp. 225–254). SNS Förlag.

Boglind, A. (2013). Volvo and a Swedish organisation and management model. In A. Sandberg. (Ed.). *Nordic Lights. Work, Management and Welfare in Scandinavia* (pp. 189–224). SNS Förlag.

Cedefop (2018). *Insights into Skill Shortages and Skill Mismatch. Learning from Cedefop's European Skills and Jobs Survey.* Publications Office of the European Union.

Coloplast. (2013). *Corporate Social Responsibility Report 2012/13.*

Council Directive of 12 June 1989 on the introduction of measures to encourage improvements in the safety and health of workers at work (89/391/EEC).

De Craecker, F., & Eeckelaert, L. (2021). *Samen op smaak gebracht. Over het organiseren van arbeid in voedingsfabrieken van de toekomst (Flavoured together. About Organising Labour in the Food Factories of the Future).* Alimento.

De Sitter, L. U. (1981). *Op weg naar nieuwe fabrieken en kantoren* (*Heading Towards New Factories and Offices*). Kluwer.

De Sitter, L. U., Den Hertog, J. F., & Dankbaar, B. (1997). From complex organizations with simple jobs to simple organizations with complex jobs. *Human Relations*, 50(5), 497–534.

DG GROW European Commission (Retrieved October 2021). *Workplace Innovation.* http://ec.europa.eu/growth/industry/innovation_en

EFFAT (European Federation of Food Agriculture and Tourism Trade Unions) (2020). *Hungry for Fairness: Raising Standards in the Meat Industry*. Policy paper. Brussels: EFFAT.

Erol, S., & Schulten, T. (2021). *Renewing Labour Relations in the German Meat Industry*. Institute of Economic and Social Research (WSI).

Eurofound & Cedefop (2021). *Innovation in EU Companies: Do Workplace Practices Matter?* European Company Survey 2019 series. Publications Office of the European Union.

EU-OSHA (European Agency for Safety and Health at Work) (2019). *The Fourth Industrial Revolution and Social Innovation in the Workplace* (Discussion Paper).

European Commission (2004). *Communication from the Commission on the Practical Implementation of the Provisions of the Health and Safety at Work Directives 89/391.*

European Commission (2019a). *Employment and Social Developments in Europe 2019, Sustainable Growth for All: Choices for the Future of Social Europe.* Publications Office of the European Union.

European Commission (2019b). *Assessment of the Europe 2020 Strategy. Joint Report of the Employment Committee (emco) and Social Protection Committee (spc).* Publications Office of the European Union.

European Commission (2019c). *Skills Mismatch and Productivity in the EU.* Publications Office of the European Union.

European Social Partners (2020). *Framework Agreement on Digitalisation.* European social partners framework agreement on digitalisation | BusinessEurope

European Commission (2021a). *Intra-EU Mobility of Seasonal Workers: Trends and Challenges.* Publications Office of the European Union

European Commission (2021b). *The European of Social Rights Action Plan.* Publications Office of the European Union.

European Commission (2021c). Industry 5.0. *Towards a Sustainable, Human-centric and Resilient European Industry.* Publications Office of the European Union.

Frick, K. (2014). The 50/50 implementation of Sweden's mandatory systematic work environment management. *Policy and Practice in Health and Safety, 12*(2), 23–46.

Gellerstedt S. (2011). *Fler arbetare måste få utvecklande jobb – inte digital Taylorism (More workers need to get developing jobs – not digital Taylorism).* LO.

Guendelsberger, E. (2019). *On the Clock. What Low-wage Work Did to Me and How it Drives America Insane*. Little, Brown and Company.

Hacker, W. (1986). Complete vs. incomplete working tasks: A concept and its verification. In G. Debus & H.-W. Schroiff (Eds). *The Psychology of Work Organization* (pp. 23–36). North Holland Publishers.

Hacker, W. (2003) Action regulation theory: A practical tool for the design of modern work. *European Journal of Work and Organizational Psychology, 12*(2), 105–130.

Hansen, Å. M., Kaergaard, A., Hviid Andersen, J., & Netterstrøm, B. (2003). Associations between repetitive work and endocrinological indicators of stress. *Work & Stress, 17*(3), 264–276.

Hasle, P., Hansen, N.J., & Møller, N. (2004). Agreements between labour unions and employers' associations as a strategy for the prevention of repetitive strain injury. *Economic and Industrial Democracy, 25*(1), 75–101.

Houtman, I.L.D., Bongers, P.M., Smulders, P.G.W., & Kompier, M.A.J. (1994). Psychosocial stressors at work and musculoskeletal problems. *Scandinavian Journal of Work Environment & Health, 20*(1), 39–45 .

ISO (2021). *ISO 45003: Occupational Health and Safety Management – Psychological Health and Safety at Work – Guidelines for Managing Psychosocial Risks*. ISO 45003:2021(en), Occupational health and safety management – Psychological health and safety at work – Guidelines for managing psychosocial risks.

Ittermann, P., & Virgillito, A. (2019). Einfacharbeit und Digitalisierung im Spiegel der Statistik (Simple work and digitisation as reflected in statistics). In H. Hirsch – Kreinsen, P. Ittermann & J. Falkenberg (Hrsg.). *Szenarien digitalisierter Einfacharbeit (Scenarios of digitised simple work)* (pp. 69–86). Nomos.

Karasek, R.A. (1979). Job demands, job decision latitude, and mental strain: Implications for job redesign. *Administrative Science Quarterly, 24*(2), 285–307.

Karasek, R., & Theorell, T. (1990). *Healthy Work : Stress, Productivity, and the Reconstruction of Working Life*. Basic Books.

Karasek, R. (2020). The Associationalist Demand-Control (ADC) Theory. In T. Theorell (Ed.), *Handbook of Socioeconomic Determinants of Occupational Health* (pp. 573–610). Springer.

Lager, H. (2019). *Anpassungsfähigkeit in Zeiten der Digitalisierung. Zur Bedeutung von Empowerment und innovativer Arbeitsorganisation (Adaptability in Times of Digitisation. On the Importance of Empowerment and Innovative Work Organisation)*. Springer.

Lager, H., Virgillito, A., & Buchberger, T.-P. (2021). Digitalization of Logistics Work: Ergonomic Improvements Versus Work Intensification. In M. Klumpp & C. Ruiner (Eds.), *Digital Supply Chains and the Human Factor* (pp. 33–53). Springer.

Leclerc, A., Landre, M.-F., Chastang, J.-F., Niedhammer, I., & Roquelaure, Y., the Study group on Repetitive Work (2001). Upper limb disorders in repetitive work. *Scandinavian Journal of Work Environment & Health, 27*(4), 268–278.

Leka, S., & Cox, T. (Eds) (2008). *The European Framework for Psychosocial Risk Management* (PRIMA-EF) PRIMA-EF Book – Psychosocial Risk Management Excellence Framework.

Niedhammer, I. Bertrais, S., & Witt K. (2021). Psychosocial work exposures and health outcomes: A meta-review of 72 literature reviews with meta-analysis. *Scandinavian Journal of Work Environment & Health, 47*(7), 489–508.

Oeij, P.R.A., Rus, D., & Pot, F.D. (Eds.) (2017). *Workplace Innovation: Theory, Research and Practice*. Springer.

Osterman, P. (2018). In search of the high road: Meaning and evidence. *ILR Review, 71*(1), 3–34.

Parding K., Sjögren, F., Petersson, C., & Pekkari, N. (2020). *The Organization of Work and Its Significance for Health and Wellbeing*. Swedish Agency for Work Environment Expertise.

Parker, S. K., & Grote, G. (2019, 30 December). Automation, algorithms, and beyond: Why work design matters more than ever in a digital world. *Applied Psychology*, 1–45. https://doi.org/10.1111/apps.12241

Pekkeriet, E., & Splinter, G. (2020). *Arbeid in de toekomst; Inzicht in arbeid en goed werkgeverschap in de tuinbouw (Work in the Future; Insight into Work and Good Employment Practices in Horticulture).* Wageningen University & Research.

Pot, F. (2021). Workplace innovation's spillover into community and political participation. *EUWIN Bulletin,* June 2021. Workplace innovation's spillover into community and political participation – EUWIN

Pot, F., Peeters, M., Vaas, F., & Dhondt, S. (1994). Assessment of stress risks and learning opportunities in the work organisation. *European Work and Organisational Psychologist, 4* (1), 21–37.

Rodrik, D., & Sabel, C.F. (2019). *Building a Good Jobs Economy*. Harvard Kennedy School/Columbia Law School. Building a Good Jobs Economy by Dani Rodrik, Charles Sabel:: SSRN

Sandel, M.J. (2020). *The Tyranny of Merit: What's Become of the Common Good?* Penguin Books.

Schmeink, L., & Schneider, R.H. (Hrsg.) (2021). *Future Work. Die Arbeit von übermorgen. 15 Kurzgeschichten aus der Zukunft (Future Work. The Work of the Day after Tomorrow. 15 Short Stories from the Future)*. KIT Scientific Publishing.

Sterud, T. (2013). Work-related psychosocial and mechanical risk factors for work disability: a 3-year follow-up study of the general working population in Norway. *Scandinavian Journal of Work Environment & Health, 39*(5), 468–476.

Swedish Work Environment Authority (2012). *Ergonomics for the Prevention of Musculoskeletal Disorders. Provisions and General Recommendations.* Stockholm: Swedish Work Environment Authority.

UNI Global Union (2021). *The Amazon panopticon. A guide for workers, organizers and policymakers.*

Vermeerbergen, L., Pless, S., Van Hootegem, G., & Benders, J. (2018). From silos to cells: Reducing repetitive jobs through sociotechnical redesign. *Economic and Industrial Democracy,42*(1), 160–178.

Maria Albin, Theo Bodin, and Eskil Wadensjö

Sustainable work for health and job longevity[1]

Abstract: While improved public health in groups with high or middle socioeconomic status permits many to work for more years, the gap is widening for less advantaged groups, such as those with only compulsory level education. Within manual jobs, individual health status and the challenges of physical demands exceed the physical capacity of many middle-aged workers, and with a low bargaining power, constitute major threats to job longevity. Artificial intelligence and digitalisation are also rapidly transforming the labour market, especially for low-mid grade white-collar workers. Young workers often have insecure job contracts, while older workers may have a permanent position but have a fear of leaving a safe position for a new one, and may be forced to leave their job when they are unable to meet the demands.

Current economic incentives to prolong working life, often combined with more restrictive unemployment and disability benefits, may overall increase work participation but may also decrease sustainability in the more disadvantaged part of the labour market.

Recent research suggests that unemployment is the most important factor behind lost working years among workers with less education, and that prevention focused on the work environment rather than individual health promotion, will enhance sustainability together with inclusive welfare systems. Resilience in the workforce on a macro- and workplace level can be achieved by well-established societal measures.

Keywords: disability pension, job longevity, resilience, physical demands, physiological ageing

Outline

This chapter highlights the tension between two trends: increased expectations on career longevity, and increasing socioeconomic inequalities in health. This is further explored as a gap between job demands and the individual capacity, and the risk of being "locked-in" or forced out when facing this scenario. Finally, macro- and micro-level measures to decrease the vulnerability for mainly manual and low-skilled workers are discussed, and more specifically in relation to the sustainable development goal: Decent work and economic growth.

---

1 This paper is partly based on an extended abstract from a research seminar published in Socialförsäkringsrapport (Social Insurance Report) 2020:5 Förlängt arbetsliv – förutsättningar, utmaningar och konsekvenser Rapport från forskarseminariet i Umeå 15–16 januari 2020 (in Swedish).

Better health but increasing inequalities

Better health and longer lives have increased expectations on career longevity. However, these expectations need to consider the development in different parts of the workforce. While life expectancy overall has increased in Europe since 2000, the health divide between socioeconomic groups has remained constant (Southern Europe) or increased (Western, Eastern and Northern Europe; Health Inequalities in the EU, 2013). In Sweden, the overall health status in the population has dramatically improved in recent decades, as reflected in, for example, life expectancy (SOU, 2017). However, the socioeconomic disparities in health have increased.[2] Using different measures of socioeconomic status (e.g. position in the income distribution, educational level) this pattern is consistent for women, and for younger men (Hartman & Sjögren, 2017). The associations between socioeconomic status and health are thought to be mediated through living and working conditions but also the individual resources in economy, social networks, and knowledge, as well as decision latitude throughout life (Health Inequalities in the EU 2013; SOU 2016): Good/sufficient resources and discretion at critical points in life enhance the likelihood of upward instead of downward trajectories in health and living conditions.

The most remarkable and challenging observation is that, as opposed to higher educational levels. life expectancy at age 30 has stagnated during the last three decades amongst women with only compulsory education (Fig. 3).[3] Life expectancy at age 30, was in 2020 by educational level, 57.1 years for women with post-secondary, 54.4 years with upper secondary, and for those with only compulsory education, 50.6 years. It is noteworthy that the variation in life expectancy displays different trends over time within each educational level, decreasing for the highest level, being constant in the intermediate, and increasing in the lowest one. This indicates that the health status is not only stagnating but becoming increasingly heterogeneous among those with low socioeconomic status, while more homogenously improving in the high ones.

---

2 Regional differences within Sweden are small after taking socioeconomic factors into account and tend to decrease. Based on available data the pattern is similar for those born in Sweden and abroad, with essentially the same life-expectancy at age 30 for different educational categories (SOU 2017), but the information is less complete for those born abroad (mortality as well as educational level may be somewhat underestimated).

3 Compulsory education in Sweden is 9 years from age 7 but was previously shorter (6–8 years). A preschool year from age 6 was recently added but is not relevant for the birth cohorts discussed in this paper.

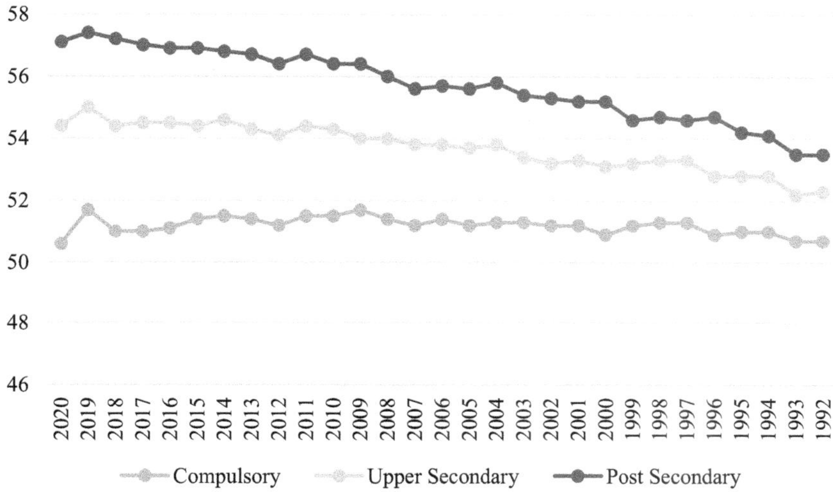

Fig. 3. Remaining life expectancy at age 30 by highest attained educational level. Women. From: Folkhälsodata (Folkhälsomyndigheten, 2021).

In the context of a sustainable working life, healthy life expectancy or years without activity limitations may be more relevant than longevity.[4] Here we find what seems to be an even more accentuated socioeconomic gradient (Fig. 4) than that for life expectancy: at age 30, women with compulsory education have on average only 39 remaining years without activity limitations due to poor health, i.e. the average age when you report such limitations is 69 years; for women with a long (3 years or more) post-secondary education the corresponding age is 80 years (Statistics Sweden, 2018). As seen for life expectancy, this is a gradient, with more expected years without activity limitations for every step of attained educational level. The pattern for men is similar, but the difference between those with the lowest and highest educational level is 10 years, i.e. one year shorter than for women.

4 Activity limitation is here defined as "Not being able to perform activities or tasks most other people can do, for health reasons, since at least six months". Based on Global Activity Limitation Indicator (GALI), according to SCB (2018), for details and confidence intervals c.f. ibid, diagram 6.27, and Table 10.

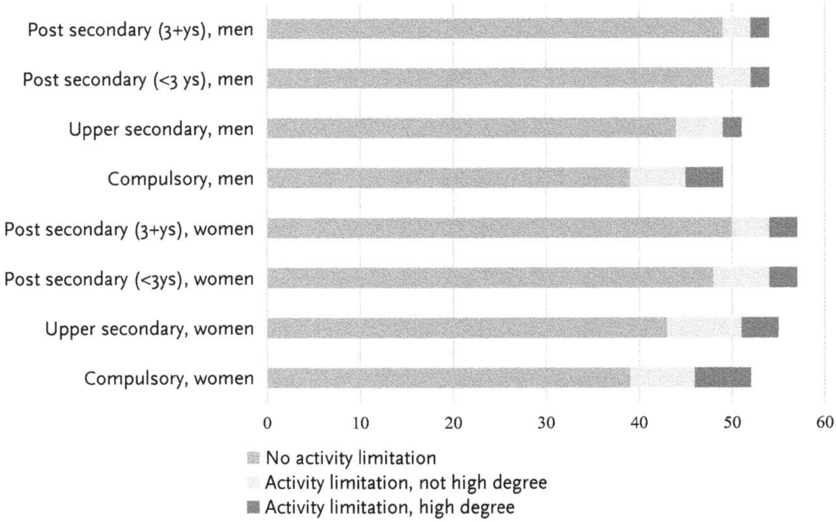

Fig. 4. Remaining years with and without activity limitations at age 30, 2016–2017. From Statistics Sweden (2018).

Gaps between job demands and individual capacity

High mental and/ or physical demands characterise many jobs. Excessive demands, either mental or physical, tend to shorten working life. However, the impact will differ over the life span. Generally, excessive mental demands are especially critical at younger ages, but can be better handled by experienced workers who have a better overview and the ability to sort out minor from major issues. Slower mental processing can often be compensated for by experience. A wise employer will use this shift in abilities as an advantage. Management research linking company and employee characteristics in Germany, suggests that age-diversity in a company with age-mixed teams may be associated with higher productivity (Göbel & Zwick, 2010), although possibly mainly for non-routine tasks (complex decision-making, innovation; Backes-Gellner & Veen, 2009).

However, age discrimination in opportunities for skills upgrade and professional development at the workplace may in the long term impair older workers' performance. These practices are often based on stereotypic perceptions of older workers' learning abilities, and underestimation of the rentability of such investments (Eurofound, 2020), but may change with expectations of a higher retirement age (i.e. gradual increase in age limits for employment protection, pension schemes etc).

The normal physiological ageing up to age 75 is in general not a limitation in relation to mental job demands (Johansson, 2016; Vingård, 2018).

Physical work demands have a different trajectory. Excessive demands are harmful at all ages, but what are excessive demands changes as we age? Physical strength decreases from age 40 and on (Kenny et al., 2008), mainly in our legs and torso. Co-ordination of movements, including balance, will also decline, implying a higher risk to fall when losing balance (Torgén, 2016).

Many manual jobs have high physical demands, often combined with a low decision latitude. In general, jobs with high physical demands are strongly associated with a low educational level, but large groups with an intermediate educational level will have physically strenuous work in the health care sector (e.g. nurses). Individual variations in physical strength and vigour are substantial, and tend to increase with age. This is especially relevant for work that requires uncomfortable or static postures or highly repetitive movements which is usually difficult at an older age (Vingård, 2018). Compared to mental demands, experience will to a lesser degree compensate for physiological ageing. Heavy physical work does, in contrast to what is often assumed, not generally enhance physical fitness. In fact, recent research suggests an accelerated cardiovascular ageing, also when considering relevant confounders (Coenen et al., 2018; Holterman et al., 2021).[5]

The prevalence of heavy work is overall decreasing, but the decline is rather slow, e.g. as indicated by Swedish data on reported lifting of heavy objects several times a day (Arbetsmiljöverket, 2016). Such work was in 2013 (the last year with available data by socioeconomic index) especially common among skilled blue-collar workers (30 % of the men, 25 % of the women), as compared to 2 % and 1 %, respectively, among higher white-collar workers (Statistics Sweden). Also, other physically strenuous tasks (uncomfortable or static postures, repetitive movements) are much more common among blue-collar workers.

Physical demands will often exceed the individual capacity at older ages, if heavy tasks are not gradually replaced over working life. Studies of physical demands in different age groups are not consistent. However, studies based on actual measurements of the physical load do not suggest such a shift in some jobs of special concern, such as in cleaning and manufacturing (Oakman et al., 2019), construction and care (Merkus et al., 2019), or find that the shift is insufficient

5 This is hypothesized to occur from an increase in blood pressure and heart rate during work that increases the load on the vascular endothelium and on the heart but is not sufficient to give a training effect.

in relation to the physical capacity of the older workers in these trades (Merkus et al., 2019).

It is well established that both excessive emotional and physical work demands will increase the risk of early exit from the labour market. An important observation is that a high physical workload interacts with age, so that it is especially harmful for older workers (Burr et al., 2017). A recent study of the entire Swedish population of middle aged and older workers observed an increased risk for disability pension, associated with heavy physical workload, also when adjusting for socioeconomic factors and job control (Falkstedt et al 2021). Danish manual workers aged 50 or more especially highlighted reduced physical workload, when asked about opportunities to prolong working life (Andersen et al., 2020). While poor psychosocial working conditions contributes most to gender differences in sickness absence and disability pension, social inequalities in health-related exit from the labour market seems to be more strongly associated to physical workload (Albin et al., 2017b).

Another critical aspect of physically demanding work is the fact that an increasing proportion of the active workforce have a chronic disease, partly due to the ageing of the workforce, but also to medical progress. Improved treatment of e.g. cardiovascular disease and cancer means that many more can return to work although they have a serious condition (Albin et al., 2017a). Those diseases will usually limit the individual capacity more in relation to physical than mental work demands. The employment gap between workers without and with chronic disease is substantially higher for workers with a low than a high educational level, and it continues to widen (Schram et al., 2019).

A well-established instrument for predicting future long-term sick-leave, disability pension and exit from the labour market, is the work-ability index, which reflects a perception of having work demands that exceed the individual capacity. A mismatch between demands and capacity may represent work demands that are excessive to most individuals, or an individual limitation. It is rather common, especially in groups with a short education, to report work demands exceeding physical capacity (Fig. 5).

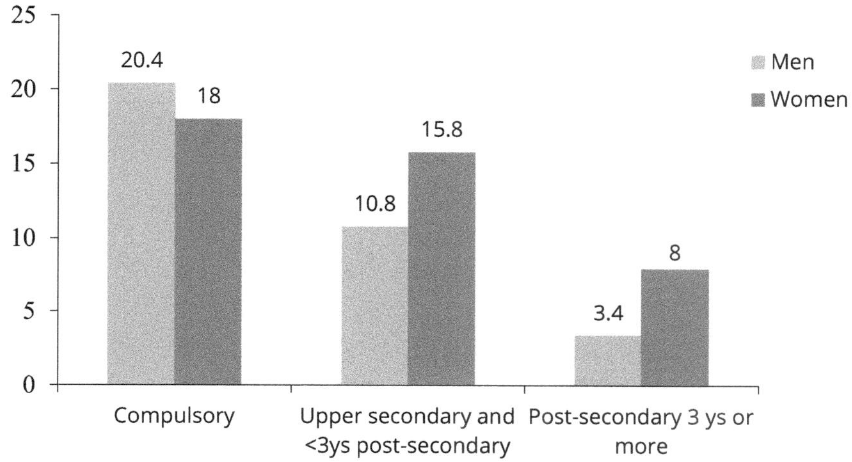

Fig. 5. Proportion (%) of occupationally active men and women by educational level, who report that physical work demands exceed their capacity, Stockholm county. From Centrum för arbets- och miljömedicin (2016).

As expected from the scenarios described above, the proportion reporting that physical work demands exceed their capacity in the population tend to increase with age (Table 4). On the contrary, the proportion reporting that mental demands exceed their capacity tend to decrease with age, which may at least partly be due to the fact that experience can make it easier to handle mental demands. A clear concern is that one out of five women 18–34 and 50–64 years of age believe that they will not be able to remain in their present job in two years for health reasons (Albin et al., 2017a, see also Tab. 4). It is noteworthy that a decreased workability in mid-life, is predictive of old age disability severity (28 years on) as measured by e.g. self-care ability in daily life (von Bonsdorff et al., 2012).

Tab. 4. Proportion (%) of occupationally active women and men reporting that mental or physical job demands exceed their capacity, and proportion believing that they will not be able to remain in present job for health reasons in two years, County of Stockholm.

Work demands exceed capacity	Age 18–34	Age 35–49	Age 50–64	Total
Women				
Physical	12	11	16	13
Mental	19	16	15	16
Not in present job in two years	21	14	20	18
Men				
Physical	6	8	13	9
Mental	11	9	10	10
Not in present job in two years	12	10	16	12

Source: Albin et al. (2017a).

Locked in and forced out?

An obvious solution to a mismatch between the job demands and individual capacity is to find a more suitable one. Being in a non-preferred job, but at the same time perceiving poor employability, has been characterised as "locked-in" (Stengård et al., 2016). According to Aronsson and Göransson (1999) one out of four workers with a permanent contract, and every second worker with a temporary contract, reported that they were in a non-preferred job. Being in such a job is predictive of developing poorer mental health (Canivet et al., 2017), especially among older workers. Along this line, Garthe and Hasselhorn (2021) found that those who reluctantly stayed with their employer, in contrast to those who preferred to stay or left willingly, not only had poor mental health already at baseline, but also experienced deteriorating physical health during follow-up.

As mentioned before, too high job demands are predictive of early exit from the labour market, and older workers face greater difficulties in getting a new job than younger ones (OECD, 2019). One could thus hypothesise that ageing workers, with low employability (i.e. skills in low demand) face both a lock-in (not daring to quit for fear of unemployment), with potential effects on mental wellbeing, but also in the long-run premature exit (forced out) because they can no longer meet the work requirements.[6] In the absence of direct empirical support for such patterns, some indirect indications are presented below.

6 Reduced working hours are common towards the end of working life and may both reflect and affect health and workability.

A detailed study of lost working years between age 30 and 66 related to educational level from the Netherlands, found that men with a low educational level on average lost 2.6 years due to disability pension, 4.3 years due to unemployment, and less than 1 year due to exit with no income or death. Men with high educational level had somewhat high losses due to early retirement schemes, studies, or emigration. The pattern among women was similar, but loss due to unemployment was higher (5.2 years) as was exit with no income (3.6 years; Robroek et al., 2020). Importantly, much of the loss occurred already between 30 and 50 years of age, suggesting that early interventions would be most effective.

Studies including the 40 most common occupations in Sweden found that, in spite of changes in the old-age pension with stronger economic incentives to prolong working life, substantial differences remained between occupational groups for loss of work-life expectancy due to disability pension, long-term sick-leave directly preceding disability pension, or death, while differences between men and women had virtually disappeared. In general, the loss of work-life expectancy was highest for unskilled manual occupations, and lowest among white collar occupations requiring a high educational level, with a difference of up to five years between high and low risk occupations (Kadefors et al., 2017).

Several European countries, including Sweden, have in recent decades restricted access to disability pension. In Sweden, this seems to have increased the use of early age retirement (drawing from the total retirement benefit so that the yearly pension will be lower) especially in blue collar occupations: 9 out of 10 occupations with the highest increase were blue collar ones, while 10 out of 10 occupations with the lowest increase were white collar occupations. (Kadefors et al., 2019).

In summary, national policies aiming at prolonging working life through economic incentives have not achieved a levelling upwards to a full working life in many blue-collar occupations. An increased claiming of early old-age pension in blue collar jobs, even though it will often be associated with economic hardship later in life, suggests that more restrictive policies on disability pension left groups of manual workers who no longer are able to do their job with no other option. Measures offering a match between demands and capacity throughout working life are required, especially for manual occupations. It also makes the workforce more dependent on options for e.g. retraining and other benefits offered by collective agreements, thus accentuating the differences between unionised versus ununionised workers, and the high-end versus the low-end of the labour market.

Building resilience

Climate change has highlighted the vulnerability of our societies, and raised a debate on how to enhance resilience. It may be argued that some global trends (i.e. globalisation, digitalisation and automation) also increase the vulnerability of significant parts of the labour force, and that strategies which enhance resilience (i.e. reduces vulnerability) are urgently needed, at the workplace as well as at the macro-level, and with a holistic approach.[7]

Workplace

One aspect of building resilience throughout working life is to identify risks associated with a certain age-span or (lack of) seniority, e.g. young and unexperienced workers have higher occupational accident rates than more senior ones (Guérin et al., 2020; Meidner, 1954). Workers with caring duties will be more vulnerable to work-family conflicts (e.g. like unpredictable working hours), and older workers more vulnerable to physical strain and insufficient recovery. An age-conscious approach can, as suggested by Nilsson (2020), easily be included as part of the statutory risk assessment at the workplace. However, the Joint Programming Initiative "More Years Better Lives" identified important knowledge gaps regarding managers' perspective on a longer working life and organisational opportunities (Hasselhorn & Apt, 2015).

It is often said that women are more vulnerable to psycho-social stress at the workplace than men, but more detailed analyses indicate that observed differences can largely be explained by differences in exposure (e.g. more job-strain in jobs with predominantly female workers; Theorell et al., 2016). Thus, resilience should build on increasing job control, rather than promoting individual coping strategies in these sectors.

Non-discrimination, fairness, respect and being listened to, are all important aspects for job longevity. Apart from gender and ethnicity, old age is, as mentioned above, a common ground for discrimination and stereotyping. In this context it is noteworthy that there seems to be a socioeconomic gradient of perceiving being listened to by the closest manager, so that workers with short education or low income most often report not being listened to. In turn, this was

---

7 The European Economic and Social Committee on "The changing world of work and the longevity/ageing population" have made several specific recommendations (2020) for the development of comprehensive national strategies.

longitudinally associated with exhaustion and depressive symptoms, most likely mediated through less job control (Theorell et al., 2012).

The importance of employment arrangements for occupational health has increasingly been seen as an additional dimension of exposure (Bodin et al., 2020; O'Connor et al., 2020). A temporary contract may or may not be associated with other disadvantages, determining whether it has negative health impacts on the individual.[8] In general, temporary workers will tend to have a weaker voice at the workplace, less familiarity with workplace routines, less access to skills upgrade, be less unionised, have less insurance benefits, and be more likely to lose employment in case of poor health (Schram et al., 2020). This accumulation of multiple disadvantages in the employment arrangement is usually referred to as precarious employment (Kreshpaj et al., 2020). Precarious employment arrangements can lead to negative health consequences, through several direct and indirect pathways. The COVID-19 pandemic has highlighted the association between precarious employment and workplace safety, e.g. outbreaks of disease related to adverse conditions including symptomatic workers feeling obliged to come to work (Dyal et al., 2020), caring workers working at multiple facilities (Department of Health and Social Care, 2020; Dyal et al., 2020), and mortality rates at nursing homes associated with unionisation (Dean et al., 2020), thus suggesting that employment arrangements should be considered in risk assessment and as a means to enhance resilience.

Flexibility aiming at accommodating individual needs is seen as important for extending working life. Andersen et al (2019) found, in a representative sample of the Danish workforce age 50 or more, that opportunities supporting a long working-life (i.e. possibilities for more vacation, reduction of working hours, flexible working hours, access to treatment, further education and physical exercise) at the workplace, were fewer among manual workers, women, and workers with disabilities. It is obviously important to identify and act upon this type of mismatch between support and needs.

The occupational health service has a dual task, to assist in risk assessment and reduction of harmful exposures, and in adapting the job to the individual worker (ILO, 1985). Access to occupational health service is thus especially important in jobs with a high risk for ill health caused by harmful exposure at work and in jobs where employees more likely have health conditions that affect

8 Another aspect of shifting employment arrangement which need further investigation with regard to working conditions and work environment are agency workers, and the self-employed outside the agricultural sector,

their work. Due to the socioeconomic gradients in both exposures and health, the need is thus especially high in blue-collar occupations. Favourable changes in physical workload among those with chronic disease was shown to reduce the risk for exit from paid employment (Schram et al., 2020).

It is thus a paradox that access to occupational health service is inversely related to needs in Sweden, with good access (over 80 %) among higher managers and about half (around 40 %) in the service sector as well as in hunting, fishing and forestry (Arbetsmiljöverket, 2020). This clearly fails to protect those at highest risk and most in need, a gap which should urgently be acted upon by the social partners or by legislation, i.e. by action at the macro-level when the workplace level is failing.

Macro level

While the workplace level is decisive in supporting a long working life, there is a strong interdependence between legislation and welfare systems. Longer additional education is often required for a necessary shift to a career outside the current employer, or to keep employability during technological changes within a sector. This, however, will rarely be financed by the employer, forcing the individual worker to rely on active labour market policies and inclusive welfare systems to support the shift, and the older unexperienced worker will need the same initial mentorship as a young worker to e.g. prevent accidents. There would be less need for such leaps if life-long learning polices were widely implemented providing a gradual skills upgrade-transition possibility (see also Halvorsen's chapter in this book).

Employment protection is also likely to contribute to resilience (decrease vulnerability), especially for older workers, workers with chronic disease, and workers with low education (Schuring et al., 2020). Low employability for those workers will in the case of unemployment easily trigger downwards trajectories in several aspects of working conditions. Multiple adverse changes dramatically increase the risk for exit from paid employment (Schram et al., 2020) and could thus motivate a strong employment protection from a sustainability perspective.

The transfer of many caring duties from the home is the key to women's work participation; this applies to childcare, meals and leisure time activities for school children, and elderly care. The Covid-19 pandemic has reminded us of this dependency. The liberation of women's potential on the labour market is still limited in many countries (e.g. unaffordable care for those with a low or medium income), and the quality of the services is affected by economic crises (i.e. austerity measures). It is remarkable that a high proportion of women of working age (32.7 % of those age 20–64 not in the workforce in EU 28, and 5.5 % to 19.7 % in the Nordic countries) report not actively seeking work due to caring responsibilities, with an increasing trend (25.7 % in 2007; Eurostat, 2020).

Finally, increasing health inequalities are a driver of an increasing gap in work longevity between occupational groups, and thus calls for decisive action at a societal level (Figure 6).

Fig. 6. Proportion of women aged 20–64 (%) outside the labour force due to caring responsibilities in 2019. European Union (EU-28) average is shown together with individual countries above average. Source: Eurostat (2022).

Decent work and economic growth

The sustainable development goal Decent work and economic growth (SDG 8) calls for providing opportunities for full and productive employment and decent work for all while eradicating forced labour, human trafficking and child labour and promoting labour rights and safe and secure working environments. Many observations suggest a polarisation of working conditions, with many improvements in the high end, and an accumulation of adverse conditions in the low end. This tends to make averages deceptive when discussing the need to develop new policies.

- While overall employment rates in e.g. EU 28 are moving upwards, the gap in employment by educational level is increasing, and 7 % of full-time workers are at risk of in-work poverty (Eurostat 2020).
- On average 15 % of all workers in the EU report exposure to smoke, gases, powder or dust at least one quarter of their working hours, among skilled blue-collar workers the corresponding proportion is 56 % and among unskilled workers 35 % (Eurofound, 2015). While substantial effort is put into decreasing the cancer burden from such exposure in the EU, permissible levels still confer unacceptably high excess mortality following a full working-life (Johanson & Tinnerberg, 2019), especially when considering the total extra disease burden (e.g. cardiovascular disease, chronic obstructive pulmonary disease; Albin & Gustavsson, 2020; Sjögren et al., 2020) in conflict not only with a sustainable working life, but with fundamental rights to safe and healthy working conditions (European Parliament, 2000). Similarly, lack of basic safety measures for frontline workers during the covid-19 pandemic, and the extent to which this has unproportionally affected not only health care but many basic occupations, highlight the vulnerability of broad groups of workers and the need for a strong joint commitment for occupational safety and health from the social partners, government and researchers.

The commitment to Agenda 2030 from many sectors of society may offer opportunities to develop new strategies and policies for Sustainable work and work longevity within the SDG Decent work and economic growth (see also Levi`s chapter in this book). As an example, universities and national and regional health services are important purchasers of goods and services with the potential to influence the development in several sectors for the better, i.e. by using a socially responsible approach.(European Commission, 2020) Here social partners and researchers can assist in suggesting how these demands can be phrased to have an impact, and how compliance can be followed up.

Simultaneously, national policies need consistently to consider the impact on inequalities when e.g. changing welfare systems, labour law, and labour market policies. In the absence of such consideration inequalities will increase, and firm action is needed to reduce them (Molander, 2017). Such actions are needed to support work longevity throughout the labour market. The means to achieve this are well known, but the changing political and economic context calls for new ways of connecting the measures, and for researchers to actively be involved in the challenges.

References

Albin M., Liljefrost E., Parmsund M., Wadensjö E. (2017a). *Äldre i arbetslivet – en omvärldsanalys* [Older workers in working life – An analysis, in Swedish]. Report number 2017/00501-1. Svenska ESF-rådet.

Albin M, Gustavsson P., Kjellberg K., Theorell T. (2017b). *Arbetsmiljö och jämlik hälsa* [Work environment and equity in health, in Swedish]. Underlagsrapport nr 5 till Kommissionen för jämlik hälsa S 2015:02.

Albin, M., Gustavsson, P. (2020). A silent epidemic: occupational exposure limits are insufficiently protecting individual worker health. *Scand J Work Environ Health*, 46(1), 110–112.

Andersen, L.L., Jensen, P.H., Meng, A., Sundstrup, E. (2019). Strong Labour Market Inequality of Opportunities at the Workplace for Supporting a Long and Healthy Work-Life: The SeniorWorkingLife Study. *Int J Environ Res Public Health*. Sep. 5;16(18):32–64.

Andersen, L.L., Jensen, P.H., Sundstrup, E. (2020). Barriers and opportunities for prolonging working life across different occupational groups: the SeniorWorkingLife study. *Eur J Public Health*, 30(2), 241–246.

Arbetsmiljöverket (2016). *Arbetsmiljön* [The Work Environment, in Swedish] 2015. Arbetsmiljöstatistik Rapport 2016:2

Arbetsmiljöverket (2020). Arbetsmiljön [The Work Environment, in Swedish] 2020. Arbetsmiljöstatistik Rapport 2020:2

Aronsson G., Göransson, S. (1999). Permanent employment but not in a preferred occupation: psychological and medical aspects, research implications. *J Occup Health Psychol*, 4(2), 152–163.

Backes-Gellner, U., Veen, S. (2009). *The impact of aging and age diversity on company performance*. Retrieved from http://ssrn.com/abstract=1346895, accessed 10 October 2020

Bodin, T., Çağlayan Ç., Garde, A.H., Gnesi, M., Jonsson, J., Kiran, S., Kreshpaj, B., Leinonen, T., Mehlum, I.S., Nena, E., Orellana, C., Peckham, T., Seixas, N., Vanroelen, C., Julià, M. (2020). Precarious employment in occupational health – An OMEGA-NET working group position paper. *Scand J Work Environ Health*, 46(3), 321–329.

von Bonsdorff, M.B., Seitsamo, J., Ilmarinen, J., Nygård, C.H., von Bonsdorff, M.E., Rantanen, T. (2012). Work ability as a determinant of old age disability severity: evidence from the 28-year Finnish Longitudinal Study on Municipal Employees. *Aging Clin Exp Res*, 24(4), 354–360.

Burr, H., Pohrt, A., Rugulies, R., Holtermann, A., Hasselhorn, H.M. (2017). Does age modify the association between physical work demands and deterioration of self-rated general health? *Scand J Work Environ Health*, 43(3), 241–249.

Canivet, C., Aronsson, G., Bernhard-Oettel, C., Leineweber, C., Moghaddassi, M., Stengård, J., Westerlund, H., Östergren, P.O. (2017). The negative effects on mental health of being in a non-desired occupation in an increasingly precarious labour market. *SSM Popul Health*, 3, 516–524.

Coenen, P., Huysmans, M.A., Holtermann, A., Krause, N., van Mechelen, W., Straker, L.M., van der Beek, A.J. (2018). Do highly physically active workers die early? A systematic review with meta-analysis of data from 193 696 participants. *Br J Sports Med,* 52(20), 1320–1326.

O'Connor A., Peckham T., Seixas N. (2020). Considering Work Arrangement as an "Exposure" in Occupational Health Research and Practice. *Front Public Health,* Aug 4;8:363.

Dean A., Venkataramani A., Kimmel S. (2020). Mortality Rates From COVID-19 Are Lower in Unionized Nursing Homes. *Health Affairs* 2020, published ahead of print September 10, https://doi.org/10.1377/hlthaff.2020.01011

Department of Health and Social Care. *Official Statistics. Vivaldi 1: coronavirus (COVID-19) care homes study report.* Published 3 July 2020

Dyal J.W., Grant M.P., Broadwater K., Bjork A., Waltenburg M.A., Gibbins J.D., Hale C., et al. (2020). COVID-19 Among Workers in Meat and Poultry Processing Facilities – 19 States, April 2020. *MMWR Morb Mortal Wkly Rep.* May 8;69(18).

Eurofound. (2015). *Sixth European Working Conditions Survey 2015* (https://www.eurofound.europa.eu/surveys/european-working-conditions-surveys/sixth-european-working-conditions-survey-2015, accessed 25 September 2020).

Eurofound. (2020). *Role of social partners in tackling discrimination at work.* Publications Office of the European Union, Luxembourg.

European Commission, Executive Agency for Small and Medium-sized Enterprises. (2020). Making socially responsible public procurement work. *71 good practice cases.* Published 2020-09-10. https://op.europa.eu/en/publication-detail/-/publication/e8cf51d0-f632-11ea-991b-01aa75ed71a1/language-en/format-PDF/source-search, Downloaded October 6, 2020.

European Parliament. (2000). *Charter of Fundamental Rights of the European Union.* 2000/C 364/01. http://www.europarl.europa.eu/charter/pdf/text_en.pdf

Eurostat. (2020). *Sustainable development indicators, SDG8*, https://ec.europa.eu/eurostat/web/sdi/decent-work-and-economic-growth, accessed 25 September 2020.

Executive Agency for Small and Medium-sized Enterprises, European Commission. (2020). *Making socially responsible public procurement work. 71 good practice cases.* Published 2020-09-10. https://op.europa.eu/en/publication-detail/-/publication/e8cf51d0-f632-11ea-991b-01aa75ed71a1/language-en/format-PDF/source-search, accessed 6 October 2020.

Falkstedt, D., Hemmingsson, T., Albin, M., Bodin, T., Ahlbom, A., Selander, J., Gustavsson, P., Andersson, T., Almroth, M., & Kjellberg, K. (2021). Disability pensions related to heavy physical workload: a cohort study of middle-aged and older workers in Sweden. *Int Arch Occup Environ Health, 94*(8), 1851–1861. https://doi-org.proxy.kib.ki.se/10.1007/s00420-021-01697-9

Folkhälsomyndigheten. (2020). Folkhälsodata. (ohm-app.folkhalsomyndigheten.se/Folkhalsodata/pxweb/sv/A_Folkhalsodata/A_Folkhalsodata__Bakgrundsfakta__Demografi/MedellivsUtb.px/), accessed 02 September 2020.

Garthe, N., & Hasselhorn, H. M. (2021). Leaving and staying with the employer-Changes in work, health, and work ability among older workers. *Int Arch Occup Environ Health, 94*(1), 85–93. https://doi-org.proxy.kib.ki.se/10.1007/s00420-020-01563-0

Göbel, C., Zwick, T. (2010). *Which Personnel Measures are Effective in Increasing Productivity of Older Workers?* (Discussion Paper No. 10-069). Retrieved from Centre for European Economic Research website: ftp://ftp.zew.de/pub/zew-docs/dp/ dp10069.pdf

Hartman, L., Sjögren, A. (2017). *Hur ojämlikt är Sverige? Sociala skillnader i dödsrisker: Utvecklingen över tid och skillnader mellan åldersgrupper och regioner* [How unequal is Sweden? Social disparities in death risk: Development over time and differences between age groups and regions, in Swedish]. Underlagsrapport nr 4 till Kommissionen för jämlik hälsa S 2015:02.

Hasselhorn, H.M., Apt, W. (Editors). (2015). *Understanding Employment Participation of Older Workers: Creating a Knowledge Base for Future Labour Market Challenges.* JPI- More years better lives 2015. https://www.jp-demographic.eu/wp-content/uploads/2015/07/JPIUEP_Brochure1.pdf, accessed October 10, 2020.

Health Inequalities in the EU – Final Report of a Consortium. Consortium lead: Sir Michael Marmot. European Commission Directorate-General for Health and Consumers. European Union 2013. https://ec.europa.eu/health/sites/default/files/social_determinants/docs/healthinequalitiesineu_2013_en.pdf

Holtermann, A., Schnohr, P., Nordestgaard, B.G., & Marott, J.L. (2021). The physical activity paradox in cardiovascular disease and all-cause mortality: the contemporary Copenhagen General Population Study with 104 046 adults. *Eur Heart J, 42*(15), 1499–1511. https://doi-org.proxy.kib.ki.se/10.1093/eurheartj/ehab087

International Labour Organisation (ILO). (1985). *The ILO convention on Occupational Health Services* No 161, ILO 1985.

Johanson, G., Tinnerberg, H. (2019). Binding occupational exposure limits for carcinogens in the EU – good or bad? *Scand J Work Environ Health*, 45(3), 213–214.

Johansson, B. (2016). *Cognitive ageing.* In: Healthy workplaces for women and men of all ages. Knowledge compilation 2016:8, Arbetsmiljöverket 2016.

Kadefors, R., Nilsson, K., Rylander, L., Östergren, P.O., Albin, M. (2017, March 20). Occupation, gender and work life exits: A Swedish population study. *Ageing and Society*, 1–18.

Kadefors, R., Nilsson, K., Östergren, P.O., Rylander, L., Albin, M. (2019). Social inequality in working life expectancy in Sweden. *Zeitschrift für Gerontologie under Geriatrie* 51(8): 1–10.

Kenny, G.P., Yardley, J.E., Martineau, L., Jay, O. (2008). Physical work capacity in older adults: implications for the aging worker. *Am J Ind Med*, 51(8), 610–25.

Kreshpaj, B., Orellana, C., Burström, B., Davis, L., Hemmingsson, T., Johansson, G., Kjellberg K., Jonsson, J., Wegman, D.H., Bodin, T. (2020). What is precarious employment? A systematic review of definitions and operationalizations from quantitative and qualitative studies. *Scand J Work Environ Health*, 46(3), 235–247.

Meidner, R. (1954). *Svensk arbetsmarknad vid full sysselsättning* [The Swedish Labour Market at Full Employment, in Swedish with English summary], PhD thesis, Stockholm University. Stockholm, Konjunkturinstitutet.

Merkus, S.L., Lunde, L.K., Koch, M., Wærsted, M., Knardahl, S., Veiersted, K.B. (2019). Physical capacity, occupational physical demands, and relative physical strain of older employees in construction and healthcare. *Int Arch Occup Environ Health*, 92(3), 295–307.

Molander, P. (2017). *The Anatomy of Inequality: Its Social and Economic Origins and Solutions.* Melville House Publishing.

Nilsson, K. (2020). A sustainable working life for all ages – The swAge-model. *Applied Ergonomics* 86; 103082.

Oakman, J., Clays, E., Jørgensen, M.B., Holtermann, A. (2019) Are occupational physical activities tailored to the age of cleaners and manufacturing workers? *Int Arch Occup Environ Health*, 92(2), 185–193.

OECD. (2019). *Working Better with Age, Ageing and Employment Practices*. Paris: OECD Publishing.

Robroek, S.J., Nieboer, D., Järvholm, B., Burdorf, A. (2020). Educational differences in duration of working life and loss of paid employment: working life expectancy in the Netherlands. *Scand J Work Environ Health*, 46(1), 77–84.

Schram, J.L.D, Schuring, M., Oude, Hengel K.M., Burdorf, A. (2019, June 1). Health-related educational inequalities in paid employment across 26 European countries in 2005–2014: repeated cross-sectional study. *BMJ Open*, 9(5), e024823.

Schram, J.L.D., Robroek, S.J.W., Ots, P., Brouwer, S., Burdorf, A., van Zon, S.K.R., Oude, Hengel, K.M. (2020). Influence of changing working conditions on exit from paid employment among workers with a chronic disease. *Occup Environ Med*, 77(9), 628–633.

Schuring, M., Robroek, S.J.W., Carrino, L., O'Prinsen, A.C., Oude Hengel, K.M., Avenano, M., Burdorf, A. (2020). Does reduced employment protection increase the employment disadvantage of workers with low education and poorer health? *J Epidemiol Community Health*, 74(10), 851–857.

Statens offentliga utredningar (SOU). (2016). *Det handlar om jämlik hälsa. Utgångspunkter för Kommissionens vidare arbete* [About equity in health: Considerations for the work of the Commission, in Swedish]. Delbetänkande av Kommissionen för jämlik hälsa. SOU, 55.

Statens offentliga utredningar (SOU). 2017. *Nästa steg på vägen mot en mer jämlik hälsa. Förslag för ett långsiktigt arbete för en god och jämlik hälsa* [Next step towards more equity in health; Recommendations for a long-term work for good and equitable health, in Swedish]. Slutbetänkande av Kommissionen för jämlik hälsa. SOU, 47.

Statistics Sweden. *Work Environment Survey*. Statistics data base. Available at https://www.statistikdatabasen.scb.se/pxweb/sv/ssd/START__AM__AM0501__AM0501B/ArbmiljoSEI2/table/tableViewLayout1/?rxid=0dddbd21-8633-4dcc-84e0-eb37675610f2

Statistics Sweden. (2018). *Skilda världar? Det demografiskt delade Sverige*. [Separate worlds? The demographically separated Sweden. In Swedish]. Statistiska Centralbyrån [Statistics Sweden]. Demografiska rapporter, 2

Stengård, J., Bernhard-Oettel, C., Berntson, E., Leineweber, C., Aronsson, G. (2016). Stuck in a job: being "locked-in" or at risk of becoming locked-in at the workplace and well-being over time, *Work & Stress*, 30:2, 152–172.

Theorell, T., Nyberg, A., Leineweber, C., Magnusson Hanson, L.L., Oxenstierna, G., Westerlund, H. (2012). Non-listening and self-centered leadership-relationships to socioeconomic conditions and employee mental health. *PLoS One*, 7(9), e44119. Doi:

Theorell, T., Jood, K., Järvholm, L.S., Vingård, E., Perk, J., Östergren, P.O., Hall, C. (2016). A systematic review of studies in the contributions of the work environment to ischaemic heart disease development. *Eur J Public Health*, 26(3), 470–477.

Torgén, M. (2016). Physiological ageing – Physical capacity and occupational performance. In: Healthy workplaces for women and men of all ages. *Knowledge Compilation*, 8, Arbetsmiljöverket.

Vingård, E. (2018). *Vad blir sämre och vad blir bättre när man blir äldre?* [What gets better and what gets worse as you age?, in Swedish] Rapport 8, Delegationen för senior arbetskraft S2018, 10.

Susan Reh, Shruti Raghuraman, Åsa Lundqvist, Victoria Tischler, Emma Jeanes, and Laura Trigg

Challenges to a sustainable working life for older women in Europe

Abstract: Older women make a significant contribution to the European labour market yet still experience age and gender discrimination, lower wages and negative workplace impacts on health and wellbeing compared to their male counterparts. This review of the literature assesses the current situation for older female workers in Europe. The authors identify issues including work and domestic conflicts, menopause, stress and income disparities that impact negatively on older female workers. Research gaps are identified with an increase in qualitative and intersectional studies recommended to better understand the experiences of older women and the multiple, interacting factors that constrain their working lives. In addition, future studies should focus on novel interventions that promote effective digital working, intergenerational solidarity and effective menopause support.

Keywords: ageing, health, labour market, older women, wellbeing

Introduction

Sustainable working life is high on the European political agenda, both in terms of quality of work, decent working, and employment conditions, as well as in political debates on social and economic rights. Although a sustainable working life is desirable, several challenges remain. In this chapter, we address some of these challenges, faced by older women in the labour force.

The number of those employed in Europe (EU-27) aged 55 years and over increased from 12 % to 20 % between 2004 and 2019 (Eurostat, 2020). Women in work aged 55–64 are increasing and further work is required to support their participation.. Research shows that women, especially older women (55 years and over) face more discrimination from a young age with a cumulative effect over time when compared to men (Kornadt, Voss, & Rothermund, 2013). To create a more sustainable working life, where discrimination against women is recognised and addressed, more knowledge is required about the challenges they experience in the workforce.

This chapter presents an overview of recent research documenting the experiences and wellbeing of older female workers in the European labour market. The purpose is to identify the challenges and facilitators experienced by older female workers entering, retaining roles, and progressing in the labour market. It is anticipated that the findings will support the labour market to become more age-inclusive, providing older female workers with sustainable work that facilitates their physical and mental wellbeing.

Research on experiences and wellbeing of older female workers in Europe

This chapter offers insight into the key challenges faced by older women working in the European labour market. We present a consolidated overview of literature reviewed from various countries in Europe, including United Kingdom (UK), The Netherlands, Sweden, Finland, Germany, and Italy. Portugal, France, Austria, Croatia, and Switzerland. The search strategy focused on four key concepts – older women, labour and employment, experiences of health and well-being, and a European context. We searched seven electronic databases including PubMed, OVID Medline, Business Source Complete, HMIC, PsycINFO, Scopus, and Social Policy and Practice. The age cut-off was 55 years and older, in order to gain insights on women who have a substantial time left in the labour market before retirement. Among the studies reviewed for this chapter, a majority used quantitative methods such as analyses of publicly available cross-sectional and longitudinal survey data (e.g., Survey of Health, Ageing and Retirement in Europe; Survey of Health Ageing & Retirment in Europe- SHARE). A few qualitative studies and previously published reviews of literature in this field were also included.

The findings are presented across two broad themes: (1) *Job quality and inequality: Towards a sustainable working life for older women,* and (2) *Challenges and the future for older women in the labour market.*

Job quality and inequality: Towards a sustainable working life for older women?

Heterogenous career trajectories

Women's career trajectories in Europe remain very different from men's, following heterogeneous, non-linear patterns with more interruptions to employment. The first difference is women's lower participation in the workforce (Edge et al., 2017), despite a positive upward trend over the last two decades (Eurostat, 2015). Women are more likely to work part-time, work fewer hours in general, have contract jobs or do voluntary work (Curvers et al., 2018; Payne & Doyal,

2010; Weber et al., 2019) resulting in only half as many full-time employment hours on average in comparison to men (Engels et al., 2020). One driver of these differences seems to be women's greater responsibility and involvement in domestic and caring duties which are accompanied by part-time paid work or no paid work at all (Engels et al., 2020). Moreover, employers appear to hold the stereotypical belief that women prefer part-time work (Edge et al., 2017) which might hinder women's greater participation in full-time employment. Later in their working life, older women can be more expensive to employ when progressive pay policies are in place due to the perception that they are less productive or are likely to have fewer qualifications compared to younger workers (Payne & Doyal, 2010). This poses challenges for older women seeking full-time employment in later life.

At the same time, the prevailing gender pay gap of 16.1 % in 2016 in the EU and lower gross incomes (Edge et al., 2017; Payne & Doyal, 2010; Weber et al., 2019) underline the lack of equal returns that women receive for their work. This could be for a variety of reasons, including but not restricted to the higher propensity for women to be engaged in part-time work over the life course. Feuvre Le et al. (2015) summarisedsuch dynamics in terms of ageing as a gendered experience with women "ageing with resentment" as opposed to men who "age with confidence" as a esult of the cumulative effects over an individuals' working lifespan. Perceived unequal returns for high effort can result in many older women experiencing frustration and resentment in their working lives. In other cases, some women are more likely to be "ageing with confidence" due to their focus on domestic and/or caring responsibilities at home, while opting to support their male spouse's career ambitions. Importantly, this may only apply to those within a conventional heteronormative relationship where the male partner is the primary salary earner. The ratio of input (effort) and output (financial reward) may be perceived as more favourable by these women, compared to women in the labour market" 'ageing with resentmen"' due to hitting the glass ceiling (Feuvre Le et al., 2015) This "glass-ceiling effect" conceptualises prevailing gender differences in leadership positions (Cotter et al., 2001).

Besides financial disadvantages, women also have more negative workplace experiences that often drive them out of employment such as negative age stereotypes, age- and gender-based, discrimination and workplace bullying (Payne & Doyal, 2010; Keeble-Ramsay, 2018). There is also a trend of fewer women occupying managerial positions e.g.,12 % vs. 34.4 % among same-age males, as reported in a study of "baby boomers" by Wanka et al. (2015).

Transition challenges into retirement

Women's heterogeneous employment trajectories with fewer accumulated working hours over the course of their working lifespan directly impact on their transition into retirement, which is also relatively atypical when compared to men's transition into retirement. These issues may result in disadvantages for older women with regards to their decision when to retire. Often women must work until an older age out of financial necessity (Edge et al., 2021; Feuvre et al., 2015). An additional reason for this is that women often engage in caring responsibilities in their early and mid-career years which results in lower accumulated pension and financial pressures in later life (Brown & Vickerstaff, 2011; Edge et al., 2021; Loretto & Vickerstaff, 2013).

Alternatively, women sometimes retire earlier than men, due to a variety of motivations and reasons. One of them is menopause, and the lack of perceived workplace support for the condition which negatively impacts older women's career trajectories, and could potentially influence earlier retirement (Keeble Ramsay, 2018). Relatedly, poor health contributed to older women at work being perceived as less competent (Payne & Doyal, 2010), which sustains discriminatory practices. On the other hand, some older women may experience financial pressure to postpone retirement due to caring responsibilities, which can impact negatively on their health and wellbeing. Caring responsibilities impose a double-burden on older working women and pose a major challenge when it comes to retirement decisions. Women may also retire earlier due to personal reasons, lower-grade positions, or other negative impacts (e.g. shift work) on their health (Edge et al., 2017). However, sometimes women retire earlier due to the financial security afforded by their their (male) partner, with retirement decisions made jointly (Loretto & Vickerstaff, 2013). This further reinforces the conventional male-breadwinner model (Brown & Vickerstaff, 2011) that reduces older women's participation in paid employment but that may not apply to those in alternative family structures.

The challenges that older female workers in Europe face with regards to sustainable transitions into retirement emerge from their heterogenous and often disadvantaged employment paths compared to males. Thus, policies that seek to resolve this challenge need to consider older female workers career trajectories over their working lifespan. Moreover, future research, as well as practitioners and policy makers, should consider how caring responsibilities and retirement can be reconciled in a way that is sustainable for older female workers financially, and to support their health and wellbeing.

Working conditions: lack of choice, control and experiences of discrimination

Women's heterogenous career patterns and their career decisions point to potential differences in the type of employment and the working conditions that older women in Europe experience, in comparison to their male counterparts. Research has demonstrated gender differences in working conditions, with older women having fewer opportunities for flexibility, autonomy, and control in their job (Damman & Henkens, 2020; Payne & Doyal, 2010). This affects areas such as their work schedule and work location (Damman & Henkens, 2020), and decision making, time pressure and general working conditions (Payne & Doyal, 2010), all of which may contribute to higher work stress and, by extension, health problems (Nilsen et al., 2014). Such gender differences are particularly negative, in light of research showing that flexibility and choice facilitate extended working lives for older women (Edge et al., 2021) including, but not limited to, easing the burden of work-family/life conflict that is still predominantly a female-specific challenge (Baptist et al., 2015; Edge et al., 2021). At the same time, flexible work can create risks as women may perceive that they must fit their work around other responsibilities (Loretto & Vickerstaff, 2015), resulting in the "double burden" effect.

Other areas to consider with regards to working conditions are training and educational opportunities. Several studies suggest that older female workers have fewer of these opportunities compared to men (Keeble-Ramsay, 2018; Payne & Doyal, 2010). This is unfortunate as Edge and colleagues (2017; 2021) point out that training and education is associated with extended working lives of women. Other research emphasises the value of age-relevant training programmes at work to improve well-being (Wilks & Neto, 2013) or policies and training to improve women's health and wellbeing during menopause (Viotti et al., 2020).

On an interpersonal level, older women face the challenge of discrimination including sexism, ageism, and harassment (Edge et al., 2017, 2021; Keeble-Ramsay, 2018; Payne & Doyal, 2010; Wilks & Neto, 2013). This is potentially fuelled by others' perceptions that older women are less competent and not as able to cope with difficult work situations (Payne & Doyal, 2010). Intergenerational conflict with younger colleagues is another negative consequence of age-related stereotypes of older women at work (Edge et al., 2021). As a result, older women report feeling isolated and lonely at work (Bjelajac et al., 2019).

Such negative experiences can result in older women increasingly reporting feeling exhausted as a result of work-related stress. Wanka and colleagues (2015) identified that 27 % of female workers reported experiencing psychological stress at work in the past week. The same study revealed that women report higher levels of physical complaints than men due to work-related stress. Björklund and colleagues (2013) found that females in their study reported higher stress than males, especially when they were in a low managerial position.

Challenges and the future for older women in the labour market

Resolving work-life conflict and unpaid caring roles

A major challenge faced by older female workers in Europe is the double-burden of juggling their professional lives with unpaid domestic work and caring responsibilities, such as taking care of grandchildren or looking after elderly relatives (Edge et al., 2017; Feuvre Le et al., 2015; Keeble-Ramsay, 2018; Payne & Doyal, 2010; Wanka et al., 2015).This double-burden may compel women to re-enter the labour market when financial pressures threaten their choice of a family-centred life (LeFeuvre et al., 2015), or if they have to conform with the "male breadwinner" model in order to address financial pressures. It has also been found that the boundaries between paid work and unpaid domestic labour become increasingly blurred as women age, especially when they include support for those outside of their own family e.g., neighbours or friends (Loretto & Vickerstaff, 2015). They are also likely to be less visible than e.g., the caring responsibilities of a young mother, signifying the interplay of both gender- and age-related disadvantages faced by older women.

Older women's dual roles are a major source of work-family/life conflict which is associated with greater stress (Payne & Doyal, 2010) and impaired health, especially in combination with low job satisfaction (Brown & Vickerstaff, 2011), sleep problems (Lallukka et al., 2010), lower work capacity amongst menopausal women (Viotti et al., 2020), and increased depressive symptoms compared to men (Baptist et al., 2015). Effectively balancing unpaid (caring) work and paid work is thus an important factor in extending older women's working lives (Edge et al., 2017; 2021). While choices around caring responsibilities have historically been viewed as individual challenges, Loretto and Vickerstaff (2015) suggest that work-life conflict is a societal issue.

Facilitating healthy work: opportunities and risks

A promising finding in a study among older Croatian workers was that being employed supported good mental health (Bjelajac et al., 2019). At the same time, the multiple challenges, difficulties, and disadvantages faced by older women at work take a toll on their health, often because of increased stress at work (Payne & Doyal, 2010). Poor physical and mental health (Brown & Vickerstaff, 2011) in turn is an important barrier to extended working lives of older women (Edge et al., 2021) and often leads to earlier retirement. This underscores the need to better understand the specific challenges faced by older women at work with regards to their health and to identify the factors that support intervention to foster older females' well-being and health at work.

Higher job demands are another factor that predicts a higher likelihood for health problems and exhaustion for older women in comparison to men (Nilsen et al., 2014; Payne & Doyal, 2010; Viotti et al., 2017). In combination with findings around work-life conflict, this points to women having fewer resources to deal with the demands that their job and family obligations pose. For instance, research by Björklund and colleagues (2013) compared stress levels among men and women in higher and lower managerial positions, with women showing significantly higher stress levels than men. Higher stress predicts sleep complaints among older women with women being more affected than men (Lallukka et al., 2010), older women suffer from more physical pain at work (Wanka et al., 2015), and more often receive unfit-to-work-diagnoses from physicians in comparison to men (Dutheil et al., 2016). In terms of mental health, two studies from Germany and Croatia respectively, reported that working women scored higher on depression than men (Baptist et al., 2015; Bjelajac et al., 2019) which was due to higher work stress in the German sample (Baptist et al., 2015).

Other research points to risk factors such as long hours, shift work, or inadequate breaks during the workday, negatively impacting older women's labour market participation (Edge et al., 2021). Interestingly, those jobs that resemble women's unpaid caring responsibilities such as teaching, nursing, midwifery and caring personal services, were those with the highest risk of losing older female workers for health-reasons.(Syddall et al, 2020).

Findings around technology point to both opportunities and risks associated with older female worker's health: On the one hand, the use of technology like desktop computers and mobile phones relates to symptoms such as exhaustion, anxiety, or neck pain among older women at work (Korpinen et al., 2017). On the other hand, technology presents opportunities to work flexibly. Cronin and colleagues (2021) noticed that more work is needed on the use of digital health technologies to support older working women, for instance, in managing symptoms of menopause.

Finally, Viotti and colleagues (2020) highlight the role of a health-oriented organisational environment in supporting women during menopause, specifically the perception of senior managers to the issue, and prioritisation of employee health creating an overall positive working environment.

In sum, older female workers in Europe are at risk of experiencing health impairments which can have negative impacts on their labour market participation and sustainable transition into retirement. Looking at the findings, we could speculate that a lot of the health-effects may be due to other challenges that women face that cause stress (e.g., discrimination, unfavourable working conditions, work-life conflict). However, this remains to be tested, requiring future research to draw clear conclusions on why women experience more health problems than men at work. Understanding these causes will also help to develop recommendations on ways that older female worker's health can be improved through interventions, policies, or individual strategies.

Discussion and recommendations for future research

In this chapter we have presented an overview of research analysing the experiences and well-being of older women workers in Europe. Several key factors impacting the workplace experiences and wellbeing of older women in Europe are identified, including financial status, physical and mental health, work decisions of partners or other close family members, caring responsibilities, and job satisfaction.

Older women's experiences of working life remain different from those of their male counterparts, participation in the workforce by women is still lower than men, and women still work part time to a higher degree than men. Moreover, there is an ongoing gender pay gap, affecting women across all sectors. In addition, women's greater responsibility for unpaid care work in the home affects their chances in the labour market. Feuvre Le et al. (2015) arguethat such gendered inequalities in the labour market may result in a situation with women "ageing with resentment" as opposed to men who "age with confidence". Ageing with resentment or with confidence is closely connected to the transition into retirement. Various reasons can be found in the literature, but for women, menopause and increasing stress and poor health, often related to lack of flexibility, autonomy and control, are some of the key factors identified.

Since (unfavourable) working conditions are directly linked to older female workers' experiences of paid employment, and have consequences for their health and decisions around employment and retirement, an important question for organisations to consider is how they can ensure equity in working conditions, and establish flexible working conditions that help older female employees in juggling the multiple roles (i.e., caring responsibilities) and age-related challenges (e.g., menopause) that they experience. The issues of caring responsibilities reflect societal concerns that should also be addressed at a policy level.

In future research, it is important to investigate work characteristics beyond autonomy, control, and training opportunities to gain a more complete understanding about existing gender differences. Managers may further support older female employees, by encouraging them to seek out and ask for more training and development in their organisation.

Despite initiatives to increase parity for female and male workers, women still experience age and gender discrimination which negatively impact their experiences in the labour market. Experiences of isolation, disproportionate domestic demands and workplace conflict are significant issues that hinder maximised engagement and progression in the workforce. Thus, for future research and any workplace intervention, it is important to clearly differentiate between creating job control and choices for older women at work, as opposed to mere flexible work that may reinforce the additional burdens that they face.

Another key challenge for future research, policy makers, and organisations is the question of how to increase the amount of sustainable full-time and part-time employment for women; namely work that is rewarding and fair, both financially and psychologically. This includes balancing work-life conflicts, which in research and policy debates often tends to focus on families with young children. However, our overview shows the importance of highlighting older women's different experiences of paid and unpaid work, and how they resolve their commitments to caring responsibilities and paid employment. Work-life conflicts are as much of a concern for older women as for younger generations and therefore in need of attention and more in-depth analysis. It is possible that novel intergenerational projects (e.g., older female workers mentoring working age new migrants) could harness older female workers expertise whilst facilitating their role in supporting younger members of the community.

Limitations of this review of literature include a lack of consensus on what constitutes an older worker, with few studies on those aged 55 and over, a lack of studies from Eastern Europe and a lack of definition and research regarding wellbeing. Studies tended to focus on experiences of professionals in specific industries such as education, healthcare, and nursing, thereby limiting application of findings. There was a lack of studies examining interactions between factors e.g., age and gender, plus the influence of other structural and systemic issues, and few that explored experiences of menopause. There was a paucity of qualitative research that may help to explore the multiple factors impacting older women's experiences in the workplace. This highlights the need to develop research on key definitions of ageing and wellbeing, intersectional studies and those using qualitative methods to obtain more nuanced accounts of older female workers experiences.

Older women workers in Europe represent a large and important demographic, who make a significant contribution to the labour market. To retain and support this population, future studies should explore intervention development, including digital technology, and sustainable efforts to improve the wellbeing and mitigate the challenges of older female workers. The transition into hybrid working that has been a significant development during the COVID-19 pandemic should also be investigated. Policy innovation within Europe that benefits the progression and retention of older women workers should also be investigated.

References

Baptist, J., Peter, R., du Prel, J.-B., & Peter, R. (2015). Work-family conflict as a mediator in the association between work stress and depressive symptoms: Cross-sectional evidence from the German lidA-cohort study. *International Archives of Occupational and Environmental Health*, *88*(3), 359–368. https://doi.org/10.1007/s00420-014-0967-0

Bjelajac, A. K., Bobic, J., Kovacic, J., Varnai, V. M., Macan, J., & Smolic, S. (2019). Employment status and other predictors of mental health and cognitive functions in older Croatian workers. *Arhiv Za Higijenu Rada i Toksikologiju*, *70*(2), 109–117. https://doi.org/10.2478/aiht-2019-70-3254

Björklund, C., Lohela-Karlsson, M., Jensen, I., & Bergström, G. (2013). Hierarchies of health: Health and work-related stress of managers in municipalities and county councils in Sweden. *Journal of Occupational and Environmental Medicine*, *55*(7), 752–760. https://doi.org/10.1097/JOM.0b013e318295681c

Brown, P., & Vickerstaff, S. (2011). Health subjectivities and labor market participation: Pessimism and older workers' attitudes and narratives around retirement in the United Kingdom. *Research on Aging*, *33*(5), 529–550. https://doi.org/10.1177/0164027511410249

Cotter, D. A., Hermsen, J. M., Ovadia, S., & Vanneman, R. (2001). The glass ceiling effect. *Social forces*, *80*(2), 655–681.

Cronin, C., Hungerford, C., & Wilson, R. L. (2021). Using digital health technologies to manage the psychosocial symptoms of menopause in the workplace: A narrative literature review. *Issues in Mental Health Nursing*, *42*(6), 541–548. https://doi.org/10.1080/01612840.2020.1827101

Curvers, N., Pavlova, M., Hajema, K., Groot, W., & Angeli, F. (2018). Social participation among older adults (55+): Results of a survey in the region of South

Limburg in the Netherlands. *Health & Social Care in the Community*, *26*(1), e85–e93. https://doi.org/10.1111/hsc.12480

Damman, M., & Henkens, K. (2020). Gender differences in perceived workplace flexibility among older workers in the Netherlands: A brief report. *Journal of Applied Gerontology: The Official Journal of the Southern Gerontological Society*, *39*(8), 915–921. https://doi.org/10.1177/0733464818800651

Dutheil, F., Naughton, G., Sindyga, P., & Lesage, F. X. (2016). Ill health-related job loss: A one-year follow-up of 54,026 employees. *Journal of Occupational and Environmental Medicine*, *58*(9), 918–923. https://doi.org/10.1097/JOM.0000000000000825

Edge, C. E., Coffey, M., Cook, P. A., & Weinberg, A. (2021). Barriers and facilitators to extended working life: A focus on a predominately female ageing workforce. *Ageing and Society*, *41*(12), 2867–2887. https://doi.org/10.1017/S0144686X2000063X

Edge, C. E., Cooper, A. M., & Coffey, M. (2017). Barriers and facilitators to extended working lives in Europe: a gender focus. *Public Health Reviews*, *38*, 2. https://doi.org/10.1186/s40985-017-0053-8

Engels, M., de Moortel, D., Weyers, S., Dragano, N., & Wahrendorf, M. (2020). Linked work lives: The interrelation of own and partner's employment history and their relationship with mental health in older European couples. *Archives of Gerontology and Geriatrics*, *89*, 104092. https://doi.org/10.1016/j.archger.2020.104092

Eurostat (2020) Ageing Europe – looking at the lives of older people in the EU https://ec.europa.eu/eurostat/statistics-explained/index.php?title=Ageing_Europe_-_looking_at_the_lives_of_older_people_in_the_EU

Eurostat. (2015). Employment rate of people aged 20 to 64 in the EU up to 69.2% in 2014: New peaks for women and those aged 55–64. *Eurostat News Release, May 2015.*

Feuvre, Le, N, Kuehni, M., Rosende, M., & Schoeni, C. (2015). Gendered variations in the experience of ageing at work in Switzerland. *Equality, Diversity & Inclusion*, *34*(2), 168–181. http://10.0.4.84/EDI-03-2014-0017

Keeble-Ramsay, D. (2018). Exploring the concept of "positive ageing" in the UK workplace – A literature review. *Geriatrics (Switzerland)*, *3*(4). https://doi.org/10.3390/geriatrics3040072

Kornadt, A. E., Voss, P., & Rothermund, K. (2013). Multiple standards of aging: Gender-specific age stereotypes in different life domains. *European Journal of Ageing*, *10*(4), 335–344. https://doi.org/10.1007/s10433-013-0281-9

Korpinen, L., Pääkkönen, R., & Gobba, F. (2017). Near retirement age (≥55 Years) self-reported physical symptoms and use of computers/mobile phones at work and at leisure. *Healthcare (Basel, Switzerland), 5*(4). https://doi.org/10.3390/healthcare5040071

Lallukka, T., Rahkonen, O., Lahelma, E., & Arber, S. (2010). Sleep complaints in middle-aged women and men: the contribution of working conditions and work-family conflicts. *Journal of Sleep Research, 19*(3), 466–477. https://doi.org/10.1111/j.1365-2869.2010.00821.x

Loretto, W., & Vickerstaff, S. (2013). The domestic and gendered context for retirement. *Human Relations, 66*(1), 65–86. https://doi.org/10.1177/0018726712455832

Loretto, W., & Vickerstaff, S. (2015). Gender, age and flexible working in later life. *Work, Employment and Society, 29*(2), 233–249. https://doi.org/10.1177/0950017014545267

Nilsen, C., Andel, R., Fors, S., Meinow, B., Darin Mattsson, A., & Kåreholt, I. (2014). Associations between work-related stress in late midlife, educational attainment, and serious health problems in old age: A longitudinal study with over 20 years of follow-up. *BMC Public Health, 14*(1), 1–12. https://doi.org/10.1186/1471-2458-14-878

Payne, S., & Doyal, L. (2010). Older women, work and health. *Occupational Medicine, 60*, 172–177. https://doi.org/10.1093/occmed/kqq030

Syddall, H.E, D'Angelo, S., Ntani, G., Stevens, M., Harris, E.C., Linaker, C.H., et al. (2020) Work participation and risk factors for health-related job loss among older workers in the Health and Employment after Fifty (HEAF) study: Evidence from a 2-year follow-up period. *PLoS ONE, 15*(9), e0239383.

Viotti, S., Guidetti, G., Converso, D., & Sottimano, I. (2020). Fostering work ability among menopausal women. Does any work-related psychosocial factor help? *International Journal of Women's Health, 12*, 399–407. https://doi.org/10.2147/IJWH.S230796

Viotti, S., Guidetti, G., Loera, B., Martini, M., Sottimano, I., & Sara, C. (2017). Stress, work ability, and an aging workforce: A study among women aged 50 and over. *Special Issue: The Role of Affect and Emotion to Cope with Stressful Situations, 24*(Suppl 1), 98–121. https://doi.org/10.1037/str0000031

Wanka, A., Kolland, F., & Psihoda, S. (2015). Job strain and coping among ageing baby boomers. *Zeitschrift Fur Gerontologie Und Geriatrie, 48*(6), 511–516. https://doi.org/10.1007/s00391-015-0929-5

Weber, J., de Lange, A., & Müller, A. (2019). Gender differences in paid employment after retirement: Psychosocial working conditions and well-being. *Zeitschrift Fur Gerontologie Und Geriatrie, 52*(1), 32–39. https://doi.org/10.1007/s00391-018-1453-1

Wilks, D. C., & Neto, F. (2013). Workplace well-being, gender and age: Examining the "Double Jeopardy" Effect. *Social Indicators Research, 114*(3), 875–890. https://doi.org/10.1007/s11205-012-0177-7

Bjørn Einar Halvørsen

High and rising senior employment in the Nordic countries

Abstract: The chapter gives an overview of the high and rising employment of older workers in the Nordic countries during the last 20 years, and the policies and reforms behind this development. Much of this development is of course due to the fact that new cohorts of seniors are consistently living longer, have better health and education, and many of them have had less physically demanding and health-risky jobs and working lives than previous generations of older workers.

The the high and rising employment rate of older workers in the Nordic countries can also to some extent be explained by the *policies* that have been implemented in key areas. Much has been done when it comes to active and inclusive labour market policies, information and awareness-raising, as well as retirement- and pension reforms. However, more could be done by promoting employers to retain and hire older workers, and by promoting their employability throughout the whole of working life (Halvørsen, 2020).

Keywords: senior employment and retirement, active labour market policies, pension reforms, employability, employers` role, Nordic, European comparisons

Introduction

Most seniors in the Nordic countries continue in gainful employment beyond the age of 55. This results in high employment rates of older workers, compared with most other countries in Europe. In addition, the employment of older workers is rising remarkably over time. Much of this is due to the fact that new cohorts of seniors are consistently living longer, have better health and education, and many of them have had less physically demanding and health-risky jobs and working lives than previous generations of older workers.

The high and rising employment rate of older workers in the Nordic countries can also to some extent be explained by the *policies* that have been implemented in key areas. In some contexts, there is talk of a "Nordic model" for the economy, working life, social security and welfare. So also, when it comes to older workers` employment and retirement. Much has been done when it comes to active and inclusive labour market policies, retirement- and pension reforms. However, more could be done by promoting employers to retain and hire older workers, and by promoting their employability throughout the whole of working life.

This article describes and analyses what is happening in the Nordic countries in respect of:

- High and rising senior employment, but still potential for further improvements
- Economic policy aimed high employment and low unemployment
- Active and inclusive labour market policy and curbed early retirement
- Old-age pension reforms
- Encouraging employers to retain and hire older workers
- Promoting employability throughout the whole working life
- Summary and concluding remarks

The chapter focuses on major national strategies, reforms and campaigns, as opposed to local measures at individual enterprises and workplaces. The text is mainly descriptive. The ambition is not to reveal causal relationships or effects of policies. This should be a task for closer research, I hope.

High and rising senior employment, but still potential for improvements

The employment rates of older workers have increased markedly in the Nordic countries during the last 20 years (Fig. 7). The only exception is Iceland, where the employment rate of older workers is stable or slightly decreasing, but at a very high level. Except for Denmark, the employment of older workers also increased during the global financial crisis 2008–2010. We can hardly see any signs of the previous "lump-sum fallacy of labour" from the crisis about 20 years earlier, where a strategy was to try to reduce youth unemployment by extended early retirement among senior workers.

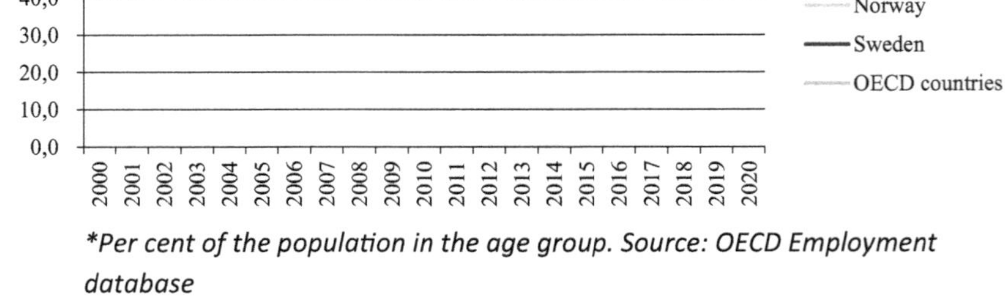

Fig. 7. Employment rates 55–64 years old* in the Nordic countries 2000–2020.
*Per cent of the population in the age group. Source: OECD Employment database

The employment rates of older workers are highest in Iceland, followed by Sweden and Norway. They are lowest in Finland and Denmark, but the senior employment rates have increased most in Denmark and Finland. The employment rates in the age group 55–64 in the years 2000/2020, respectively, were: Denmark 56/71, Finland 42/68, Iceland 84/77, Norway 65/73, Sweden 65/78 and OECD total 48/60.

The employment rates are relatively high among *both men and women* in the Nordic countries, with relatively small differences between the sexes (Fig. 8). In Finland there is even slightly higher employment among women than among men in this age group (55–64). The employment rates (%) among men / women respectively in this age group in 2020 were: Denmark 76/67, Finland 67/68, Iceland 83/71, Norway 76/69, Sweden 80/76.

In other European countries with relative high employment rates, they have greater differences between men and women (Germany, Netherlands, Switzerland, Czech republic). In other European countries, the employment rates are considerably lower among both women and men (Belgium, France, Italy, Greece and Poland).

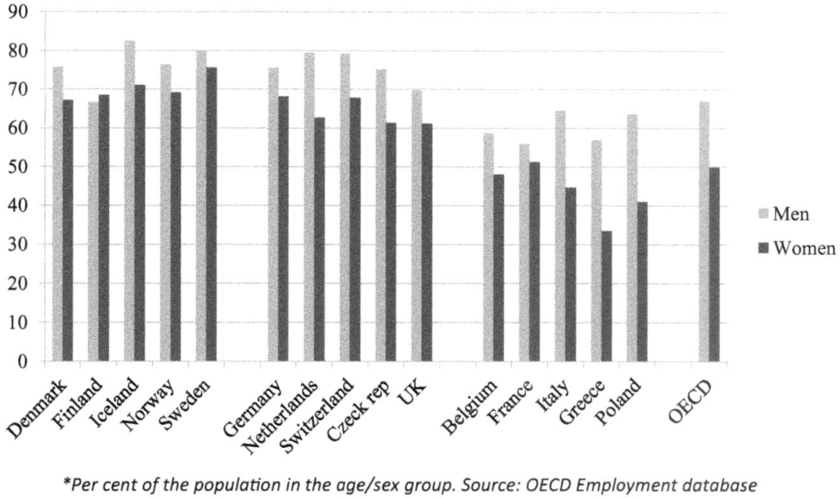

Fig. 8. Employment rates 55–64 yo. Men and women. Selected European countries 2020.

*Per cent of the population in the age/sex group. Source: OECD Employment database 2020

Tab. 5. Senior employment rates in the Nordic countries. Percentage of five-year age groups.

	Denmark		Finland		Iceland		Norway		Sweden	
Age group	2000	2020	2000	2020	2000	2020	2000	2020	2000	2020
55–59 years	73	81	59	79	88	80	77	80	78	85
60–64 years	34	61	23	56	80	75	54	65	48	70
65–69 years	8	22	5	15	49	45	18	29	15	25
70–74 years	4	8	2	7	17	15	4	7	6	11

Source: OECD Employment database 2020. Labour force surveys (LFS).

Table 5 shows employment (%) in five-year age groups between the ages of 55 and 75 years in the Nordic countries in the years 2000 and 2020. There has been strong employment growth in all the senior age groups in all Nordic countries, except for Iceland, where they are slightly decreasing. The increase has been especially high among people in their sixties and among women. The Nordic countries have higher senior employment rates than in most other European countries, especially in the age groups between 60 and 70 years old.

There are stepwise decreases in employment rates around the ages of 60, 65 and 70 years in all the Nordic countries. This is at the ages where it was previously more formal or fixed retirement ages. The retirement ages and options have been more flexible during the last 10–20 years. This means that there is potential for higher employment among people aged 60 and older in the Nordic countries.

Table 6 shows a number of supplementary indicators for the situation in the labour market and working life environment, for seniors in the Nordic countries and for the OECD.

Tab. 6. Working life indicators for older workers in the Nordic countries and OECD 2018.

	Denmark	Finland	Iceland	Norway	Sweden	OECD
Employment rate 55–74 years (%)	52	49	69	56	58	51
Employment gap W/M 55–64 years (%)	9	−2	11	8	4	14
Part-time job 55–64 years (%)	15	16	19	24	21	20
Temporary job 55–64 years (%)	4	9	3	2	7	7
Self-employed (%)	10	17	19	8	14	21
Retention rate 60–64 years (%) 1)	50	51	80	70	64	47
Hiring rate 55–64 years (%) 2)	8	10	5	4	9	9
Unemployment 55–64 years (%)	4	7	2	2	5	5
Of which unemployed > 1 year (%)	42	40	27	31	29	46
Higher education 55–64 years (%)	29	40	31	34	33	27
Participated in learning 55–64 years (%)	44	40	..	54	57	42

Source: OECD Older Workers Scoreboard 2018.

Notes: (1) The proportion of workers aged 60–64 years who were in the same job five years earlier. (2) Proportion of workers aged 55–64 years who have been employed for less than one year in the same job.

Table 6 indicates that working life quality for older workers is generally good on average, as measured by these indicators. There are also certain nuances and differences between the Nordic countries. The table shows that:

- *The employment rate among people aged 50–74 years* is higher than 50 %, and highest in Iceland, followed by Sweden and Norway.
- *The employment gap between older women and men* is fairly low: 8–10 % difference in Denmark, Norway and Iceland, and 4 % difference in Sweden. Finland has slightly (2 %) higher employment among older women than among older men.

- The proportion of seniors (55–64) in *a part-time job* is quite low, and varies between 15 % (Denmark) and 24 % (Norway).
- The proportion of older workers (55–64) in *a temporary job* is lower than 10 %, and is especially low in Norway, Iceland and Denmark (2–4 %)
- The proportion of *self-employed* older workers (55–64) varies between 8–10 % in Norway and Denmark and as high as 17–19 % in Finland and Iceland respectively.
- More than 50 % of older workers (60–64 years) have been *in the same job for more than five years*. This retention rate is highest in Iceland (80 %), followed by Norway (70 %) and Sweden (64 %).
- Less than 10 % of older workers (55–64) have recently *beent hired for a new job*. They have been employed in their current position for less than one year. Iceland and Norway have the lowest hiring rates, and Finland and Sweden have the highest ones.
- *Unemployment* among older workers (55–64) is low. It is lowest in Iceland and Norway (around 2 %) and highest in Finland (7 %).
- By contrast, *the proportion of long-term unemployed (>1 year)* among the unemployed older workers (55–64) is high: About 25 % in Iceland, 30 % in Norway and Sweden, and 40 % in Denmark and Finland.
- The proportion of older workers (55–64) with *higher education* is around 30 % in all the Nordic countries except in Finland, where 40 % have higher education.
- Between 40 % (Finland and Denmark) and 50–60 % (Norway and Sweden) of older workers (55–64) have participated in *learning activities* during the last year.

The OECD report *Working Better with* Age (2019) gives a broad status and analysis about the situation and development for older workers in the OECD countries. The report confirms the relatively good situation and development in the Nordic countries. The conclusion is still that all countries: the Nordics included, should take further actions to boost the job opportunities at an older age. OECD recommends governments to take further actions in three broad areas:

- ➢ Rewarding work at an older age
- ➢ Encouraging employers to retain and hire older workers
- ➢ Promoting employability of workers throughout their whole working lives

Most political focus and reforms have been implemented within the first one of these broad areas, mainly by better work incentives, old-age pension reforms and early retirement reforms. However, more can be done especially within the two other areas, says the OECD. Within the second area by addressing negative ageist attitudes and age discrimination in recruitment, promotion and retention, and by encouraging good practice by employers and leaders in managing an age-diverse workforce. Within the third area by improving lifelong learning and skills recognition, by improving working conditions and job quality at all ages, and by providing effective employment assistance for older workers facing job loss or wish to find another job. These are important challenges and areas for improvement in the Nordic countries as well.

Economic policy aimed high employment and low unemployment

An important underlying factor behind the high and rising employment of older workers in the Nordic countries is a proactive, stabilising, and inclusive economic policy. This has led to stable economic growth, high and stable employment, and low unemployment rates in countries.

Like most other countries, the Nordics suffered a sudden decline in the economy during the global financial crisis of 2008–2010, but the economic development stabilised rather quickly thereafter. The financial crisis had greater impact on the economy of most other European countries than in the Nordic countries, except for Iceland. The reasons are related to the economic policy and the labour market systems in the Nordic countries. Important advantages in the Nordic countries include:

- Stable, predictable institutional framework conditions
- Stabilising fiscal policy and monetary policy
- Tripartite collaboration on wage development, employment and social welfare policies
- Active and universal labour market policy
- A relatively high overall level of education in the population
- Social security for all through universal and relatively good social insurance schemes

This both presupposes and entails joint responsibility and mutual confidence among people and between the people and the governmental institutions (Andersen, Dølvik & Ibsen 2014).

During the Corona Pandemic 2020–2021, the national economic and labour market policies were further strengthened and expanded. Unemployment benefits were increased and several enterprise and employer subsidies were introduced to help the most severe enterprises survive financially during the close-down. Such kinds of measures have been important types of countercyclical interventions in many European countries. Late 2021 the economic activity seems to return rather quickly back on quite good track in the Nordics. The economic and social inequality among people have increased further, however. This is a political challenge, even in the Nordic countries.

Active and inclusive labour market policy and curbed early retirement

The Nordic countries pursue an active and inclusive labour market policy and working environment policy, based on good regulations and institutions. Most policies and instruments are *universally designed*, with mainly equal individual rights and duties for everyone, regardless of their age, gender, and other characteristics. Older workers are covered by the universal instruments in the same way as everyone else. There are also several measures and programmes that target older employees and jobseekers in particular. The situation for seniors on the labour market in the Nordic countries must therefore be considered considering both universal schemes as well as more targeted programmes.

Senior workers have not been more severely hit by lay-offs and unemployment than younger workers during the Corona Pandemic 2020/2021. Rather on the contrary. Young people have been hardest hit by reduced economic and social activities and business closures due to pandemic.

Denmark: Denmark has attracted international interest for its *"flexicurity model"* in the employment market ("easy to hire and easy to fire"). This entails relatively weak, by Nordic standards, employment protection rights, combined with fairly good social insurances and a very active labour market policy. Denmark's labour market policy in recent years represents something of a U-turn from its previous policy of encouraging early departure from working life. The voluntary early retirement pension scheme (*"efterløn")* and other early retirement schemes have gradually been reformed and curbed, in favour of economic incentives to continue working for longer. Several political reform packages have been implemented. *The Employment Reform (2015)* was specifically aimed at people over the age of 50 at risk of long-term unemployment and possibly falling out of the labour market.

Finland: Finland's working life policy in the 2000ies has mainly focused on addressing a combined stagnation and transition in the economy, combined with extensive early departure from working life. Several programmes and schemes have been implemented to promote a return to work and retraining for a new job and education in connection with staff cuts. In addition, there have been various working environment programmes to promote human relations management with a focus on older workers and a life-cycle approach, as well as for a good health and quality situation at the workplaces. An "unemployment tunnel" of extended and longer unemployment benefits for older people (55–65) into retirement has gradually been dismantled.

Iceland: The labour market in Iceland is quite flexible. There have been tremendous changes in the wake of the financial collapse in 2008–2010. Iceland has the highest employment rate and lowest unemployment rate in the whole OECD area. Iceland has mainly *not* implemented new types of extensive active labour market measures nor programs. However, the government has recently drawn up a policy to help older workers stay even longer in the workforce. Older workers can gradually switch to less physically demanding jobs and perhaps slightly less responsibility and a slower pace: – in a mutual understanding of their own and the company's preferences. There is however, a significant early departure from working life by a disability pension.

Norway: Tripartite collaboration between the government and the social partners by income negotiations and in the labour market- and social policies is essential in Norway. This has led to good overall achievements when it comes to employment and working conditions, also for older workers. The Labour and Welfare Administration (NAV) offers several types of labour market measures, and NAV also offers all types of public social insurance benefits for all Norwegians. Older workers are not a certain priority group for active labour market schemes, but they are overrepresented among the long-term unemployed, which is a priority group. However, there is a widespread early departure from working life through disability pension in Norway. Much of this has its background in restructuring and downsizing of enterprises and workplaces. The prevalence of disability beneficiaries is very high among older workers (20 % in age group 55–59 and 26 % in age group 60–64), but these rates have been slightly decreasing over time.

The upper age limit for protection against dismissal has been increased from 70 to 72 years in the private sector, and the same has been proposed for the public sector as well. A government-appointed *Employment Committee* has recently delivered a report on improved policies and measures that can contribute to include more people in the labour force and fewer people ending up on disability benefits or other social benefits (NOU 2021: 2). The new government will follow up this report.

Sweden: There are few ALM programmes that are specifically aimed at seniors in Sweden. However, how they are implemented, dimensioned, and practised can often be adjusted to target specific groups, such as older workers and long-term unemployed. Sweden has had good results by using positive economic incentives to promote employment of older jobseekers and other more vulnerable groups in the labour market. Sweden has also a good tradition and good achievements by supporting and managing organisational restructuring and downsizing in businesses and working life in the best possible way for affected employers and employees. There was previously a high prevalence of sickness absence and disability retirement in Sweden. Introduction of guideline-limits on the duration of sickness benefit combined with an active rehabilitation chain, are the key reform elements to curb this trend. The result is lower sickness absence and fewer people on disability pension, but on the other hand also higher unemployment and more people receiving social cash benefits.

Old-age pension reforms

During the last 30 years, all European Union member states have reformed their old-age pension systems. In view of ongoing and future population ageing, reforms have aimed at containing the rise of the demographic old-age dependency ratio and lowering the pension benefit ratio. The pension systems have moved towards a mulita-pillar system, giving larger roles to occupational pensions and individual pensions. The pension reforms focusing on long-term financial sustainability may increase the risk of old-age poverty, however (Hinrichs 2021).

There have been, and is still being, extensive pension reforms implemented in all the Nordic countries. The main objective is to make the pension systems more sustainable in the long term with fair intergenerational balances of benefits and costs. Incentives and mechanisms to stimulate to longer working lives and greater flexibility in the transition between work and retirement are central.

Denmark: The retirement reforms in Denmark have mainly focused on gradually raising the official retirement age and early retirement ages:

- The general retirement age is being raised gradually from 65 years to 67 years.
- The voluntary early retirement pension age is being raised from 60 to 62 years.
- Longevity indexing of these age limits for receiving a pension in the longer term.
- Reductions of voluntary early retirement benefits against old-age pension.
- More favourable deduction of old-age pension against earned income.

Work has also been initiated to simplify and improve the incentives to carry on working in respect of means-testing and reduction of different types of pension benefits against each other and against earned income. A new *"years-of service" early retirement pension* will be implemented in 2022, targeted towards persons 61 years and older with long and physically hard working lives behind them.

Finland: Finland has implemented several pension reforms and has others in the pipeline. The main objective is more sustainable pensions in the long run by encouraging higher employment and a longer and better working lives for older workers. *The 2017 pension reform* shall contribute to this, while also ensuring adequate income for future retirees. A longer working life will yield higher annual pensions. The earliest possible retirement age is gradually being raised from 63 to 65 years up to 2027. From 2030, the future retirement age will be indexed in accordance with development in the expected remaining life expectancy of the relevant age cohorts. The reform also introduces incentives to continue working beyond the retirement age. Longevity indexation of accumulated pension rights earned from work has been introduced.

A flexible partial pension can be drawn as 25 % or 50 % of the accumulated pension from the age of 61, and from 64 years for people born in 1964 or later. This lower age limit will also be indexed based on expected remaining life expectancy starting from 2030. *A new "years-of-service pension"* was also introduced in connection with the 2017 pension reform. The pension is targeted towards older persons (61+) with reduced work capacity after long and physically demanding working careers.

Iceland: The general retirement age is 67 years, with a requirement of 40 years' residence to receive a full basic pension and 40 years' accumulation of pension savings to qualify for a full supplementary pension. The law on mandatory supplementary occupational pension entered into force in 1998, so no-one has yet earned a full supplementary pension. The earned supplementary pension can be drawn from the age of 60 years or deferred up until the age of 72 years, against deductions from – or additions to the annual pension respectively. From 2018, it is possible to draw half the supplementary pension against a corresponding reduction in working hours. The government aims to rise the general retirement age gradually from 67 to 70 years.

Norway: The 2011 pension reform: The overall pension system in Norway has gradually been reformed since 2011. The reform is inspired by the Swedish pension reform some ten years earlier, and based on the report from a public Pension Commission in 2004. The objective is a more sustainable system with better intergenerational balance. The main elements of the pension reform in the Norwegian National Insurance Scheme are:

- Pensions earnings on all earned income throughout the entire working life. 18 % of the annual work income up to a certain threshold is being accumulated into an individual pension account, which is to be distributed over all the years of retirement.

- A guaranteed minimum pension for people with low pension earnings. Minimum level approx. NOK 200,000 (EUR 20.000) with 40 years' residence in Norway, and a lower level with shorter length of residence. Reduced by 80 % against the earned pension.
- Flexible retirement age and pension withdrawals between the ages of 62 and 75, based on cost neutrality. Early pension withdrawal results in a lower annual pension, and vice versa.
- Longevity indexing of the accumulated pension accounts. Increasing longevity leads to lower pension per year, or you have to work longer for a certain pension level per year.
- Accumulated pension assets are indexed in line with the overall wage increases, while the paid pension is adjusted 0.75 % lower than the annual wage increases. From 2020 changed to the average development of wages and prices.

Pension payments are not means-tested (reduced) against income from work. Individuals are free to draw pension and continue working. Supplementary contractual pensions and occupational pensions are gradually being adapted to the reformed Norwegian National Insurance Scheme.

Sweden: The Swedish pension reform that took place some 20 years ago has acted as a template for pension reforms in many other countries. The core of the reform was to combine good characteristics of a defined-benefit system and a defined-contribution system. The main elements of the reform are:

- A transition from a "defined-benefit" system to a "listed defined-contribution" system. An annual pension premium of 16 % of the annual income is accumulated over the individual's entire working life, in an individual pension account that is to be distributed over the expected number of years of retirement – The General Pension (AP).
- The individual's pension earnings are proportional with their annual income, with premiums paid over their entire working life, as compared with the previous system based on the income in the 15 best of 30 years.
- Flexible access to draw a full or partial pension from the age of 61 years. The longer the individual waits to start drawing their pension, the higher the annual pension they receive.
- A fund-based, individual, premium pension was introduced. 2.5 % of the annual income is paid into an investment fund with individual investment choices.

- Guaranteed minimum pension from the age of 65 years for people with low or no earnings in the General Pension (AP) scheme.

The future rules regarding retirement age and other age limits will be linked to the development in average life expectancy through a "target age" (*"riktålder"*) system. This means that all the age limits in the pension system and in the social security system will be linked to life expectancy. The lowest age at which people can start drawing the general pension (AP) is going to be raised gradually from 61 years to 64 years. The age from which the guaranteed minimum pension can be drawn is going to be raised gradually from 65 to 66 years and eventually up to the future new "target age". An additional income pension element has been proposed for persons with a long working life and low wages,

Encouraging employers to retain and hire older workers

Most initiatives and reforms to increase the labour market participation of older workers have so far been implemented on the *supply side* of the labour market. In particular by strengthened work incentives in pension reforms and active labour market measures. There have been fewer and weaker initiatives on the *demand side* of the labour market. Namely by encouraging employers to retain and hire older workers. Employers are usually more willing to retain than to hire older workers. The retention rates of older workers are high and the hiring rates pretty low in the Nordic countries (OECD 2019 and Tab. 6.

Age discrimination in the labour market is forbidden by law in the Nordic countries, but age stereotypical attitudes and behaviour exist (SOU 2020:69). This is most common when it comes to recruitment and hiring processes. Employers and line managers often appreciate their older employees, but they are more hesistant to hire older workers: the main reason may be actual or perceived obsolete competence and/or reduced productivity.

In three of the Nordic countries: Denmark, Norway and Sweden, the governments have set up national and tripartite anchored institutions to provide knowledge-based information, advice and awareness-raising about such kinds of issues and questions:

Denmark: The Seniors Think Tank for a longer, good working life. www.seniortaenketanken.dk The Think Tank was set up in 2018, with the objective to help ensure that seniors can have a better and longer working life, and to get more people to defer starting to draw their pension.

Norway: Centre for Senior Policy (CSP). www.seniorpolitikk.no CSP is a national resource centre that aims to stimulate the integration and promotion of a seniors perspective in companies' human relations (HR) policy and management.

Sweden: Delegation for Senior Labour. www.seniorarbetskraft.se The delegation was set up by the Government in 2018 to promote older workers, counteract age discrimination, and identify opportunities to make better use of older workers' experience and competencies. The objective is to work for a more inclusive and age-neutral working life.

The Danish think tank and the Swedish delegation completed their work in 2019 and 2020 respectively, while the Norwegian CSP is permanent. However, the two former institutions in their final reports have recommended permanent solutions for such purposes in Denmark and Sweden, like there is in Norway.

The Danish Think Tank has published a range of analyses, and good practice examples of senior policies and how to improve the senior policy at enterprise level. Their final report contains 20 concrete recommendations to the government and the social partners about how more seniors can experience more good years in working life. The recommendations are divided into three main strategies: (1) Better opportunities and conditions for long and good working lives, (2) Help unemployed seniors rapidly back to work, and (3) Help seniors to see the advantages by postponing retirement. The main recommendation is that the Government and the social partners should establish a permanent partnership for further increasing of senior employment. (Seniortænketanken 2020)

The Norwegian Centre for Senior Policy (CSP) is providing knowledge-based information on scientific research as well as good practical examples of senior policy in the working life. CSP initiates research and pilot projects, they arrange seminars and conferences and issues publications on senior policy questions. A *«Senior Policy Barometer»* measuring attitudes among employees and employers/leaders is each year being issued, presented, and discussed by the social partners, policy makers, enterprises and researchers (Norsk Seniorpolitisk barometer 2020/2021). A core priority for CSP is to stimulate good human relations policy and -practice with a life-long perspective. Such kinds of studies and projects are being carried out in a practical setting in specific sectors and branches of the labour market, such as industry-, trade-, education -and care sectors.

The Swedish Delegation for Senior Labour has published a number of papers and reports on different kind of issues pertaining to senior workers. The delegation also undertook study- and co-operation visits to labour market organisations and enterprises, in order to learn about- and provide information on current senior policy issues and programmes. "Delegation ambassadors" have published articles and made presentations about such issues in the mass media, and have participated actively in public debate. The Delegation`s main, final considerations are that (1) the competencies and experiences of senior workers should be better acknowledged, apprecieated and used, (2) a longer working life presupposes lifelong learning, and (3) formal age limits and regulations are affecting the length of the working life. Their main recommendation is to continue and develop the knowledge and information about seniors and work, and to influence attitudes and behaviour on a permanent basis (SOU 2020:69)

Promoting employability throughout the whole working life

The OECD-report *Working Better with* Age (2019) pointed out skills development and lifelong learning as an important area for further development and improvements of the future employment of seniors and older workers. Results from the OECD Survey of Adult Skills (PIAAC) suggest that older workers across the OECD are not, on average, well equipped to deal with changes in skill requirements brought about by technological progress and globalisation. The ability to solve problems in tehnology-rich environments are lower than among their younger colleagues. Older workers with less recent vintages of skills are particularly exposed to the risk of skills obsolescence. In addition, older workers participate far less than younger workers in job-related training. Older jobseekers have also often severe problems by getting a new job after enterprise restructuring and downsizing. A lot of them leave the labour market into (too) early retirement (OECD 2019).

Such challenges are broadly acknowledged in the Nordic countries and highlighted in several governmental policy documents and initiatives. Some concrete policy initiatives have also been implemented, but more could be done, especially in practice and at the enterprise level.

The Danish public employment centres (PES/Jobcentre) provide a wide range of active labour market service measures in their toolbox. Among them also several programmes for job-oriented adult training, learning and education, both for jobseekers as well as for employed workers. The programmes contain both short-time job-training courses and vocational educations, as well as supplementary educations up to bachelor-level. The duration varies from 3–4 months up to 3–4 years. Most programmes are free of charge, and the participants usually receive a wage- or financial support during their participation in training or education programmes. For academic education you usually do not receive a wage remuneration, and usually you have to pay a subsidised participants fee.

In *Finland* there are several programmes and initiatives to promote reemployment after redundancy, such as the *«New security, new skills»* programme. This is a programme that provides early intervention in the form of personal advice, guidance, support and follow-up services for workers who are laid off or made redundant due to organisational restructuring, as well as for employers and line managers, to help them carry out such restructuring processes in a best possible way. The programme is more tailored towards white-collar workers than towards blue-collar workers. A *National Working Life Development Strategy* aims at increased employment, productivity and quality in the working life, as well as employee`s wellbeing at work. A programme *«Competence Based Qualifications»*, recognises competencies acquired during the worklife, and offers the possibility to complete a vocational upper secondary qualification, further and special vocational qualifications.

In *Iceland* a law on adult education was adopted in 2010. The goal is to raise the level of education in the adult population, and especially among people with little formal education. The principle is that everyone should have the opportunity to take education, and develop their competences during their whole lives.

In *Norway* there is a tripartite *National Competence-policy Strategy* (2017–2021). Lifelong learning and competence acquirement at work is one of the (3) main goals for the strategy. Among the more concrete initiatives are: Strengthen and develop the digital competence in the entire workforce. Improved regional career-guidance services. More active use of training and competence-building measures in the labour market- and integration policies. Strengthen the PES`s (NAV`s) learning- and training services for jobseekers who need better qualifications to get a job. The Government in 2020 launched a White Paper for the Parliament on *Competencereform on lifelong learning* (Melding til Stortinget 14 for 2019–2020). The main goals are that nobody should be outdated because of lack of competence, and to tighten gaps between the workers`s competencies and what working life needs. Three main programme-areas for action are pointed out: (1) Financial support to flexible, higher education for adults, (2) Tripartite sector-programmes for competence-development, and (3) Pilot projects for financial incentives for life-long learning.

Sweden has a good tradition of working systematically to handle and manage necessary restructuring and downsizing of enterprises and workplaces, in the best possible ways for affected employers and employees. *The Security Council (Trygghetsrådet TRR)* works as a long-term consult and partner and provides professional counselling, guidance and support to managers, employees and local trade unions during major restructuring or downsizing processes. *The Employment Transition Fund (Trygghetsfonden TSL)* is another, similar agency, more aimed at blue-collar workers than TRR. The achievements of the TRR and TSL services are pretty good: Around 8–9 out of 10 of the affected workers get a new job or a career shift through the co-operation with TRR or TSL. To facilitate the continous restructuring in the labour market, the government have introduced opportunities for employees to develop and their competencies, or to learn new skills during their whole working lives. A paid period for personal professional development for up to one year will be provided.

In all the Nordic countries, several packages of extended financial support to job-oriented adult training, learning and further education have been launched during the last year, as elements of the Governments`Corona Pandemic strategies.

Summary and concluding remarks

The employment of older workers is high and rising in the Nordic countries during the last 20 years. The employment rates among people 55 years and older are highest in Iceland, followed by Sweden and Norway, but have increased most in Denmark and Finland during the last 3–5 years. The senior employment rates are relatively high both for men and women, compared to most other European countries. There are stepwise decreases in employment rates around the ages of 60, 65 and 70 years in all the Nordic countries. This is at the ages when it previously was normal (or compulsory) to retire, due to formal retirement ages. This means that there is potential for higher employment among people older than 60 years in the Nordic countries in the future.

The OECD has recommended governments to take actions for further improvements of the seniors` employment in three broad areas (OECD 2019):

- Rewarding work at an older age
- Encouraging employers to retain and hire older workers
- Promoting employability of workers throughout their whole working lives

Most political focus and reforms have been implemented within the first of these broad areas, mainly by better work incentives, old-age pension reforms and early retirement reforms. However, more can be done within the two other areas, say the OECD. This is relevant for the Nordic countries as well.

An important underlying factor behind the high and rising employment of older workers in the Nordic countries is the *stabilising and inclusive economic policy* that has been pursued. This has led to stable economic growth, high and stable overall employment and low unemployment rates.

All the Nordic countries pursue an *active and inclusive labour market policy and working environment policy*, on the basis of pretty good regulations and institutions. Tripartite co-operation between the governments and the social partners is essential. Most programmes and measures are *universally designed*, with mainly equal individual rights and duties for everyone, regardless of their age and gender and so on. Older workers are covered by the universal measures in the same way as everyone else. There are also some measures and programmes that are more targeted and tailored towards older employees and jobseekers.

A big challenge is the severe ongoing and future s*tructural transitions in the labour markets*. This has accelerated tremendously during the ongoing global corona pandemic crisis. We know that older workers have great problems in getting a new job after enterprise downsizing, and many of them leave the labour market into (too) early retirement. In Sweden and to some extent also in Finland they have good programmes and results with systematic and proactive support to enterprises, employers and employees who are facing severe restructuring and downsizing.

Extensive pension reforms have been and are being implemented in all the Nordic countries. The main objective is to make the pension systems more sustainable in the long term, with good intergenerational balance of benefits and costs. Central elements of the pension reforms implemented are improved incentives and mechanisms to stimulate to longer working lives, curbing early retirement schemes, and by giving more flexibility in the transition between work and retirement.

One upcoming pension policy challenge may stem from a bit too one-sided focus on work incentives to the expense of social redistribution and poverty prevention in the pension reforms. In some Nordic, and other European countries they are now considering or implementing improved pension solutions for people with long working lives and low wages, and demanding or unregulated working conditions.

Encouraging employers to retain and hire older workers. Most initiatives and reforms to increase the labour market participation of older workers have so far been implemented on the *supply side* of the labour market. In particular by strengthened work incentives in pension reforms and active labour market measures. There have been fewer and weaker initiatives on the *demand side* of the labour market. Employers are usually more willing to retain than to hire older workers. The retention rates of older workers are quite high and the hiring rates quite low in the Nordic countries.

Age discrimination in the labour market is forbidden by law in the Nordic countries, but both age discrimination and age stereotypical attitudes and behaviour exist (SOU 2020:69). This is most common when it comes to recruitment and hiring processes. Employers and line managers often appreciate their older employees, because of their work experience, loyalty and responsibility. But they are more hesistant to hire older workers; the main reason may be actual or perceived obsolete competence and reduced productivity. In three of the Nordic countries: Denmark, Norway and Sweden, the governments have set up national and tripartite anchored institutions to provide knowledge-based information, advice and awareness-raising about such kinds of issues and questions.

Promoting employability throughout the whole working life. Results from the OECD Survey of Adult Skills (PIAAC) suggest that older workers across the OECD are not so well equipped to deal with changes in skills requirements brought about by technological developments and globalisation. This is the situation in the Nordic countries as well. Older workers with less recent vintages of skills are particularly exposed to the risk of skills obsolescence. In addition, older workers participate far less than younger workers in job-related training (OECD 2019).

Such challenges are quite broadly acknowledged on a national level in the Nordic countries and highlighted in several governmental policy documents and initiatives. Some concrete policy and practice initiatives have also been implemented. But more could be done, especially in practice, on regional and local level, on industry- and enterprise level, and last but not least on the individual level.

Policy matters! A recent comparative study has examined the effects of macro-level institutional policy factors on effective retirement age and employment rate of older workers (55–64) in 15 OECD countries (Finland, Norway and Sweden included) from 1992 to 2010 (Kuitto and Helmdag 2021). They found that policies do matter for retirement and labour market outcomes, and that different (but not all) pull, push and retention factors have a substantial impact on extending working lives. The study reveals that public pension reforms geared towards postponing retirement in many countries are significant determinants of lengthening working lives. In particular, statutory retirement age and financial disincentives for early retirement proof important. Institutional effects differ by gender, though. Furthermore, the results point to the importance of social and active labour market policies supporting labour market participation throughout the life-course: social investment in human capital and public services clearly supports extending working lives.

I hope that such kind of comparative policy studies could be carried out for years after 2010 as well.

References

Andersen, S.K., Dølvik, J.O., & Ibsen, C.L. (2014): De nordiske aftalemodeller i åbne markeder – udfordringer og perspektiver. Fafo-rapport 2014:08. NordMod 2030. Delrapport 9.

Beskæftigelsesministeriet DK (2019): *Fremtidens seniorarbejdsliv – anbefalinger fra Seniortænketanken.* www.seniortaenketanken.dk/anbefalinger

Halvørsen, Bjørn (2020): *Senior citizens: Work and pensions in the Nordics.* Report 17. Swedish Governmental Delegation for Senior Workforce. www.seniorarbetskraft.se

Kuitto, Kati and Helmdag, Jan (2021): *Extending working lives: How policies shape retirement and labour market participation of older workers.* Social Policy & Administration / Volume 55, Issue 3 /pp. 423–439. https://onlinelibrary.wiley.com/doi/10.1111/spol.12717

Meld. St.14 (2019–2020): *Kompetansereformen – Lære* hele *livet.* www.regjeringen.no/no/dokumenter//meld.-st.-14-20192020/id26988284

Norsk seniorpolitisk barometer (2020 og 2021) Oslo: Senter for seniorpolitik.: www.seniorpolitikk.no/kunnskap/norsk-seniorpolitisk-barometer.

NOU (2021): 2 *Kompetanse, aktivitet og inntektssikring. Tiltak for økt sysselsetting.* www.regjeringen.no/no/dokumenter/nou-2021-2/id2832582

OECD (2019): *Working Better with Age, and OECD Older Workers Scoreboard.*

SOU (2020:69): *Eldre har aldrig varit yngre – allt fler kan och vill arbeta lengre.* www.regeringen.se/rattsliga-dokument/statens-offentliga-utredningar/2020/11/sou-202069

Russell D. Lansbury

Sustainable work and creative leisure? Some reflections

The issues discussed in the first section of this book are very important for the times in which we live, whether in Europe or other countries around the globe. Generating jobs for those who are seeking or needing work is a challenging issue. While we continue to have problems of both unemployment and underemployment, it may seem a diversion to focus on "sustainable work", yet this what is required if meaningful and productive forms of work are to be achieved.

Three important key themes emerge from the chapters in the first part of this book.

First, achieving sustainable work is not a "quick fix". As reflected by several authors in this first section, implementation of sustainable work policies requires a whole life course perspective. The United Nations' sustainable development goal of "decent work and economic growth" (SDG8) calls not only for full and productive employment but also the eradication of various forms of abuse at work such as forced labour, human trafficking and child labour. While overall rates of employment and decent work are improving in Europe, the gap between rich and poor countries in terms of job quality and equality is growing wider each year. Improving working conditions and attaining sustainable work are becoming an increasingly important and urgent objectives not only in Europe but also for the world as a whole.

Second, achieving long-term improvement in sustainable work is a complex issue involving the interaction and interdependency of many variables, including: technology, innovation and the quality of jobs. Many of the breakthroughs to achieve greater sustainable work in recent decades emerged from Swedish manufacturing, such as Volvo and Saab, which demonstrated that technology could be used to redesign work in a more "human-centred" manner. The research underpinning these changes drew on the "sociotechnical systems" approach developed by the Tavistock Institute in the UK. Outstanding examples of this approach were undertaken by Emery and Thorsrud (1976) in the Norwegian off-shore oil and gas fields. The key lesson from this experience was that when the technology is used to enhance human skills, there are more efficient and socially productive outcomes. Many of the current applications of technology in the service sector, such as automated banking, are being used to eliminate jobs rather than rendering work more sustainable. However, some positive examples can be found in iron ore mining at LKAB in northern Sweden where automation is being used to create more sustainable jobs. These initiatives use "intelligent" technology to replace arduous and dangerous work (Cooney and Lansbury, 2018).

Third, achieving sustainable work requires fundamental transformation of our current economic and social policies. The triple challenge of digitalisation, green transition and the pandemic raises the need for increasing transition capacity on the European labour market and in global contexts. They have also raised the important question: are we finally witnessing the "end of work"? While work provides economic security, it is also is an important source of identity for people. Hence, if work is to occupy less time in people's lives, how will society address both issues of income maintenance as well as the social and psychological importance of work to individuals? Data from *Eurofond* indicates that those who opt for early retirement do so because they have access to a pension. Governments should be legislating for more flexible pension schemes. These would enable workers to retire earlier or more gradually with a blend of work and semi-retirement, thus making the transition to retirement easier. More emphasis should be placed on sustainable and creative leisure. This is important not only throughout the "life course" of workers' careers. It should also be possible for workers to make a transition towards greater leisure as they begin to age and find work more arduous and stressful.

While sustainable work is clearly a subject that requires more thought and discussion, greater attention needs to be directed at how leisure can be made more affordable and attractive to workers, employers and governments. During the 1960s and early 1970s, it was frequently asserted by prominent sociologists in North America and Western Europe that affluent societies were on the verge of a new era of "mass leisure". It was argued that the population would increasingly relocate from overcrowded and polluted cities to the fast-expanding suburbs where they could enjoy a more tranquil environment and spend their increasing leisure time (Lansbury, 1970). Some Nordic sociologists, such as Harald Swedner at Lund University, raised concerns about how workers would spend their increased leisure time and campaigned for an expansion in life-long learning opportunities so that people would put their new-found leisure to increasing their education and undertaking productive activities in their communities

In retrospect it is evident that neither of these predictions was fulfilled. The union campaigns to reduce working hours resulted in minor reductions for some but there has been a reversal of trends with many people working longer hours. Furthermore, urban renewal has seen people moving back to the cities, sometimes to be closer to their place of work and reduce commuting time. But the COVID pandemic may usher in a new era. An increasing percentage of the workforce are opting to work remotely or in hybrid forms of work which blend traditional and new approaches to the location and methods of work. Will the trend towards "contingent" and "insecure" forms of work continue or evolve into more sustainable forms of employment? If workers have more autonomy and control over their working lives, will they opt for more leisure or a blend of work and free time?

In the 1930s, Bertrand Russell wrote that: "Modern methods of production have given man the possibility of ease and security for all, yet he has chosen to have over-work for some and starvation for other"' Russell also argued: "a great deal of harm is being done in the modern world by belief in the virtues of work … (whereas) the road to happiness and prosperity lies in the diminution of work" (Russell, 1935). In his classic novel, *The Heart of Darkness*: Joseph Conrad has one of his characters state: "I don't like work – no man does, but I like what is in the work – the chance to find yourself, your own reality … for yourself, not for others … what no other man can ever know". Hence, work is important for our sense of identity, but it may also form part of an implicit social contract between workers and their employers.

Kochan and Dyer (2021) have defined the social contract at work as "the mutual expectations and obligations that employers, employees and society at large has for work and employment relations … It is a set of norms that holds us all accountable for adding value at work and providing work that is a productive, meaningful life experience".

A new social contract for sustainable work should be based on three pillars: a full employment policy combined with a strong social safety net for those unable to work; a comprehensive system of life-long learning which provides free access to post-secondary education and retraining for those who lose their jobs or wish to change their field of work, and an industrial relations system which give workers greater rights and voice in decisions which affect them in the workplace (Lansbury, 2021).

The Nordic countries have been to the fore in pursuing these kinds of social policies in the past, particularly for several decades following the Second World War. However, with the rise of neoliberal political parties during the past couple of decades, many of the earlier progressive economic and social policies have been wound back not just in the Nordic countries but other parts of Europe. New impetus is needed to revive and redefine policies which will achieve not only more sustainable work but also more productive leisure time which frees workers from arduous labour and adds to the well-being of society.

References

Cooney, R. and Lansbury, R.D. (2018) Socio-technical Transitions in Mining: Sweden and Australia Compared. Proceedings of the SASE 30th Annual Conference. Doshida University, Tokyo.

Kochan, T.A. and Dyer, L. (2021) Shaping the Future of Work: A Handbook for Building a New Social Contract. New York: Routledge.

Lansbury, R.D. (1970) Leisure in the New Suburbs. Sociologiske Meddelelser, 14 (1–2): 79–92.

Lansbury, R.D. (2021) Crossing Boundaries: Work and Industrial Relations in Perspective. London and New York: Routledge.

Russell, B. (1935) In Praise of Idleness and Other Essays. London: George Allen and Unwin,.

II Sustainable workplace innovations, digitalisation, and the green revolution

Christopher Mathieu and Susanne Boethius

The dynamics and (job) qualities of sustainable work

Abstract: This chapter argues that understanding and pursuing sustainable work can be greatly improved by adopting an approach that recognises the centrality of the mutually generative interaction between innovation and job quality. Such an approach de-mysitifies change as largely an effect of innovation, while also inherently linking innovation to job quality, which has direct bearing on the sustainability of work. Based on quantitative and qualitative empirical studies, the association between innovation and various dimensions of job quality is established and two ideal-typical spirals are elaborated. The virtuous spiral is premised on employee participation in innovation activities and job quality improvements largely in keeping with the sustainable work agenda, while the vicous spiral is premised on innovation from above, Tayloristic work processes and little consequent investment in employee capabilities and innovation participation, resulting in low and often declining job quality, characteristic of unsustainable work. The chapter thus shows how sustainable and unsustainable work are produced along different trajectories, based on the interlinked innovation and job quality choices that are made by firms and organisations already now in the present.

Keyword: Organisational change, improvement, innovation, job quality, participation, sustainable work

That sustainable work is inherently dynamic and multidimensional is widely recognised (Blonk et al., 2015; Docherty et al., 2009). However, most often the dynamism or change are treated as framework conditions, and multidimensionality as generalised sources of inputs and destinations for outcomes. In this chapter we nuance these understandings, by arguing that dynamism and change is largely a product of innovation, and that the multidimensional inputs and outputs relevant to sustainable work can largely be seen as consisting of, or running through, job quality factors. Furthermore, recent research shows that there are mutually generative relations between innovation and various dimensions of job quality, expressly linking the two (De Spiegelaere et al., 2016; Duhautois et al., 2018, 2020; Grande, et al., 2020; Laursen & Foss, 2014; Lorenz, 2013; Mathieu & Boethius, 2021).

In focusing on this core relationship between innovation and job quality, we gain greater insight into an important interactional dynamic driving sustainable work. We argue that the innovation-job quality relationship can operate positively or negatively for sustainable work, comprising virtuous spirals conducive to sustainable work on the one hand, or vicious spirals undermining sustainable work on the other. In looking at sustainable work as an inherently multidimensional concept, this chapter traces the implications of the innovation-job quality dynamic, via sustainable work, to and from the three generally acknowledged arenas of sustainability: economic/business sustainability, individual/societal sustainability, and environmental/ecological sustainability.

However, rather than seeing sustainability or unsustainability merely as outcomes or effects of the innovation-job quality relationship, it is recognised that sustainability as policy, strategy and individual goals also exerts direct force on innovation and job quality, i.e. though purposive and sometimes externally supported sustainability-oriented innovations and job quality improvements. Here the roles of national and international agencies promoting the sustainability agenda link in. Support for sustainability per se is important, but an objective of this chapter is to promote an understanding of the innovation-job quality dynamic on sustainability, and sustainable work in particular, which can lead to more sophisticated and poly-directional policy and social-partner based approaches to promoting sustainability. By showing the interrelatedness of innovation, job quality and sustainable work, it should be possible to link the innovation agenda, with its competitiveness roots, to the sustainability agenda, which often has an existential and normative base.[1] Thus, we merge the sustainable work agenda with the (sustainable) innovation agenda.

This chapter is structured in the following manner. Directly below we start by making some basic definitional statements regarding innovation, job quality, sustainability, work, and sustainable work. We then develop the empirical argument regarding the mutual generative relationship between innovation and job quality and the role of innovation in worklife change. The empirical arguments draw largely on the research and findings of the Horizon 2020 project *Quality of Jobs and Innovation Generated Employment Outcomes* (QuInnE).[2] From the

1 There is also an increasing competitive logic developing around business cases for sustainability (Schaltegger et al., 2019).

2 QuInnE – Quality of jobs and Innovation generated Employment outcomes – was an interdisciplinary project investigating how job quality and innovation mutually impact each other, and the effects this has on job creation and the quality of these jobs. The project ran from 2015 through 2018. The QuInnE project was financed by the European Commission's Horizon 2020 Programme 'EURO-2-2014 – The European growth agenda', project reference number: 649497 (See Mathieu & Boethius, 2021 for more detailed descriptions of the QuInne-project).

empirical studies, two models of the innovation-job quality dynamic are derived. One is an upward spiral, activating participation in innovation activities and characterised by better job quality, the other a downward spiral of pacifying innovations leading to restricted participation in innovation, and characterised by worse job quality. Links are then made from the two models to various dimensions of sustainability.

Concepts and definitions

In the following section we clarify how the central concepts of innovation, job quality, sustainability, work, and sustainable work are used in the discussions below.

The definition of innovation used in this chapter is taken from the 3rd edition of the OECD/Eurostat Oslo Manual (2005).[3] In this edition, four types of innovation are delineated: product, process, organisational, and marketing innovations. The first two (product and process) are grouped as technological innovations, and the latter two (marketing and organisational) as non-technological innovations. Product innovation is defined as the introduction of a good or service that is new or significantly improved with respect to its characteristics or intended uses. Process innovation is defined as the implementation of a new or significantly improved production or delivery method.

This definition includes significant changes in techniques, equipment and/or software. Marketing innovation is defined as the implementation of a new marketing method involving significant changes in product design or packaging, product placement, product promotion or pricing. Finally, organisational innovation is defined as the implementation of a new organisational method in the firm's business practices, workplace organisation or external relations. As the discussions below focus mostly on work processes, marketing innovations are omitted from the analyses.

Jensen et al. (2007) introduced a differentiation between two modes of innovation, what they term the Doing, Using and Interacting (DUI) mode and the Science and Technology-based Innovation (STI) mode. The DUI mode is primarily based on informal practical interaction, developing innovations by learning by doing and experimentation. The STI mode is largely based on formal large-scale Research and Development efforts to produce explicit, codified

3 These definitions were embedded in the OECD and Eurostat's surveys at the time the QuInnE-project was carried out.

scientific knowledge as the basis for innovation development. The DUI mode has been associated with incremental and non-technological innovations, especially those classified as employee-driven, co-created and workplace innovations (Høyrup, 2012; Oeij et al., 2017), whereas the STI mode is more associated with largescale technological innovations (Parrilli & Heras, 2016). While these are investigated as distinct modes (Alhusen et al., 2021), from the outset in Jensen et al. (2007) they have not been seen as mutually exclusive, and in practice they are frequently used in combination.

The substantive approach to job quality adopted here derives from the index developed for the studies carried out in the QuInnE research project (Mathieu & Boethius, 2021). It is multi-dimensional and cross-disciplinary, comprising six main categories: wages, employment quality, education and training, working conditions, work life balance, and employee participation. These dimensions and their indicators are presented in Tab. 7.

Tab. 7. QuInnE's bespoke approach to job quality.

Dimension	Indicators
Wages	Pay level relative to national minimum pay and average for required qualifications; Pay variability
Employment quality	Permanent/temporary status; job security; internal progression opportunities; predictability of weekly hours; presence/absence involuntary long hour work/part-time work
Education & training	Learning opportunities on the job; training incidence; training quality; opportunities for general vs specific skill acquisition (transferability)
Working conditions	Individual task discretion / autonomy; semi-autonomous teamwork; job variety; work intensity; health and safety (physical and psychosocial); supervisory social support; peer group social support
Work life balance	Work time scheduling (unsocial hours); hours of work (duration); working time flexibility – provisions for time off for personal needs
Employee participation	Direct participation regarding organisational decisions; consultative committees / works councils; union presence; union decision making involvement

This approach to job quality focuses on a broad range of objective intrinsic, extrinsic, physical, social, and material dimensions tied directly to work and employment, avoiding subjective assessments, such as satisfaction (see Muñoz de Bustillo et al., 2022; Warhurst et al., 2018a,b).

Sustainability, especially in relation to work, is defined in many ways. At its most basic and semantic level, sustainability is the ability of a system to persist over time, or, defined negatively, that which will not in the foreseeable future lead to system collapse. Some definitions focus on single systems, others take a broader perspective in which a system is unsustainable if it causes another system with which it interacts to collapse through exploitative exhaustion of that system's essential resources (Zink, 2014). Sustainability can be attained via different mechanisms.

The primary mechanism discussed in the literature is regeneration. Regeneration of utilised resources can either be a largely passive process where boundaries or tipping points for exhaustion are known and respected, and subsystems can regenerate requisite resources on their own. Regeneration can also be actively assisted or accelerated, via the direct injection of inputs to aid the regeneration process. Another mechanism is partially or wholly alleviating a system nearing collapse via substitution. Substitution can either entail substituting a particular resource at risk of depletion within a system or that causes internal or external damage, or creating a novel functionally equivalent system based on more plentiful or regeneratable resources. The latter can either partially relieve or entirely replace the system at risk.

Work, jobs and employment are sometimes used as synonyms, and conflated as concepts or in their application. However, as social scientific concepts it is important to pay attention to the analytical division of labour accomplished by these concepts. The broadest of the terms, *work*, is defined by Tilly and Tilly (1994: 285) as "any human effort that adds use value to goods and services." They go on to add that, "Only a prejudice bred by Western capitalism and industrial labour markets fixes on strenuous effort expended for money payment outside the home as real work, relegating other efforts to amusement, crime, and mere housework." What they point out in the latter passage is the fallacy of conflating work with remunerated work, i.e. work carried out under various forms of employment.

Thus, only some work takes place under employment. Usually occurring under employment, *jobs* are relatively durable bundles of tasks, usually assembled by employers, to which employees are recruited and assigned as part of a production process. *Employment* is the terms upon which labour is contracted, usually to carry out more or less specifically defined jobs. Putting these concepts in relation to each other, according to Warhurst et al., (2022) "Jobs comprise both work (the application of labour to tasks using technologies to produce use or exchange value) and the terms and conditions of employment through which that work is contracted, importantly, that it is paid." To revisit the operational definition of job quality given above in more general terms based on the discussions directly above, the quality of a job entails assessment of both the conditions of the actual work that is undertaken, and the employment conditions under which it is carried out.

Combining the concepts *sustainability* and *work,* to render *sustainable work,* in fidelity with the definitions above, brings us to a different place than where most of the sustainable work literature takes its point of departure. Work, as defined above, points at all work, that is to say all productive labour, regardless of whether it is carried out in an employment context or not. However, most of the discussions about sustainable work deal exclusively with paid work in employment contexts, rather than for example household or volunteer work. Likewise, when assessing the sustainability of "work", the terms and conditions under which this work is carried out are usually considered as well: i.e. the *employment* dimensions under which work is carried out. In light of the discussions above, it can be argued that the term *sustainable work* is a misnomer. What is discussed in the literature on sustainable work is more precisely sustainable jobs.

A further problematic aspect of the sustainable work discourse is the predominant role of the exhaustion perspective in sustainable work thinking. The understanding of temporally finite resources that can be exhausted is appropriate in some regards, and inadequate in others, regarding work. For example, at the individual worker level, physical and mental capacities can be exhausted, and up to critical levels be replenished via rest and recovery. However, with regard to knowledge and skills, the greater threats are obsolescence, lack of acquisition, or falling into disrepair, due to lack of use rather than over-consumption and exhaustion.

Thus, we contend that sustainable work discussions need to do at least two things. One is to recognise that work is not synonymous with work in employment, but much broader, especially in light of the extensive literature on "work-life spillover" and "second-shift" work (Brandon et al, 2021)(Hochschild, 1990), or talk directly about sustainable jobs when that is the actual focus. The second is the explicit recognition of obsolescence and non-acquisition and use of knowledge and skills as central to sustainable work (jobs), rather than the primary paradigm being exhaustive use, which is only part of the problem.

The innovation-job quality nexus

Training and education, discretion and autonomy, trust and support from managers, are recognised as important factors facilitating innovation (Beugelsdijk, 2008; Laursen & Foss, 2014). Rarely however in the innovation context are these factors acknowledged, individually and collectively, as aspects of job quality. In other words, there is a widespread conceptualisation of these as *innovation inputs*, but scant recognition that they are also highly significant in another regard, that is as job quality factors. This connection is absent both in the research literature (Duhautois et al., 2020), and in policy spheres.

The non-connection, especially in the policy sphere, is puzzling as aspects of job quality such as training and skill development are also a flagship initiative in the Europe 2020 Strategy.[4] But no explicit connection between the two flagship initiatives in the Europe 2020 Strategy, the Innovation Union on the one hand, and the Agenda for new skills and jobs on the other, nor innovation and job quality per se, is made.

The connection between innovation and job quality was explicitly investigated in several studies carried out under the Horizon 2020 financed project QuInnE (see Mathieu & Boethius, 2021). These studies empirically analysed the relationship between product, process, and organisational innovation, and a battery of job quality factors (listed in Tab. 7). Regarding the association between innovation and job quality, Muñoz de Bustillo et al., (2016) found a positive and significant correlation between both types of technological innovation, but not organisational innovation and job quality in general. In detailed analysis of which aspects of job quality are associated with innovation in the same study, they found very high correlation for intrinsic (skills, autonomy, personal support) and employment (contract stability and development opportunities) dimensions of job quality, with moderate outcomes for health and safety and work life balance dimensions. A subsequent study by Muñoz de Bustillo et al. (2017) found similar results, with process innovation being strongly correlated to job quality, while product innovation correlated more weakly, and organisational innovation insignificantly. The finding regarding process innovation can be viewed as surprising, in light of the frequent association of process innovation with workplace rationalisation. While the finding for organisational innovation may also look surprising, due to its direct bearing on job quality, as discussed elsewhere (Muñoz de Bustillo et al., 2017; Mathieu & Boethius, 2021), this probably has to do with the heterogeneity found within the conceptual construct of organisational innovation, rather than a lack of mutual effects between the discrete elements contained within the organisational innovation construct, and dimensions of job quality.

---

4 The European Union's concern with increasing and improving employment, social inclusion, innovation, and competitiveness were core to the Europe 2020 Strategy (European Commission, 2010).

In another QuInnE-study using large firm-level datasets for France, Germany and Spain, Duhautois et al. (2018) also analysed which types of innovation are associated with positive and negative effects on different aspects of job quality. Product innovation was found to increase wages, skilled jobs, and job security in France and Germany, while also increasing non-skilled jobs in Germany. Process innovation increased pay, lowered turnover, and increased part-time jobs in Germany, while having negative effects on wages and employment conditions in France. Organisational innovation had a negative impact on wages in France, while increasing low-paid jobs in Germany.

The general conclusion from these transnational studies is that technological innovation (product and process innovation) is associated with better job quality, though not obtaining for example in one study for process innovation in France. The results for organisational innovation are largely ambiguous or negative, at least in the case of France according to Duhautois et al. (2018). However, regarding organisational innovation, one significant finding by Muñoz de Bustillo et al. (2016) is that worker representation and organised labour tips the valence of organisational innovation towards being more favourable for job quality, underscoring the opportunity for effects to be changed under specific institutional and action circumstances. Thus, outcomes are not predetermined, but swayed by the agency of differently empowered actors under specific industrial relations regimes. Employee participation is therefore not just important for increasing innovation, but also at a collective level in ensuring that innovation takes place in a more equitable manner.

Another way in which innovation and job quality are linked is demonstrated in Gallie's (2018) finding that incumbents in jobs high in "innovation-conducive job quality" (ICJQ) elements (training and learning; task discretion and initiative; and job security) are 4.7 times (66 % versus 14 %) more likely to be engaged in innovation activities than those low in these job quality factors. This also displays the gravity of the gap between the inclusion of high-skill workers in innovation activities, and the exclusion of low-skill workers from innovation activities. Another of Gallie's (2018) findings, a longitudinal trend towards an increase in ICJQ jobs in the EU from 2005–2015, and convergence between regions, is positive. However, a further finding is that temporary jobs are decreasing in ICJQ, i.e., temporary jobs were found to be continuously declining in terms of the aspects of job quality that contribute most to innovation processes.

To further investigate the intricacies of the innovation-job quality relationship, an extensive set of qualitative studies was carried out as part of the QuInnE-project, and reported in Jaehrling (2018). The qualitative studies were undertaken in eight industries across seven countries (see Tab. 8).

As radical innovation is quite infrequent, the case studies found primarily examples of incremental innovation along the DUI mode. Some examples were found of DUI adaptations to or within more radical STI innovations, such as the introduction of AI in the banking sector, or digital 3D blueprints in the aerospace industry, discussed further below.

Tab. 8. Number of case studies and interviews per industry and country.

	UK	FR	NL	SE	ES	HU	GER	Total no. of case studies (total no. of interviews)
Manufacturing sector								
Aerospace	1	3		2				6 (78)
Automotive						3	2	5 (34)
Agri-food					4	3		7 (59)
Private service sector								
Computer games	2		6	3			3	14 (86)
Banking		3			2			5 (42)
Retail Logistics		2	2				3	7 (52)
(quasi) Public sector								
Elderly / Home care	3	inline	2			3		8 (56)
Hospitals				4	2			6 (54)
Total	6	8	10	9	8	9	8	**58 (461)**

Abbreviations: UK: United Kingdom, FR: France, NL: The Netherlands, SE: Sweden, ES: Spain, HU: Hungary and GER: Germany
Source: Jaehrling (2018:13)

The linchpin in the connection between job quality and innovation was found in the case studies to centre around worker participation. Many of the managerial innovations introduced were aimed at promoting participation, via two-way communication channels between managers and workers, and exploration and experimentation. The former often took the form of well-known mechanisms, such as regular meetings between managers and workers, that are part of agile, scrum, and lean processes; employee suggestion channels and competitions; and co-locating cross-occupational development groups.

A significant finding in industries where design and execution are separated (in contrast for example to computer games development work, which was found to constantly blur this boundary) was the role of two-way communication channels allowing implementation employees to question, comment on, and make suggestions back into the design phase of the processes they were to implement. This erodes the classic linear design-implementation dichotomy and division of labour. This was found most explicitly in the aerospace industry with the introduction of 3D CAD/CAM or digital blueprints, where comments could be made directly back to design engineers via the same technology platform (Gautié et al., 2018). Similar technologies also facilitated workers at automotive OEMs to communicate with suppliers (Makó et al., 2018). Similar activities took place in services, notably in social and health care, but based on a social rather than technological channels (Green et al., 2018; Mathieu et al. 2020).

Opening up technologies and social spaces for contributions from employees further along the production process turned this from a linear to a looped process. Importantly, this shifts the innovation contribution from the workers' very proximate task operations, to decisions more distant and profound in their implications than the immediate realm of the given employee. Routine task performance becomes punctuated by creative contributions. These are situations where more durable, comprehensive incremental contributions were made. This can be contrasted with situations where creative contributions were either continuously demanded and required as in the computer games industry (Keune et al., 2018), or in the banking industry where customer service agents continuously modified and "personalised" standard AI-generated replies to customers (Perez & Martín, 2018).

Regarding employee exploration and experimentation, nowhere was managerial support for this found to be greater than in the computer games industry towards game developers. Here continuous individual and collective problem-solving was required, and high-degrees of discretion were accorded individuals and workgroups to accomplish their essentially creative tasks (Keune et al., 2018). Further evidence of employee participation and managerial support for employee discretion in this industry is the extensive use of firm-external knowledge networks among developers, i.e. that developers contacted other developers and communities outside their firm for advice or inspiration on problem-solving.

One of the organisational innovations found in several case studies was the introduction of established innovation-promoting management programmes: Lean in manufacturing and healthcare (Makó et al., 2018; Mathieu et al., 2018); the liberated firm in aerospace (Gautié et al., 2018); and agile/scrum in the computer games industry (Keune et al., 2018). In these cases, codified knowledge management programmes derived from management science are implemented in order to promote the Doing, Using and Interacting (DUI – Jensen et al., 2007) innovation mode based on immanent, tacit and discretionary learning knowledge production (Lorenz, 2015). As noted by Gallie (2018) these variants on High-Involvement or High-Performance Work Systems promote worker participation in the innovation process and job quality simultaneously. The introduction of these management programmes underlines the importance of incremental innovation (Mathieu & Warhurst, 2018) in line with the DUI innovation mode, especially in mature fields where radical innovations are less likely, due to an emphasis on exploitation rather than exploration (March, 1991). Such conditions were reported particularly in the aerospace (Gautié et al., 2018) and automotive industries (Makó et al., 2018) where firms in particular positions in value or supply chains are locked into an established technological configuration network.

The industry where case studies displayed the greatest variation in approaches towards innovation and job quality was social care. At one end there are highly Tayloristic systems, so-called time-and-task approaches, where a rigid schedule and reporting regime specifies particular activities to be undertaken by a caregiver in a given order and time allotment. At the other end is a Dutch example of multi-occupational self-governing teams that are given resources and responsibility for a specific geographic area, then accorded tremendous discretion in the planning and execution of care activities in consultation with the recipients. Variants of both high and low-trust/discretion systems were found in the three countries analysed, a variation which is impacted by both basic managerial choices made by firms, as well as the reporting and accounting directives imposed by the (usually municipal) bodies that fund and contract social care services (Green et al., 2018).

In the more Tayloristic systems, whether they are technologically-led as in retail logistics (Jaehrling et al., 2018), or scheduling-led in social care (Green et al., 2018), it was found that employees in low, de-skilled work are not invested with the required level of training, skill-development, tenure at work, and decision latitude to develop innovation contributions. A second mechanism is disenfranchisement due to lack of employee motivation to participate in innovation activities, as a result of a feeling of lack of investment and trust in them by management as innovation actors. A third is low job quality employees being in jobs, and having tasks so rigidly controlled, Taylorised and mechanistically interlinked, that jobs and tasks are only developable through system-changes from above (Jaehrling et al., 2018). A more universal factor found across industries inhibiting innovation, and acutely evidenced among high-skill workers in hospitals, but disproportionately impacting workers with lower job quality, is work intensification, rendering little time and energy left after mandatory tasks are accomplished. The reversal of the listed conditions becomes a recipe for increasing the propensity for innovation.

Condensing the findings across the 58 qualitative case studies found in Jaehrling (2018), and the quantitative analyses above, two basic models of the interaction between innovation and job quality were discerned; one activating and the other pacifying employee participation in innovation activity. These are rendered in Fig. 9.

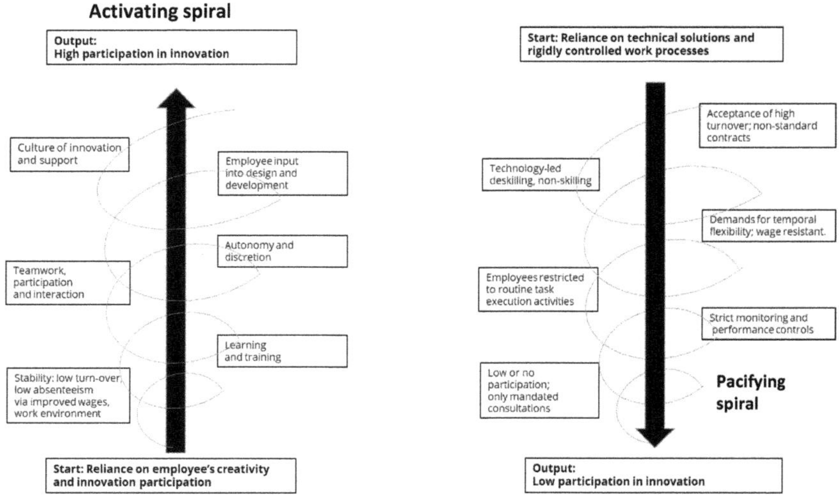

Fig. 9. Activating versus pacifying spirals.

The two spirals arise from different perceptions or experiences of contextual conditions by management. The vicious spiral resulting in low employee participation in innovation activities is premised on a perception of a rigid regime of cost constraints, that can derive from a competitive market situation with low opportunities to raise quality and receive compensation for this, or from strict public sector budgets aggravated by austerity or race-to-the-bottom cost-focused public procurement processes (Green et al., 2018). The virtuous spiral emanates from a context where firms and organisations are dependent upon and/or recognise and can leverage employees' contribution to innovation processes to create value and organisational benefits. As employees are central to the value-creation-through-innovation process in such contexts, investment (in training, working conditions, and retention) is oriented towards them.

From these different points of departure, the spirals develop in different, roughly mirror opposite trajectories. The vicious spiral exhibits a reliance on standardised procedures and technology-led production processes, to simplify and direct work leading to an acceptance of high turnover. This leads to, and is exacerbated by, the frequent use of non-standardised contracts and high demands for temporal flexibility, including shift-work of varying duration with night and weekend work common. The predominance of technology-led and Taylorised production systems leads to de-skilling or non-skilling of the labour force, and thus low necessity and incidence of training and education. Employees are largely restricted to routine task execution, though there may be rotation to different workstations, or a limited number of varied tasks carried out during a shift, found both in work-settings as diverse as warehouses and social care. Though for example in social care there may be high intrinsic rewards in meeting client needs, the scope for creativity and discretion in the Taylorised social care regimes are limited (Green et al., 2018; Mathieu et al., 2020). The work is also subject to strict monitoring and performance controls by management, which can be technologically or digitally mediated. This can be in real-time or retrospectively, with the employees highly aware of the monitoring (Green et al., 2018; Gautié et al., 2018. Jaehrling et al., 2018).

With little expectation of valuable employee input, employee voice at the individual and collective level is marginalised or kept to the minimum of legally mandated co-determination consultations. The ultimate result is low-skill, low-wage, high turnover jobs, with little scope for employee input and voice – hallmarks of low individual and societal sustainability. Likewise, the resulting low likelihood of innovation and improvement from the employee side can be seen to lower the prospects for firm or organisational sustainability unless it can be argued that reliance on external innovation and innovation from above, and the high employee turnover, can continue to be fed and socially and politically accepted in contemporary societies. In other words, that there is a socially and politically sustainable low-road model beyond mere economic viability. Furthermore, as employees in this downward spiral model are largely excluded from the innovation process, which is a key driver of organisational change, the prospects for improvement via internal innovation processes greatly diminish.

The virtuous spiral is based on broad-based participation in DUI activities as a key to organisational performance largely via incremental innovation. A foundational condition is workforce stability, as many of the processes are premised on cumulative, informal knowledge production and trust. Thus, positive working and employment conditions, ranging from wages, to the physical and psychosocial work environment, to work-life balance accommodation, are instrumental to both employee retention and lowering absenteeism, as well as being goods in and of themselves. Workforce stability both makes it worthwhile and possible to provide training and educational activities for upskilling employees with a return on human capital investment. Likewise, workforce stability also makes teamwork and cross-functional group collaboration practicable, with both continuity of interaction leading to collective knowledge development as well as trust. Teamwork and participation are central to the (I)nteracting in DUI. Individual and group discretion and autonomy are also premised on trust, especially from management and central to the creative and experimental dimensions of (D)oing and (U)sing. Rejection of monitoring and control opportunities, as found in the French aerospace case in order to pursue a more respectful and trust-based system, are evidence of conscious choice between courses of action (Gautié et al., 2018). Being able to feed one's observations and suggestions from application and implementation activities back to the design phase as discussed above, becomes a central dimension of innovation. The empirical observations from the case studies show how both technologies and social mechanisms can be used for these purposes (Gautié et al., 2018; Makó et al., 2018; Green et al., 2018).

The preconditions and active practice of creative and experimental activities across organisations lead to opportunities and even expectations to participate in innovation development, or an innovation culture, whether it is recognised as such, or as a routine of participation, where opportunities, motivation or dispositions and abilities and are concurrently developed and practiced, leading to innovation. As a broad range of employees are engaged in such processes, they not only enjoy high job quality, but also have the opportunity to retain and develop it, as they are active in innovation processes driving organisational change.

The two spirals are empirically derived ideal-types. Actual firms and organisations combine these, and of course other elements to varying degrees and fall somewhere in between on the continuum between the models. However, some case organisations match these extreme, ideal forms quite well. Sometimes we see general differences across industries. For example, retail logistics (Jaehrling et al., 2018) versus computer game development (Keune et al., 2018) are the most representative industries of the vicious respective virtuous spirals. But there are also several examples where the two different strategies, and spirals derived from them, exist in the same industry within the same country, with the automotive (Makó et al., 2018), social care (Green et al., 2018) and to a certain extent also retail banking (Perez & Martín, 2018) fitting this description. This indicates that some degree of choice between systems, as well as specific interventions, exists.

What the innovation-job quality dynamic means for sustainable work

Innovations change the broader environments that work takes place in and responds to. Innovation is also the primary manner by which work changes, be it technological product and process innovations, or non-technological organisational innovations that adapt to wider environmental pressures, challenges, and opportunities. Instead of taking "change" as an extraneous factor challenging sustainable work, the argument made in this chapter is that the very same basic phenomenon driving change and responding to change is innovation. Thus, innovation has a double relevance to work, and thereby sustainable work as well. Furthermore, as also displayed in through the quantitative and qualitative studies presented, it is established that job quality, which is central to sustainable work, is inherently and bidirectionally related to innovation.

Understanding change as largely a result of innovation leads us to understanding change as the result of specific activities. Innovation by definition is implemented, and thereby the result of conscious action. Innovation is authored, takes place in specific contexts, and is a solution to a challenge or exploitation of an opportunity that changes a context that further innovation responds to. As such there is a reflexive opportunity to consider the wider, multidimensional, and especially the job quality and sustainability implications of a given innovation. Previously we have suggested "innovation impact assessments" as a systematic means of understanding the individual, firm, and societal implications of innovations beyond their manifest goals (Mathieu & Warhurst, 2018). By introducing other primary considerations, such as sustainability or job quality for employee wellbeing, or further innovation capacity in addition to competitiveness, profit maximisation or cost-reduction, one can justify and inspire innovation to accomplish a variety of societal, political and economic goals and values.

Contrasting the two innovation-job quality spirals or systems, the coupling to sustainability becomes quite clear. With regard to physical health and illness, the need for workplace stability, that the upward spiral builds upon, mandates investment in a healthy work environment to lower absenteeism, prevent burnout and health related turnover. Less of a concern with employee turnover, in the downward spiral, leads to less proactive consideration and remedy of long-term health effects, though concern with absenteeism can spur strategic investments in preventing absenteeism. Regarding psychosocial health, the stimulus involved in problem-solving and social interaction, and recognition involved with collective consultation and collegial and managerial support are important salutogenic factors, whereas less consultation, inclusion and opportunity to contribute to the modification of one's work through innovation processes, coupled with strict monitoring and control whether by technology/algorithms and/or a human manager can have negative psychosocial health implications. Furthermore, it is widely recognised that varied work and the possibility to modify one's work over time promotes longevity (Albin et al., in this volume; Edwards & Jensen, 2014).

Aside from the psychosocial health benefits of learning and skills development for individual workers, such investments promote both "workability" (the ability to accomplish current tasks) as well as "employability" (the probability to be able to acquire a different job in the future). This benefits both current and possible future employers, as well as the individual worker both in terms of being able to better accomplish one's current work tasks, as well as gain future employment in the event of either voluntary or involuntary turnover. Learning and skills development have benefits at multiple levels; increasing the human capital of individuals, firms and organisations, and society. While undoubtedly some of this learning and skill acquisition is firm specific, invariably some will be transferable or developable in other contexts, in addition to the generic "learning to learn" meta-capacities developed in learning and skill acquisition.

Innovation dividends also accrue at several levels. As shown above, increased innovation and higher employee involvement in innovation usually corresponds to improved wages accruing to workers, which usually also increases tax revenue accruing to states. Studies cited above find that innovation not only increases job quality, and high quality jobs (in accordance with the skill-biased technological change thesis), but also the volume of employment, aiding moves towards state goals of full employment if the labour force is sufficiently qualified to gain access to high-qualification jobs.

There are also wider individual and societal benefits to broad employee participation and inclusion in consultation and innovation development. Collaboration and participation at the workplace promotes social skill, the ability to induce co-operation with others (Fligstein, 2001) and democratic practice, not just at the workplace but also in wider society. Participation in innovation processes not only brings more appropriate and balanced benefit innovations, as shown above, but it also instructs all parties to consider divergent interests and mutual benefits in both specific processes and outcomes, as well as a general approach. Such thinking is in line with both the more macro-oriented pluralist industrial relations approach (Befort et al., 2022) as well as the concept and methodology of Workplace Innovation (WPI; see Oeij et al., 2017). The virtuous, activating spiral builds both aptitude and inclination to engage in innovation activities, and support for innovation, if the experience is that it is for mutual rather than of selective or inordinately one-sided benefit or to one's own detriment.

As displayed above, not all innovation is favourable to job quality. There are industries with high innovation and low and declining job quality, which has a limiting or pacifying effect on innovation participation (Erhel & Guergoat-Larivière, 2016). The retail logistics industry is one example taken up in this chapter and is archetypical for the pacifying, vicious spiral. As Gallie (2018) shows, participation in innovation activities is far from evenly distributed across the workforce, and clearly skewed towards those with high ICJQ jobs. Coupled with his findings on the diminishing job quality in flexible, non-standard jobs, this leads to the obvious questioning of the sustainability of flexible employment. Furthermore, the move to more "flexible" workforce use erodes innovation capacity, corroborating the findings of Beugelsdijk (2008; also Zhou et al., 2011), in addition to being a general job quality problem. There appears to a trade-off between flexibility and innovative capacity, and policy makers should consider what it might take to tip the balance in favour of more secure employment forms for their associated benefits, not the least being sustainability.

Conclusion

The empirical studies presented in this chapter show that the animating dynamic behind sustainable as well as unsustainable change in working life, innovation, is inherently linked to job quality. As sustainability becomes an increasingly powerful and encompassing agenda and metric, it should increasingly permeate the established innovation-job quality dynamic via normative and practical and instrumental pressures. Sustainability's increased prominence and permeation is urgent, and can be hastened by bringing thinking about sustainable work more in line with the approach outlined in this chapter.

Rather than being a future-oriented project, this chapter argues that sustainable work must be a continuous project that is engaged with current practice: that of innovation. The tendency toward "projectification", with its inherent "futurification" of sustainable work, shifts our focus from what we know, can, and should do regarding on-going processes at existing workplaces today, to goals and visions to be attained in the future. Our argument is that sustainable work must be about trimming the sails now, rather than waiting for the winds to change, and doing so largely within firms and organisations. It is about assessing the innovations which we are currently developing and implementing, in terms of their wide-ranging sustainability impacts. But, as we also have argued, it is not just a matter of assessing innovations' effects, but equally the processes whereby these innovations are conceived. With inclusive innovation, multi-party assessment is part of the development, adaptation, implementation and revision process. This does not mean that distanced reflection and assessment is unnecessary at critical junctures, but it does mean that acceptance for such processes and input is already practiced and familiar; being built into the system rather than alien and tacked on.

This chapter demonstrates the actual and inherent linkages between innovation and job quality, job quality and sustainable work, and how the sustainable work agenda can advance more effectively, by understanding, embracing and working with the job quality-innovation dynamic in practice and policy.

Acknowledgements

We would like to acknowledge the researchers in the QuInnE project partners upon whose contributions this chapter is partially based, and financing from the European Commission's Horizon 2020 Programme "EURO-2-2014 – The European growth agenda", grant 649497 that made the QuInnE project possible.

References

Alhusen, H., Bennat, T., Bizer, K., Cantner, U., Horstmann, E., Kalthaus, M., … and Töpfer, S. (2021). A new measurement conception for the "doing-using-interacting" mode of innovation. *Research Policy, 50*(4).

Befort, S.F., Borelli, S., and Budd, J.W. (2022). Using efficiency, equity and voice for defining job quality, and legal regulation for achieving it. In Chris Warhurst, Chris Mathieu and Rachel Dwyer (eds). *The Oxford Handbook of Job Quality*. Oxford: Oxford University Press.

Beugelsdijk, S. (2008). Strategic human resource practices and product innovation. *Organisation Studies, 29*(6), 821–847.

Blonk, R., Vuori, J., and Price, R. H. (2015). *Sustainable Working Lives: Managing Work Transitions and Health Throughout the Life Course*. New York: Springer.

De Spiegelaere, S., Van Gyes, G., and Van Hootegem, G. (2016). Not all autonomy is the same. different dimensions of job autonomy and their relation to work engagement & innovative work behaviour. *Human Factors and Ergonomics in Manufacturing and Service Industries, 26*(4), 515–527.

Docherty, P., Kira, M., and Shani, A. (eds) (2009). *Creating Sustainable Work Systems*. Abingdon: Routledge.

Duhautois, R., Erhel, C., Guergoat-Larivière, M., Mofakhami, M., Obersneider, M., Postels, D., Anton, J., Muñoz de Bustillo, R., and Pinto, F. (2018). *The Employment and Job Quality Effects of Innovation in France, Germany and Spain: Evidence from firm-level data*. QuInnE Working Paper No. 7. Available at: http://quinne.eu

Duhautois, R., Erhel, C., Guergoat-Larivière, M., and Mofakhami, M. (2020). More and better jobs, but not for everyone: Effects of innovation in French firms. *Industrial and Labor Relations Review,* 1–27. DOI: 10.1177/0019793920925806

Edwards, K. and Jensen, P. L. (2014). Design of systems for productivity and well being. *Applied Ergonomics*, *45* (1), 26–32. https://doi.org/10.1016/j.apergo.2013.03.022

Erhel, C. and Guergoat-Larivière, M. (2016). *Innovation and Job Quality Regimes: A Joint Typology for the EU*. QuInnE Working Paper No. 3. Available at: http://quinne.eu

European Commission. (2010). EUROPE 2020: *A Strategy for Smart, Sustainable and Inclusive Growth*. Available at: https://ec.europa.eu/eu2020/pdf/COMPLET%20EN%20BARROSO%20%20%20007%20-%20Europe%202020%20-%20EN%20version.pdf

Fligstein, N. (2001). Social skill and the theory of fields. *Sociological Theory*, 19(2), 105–125.

Gallie, D. (2018). *Quality of Work and Innovative Capacity: Implications for Social Equality*. QuInnE Working Paper No. 8. Available at: http://quinne.eu

Gautié, J., Ahlstrand, R., Green, A., and Wright, S. (2018). Innovation, job quality and employment outcomes in the aerospace industry: Evidence from France, Sweden and the UK. In K. Jaehrling (ed.). *Virtuous Circles between Innovations, Job Quality and Employment in Europe? Case Study Evidence from the Manufacturing Sector, Private and Public Service Sector*, 36–87. QuInnE Working Paper No. 6. Available at: http://quinne.eu

Grande, R., Muñoz de Bustillo, R., Fernández Macías, E., and Antón, J. I. (2020). Innovation and job quality. A firm-level exploration. *Structural Change and Economic Dynamics*, *54*, 130–142. https://doi-org.ludwig.lub.lu.se/10.1016/j.strueco.2020.04.002

Green, A., Illéssy, M., Koene, B., Makó, C., and Wright, S. (2018). Innovation, job quality and employment outcomes in care: Evidence from Hungary, the Netherlands and the UK. In K. Jaehrling (ed.). *Virtuous Circles between Innovations, Job Quality and Employment in Europe? Case Study Evidence from the Manufacturing Sector, Private and Public Service Sector*, 333–386. QuInnE Working Paper No. 6. Available at: http://quinne.eu

Hochschild, A. (1990). *The Second Shift*. Avon Books.

Høyrup, S. (2012). *Employee-driven Innovation. A New Approach*. London: Palgrave Macmillan.

Jaehrling, K. (ed.). (2018). Prospects for virtuous circles? The institutional and economic embeddedness of companies' contemporary innovation strategies in Europe. In K. Jaehrling (ed.). *Virtuous Circles between Innovations, Job Quality and Employment in Europe? Case Study Evidence from the Manufacturing Sector, Private and Public Service Sector*, 1–34. QuInnE Working Paper No. 6. Available at: http://quinne.eu

Jaehrling, K., Gautié, J., Keune, M., Koene, B., and Perez, C. (2018). The digitisation of warehousing work. Innovations, employment and job quality in French, German and Dutch retail logistics companies. In K. Jaehrling (ed.). *Virtuous Circles between Innovations, Job Quality and Employment in Europe? Case Study Evidence from the Manufacturing Sector, Private and Public Service Sector*, 280–332. QuInnE Working Paper No. 6. Available at: http://quinne.eu

Jensen, M.B., Johnson, B., Lorenz, E., and Lundvall, B.-Å. (2007). Forms of knowledge and modes of innovation. *Research Policy, 36*(5), 680–693.

Keune, M., Payton, N., Been, W., Green, A., Mathieu, C., Postels, D., Rehnström, F., Warhurst, C., and Wright, S. (2018). Innovation and Job Quality in the Games Industry in Germany, the Netherlands, Sweden and the UK. In K. Jaehrling (ed.) *Virtuous Circles between Innovations, Job Quality and Employment in Europe? Case Study Evidence from the Manufacturing Sector, Private and Public Service Sector*, 234–279. QuInnE Working Paper No. 6. Available at: http://quinne.eu

Laursen, K. and Foss, N. (2014). Human resource management practices and innovation. In Dodgson, M., Gann, D., and Phillips, N. (eds). *The Oxford Handbook of Innovation Management.* Oxford: Oxford University Press, 506–529.

Lorenz, E. (2013). Innovation, work organisation and systems of social protection. In E. S. Andersen, J. Fagerberg, and B. R. Martin (eds). *Innovation Studies: Evolution and Future Challenges.* Oxford: Oxford University Press.

Lorenz, E. (2015). Work organisation, forms of employee learning and labour market structure: Accounting for international differences in workplace innovation. *Journal of the Knowledge Economy*, 6(2), 437–466.

McDaniel, B.T., O'Connor, K., and Drouin, M. (2021). Work-related technoference at home and feelings of work spillover, overload, life satisfaction and job satisfaction. *International Journal of Workplace Health Management*, *14*(5), 526–541. https://doi.org/10.1108/IJWHM-11-2020-0197

Makó, C., Illéssy, M., and Latniak, E. (2018). The relationship between employment, job quality and innovation in the automotive Industry: A nexus of changing dynamics along the value chain. Evidence from Hungary and Germany. In K. Jaehrling (ed.). *Virtuous Circles between Innovations, Job Quality and Employment in Europe? Case Study Evidence from the Manufacturing Sector, Private and Public Service Sector,* 88–130. QuInnE Working Paper No. 6. Available at: http://quinne.eu

March, J. (1991). Exploration and exploitation in organizational learning. *Organization Science*, *2*(1), 71–87.

Mathieu, C. and Boethius, S. (2021). The generative relationship between job quality, innovation, and employment. *European Journal of Workplace Innovation*, *6*(2), 163–186. https://doi.org/10.46364/ejwi.v6i2.803

Mathieu, C., Wright, S., Boethius, S., and Green, A. (2020). Innovations on a shoestring: Consequences for job quality of public service innovations in health and social care. *European Journal of Workplace Innovation*, *5*(2), 4–30.

Mathieu, C., Boethius, S., and Martín, F. (2018). Innovation, job quality and employment in hospitals in Spain and Sweden. In K. Jaehrling (ed.). *Virtuous*

Circles between Innovations, Job Quality and Employment in Europe? Case Study Evidence from the Manufacturing Sector, Private and Public Service Sector, 387–431. QuInnE Working Paper No. 6. Available at: http://quinne.eu

Mathieu, C. and Warhurst, C. (2018). *QuInnE Policy Recommendations*. QuInnE Working Paper No.14. Available at: http://quinne.eu

Muñoz-de-Bustillo, R., Grande, R., and Fernández-Macías, E. (2016). *Innovation and Job Quality. An Initial Exploration*. QuInnE Working Paper No. 5. Available at: http://quinne.eu

Muñoz-de-Bustillo, R., Grande, R., and Fernández-Macías, E. (2017). *An Approximation of Job Quality and Innovation Using the 3rd European Company Survey*. QuInnE Working Paper No. 4. Available at: http://quinne.eu

Muñoz de Bustillo, R., Fernández-Macías, E., and Antón, J. (2022). Job quality: A family affair? In Chris Warhurst, Chris Mathieu, and Rachel Dwyer (eds). *The Oxford Handbook of Job Quality*. Oxford: Oxford University Press.

OECD. (2005). *Oslo Manual: Guidelines for Collecting and Interpreting Innovation Data*, 3rd Edition. OECD Publications.

Oeij, P., Rus, D. and Pot, F. (2017). *Workplace Innovation: Theory, Research and Practice*. New York: Springer.

Perez, C. and Martín, F. (2018). Digitalisation and artificial intelligence: The new face of the retail banking sector. Evidence from France and Spain. In K. Jaehrling (ed.). *Virtuous Circles between Innovations, Job Quality and Employment in Europe? Case Study Evidence from the Manufacturing Sector, Private and Public Service Sector*, 178–233. QuInnE Working Paper No. 6. Available at: http://quinne.eu

Parrilli, M. D. and Heras, H. A. (2016). STI and DUI innovation modes: Scientific-technological and context-specific nuances. *Research Policy*, 45(4), 747–756.

Schaltegger, S., Horisch, J., and Freeman, R. E. (2019). Business cases for sustainability: A stakeholder theory perspective. *Organization and Environment*, *32*(3), 191–212.

Tilly, C. and Tilly, C. (1994). Capitalist work and labour markets. In Smelser, N. and Swedberg, R. (ed.). *The Handbook of Economic Sociology*. Princeton, NJ: Princeton University Press.

Warhurst C., Erhel, C., Gallie, D., Guergoat-Larivière, M., Muñoz de Bustillo, R., Obersneider, M., Postels, D., Sarkar, S., and Wright, S. (2018a). *Data Evaluation Report: An Evaluation of the Main EU Datasets for Analysing Innovation, Job Quality and Employment Outcomes*. QuInnE Working Paper No. 14.

Warhurst, C., Mathieu, C., Keune, M., and Gallie, D. (2018b). *Linking Innovation and Job Quality: Challenges and Opportunities for Policy and Research*. QuInnE Working Paper No. 11.

Warhurst, C., Wright, S., and Mathieu, C. (2022). Job quality: A family affair? In Chris Warhurst, Chris Mathieu, and Rachel Dwyer (eds). *The Oxford Handbook of Job Quality*. Oxford: Oxford University Press.

Zhou, H., Dekker, R., and Kleinknecht, A. (2011). Flexible labor and innovation performance: evidence from longitudinal firm-level data. *Industrial and Corporate Change*, *20*(3), 941–968.

Zink, K. J. (2014). Designing sustainable work systems: The need for a systems approach. *Applied Ergonomics*, *45*(1), 126–132. https://doi.org/10.1016/j.apergo.2013.03.023

Lena Abrahamsson and Jan Johansson

Digitalisation and Sustainable work: obstacles and pathways

Abstract: The aim with this chapter is to identify obstacles, and find pathways for sustainable work, in a digital future. We are all concerned about how our work will be in the future; will we be able to handle the new technology, or will technology control us? The development is often described in black and white, either as *God's gift to mankind,* or as *the wolf is coming.* However, the question is not that simple. New technology, such as digitalisation, does not in itself have a particular way to change our work, whether positive or negative. Future work is shaped here and now, and it is always possible to influence and control the development. Based on the vision of Industry 4.0, and observations of the latest technological development that already concretely affects workplaces and people, we have, with the help of theories of sustainable work, discussed what digitalisation can mean for work in the future. We have identified four critical issues that need to be discussed further: (1) The Swedish labour market model under attack, (2) Upskilling, deskilling, or reskilling, (3) Changed gender patterns and (4) Shaping an A and B labour market. The theories of sustainable work are well known and used in working life, in Sweden as well in many other countries, but the road towards digitalisation is complex and filled with traps and pitfalls that need to be handled. To enable positive development, the technical and organisational development also needs to include knowledge of the society, the human and the working environment.

Keywords: sustainable work, Industry 4.0, skills, digitalisation, gender, Sweden

Introduction

Green industrial transformation comes by leaps and bounds, especially in Norrbotten and Västerbotten, with green mines and green steel plants powered by green electricity. This development is forced by climate change, and made possible by digitalisation and what we usually call Industry 4.0. This is basically good, in the sense of being a positive development, and cannot really be questioned. However, this transformation creates a new arena for future work, and there is an urgent need to investigate not only how these technologies are designed, chosen and implemented, but also their impacts on work and workplaces in a green industrial context. Without social acceptance of the new technology and functioning co-operation at the workplace, it will be difficult to implement necessary changes, no matter how good they are. New questions must be addressed if we are to succeed in the green transformation of our industries, and they must be asked now: green industrial transformation will not wait.

In this chapter we discuss some obstacles and pathways to green transformation in the context of digitalisation. "The wolf is coming" and "God's gift to mankind" are two common positions or reactions that follow many technical innovations. This also applies to today's debate on digitalisation, automation and artificial intelligence in working life. "The wolf is coming" indicates a fear that our lives will be deprived of something we want to maintain, while we neither can nor really want to refrain from the digitalised society. Here we can recognise the fear that the robots will take over and that our jobs will diminish. "God's gift to mankind" emphasises the advantages and new opportunities that facilitate and enrich our lives. Here we find techno-optimistic and often technology driven ideas. Society has participated in the technological development with these mixed emotions over the last 20 years, and now there are clear signs that digitalisation will take a greater leap, into not only our everyday lives, but also our work lives in very concrete ways. Conditions that have been considered as given may not be so sustainable in the future. In other words, future work is shaped here and now. In order to find pathways to handle the new technology and design sustainable workplaces for the future, we need to get a picture of what is happening, but we also need a vision of where we want to go, and how to get there. In these times of change, we as researchers have to take on the role of the wolf and ask the uncomfortable questions, but also to go between or beyond the two positions "The wolf is coming" and "God's gift to mankind".

The role of work in a digital industrial context?

The German's vision Industry 4.0 (Lasi et al. 2014), and its Swedish companion Smart Industry: a strategy for new industrialisation for Sweden (Regeringskansliet, 2016), paint a bright picture of future working life, where smart machines continuously exchange information with each other, as well as with human workers. The industrial worker will be an expert who makes sure that production runs smoothly. The worker may no longer be "locked" in a control room; instead, real-time process data and status of machines follow the worker as she moves around the factory. She can solve problems on the spot by remotely interacting with other production operators, experts, suppliers, or customers in multi-competent teams, or she can interact with a humanoid robot that assists in decision-making and analyses. Production control can be done in a digital model far away from the factory. In short, the augmented worker has extended senses and extended memory through technology that takes advantage of and supports human skills, increasing situational awareness, for example, through sensors embedded in the operator's clothes while keeping an uninterrupted operational vigilance.

An interesting and perhaps in part a scary vision is presented by Romero et al. (2016), who, based on the technical core of Industry 4.0, form a typology of future operators, Operator 4.0. This typology is built on eight characteristics that can be seen as the effects or possibilities of the new technology: *Super-Strength Operator* (physical interaction) using biomechanical support for increased limb movement, increased strength, and endurance; *Augmented Operator* (cognitive interaction) using Augmented Reality (AR) for integrating information from the digital to the physical world; *Virtual Operator* (cognitive interaction) using Virtual Reality (VR) for simulation and training of real situation that might contain risks; *Healthy Operator* (physical and cognitive interaction) using wearable sensors for monitoring health-related metrics as well as GPS location; *Smarter Operator* (cognitive interaction) using Intelligent Personal Assistant (IPA) for interfacing with machines, computers, databases, and other information systems; *Collaborative Operator* (physical interaction) using Collaborative Robots (CoBots) for performing repetitive and non-ergonomic tasks; *Social Operator* (cognitive interaction) using Enterprise Social Networking Services (E-SNS) for interaction between operators and between operators and Internet of Things; and *Analytical Operator* (cognitive interaction) using Big Data Analytics for discovering useful information and predict relevant events.

The classification points to the numerous possibilities of integrating Industry 4.0 with human labour: some good and some bad. Nevertheless, there is an urgent need to investigate, not only how these technologies are designed, chosen and implemented, but also their impacts on work in the industry. There are a number of questions that need to be asked, and as academics we have a mission to be the social prosecutor who poses the uncomfortable questions. We have identified four such critical issues to discuss further in this chapter:

- The Swedish labour market model under attack
- Upskilling, deskilling, or reskilling?
- Changed gender patterns
- Shaping an A and B labour market

The Swedish labour market model at risk

Over the years we have witnessed an increase in labour flexibility, the decline of standard labour contracts, the subcontracting or outsourcing of work (Taylor, 2010), increasing self-employment, and mounting insecurity (Thompson, 2013).

However, it is the use of digital platforms by global enterprises, to crowd-source labour to small and micro sized companies all over the world, that is reshaping work and employment conditions in the most visible way so far.

The term crowdsourcing was coined by Howe in 2006, and was presented as a new level of subcontracting. For example, rather than relying on offshore jobs at low-cost locations, companies can outsource functions, once performed by employees, to an amorphous and generally large pool of individuals using an open call over the Internet (Howe, 2008). The most significant differences between crowdsourcing and a traditional workforce are the higher levels of flexibility, scalability, access to a broad range of skills, and experiences at significantly less cost, coupled with the lack of employment regulations. This strategy appeals to industrial firms as they are able to access a labour force that can expand and contract on demand, without any significant transaction costs or logistical hurdles. Management control is simultaneously "at a distance" while remaining all-powerful when directing work tasks and determining the nature of reward. Relationships are fleeting and largely anonymous, with no obligation to provide support or facilities for the workforce.

Another aspect of the new technology is related to Scandinavian industrial sociology. In this field, Lysgaard's (1961) book on the workers' collective is regarded as seminal, one of the classics of its time. Although it is well researched, and documented how workers act collectively in the workplace, the term "workers' collective" is rarely used in current Nordic research. It is, for example, well-known that the workers' collective functions as a set of norms, controlling the workers' relations to each other, as well as the extent to which deviations from these norms (e.g., a certain type of masculinity, negative attitudes to management, and technological change) are counteracted or accepted. Materialised by this normative system, the workers' collective is based on a culture of resistance that attempts to gain informal control over the work situation. It can also function as a protector of practical and hard physical work, referred to as "embodied competence" or "body capital". Consequently, new technology and new management models are often resisted by the collective system. In this context, Industry 4.0, automated factories, and Internet of Things represent a new technological and managerial landscape to which several reactions are possible. There is a need to analyse the opportunities and challenges represented by the current technological and organisational development, and to create a theoretical platform for the understanding of the transformation of work and workers based on the workers' collective.

On an aggregated level, this is about the survival of the Swedish labour market model. The Swedish labour market is one of the most harmonious in the world, based primarily on bi-lateral agreements between the parties, rather than on legislation. In a global internet-based labour market, there is hardly any space for collective agreement, and the Swedish labour market model, instead of the legislative path seems to be the only way possible. Here is an interesting opening where Swedish trade unions have long been more co-operative than their European colleagues. Relationship to new technology has often been characterised by "If you can´t beat them, join them" (Johansson et al., 2013).

Upskilling, deskilling, or reskilling?

The visions of fully automated factories, Industry 4.0, and Internet of Things not only change the technological landscape of industrial workplaces and organisations, but also cause a qualitative knowledge transformation: from bodily and tacit, into more abstract and theoretical knowledge and skills. In the optimistic view, we can read that Industry 4.0 requires workplace learning, as well as continuous education and systems that make use of the workers' skills: i.e., a learning organisation. Using Kern and Schumann's concepts (1974), we can see a clear transformation from craftsman-like qualification into more technical qualifications. New demands for teamwork, responsibility, and comprehensive understanding of production flow can be seen as a movement, from qualifications dependent on the process, to qualifications more independent of the process (cf. Bright, 1958; Blauner, 1964; Kern & Schumann, 1974, 1987; Johansson, 1986). What was earlier the workers' tacit knowledge (Polanyi, 1967) will be formalised into theoretical knowledge, digitalised, and used in computers and smart phones. In this transition, we can see contradictory movements of upskilling: rapidly changing skill demands and more theoretical, comprehensive, and communication tasks; and deskilling: fragmentation of individual craft knowledge and whole tasks (Abrahamsson & Johansson, 2006).

Whether it is a question of upskilling, deskilling, or reskilling, the transformation of knowledge affects workplace cultures, communities of practice, and identities. Individuals and organisations will have to create and recreate qualifications, identity, and gender, when meeting new technology in a changing context. For example, the new knowledge and skills needed may be more abstract and theoretical, but still based on bodily and tacit knowledge, although in new and less physically demanding forms. A common optimistic scenario gives women and other previously underrepresented groups a chance to enter and master different types of industrial work, such as in mining and process industries. Given that this scenario is realised, it does not entail a smooth and unproblematic process. The identity and symbolic aspects of work often lag behind developments in, for example, technology and qualification demands, resulting in restoring responses during processes of organisational changes (Abrahamsson, 2014). As the workers' collective (cf. Lysgaard, 1961; Fältholm, 1998) is built and sustained by processes of homosocial interaction and identification, and on norms controlling similarity between workers, there is reason to investigate how new technology affects these processes. The seemingly robust gender and power relations will be challenged, renegotiated, and ultimately transformed.

Changed gender patterns

One of the hopes of technological development in industry is that it will allow for changed gender patterns: a better work environment, combined with higher qualification demands that will enable more women to work in the industry, creating better gender equality. But the picture is not so clear-cut. At many industrial workplaces where digitalisation is taking place, it is quite common that technology is associated with masculinity (Berner, 2003; Mellström, 2004). This masculinisation of technology is evident in the discourse of the technology, as well as in the culture of these companies. At traditional male-dominated industrial workplaces, even if the workplaces undergo digitalisation, the connection to masculinity lingers, because of the old strong symbolic links to a traditional blue-collar masculinity (Abrahamsson, 2006; Andersson, 2012; Eveline, 2001; Lahiri-Dutt, 2007, 2012, see also Collinson, 1992; Whitehead, 2002; Willis, 1979). For example, the work is often associated with explicit expressions of a special type of masculinity, "macho-masculinity", which is almost difficult to take seriously and analyse (Somerville & Abrahamsson, 2003). The fear of being seen as less masculine is a common theme in these kinds of workplaces. Here men, more than in other workplaces, find it difficult to be associated with competences, attitudes, or behaviours that have a female gender-code (Ely & Meyerson, 2008; Eveline, 2001, 1989; Gherardi & Nicolini, 2000; Somerville & Abrahamsson, 2003) or have associations with unmanliness (Connell, 1995). As a result, we can see an interesting and seemingly paradoxical tendency that workplaces and work tasks introduced as a result of automation, computerisation, and robotisation can undergo a process of "feminisation," while the men hang on to the old technology (Olofsson, 2010). One example of this is when mining workers underground, half-jokingly give the remote-control workers sitting above ground nicknames such as "the velour workers" (Abrahamsson & Johansson, 2006; Andersson, 2012), meaning that they are of a soft unisex type of men, almost feminine, and not "real" workers. On the one hand, this trend opens up new gender constructions in industry; on the other hand, this trend can be seen as a symptom of a conservative organisation, i.e., barriers to implementing the new technology, and therefore important to study and understand.

At workplaces with a more gender-balance, male workers may attempt to restore the existing local gender order by telling macho-masculine stories, refusing to do "women's work" or "womanish work", and openly resisting women at the workplace (Abrahamsson, 2014; Eveline & Booth, 2002; Lahiri-Dutt, 2012). In these workplaces, ideas about gender: femininities and masculinities, often are so conservative they can create trouble during organisational changes and the implementation of new technology (Abrahamson, 2002; Hollway, 1996; Collinson & Hearn, 1996).

Gender is something that people do and construct in social interactions (Gherardi, 1994; West & Zimmerman, 1987, 2009), embedded in work identities, work organisations, and technology (Acker, 1990), formed by complex societal processes and notions of masculinity and femininity. Many attitudes, norms, and cultural symbols at work that are learned through workplace socialisation are connected to gender and the (unequal) gender order (Hirdman, 1988, 2001). Tacit collective agreements, and a continuous dramatisation of gender, both restore and change our ways of seeing masculinity and femininity. This play does not become really visible unless the existing masculinity and femininity are threatened (Butler 1990, 1993), such as in the transformation towards a digital industrial context. Even if such processes often are connected to the restoration of the unequal gender order they are situated in, these processes are continuously changing, and there is a possibility to challenge and transform these processes (Abrahamsson, 2014).

Shaping an A and B labour market

In the optimistic visions, smart systems, automation, and remote control will take over dangerous as well as routine work, so that production personnel can focus on learning, creating, and valuing work tasks in a safe environment (Gill, 2014). Even if the development will not be as the positive visions predict, depending on how the new technology is developed and interpreted, there will most likely be new types of industrial work, new types of work environments, and thus new work environmental problems. For example, digital technology and remote control, together with the emerging global and sometimes boundary-less work, not only results in increased freedom to decide how and where to work, but also results in higher demands of availability, perhaps 24 hours a day, seven days a week. This change may blur the boundaries between work and private life. Moreover, since the ability to control and monitor the individual increases, there will be a risk of new psychosocial stress. An increased information flow and accessibility could also lead to anxiety and job strain (Hoonakker & Korunka, 2014).

Other examples come from enhanced possibilities of production distribution, decentralisation, and outsourcing, both locally/regionally and in the global context. This creates dynamic systems of contractors, agency staff, and other actors temporarily active in the same physical workplace or in the same virtual/digital workplace. As mentioned above, employment form as we know today might dissolve and be replaced with crowdsourcing, and what can be called liquidised employment (Holtgrewe, 2014), complicating the co-ordination of work environment interventions and responsibilities (Johansson et al., 2010).

We might also expect that old work environmental problems will appear in new contexts and for other groups of workers. Some workers may participate in shaping the systems, while others will become machine assistants, or handle the repetitive and low qualified work tasks that could not be integrated into automated and smart systems, and the learning organisation. Maybe it is time to revive the old debate about the A and B labour market (Braverman, 1974; Kern & Schumann, 1974)?

Future work: pathways and implications

Although the climate change hangs over us like the sword of Damocles, it is a human right, for citizens of a democratic social context, to be involved in shaping their own future. For many, however, in organisational work contexts characterised less by democracy, and more by hierarchical power asymmetries and (increasingly precarious) wage labour contracts, the diffusion of new technology into their working life is sometimes perceived as a rather deterministic process, where their discretion is viewed as very limited. Our ambition is to create awareness of what the new technology can mean and for whom, and at the same time generate knowledge that development is possible to influence and control. There is always room to manoeuvre, for shaping how new technologies can be useful and relevant to people and society. The social dimension must have a prominent place in this process, both in designing the technology, and in analysing it from several perspectives.

However, there is no lack of knowledge about the significance of the social dimension. Based on extensive and relatively coherent international research on work environment and work organisation, it is possible to formulate a summary list of requirements, almost a utopian vision, of what constitutes a sustainable work (Johansson& Abrahamsson 2009). Such a list could for example include demands that, not only are physical risks and problems eliminated, and equipment and work sites are adapted to suit people's different physical and psychological set-up and designed to make work easier, but employees also enjoy autonomy, and a sense of participation and influence in matters both large and small. These involve being able to influence the division of duties and the pace and method of working, in relation to both other people and to the technical system used. The list could also include that the work and workplace provide physical, intellectual and cultural stimulation, variety, opportunities for social interactions, context and opportunities for learning and for personal and professional development. Here, workloads, demands, and challenges (both physical and psychological) are balanced at a reasonable level. The list would also include gender equality, fairness, respect, trust, democratic leadership, and open communication and opportunities for enjoyment and social support for all employees. There should also be good opportunities for a fair, stable and predictable income, and to combine work with a rich and sustainable life outside work.

To conclude, the vision of sustainable work is known and accepted by most people. It is rather the road towards it that is unknown, and filled with dangers and pitfalls. The design of new technology and new work organisation must be harmonised with both good working conditions and efficient production that can compete in a global market, but the quite optimistic scenario described in the Industry 4.0 texts is not likely to become a reality by itself. New technology does not in itself have a particular way to alter the effectiveness or working conditions, whether positive or negative. To enable a positive development, technical and organisational development needs also to include knowledge of the human, the working environment and the organisation of work, both the formal and informal.

Industry 4.0, essentially a technology-driven vision, generally refers to a technological revolution with a strong focus on production rationalisation, but we can also see that the organisational recommendations set up for the implementation of Industry 4.0 (e.g., production flow, connected processes and systems, horizontal integrated and flexible organisation, learning and production standardisation, and diagnosis) (see Kagerman et al. 2013) have clear similarities with BPR, The Boundaryless Organisation, Learning Organisation, TBM, TQM, Six Sigma, and Lean. Therefore, there is a need for critical organisational analyses, discourse analyses, analyses of embedded conflicts in Industry 4.0, power shifts, and invisibility of power. In addition, there is a need for analyses related to other current organisational trends (e.g., centralisation, monitoring, requirements for voluntary, storytelling, and corporate branding) and wider social changes.

In general, technical development is positive, but there are many questions that must be clarified, and we have discussed four of them. The development cannot and should not be stopped, but it requires reflections and considerations, so we do not create more problems than we solve. Research has an important role to play when new technology should be valued and introduced, but that role is not pregiven to us; we have to mark our position by highlighting issues that are perceived as important and relevant. We cannot let Industry 4.0's advocates set the discourse, alternative questions must be asked, other type of experts, such as academics, must be engaged, and alternative issues must be communicated and discussed by a wider audience. In the title of the chapter, we ask the question: *The wolf is coming or God's gift to mankind*? In order to experience the sustainable work, we as researchers sometimes have to take on the role of the wolf and ask uncomfortable questions.

References

Abrahamsson, L. (2002, November). Restoring the order: Gender segregation as an obstacle to organisational development, *Applied Ergonomics*, 33 (6), pp. 549–557.

Abrahamsson, L. (2006). Exploring construction of gendered identities at work, pp 105–121. In Billet, Stephan; Fenwick, Tara & Somerville, Margaret (eds). *Work, Subjectivity and Learning. Understanding Learning through Working Life*. Dordrecht: Springer.

Abrahamsson, L. (2014, December). Gender and The Modern Organization, Ten Years After. *Nordic Journal of Working Life Studies*, 4 (4), 109–136.

Abrahamsson, L. & Johansson, J. (2006). From grounded skills to sky qualifications. *Journal of Industrial Relations*, 48(5), 657–676.

Acker, J. (1990). Hierarchies, jobs, bodies. *Gender and Society*, 4(4), 139–158.

Andersson, E. (2012). *Malmens manliga mysterium*. Luleå tekniska universitet.

Berner, B. (2003). *Vem tillhör tekniken?* (red.) Arkiv: Lund, 311s.

Blauner, R. (1964). *Alienation and Freedom*. Chicago: UCP.

Braverman, H. (1974). *Labour and Monopoly Capital*. New York: Monthly Review Press.

Bright, J. (1958). *Automation and Management*. Boston: Harvard Business School.

Butler, J.P. (1990). *Gender Trouble: Feminism and the Subversion of Identity*. New York: Routledge.

Butler, J.P. (1993). *Bodies that Matter: On the Discursive Limits of "Sex"*. New York: Routledge.

Collinson, D. (1992) *Managing the Shop Floor*. Berlin: Walter de Gruyter.

Collinson, D. & Hearn, J. (eds). (1996). *Men as Managers, Managers as Men*. London: Sage.

Ely, R.J. & Meyerson, D. (2008). Unmasking manly men. *Harvard Business Review*. nos 7/8: 20.

Eveline, J. (1989). *Patriarchy in the Diamond Mines*. Australia: Murdoch University.

Eveline, J. (2001). 'Keeping the Boys Happy': Managerialism and the resistance of women miners in Australia. Unpublished paper, *Gender, Work and Organization Conference*, University of Keele, UK.

Eveline, J. & Booth, M. (2002, November). Gender and sexuality in discourses of managerial control. *Gender, Work and Organization*, 9(5).

Gherardi, S. (1994). The gender we think, the gender we do in our everyday organisational lives. *Human Relations*, 47 (6), 519–610

Gherardi, S. & Nicolini, D. (2000). The organizational learning of safety in communities of practice. *Journal of Management Inquiry*, 9(1), 7–18.

Gill, S. (2014). Industry prepares for the next industrial revolution. *Control Engineering*. https://www.controleng.com/articles/industry-prepares-for-the-next-industrial-revolution/

Hirdman, Y. (1988). Genussystemet: Reflexioner över kvinnors sociala underordning. *Kvinnovetenskaplig tidskrift KVT*, nr 3.

Hirdman, Y. (2001). Genus – om det stabilas föränderliga former. Malmö: Liber.

Hollway, W. (1996). Masters and men in the transition from factory hands to sentimental workers. In Collinson, D. and Hearn, J. (eds), *Men as Managers, Managers as Men*. London: Sage.

Holtgrewe, U. (2014). New new technologies: The future and the present of work in information and communication technology. *New Technology, Work and Employment*, 29(1), 9–24.

Hoonakker, P. & Korunka, C. (2014). Introduction. In Korunka, C. and Hoonakker, P. (eds). *The Impact of ICT on Quality of Working Life* (pp. 1–7). Dordrecht: Springer.

Howe, J. (2008). *Crowdsourcing*. New York: Crown Publishing Group.

Johansson, B., Johansson, J., & Abrahamsson, L. (2010). Attractive workplaces in the mine of the future: 26 statements. *International Journal of Mining and Mineral Engineering*, 2 (3), s. 239–252

Johansson, J. (1986). *Teknisk och organisatorisk gestaltning*. Sweden: Luleå tekniska universitet.

Johansson, J., & Abrahamsson, L. (2009). The good work – a Swedish trade union vision in the shadow of lean production. *Applied Ergonomics*, 40(4), 775–780.

Johansson, J., Abrahamsson, L., & Johansson, S. (2013). If you can't beat them, join them? The Swedish trade union movement and lean production. *Journal of Industrial Relations*, 55(3), 445–460.

Kagerman, H., Wahlster, W., & Helbig, J. (2013). Recommendations for implementing the strategic initiative Industry 4.0. München: Acatech.

Kern, H. & Schumann, M. (1974). *Industriearbeit und Arbeiterbewusstsein* (EVA). Frankfurt am Main/Köln

Kern, H. & Schumann, M. (1987). Limits of the Division of Labour, *Economic and Industrial Democracy*, 8(2), 151–170.

Lahiri-Dutt, K. (2007). Roles and status of women in extractive industries in India: Making a place for a gender-sensitive mining development. *Social Change*, 37, 37.

Lahiri-Dutt, K. (2012). Digging women: Towards a new agenda for feminist critiques of mining. *Gender, Place and Culture*, 19 (2), 193–212.

Lasi, H., Fettke, P. D. P., Kemper, H. G., Feld, D. I. T., & Hoffmann, D. H. M. (2014). Industry 4.0. *Business & Information Systems Engineering*, 6(4), 239–242.

Lysgaard, S. (1961). *Arbeiderkollektivet*, Oslo: Universitetsforlaget.

Olofsson, J. (2010). *Taking Place – Augmenting Space*. Sweden: Luleå University of Technology.

Polanyi, M. (1967). *The Tacit Dimension*. London: Routledge.

Regeringskansliet. (2016). Smart Industry – A strategy for new industrialisation for Sweden.

Romero, D., Stahre, J., Wuest, T., Noran, O., Bernus, P., Faet-Berglund, Å. & GoreckyY, D. (2016). *Towards an operator 4.0 typology: A human-centric perspective on the fourth industrial revolution technologies*. International Conference on Computers & Industrial Engineering CIE 29–31 October 2016.

Somerville, M. & Abrahamsson, L. (2003). Trainers and learners constructing a community of practice. *Studies in the Education of Adults*, 35 (1), 19–34.

Taylor, P. (2010). The Globalization of service work. In Thompson, P. and Smith, C. (eds), *Working Life*. London: Palgrave MacMillan, 244–268.

Thompson, P. (2013). Financialization and the workplace. *Work, Employment and Society*, 27 (3), 472–488.

West, C. & Zimmerman, D.H. (1987). Doing gender, *Gender and Society*, 1 (2), 125–151.

West, C. & Zimmerman, D.H. (2009). Accounting for doing gender. *Gender & Society*, 23, 112–122.

Whitehead, S.M. (2002). *Men and Masculinities*. Cambridge: Polity Press.

Willis, P. (1979). Shop flour culture, masculinity and the wage form. In Clark, J., Chricher, C. & Jonson, R. (eds). *Working Class Culture*, London: Hutchinson.

Ulrika Harlin, Martina Berglund, Katrin Skagert, Andreas Wallo, and Mattias Elg

Towards competitive sustainable work and green industrial transformation

Abstract: Green industrial transformations contributing to European climate goals and a fossil-free society require new knowledge and the ability of industrial companies to develop production systems from a systems perspective. This includes considerations of value chains, a life cycle perspective, and in parallel to regard social, ecological, and economic dimensions of sustainability over time. However, attention to social sustainability related to work is not as clear in industry´s agendas and has increasing importance as radical changes have impact on work and workplaces. This chapter illustrates industrial approaches addressing sustainability dimensions from a start-up firm's major greenfield project to establish a large-scale production of battery cells and solutions for energy storage in Europe, with Sweden as the starting point. This entrepreneurial firm had a strategic business-oriented sustainability approach and initiated solution-oriented collaborations with trade unions to proactively create conditions for a world-class concept for future production facilities, focussing working conditions and work organisation. Key elements for green transformation, competitiveness, and development of socially sustainable industry are addressed, with a focus on organisational resilience, supply of competences, sustainable work, and enablers for sustainable change processes in organisations.

Keywords: social sustainability, competence, work environment, trade union collaboration, resilience, start-up, innovation, organisational development

Workplace innovations towards sustainable industry

Europe is rapidly moving towards electrification, and green industrial transformation is vital for European industry's growth, jobs, and prosperity. This requires technology development for fossil-free production and reduction of carbon emissions, material development, and approaches towards a circular economy. Green industrial transformation also implies new forms of relationships with strategic stakeholder collaborations, e.g. in value chains and in society. Thus, development of workplace innovation through creative stakeholder collaboration is important for building skills and competence in a fast changing environment (Pot et al., 2021). In a fast pace of change, resource efficiency, flexibility, and rapid decision-making are needed, as well as the ability to create resilience to disruptions (Bjerkesjö, 2021). It is crucial that changes and transitions do not take place at the expense of poor working conditions, for example preventing work environments with high job demands, or occupational health and safety risks (Fagerlind Ståhl et al., 2018; Klofsten et al., 2020; Westgaard & Winkel, 2011). To gain sustainable health effects, organisational approaches, are needed along with an individual perspective (Docherty et al., 2002). Socially sustainable work has not usually been treated in a systems perspective together with economic and ecological sustainability in early design phases of production development (Sutherland et al., 2016; Zink, 2014), nor in early production development processes or industrial start-ups (Harlin & Berglund, 2020). Industrial strategies for green transformation need to be developed to maintain competitiveness. These aspects require innovations for the development and realisation of new solutions where competences within new fields are needed (Berglund, 2020)

Contextual understanding is needed while studying changes, as well as considerations of two interrelated perspectives: process and content, that characterise the notion of change (Pettigrew, 1990). This increases the understanding of development towards socially sustainable, green, and competitive industry. This chapter is organised in three main parts: describing an industrial context based on an industrial case, contents in terms of enablers for balancing competitiveness and sustainable work, and a process perspective for sustainable change in organisations, Tab. 9.

Tab. 9. Structure of the chapter: Context, content and process.

	Topic	**Description**
Context	Case description A start-up firm´s greenfield project towards green industrial transformation	Overview of strategies and initial approaches from a high-growth start-up firm´s ambition to accelerate green industrial transformation in Europe through development of a socially sustainable, green and competitive large-scale battery factory.
Content	Balancing competitiveness and sustainable work	Enablers and illustrative examples for ability to balance result orientation and good working conditions focusing (i) organisational resilience, (ii) supply of competences, and (iii) sustainable work.
Process	Sustainable development in organisations in fast pace of change	Process enablers for sustainable changes in organisations including Illustrative example of a start-up firm´s process building relations with trade unions – a strategic stakeholder collaboration chain knitting the change process towards sustainable industry together

The context: A case study of a start-up firm´s greenfield project towards green industrial transformation

An entrepreneurial high-growth company carried out a major greenfield project of establishing a large-scale production of battery cells and sustainable solutions for energy storage in Europe, with Sweden as the starting point. During the first three years of the new firm's start-up, a longitudinal case study was carried out (see Harlin, 2020; Harlin and Berglund, 2020; Harlin et al., 2021), where this chapter highlights practical approaches towards sustainable industry and green industrial transformation.[1] This new industrial domain in Europe was considered important for European industry to reduce dependence on, and challenge, the Asian dominance in the battery field. Major challenges were (i) the pace: a rapid company growth in parallel with developing production facilities, production processes, product development, and the entire work organisation; (ii) the speed: to quickly become competitive; and (iii) the scale: to produce large volumes. From the start, sustainability was clearly on the start-up firm´s strategic agenda, regarded as a core competitive advantage. The company's sustainability ambitions were bidirectional, focusing both on products and production, with an overarching vision to contribute to a cleaner and greener world:

- *to develop products* (the world's greenest batteries) and energy storage solutions aiming to accelerate the pace for industrial green transformation in Europe,
- *to develop production concepts* for re-creation of battery factories and large-scale production of battery cells in Europe, taking local strengths and conditions into account from a sustainability perspective.

The ambition was to accelerate the pace of change towards electrification, and to serve as a role model for development towards a sustainable industry. However, the mission was a major challenge, because of the enormous consumption of energy battery production requires, as well as access to raw materials and vital competences within a new domain, etc. The start-up firm developed a strategic concept for battery manufacturing, including replicable approaches for large-scale production, deep vertical integration with a high degree of control throughout the supply chain, traceability through advanced information technologies, standardisation and customisation, sustainability including integrated

---

1 This study was funded by Vinnova, Swedish Governmental Agency for Innovation Systems with additional funding from the XPRES (Initiative for Excellence in Production Research).

recycling, and innovative business models. The development of an initial demonstration line and R&D facility in a knowledge-intense region for product and production development was of great importance, as it should serve as a concept model for a planned large-scale factory in northern Sweden, and in the long term become scalable concepts for the re-creation of forthcoming factories in Europe.

Sustainability on the strategic agenda

The start-up firm initially had a strategic business-oriented sustainability approach. This included sustainable solutions designing for circular economy, as described by the manager of sustainability, in early phases of building up the recycling unit in the company:

- *We have the ambition to solve circular issues "key strategic", and build a business around it. For example, handling raw materials through recycling will reduce our need for new materials, Zero CO_2 in production will become a huge competitive advantage over our competitors.*

Sustainable and responsible investments were regarded as a growing movement, in which investors increasingly want to take environmental and social responsibility into their investments. Thus, it was important for the start-up firm to show a sustainable business that creates value over time. This included ensuring that legal requirements could be met, having the ability to attract competent employees, as well as establishing trusting relationships with stakeholders such as authorities, partners, customers, etc. Hence, these examples were considered as drivers towards green transformation within industry, that have the potential to strengthen the prerequisites to create value for shareholders with a strong long-term return. Examples of work practices approaching circular economy are illustrated as "closing loops" in Tab. 10.

Tab. 10. Industrial examples on circularity approaches "closing loops".

Closing "big" loops – Circularity in products life cycle creating raw material reuse	*From a long-term perspective, strategic R&D and stakeholder collaboration approaches were initiated to enable future production and battery recycling in a big loop to utilize and refine raw materials for new battery cells. The aim was to develop a business-oriented circular system where end-of-life batteries (in a 10-year perspective) could be used for the production of new batteries.*
Closing "mixed" loops – Circularity creating symbiosis, i.e., one´s waste to another's business value.	*From a medium-term perspective, solutions were developed to close "mixed" loops, e.g. where the company could create symbiosis with external stakeholders, turning one company´s waste to another company´s value, as expressed by an engineer working with finding solutions of the large amount of sulfate salt coming out as waste from the production: "In other cases people might see a problem with this waste – but we see it as an opportunity because we are going to reuse or sell it". After two years they developed a collaboration in symbiosis with a new start-up establishing two new factories, where 200,000 tons of salt are planned to be recovered from battery manufacturing processes and repurposed for commercial use of sustainable and circular fertilizer.*
Closing "inner" loops – Circularity in production process steps creating substance reuse and minimized emission exposure	*From a shorter term and in-house circular production perspective, solutions were developed in "inner loops" enabling possibilities to design for circularity in different production process steps. The ambition was to transform waste to added value through solutions for refining, recovering and reuse of substances, well as to create a recycling system in a specific manufacturing step. These solutions required integration of sustainability requirements in procurement processes and close collaboration and adjustments together with equipment and system suppliers, with outcomes of both providing circular solutions in production steps, as well healthier workplaces due to less exposure to emissions.*

In addition to attention to ecological sustainability aspects, social sustainability aspects focussing Corporate Social Responsibility had high attention in very early phases, as well as aspects related to sustainable work, where strategic approaches were developed on leadership, work organisation, and work environment. It was also expressed by top management that in addition to contribute to industrial transformation with access in Europe to key competences for battery development and production, they regarded this start-up as "a *great opportunity for driving social sustainability – to make this industrial project a platform to integrate people into society*".

During the start-up period 2017–2021, the new firm grew from scratch to over 2000 employees representing 100 nationalities, striving towards inclusion and diversity taking advantage of the potentials of having different backgrounds and experiences that enrich the company, the teams and the individuals. Thus, there was high attention on recruitment, onboarding work processes, management, mentorship, culture, and training approaches. Hence these challenges were driving forces to highlight early in industrial development projects social sustainability aspects on the strategic agenda resulting in a unique process building relations and structured collaboration processes with trade unions already during the start-up. They shared the overarching vision of green industrial transformation and to jointly create conditions for successful establishment of a new industrial domain in a Swedish context, and to build an attractive, innovative and inclusive company culture inspired by the Nordic model.

Site selection perspectives

Advantages for establishment of its first large-scale factory for battery production were found in the Nordic parts of Europe, offering climate-smart and cost-efficient energy systems with advanced electricity generation and distribution systems, as expressed by the start-up company´s CEO:

- *Sweden has a unique position to establish large-scale battery production to support the transition towards electrification, with its clean and affordable energy, proximity to raw materials, and a strong industrial tradition deep in its DNA.*

From a societal perspective, investments in industrial green transformations and new industries with demanding time schedules are opportunities, but also subject to major challenges for a region. The start-up firm´s criteria for site selection for initially planned large-scale factory and R&D facility establishment were the possibilities in a region to provide (i) access to land planned for industrial use; (ii) access to energy needed for production; (iii) environmental factors that do not complicate permitting processes when building and expanding powerlines, production plants, and other circularity possibilities such as handling water effluent; (iv) infrastructures in place for logistics; (v) attractiveness and conditions in the region for innovation and R&D, collaboration with universities, experts, and other companies; (vi) attractiveness for workforce ensuring supply of needed competences; and (vii) entrepreneurial spirit and engagement for the establishment in the municipality and local communities.

The case study indicated beneficial effects through collaboration across traditional boundaries where driving forces were based on a joint overarching purpose-driven mission: acceleration towards a greener and cleaner world. As the new domain was subjected to a high degree of uncertainties, and lack of previous experiences and knowledge, estimations were needed, as well as new ways of innovative collaborations between the start-up firm and actors in the entire society. Examples of lessons learned in the start-up firm´s establishment process towards the development of a sustainable industry was the municipality´s site readiness processes for such industrial investments and dynamic solution-oriented work practices. The selected municipality applied a concept characterised by "reversed crisis management", i.e., a scenario-based approach resulting in a positive rapid decision-making spiral, beneficial for the start-up as well as for other actors and stakeholders in and beyond the region. It included proactive customer-oriented approaches, and active support to the start-up firm through their local, regional, and national contextual understanding and ability to respond to questions they hadn't even asked, thus went beyond their requirements. As expressed by the marketing manager in the municipality:

- *What is the start-up firm thinking about right now? What are their questions? We're going to understand their questions … their problems. That's what we think about all the time … how can we contribute to their knowledge of our region … We're going to try to help them, we want to skill them in their mission.*

Furthermore, transparency, and trustful relations with social partners, authorities, public and private organisations, and structured collaborations across municipalities were regarded as key enablers for success of the start-up firm´s greenfield project. For example, the municipality worked with communication and collaboration needed for enabling establishment of new sustainable industry investments in the society´s three partnerships: (i) the region's general communication, both business communication, visitor communication and to residents; (ii) communication within actors in the municipality such as schools, universities, healthcare, transportation, housing projects, and authorities; and (iii) communication with the industrial investors' stakeholders and partners of the actual start-up firm. Altogether this was crucial to find the important intersections and create prerequisites, as the major industrial establishment within this new domain would have an impact in the whole society.

Another finding from the case study was learnings in other participating municipalities in the competition in the start-up firm´s site selection process, as expressed by management in another region:

- *'Thank you for letting us participate! We've learned a lot! We will be much better in the future when it comes to working on such issues. We have learned to work with the neighbouring municipality in a different way.'*

Lessons learned were for example that trustful, structured cross-regional collaboration *between* municipalities was regarded as a success factor for creating sustainable conditions for industrial establishment. Findings from studies showed impacts where new cross-collaborations were initiated in other regions with potential for new business opportunities. Furthermore, competences increased among other stakeholders on aspects and approaches related to industrial green transformation, such as how to operationalize environmental targets, circularity approaches, environmental permits, and approaches for future-proofing supply of competences. This is increasingly essential for employer branding and industrial workplace attractiveness in the short term but also for future generations of workforce, with increased demands on sustainability dimensions, and efforts to accelerate changes towards a greener, cleaner, and healthier world.

The content: Enablers for balancing competitiveness and sustainable work

For sustainable change, a balance is required between result orientation and good working conditions (Elg et al., 2015). Thus, there is a need in parallel to consider aspects such as efficiency, effectiveness, innovation or economic growth, health, gender equality, learning and development. There is a challenge, however, as these efforts require handling and managing sometimes conflicting demands and needs that may be associated with a change process. In the context of green transformation within industry, this chapter focuses on three enablers related to this balance: organisational resilience, strategic supply of competence, and sustainable work, part of social sustainability.

Organisational resilience

Organisational resilience refers to the ability of a system to manage expected and unexpected conditions in a resilient way, and have an ability to adjust its functioning prior to, during and following changes and disturbances. In faster pace of changes and transformations in organisations, knowledge of organisational resilience is vital for organisations to maintain functions when they are subjected to a variety of conditions (Hollnagel, 2013; Patriarca et al., 2018). Due to changes and dynamics created within the system or from the environment, these conditions may range from minor variations to disruptions and surprises. (Hollnagel, Woods, & Leveson, 2006). Thus, ability for organisational resilience is important, as industries need to manage increased uncertainties and critical events, where uncertainties may expand in movements and investments towards green transformation.

For industrial firms to become more sustainable in the future, there is a strong need to create new strategic collaborative ventures both within the organisations but also together with various stakeholders in value chains, and actors in society: for example, customers, suppliers, other companies, intermediaries and authorities. Commonly these strategic ventures have an inherent risk that unexpected disruptions can occur, and severely threaten the sustainability of these efforts. Even further, the global reach of supply chains, shorter product life cycles, and increasing customer requirements have made industrial organisations aware that disruptions to flows can cause undesirable operational and financial impacts.

Successful industry requires, among other things, operational competence for transformative processes, as well as knowledge of how to develop world-leading innovation cultures and ecosystems. As stressed in the industrial roadmap (Larsson et al., 2020), crucial tasks for sustainable industry are related to "dynamic capability" requiring skills such as identification and concretising threats and opportunities, taking advantages of challenges and opportunities, and strengthening, combining, protecting and allocating the company´s tangible and intangible assets. Companies with these capabilities are prone to change adapt more efficiently, and take better advantage of new knowledge and new experiences.

Green transition and digitalisation can lead to a paradigm shift in working methods, the possibility of advanced decision-making, etc. The division into different teams in the organisation, or in division of "white collar" and "blue collar", will possibly be blurred during major changes when new solutions need to be developed. Where and who you work for will be less in focus, but how and for what overarching goals and values all work towards will govern more. The importance of renewable capacity at both organisational and individual level will increase, which is why seamlessness also needs to be characterised by the interaction between work, competence development and studies for lifelong learning from an individual perspective in combination with organisational learning.

The industrial case illustrated approaches that create conditions for crossing boundaries, systems view, transparency, supporting organisational resilience, Tab. 11.

Tab. 11. Industrial examples enabling organisational resilience.

Vertical integration and strategic partnerships in value chains – deep control of sustainability perspectives	*From the perspective of green industrial transformation, vertical integration was an industrial approach enabling control over the value chain and optimizing processes. This was an approach to enable deeper insight and possibility to proactively foresee, and manage potential challenges, as well as to develop and control different sustainability perspectives. That includes even the social, ranging from mining and handling raw materials to recycling of battery cells, decreasing the need for new raw material, etc. Through increased control as well as close trustful collaboration with stakeholders in the value chain, the space of control and solution-oriented actions are enabled contributing to addressing potential uncertainties, circularity, traceability solutions, and socially sustainable aspects in the product life cycle.*
Artificial intelligence enabling traceability, connected systems, advanced decision support – Data is the new gold	*A strategy for achieving advanced decision support was investments in cutting edge technologies such as advanced information technology/artificial intelligence (AI), enabling data collection during a product's life cycle as well as from production processes. They saw potentials of data supporting improvements related to design, sourcing, work procedures, safety, manufacturing, performance, product cycle life, predictive maintenance, costs, etc. Thus, a key source for efforts towards improvements, and designing for future opportunities for customers as well as for resilient and sustainable production in forthcoming factories.*
Stretching targets, parallel work processes, and transparency enabling innovative sustainability solutions, and speedy environmental permits	*A major challenge for industrial establishments was achieving environmental permits for the planned production facilities. An example of cutting the lead time significantly, was to aim far beyond the legal environmental requirement targets, and work transparently in parallel rather than in a serial sequence in the decision process. This also had impact on building trustful relations and cross-boundary collaborations in the society, competence development and proactive attention to uncertainties and potential challenges, which also drove development of sustainable solutions.*

Strategic supply of competences

The transformation to a sustainable, green industry requires more than the development and implementation of new technically and environmentally viable solutions. To keep up with the challenges facing industrial corporations, such as societal disruptions, automation and digitalisation, new ways of working, and the urgent need to address well-being issues, the spotlight is shining brightly on matters of how to manage and develop the human resources (Deloitte, 2021).

There are clear indications that the organisation's capacity for learning combined with the innovative behaviours of the employees are crucial to match the increasing pace of change (Dirani et al., 2020; McLean & Jiantreerangkoo, 2020; Yawson, 2020).

For industrial start-up firms, such as the one featured in this chapter, a potential bottleneck concerns their ability to secure the "supply of competence". The supply of competence concerns ensuring access to education at all levels, having a good match between supply and demand in the labour market, as well as opportunities for learning and at work. For instance, there are urgent needs for competence in technology-related areas, in designing industrial prerequisites for economic, ecological and social sustainability, requiring a system understanding. For example, to fully benefit from digitalisation opportunities, there is a need for AI competence enabling advanced rapid decision-making and traceability along with cybersecurity and ethical challenges, knowledge of business and organisation models, innovation, change and transformation management.

A strategic approach to the competence supply chain involves having a systems perspective on the management and development of human resources, which means that there must be an understanding of how the flow of competences into, within, and out of the organisation is intertwined (Wallo et al., 2016). Starting with an analysis of the current employees' competence levels and the company's need for competences, there should be a strategy that determines what proactive actions are taken in regard to attracting, recruiting, onboarding and training future talents (Nilsson et al., 2018). From a sustainability perspective, a green strategy may have significant implications for an organisation's employer brand, and the ability to attract high-quality candidates (Pham & Paillé, 2019). It is also crucial that the strategy includes a plan for how competence can be transferred between individuals in organisations, so that organisational learning can take place (Crossan et al., 1999). Furthermore, it is also important to decide whether the competence supply issues, such as recruitment and staffing, should be managed internally, or outsourced to HR intermediaries and other external vendors (Kock et al., 2012). A strategy for competence supply should also comprise appropriate qualitative and quantitative measurements that can contribute to the evaluation of the HR practices being used (Wallo et al., 2020). The industrial case illustrated approaches related competence strategies, Tab. 12.

Tab. 12. Industrial examples of competence strategies.

Recruitment and attracting talents	*The greenfield project within a new industrial domain required major recruitment efforts striving for in-house competence within all work processes. As there was a lack of competences in Europe, experts needed to be recruited globally. In parallel, to provide the forthcoming large-scale factory with personnel, approximately 2,500 – 3,000 people will need to be recruited within a few years. Hence, the firm took strategic initiatives and initiated partnerships with public and private organisations in the society to find, attract and create collaboration with potential employees, also currently outside the labour market.* *As it was a new industrial domain, recruitments were needed worldwide, as well as a need to develop new competences during the start-up journey. Specific competences were needed within domains such as energy storage, battery development, artificial intelligence, process-, and production system development, logistics, finance, circular economy, construction, commissioning, marketing in combination with entrepreneurial and teamwork skills. However, specific competences need to be complemented with skills such as flexibility, power of initiative, willingness to do the extraordinary and continuously learn more together with others, cross-boundary teamwork beyond titles and traditional blue- and white-collar work, questioning established ways of working and contribute to innovative solutions.*
Onboarding, competence development, and retaining employees	*There was a structured onboarding process, leadership training, and digital solutions enabling efficient communication, transparency, and documentation of learning. Furthermore, newly hired employees were offered mentorship, and management at all levels was trained in work environment and culture issues towards creation of an inclusive and open culture, striving to constantly support individuals and teams in the fast-moving work environment. The organisation was expanding continuously, where each newly hired employee apart from their competences of specific fields, needed skills and ability immediately, in parallel to adapt to a start-up work environment within a new business domain where "everything was not in place". They could not rely on existing work practices, and work according to traditional roles and hierarchies. Instead, a mindset was needed for strong teamwork, working seamlessly across traditional boundaries, characterised by mutual support, trust, transparency and connecting work processes.*

Tab. 12. Continued

Building a collaboration concept around each factory, and a "competence ecosystem" beneficial for the company, region, and country	*In the regions for factory establishment, collaboration with stakeholders around each factory was initiated, including partners from municipalities, education actors, social partners, and other companies. On the one hand with the purpose to support the start-up firm with components, material, competences etc., and on the other hand to jointly strengthen and achieve benefits for the region and society as a whole.* *Furthermore, to be in the forefront, the start-up firm initiated several competence clusters within domains such as energy and electrification, circular economy, culture, and socially sustainable work. For example, they initiated collaboration communities in society including different educational organisations in the region together with municipalities and social partners as well as started a strategic and proactive dialogue with trade unions and employer associations at very early phases of the new firm. Furthermore, an opportunity of a high learning curve, building a new competence area beneficial for many stakeholders also striving towards green transformation within their businesses.*

Sustainable work, part of social sustainability

Several enabling technologies that support the so-called 5th Industrial Revolution, such as energy efficiency, data and AI technologies, IoT, digital twins and simulation, and human-machine interaction need to be complemented with attention to human demands, resilience and sustainability. Hence approaches expressed as Industry 5.0 complements the existing Industry 4.0 approach by specifically addressing the transition to a sustainable, human-centred and resilient European industry. In this respect, dimensions related to sustainable work, part of social sustainability, are regarded as enablers for the industry to be at the forefront of achieving a socially sustainable, competitive, and green industry at an accelerating pace of change.

Companies' (and in the long run countries') competitiveness relies not only on the resources employees have in terms of relevant competences, but also on their motivation and health for achieving intended goals. The workplace can in turn also promote health and well-being (Chu et al., 2000; Nordenfelt, 1995; WHO, 1986). This is also addressed in other research showing that individual conditions, how teams and management work and that the organisation's structures and systems are significant for well-being and performance (Nielsen et al., 2017). Examples of factors highlighted that both strengthen well-being *and* performance include (a) optimism, confidence in one's own ability, ability to adapt and recover on the individual level; (b) social support and team climate on the group level; (c) transformational leadership, social support and relationship leader-employee on leader level; and (d) work content, independence and variety, development opportunities and reward systems on the organisational level (Nielsen et al., 2017). All in all, it can be expressed as "good working environments" that create win-win for both employees and the organisation, and incentives for aspects related to human factors such as well-being are crucial to consider when developing or changing production systems (Gregori et al., 2017). However, sustainable work includes not only the health perspective but also the ability to manage increased complexity and when new-generation workplaces are developed (Romero et al., 2020; Sutherland et al., 2016). Furthermore, research points out that social, ecological and economical dimensions of sustainability are not isolated, and need to be considered in parallel, and constantly over time, specifically in a faster pace of change at workplaces (Backström et al., 2002; Zink, 2014).

From a Nordic perspective, the culture of trade union collaboration at workplaces may lead to positive effects for both individuals and organisations (Huzzard & Nilsson, 2004). Enabling factors addressed in previous studies are early employee participation in major change processes, with shared vision and mission to create value for people and the company. For example, previous industrial studies witness that this approach may create prerequisites for proactive and solution-oriented collaboration that is beneficial for both employees and employers (Garmann-Johnsen et al., 2018). Furthermore, Kjellberg (2011) stresses that there are competitive advantages, as a trustful collaboration may create drivers for active engagement both in daily operations as well as during change processes, instead of needing to manage contradictions. Other literature highlights mutual gains by improved possibilities to implement difficult decisions, achieve a better perceived working environment climate, increased flexibility, efficiency and productivity, improved job security and increased employee influence (Geary & Trif, 2011; Glover et al., 2014). Hence, development of workplaces with a high degree of employee participation in development and change processes (Sarfati, 2014) deserves reflection in change processes striving towards green transformation in industry. The industrial case illustrated approaches contributing to sustainable work, Tab. 13.

Tab. 13. Industrial examples on designing for sustainable work.

Building a sustainable company culture	*Three core value words – passion, boldness, and excellence – were used in the strategy to build a strong culture aiming towards the same vision and mission. In leadership and team training these values were operationalized by teams, given the task of transforming the value words to their own work situation and further set up actions. The aim in the demanding work tasks within the new domain was to create a united team spirit, positive attitude facing challenges, offer attractive work and workplaces, achieve commitment to challenge and push targets beyond traditional goals, and to expect and offer feedback during challenging work tasks and new situations. Challenges were related to peaks of workload, new types of safety issues, creating a socially sustainable work environment during high pressure of the start-up, culture varieties, and acceptance for flexible ways of working across borders. Proactive countermeasures were early establishment of flexible collective work agreements that were suitable for a fast-changing work environment in the start-up phase paying attention to both flexibility and working environment (taking working hours, working conditions, and roles into account). Furthermore, English was decided as the business language to facilitate a common culture, mutual learning and transparency, while there were advantages for competences in Swedish in a longer perspective in the large-scale factory planned in a Swedish region.*
Integration of social dimensions with ecological and economical dimensions of sustainability in work processes for development of the new factory	*The strategic approaches to sustainability also included attention to sustainable work, part of social sustainability. Drivers where the need of attracting and development of talents from all over the world, create long-term good working conditions, an agile work organisation, and an innovative work environment with rapid decision making in an inclusive environment with creative teamwork. Altogether these are considered competitive advantages. In practice, the case study showed that their approaches had reciprocal impact on social, ecological, and economic dimensions. Hence, that dimensions of sustainability in practice are integrated, rather than isolated.*

(*Continued*)

Tab. 13. Continued

Creative connected teamwork, transparency, and seamless collaborations across borders	*There were challenges of managing complexity and integrating sustainability aspects in interdependent work processes, where "creative connected teamwork" was performed in the agile work organisation. In this example, the technical team was the support, and the sustainability team was the main contact point for this specific purchase and integrating green perspectives. Hence, it was a strong cross-functional effort with seamless collaboration, and the final negotiations were led by the procurement team. Furthermore, during fast pace of change, as an employee asserted: "You have to trust that all people also are involving you in decision making!". Thus, meeting structures and documentation needed to be developed to ensure transparency and support decision making in relation to individuals´ parallel activities at other workstreams and work processes.*

The process: Sustainable development in organisations with a fast pace of change

Sustainability from a *process perspective*, is about enablers that promote sustainable development in organisations, where Svensson and Brulin (2014) have identified three key elements: (i) active; (ii) broad ownership collaboration in partnerships; and (iii) developmental learning, further developed in EJWI Fig. 10.

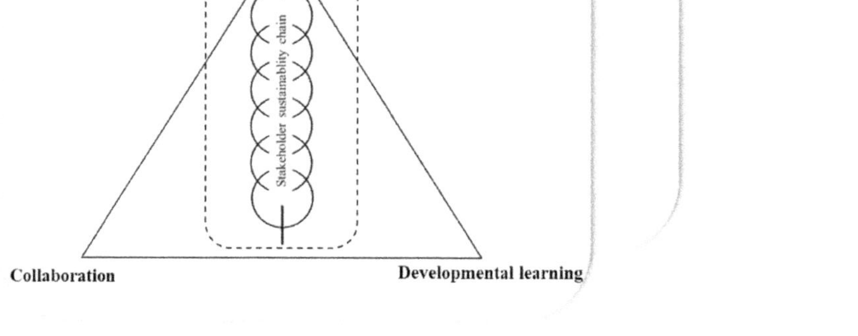

Fig. 10. Enablers for sustainable development of organisations, exemplified by change processes related to approaches towards sustainable industry and green industrial transformation, modified from Harlin and Berglund (2020) and Svensson and Brulin (2014).

Change processes towards sustainable industry and green industrial transformation require several perspectives, where this chapter focusses on dimensions related to sustainable work in early phases of factory establishment with this explicit aim.

In general, change processes can be referred to "the aim and purpose of the change process", for example, a present state X, the point of departure, aiming to a new present state Y, the point of destination. Thus, the vision in this context of change processes towards sustainable industry and green industrial transformation, are considered from mechanisms promoting enablers to succeed in the long term, i.e., enabling sustainable development. Specifically in an increasing speed of change the need increases for innovative activities in stakeholders' collaborations that promote both flexibility and efficiency and development of sustainable work (Hasle, 2014).

The first key element, *active ownership*, is described as a core driver for sustainable change, where balancing different stakeholders' interests and perspectives plays a crucial role. During major changes, and specifically at a fast pace, this is a challenge. However, a supportive factor is to consciously strive to gain involvement and a common view upon a desired change process from different stakeholders' perspectives, as well as to involve new stakeholders during a roll out phase. Constant interconnections are needed in a dynamic process, involving more actors, and being aware of keeping the chain together to prevent parts of the chain breaking, which has impact on possibilities for sustainable development of the desired change process. Here this is described as "a stakeholder sustainability chain", knitting together considerations and issues during the change process. Issues addressed to assess the status of active ownership are for example:

- How do we create the right conditions for the change process in terms of resources, governance and attention?
- How are the results taken care of during the change process and how can they become part of the usual business?

The second key element, collaboration, is described as enablers to perceive a broad involvement and inclusion of actors in partnerships, where the anchoring and robustness of planned change are secured. Issues that need to be addressed are:

- How can collaborations between strategic organisations be built for development in this direction and how can prerequisites be shaped for joint knowledge creation?
- What are relevant levels of collaborations, both within and between work processes?

The third key element, developmental learning, is described as the ability to utilise learnings initiated from problems, disruptions or new challenges requiring rethinking or new approaches (Ellström, 2001). Relevant issues are:

- How to achieve transparency and efficient communication?
- How to create an agile work organisation with the ability to adapt to changing conditions?
- How to utilize learning opportunities during the change process?

The industrial case illustrated approaches of stakeholder collaboration towards sustainable work during initial factory development, Tab. 14.

Tab. 14. Industrial examples of stakeholder collaboration during changes.

Aim and purpose of start-up firm´s collaboration with trade unions	*A strategic approach was to initiate and build competence clusters and stakeholder collaborations for co-creation of new knowledge within several domains, i.e., "partnering-up with people taking you to the next level". Regarding expertise on "sustainable work and competitiveness", expertise is found in trade union organisations' collaboration within industry in Sweden. Based on the joint purpose-driven vision and the start-up firm´s mission, a "Purpose of declaration" inspired by the Nordic model related to work, was jointly formulated by the start-up firm and trade union parties. The ambition was to co-operate to create appropriate conditions for development of an agile work organisation with the best industrial workplace of the future demonstrating flexibility, power of innovation and excellent manufacturing results. An industrial expert with strategic roles and former head of national trade union organisation, was assigned as process leader to build strategic and operational relations and partnerships with social partners, both employer associations and relevant employee organisations such as trade unions.*
Active ownership	*To achieve ownership during a fast-growing organisation, it was important to constantly offer local employee participation at workplaces, and to gradually organize regional and local union communities. This was observed in the case as the change process was carried out in a high-growth start-up firm with "constantly moving work, and working environment", where contextual understanding was crucial for the change processes. Furthermore, as it was an international multi-cultural firm, management and employees had various experiences of trade union co-operation, the firm operationalized activities and approaches in recruitment processes as well as within the organisation, e.g. integration in introduction, and onboarding activities, management and employee training education to strengthen the development of the desired company culture inspired by the Nordic model.*

Tab. 14. Continued

Collaboration	*Building trustful relations and strategic partnerships at all levels with social partners such as trade unions early during the start-up was considered important to successfully realise planned changes, i.e., go from "vision to action". This trade union collaboration was considered part of the start-up firm´s sustainability strategy and driven as a mission by top management.* *Topics for collaboration included topics such as work environment (working methods when everything is not in place), flexible collective agreements adapted to specific needs during the start-up, collaboration with subcontractors, social sustainability in working life and private life, skills and competences needed, work structures, and the trade union collaboration process itself and its potentials. An outcome was a strategic and structured process developing the union collaboration with activities in an annual cycle, interconnected to parallel work processes in the start-up firm. Challenges during the fast development pace and high growth organisation were for example operationalisation of social sustainability dimensions beyond organisational boundaries. Specifically managing cultural challenges related to the large amount of subcontractors assigned for ground preparations and construction of facilities, highlighting the need to strengthening collaboration in the stakeholder collaboration chain. Hence it is even more important to build strong relationships with social partners such as trade unions during early phases of industrial start-ups.*
Developmental learning	*The new industrial domain in combination with the fast-growing pace of the start-up firm required solution-oriented problem- solving in combination with strategic replicable concepts for new factories. Hence there was a high learning curve for all stakeholders, where each person became carriers, both within and across organisations. For example, key learnings from the union collaboration were planned to be utilized in the development of a global concept model for union collaboration in further recreation of battery factories in Europe. Furthermore, the external trade union stakeholders saw opportunities to serve as agents in other industrial involvement and in society, utilizing learnings related to industrial establishments, green transformation and designing for sustainable work in early development phases.*

Reflections and final remarks

Attention on addressing sustainable work as a competitive factor is growing, as the work environment and working conditions affect engagement, health, opportunities for innovations, and supply of competences. The industrial case illustrated several approaches beneficial from a combined sustainability perspective. For example, the vertical integration approach strove to solve circular processes proactively and cost-efficiently. It is an example that enables organisational resilience, as it incorporates more production processes in the factory than manufacturing companies normally do. Through trustful collaborations in strategic partnerships in value chains, possibilities were provided to develop innovative circular solutions, proactively foresee and manage potential challenges, as well as efficiently handle actual problems. This approach widens the management space, i.e., the space of control and actions to ensure that environmental impact is minimised throughout the production flow, social sustainability aspects can be regarded, and that the planned factory can be designed to minimise the impact on the local environment. A reflection from the start-up firm was the potential advantages of increasing control of the sustainability dimensions, including social aspects from mining to recycling, and the strengths of building in-house skills and competences.

A number of key learnings were derived from industrial case. First, the power of a jointly shared overarching mission in strategic network collaborations, far beyond the individual visions and missions. The combination of co-creative teamwork within and across traditional borders and passion-driven employees with strong ambitions to actively contribute to a greener, cleaner world, were drivers for new development of sustainable solutions. Furthermore, utilising cutting-edge technologies, business-oriented circularity approaches, together with flexibility, trustful stakeholder collaborations, capability of managing uncertainties, stretching targets, and organisational learning during a high pace of change, were regarded as differentiating competitive factors. Here the case illustrated an approach to both speed the production establishment and ability to speedily drive innovative circularity solutions avoiding sub-optimisation, through an entrepreneurial spirit in the company culture "stretching environmental targets" and not accepting "no for an answer".

Second, a broad collaboration crossing boundaries integrating sustainability dimensions in work processes within industries, between organisations, and in society are enablers. That included cross-boundary collaboration in supply chains, between organisational functions and work processes related to due diligence, procurement of machines and equipment, between individuals and teams in an international company culture, as well as with actors in the society such as authorities, municipalities, social partners, and education organisations. To jointly develop innovative sustainability solutions, with a competitive mindset regarding obstacles and hindrances as incentives, thus has potential for developmental learning and creating competitive advantages for all stakeholders.

Third, an area of knowledge creation considering social sustainability dimensions in combination with development of a new industrial domain towards green transformation, was reached through early stages of collaboration with experts, in this case, trade union parties. Building trustful relations and union collaboration structures in early development phases, potentials for proactiveness were found, combining aspects of sustainable work and competitiveness.

Designing for competitive sustainable work and green industrial transformation requires a systems perspective on sustainability, including social, ecological, and economical dimensions, over time. This chapter contributes industrial experiences of developing concepts and approaches in practice. This includes a contextual understanding in balancing competitiveness and sustainable work, and how to manage sustainable development in fast changing organisations.

References

Backström, T., van Eijnatten, F. M., & Kira, M. (2002). A complexity perspective. In P. Docherty, J. Forslin, & S. A. B. (Rami) (eds), *Creating Sustainable Work Systems – Emerging Perspectives and Practice* (pp. 65–75). Routlegde. Taylor and Francis Group. https://doi.org/10.4324/9780203995389.pt1

Berglund, H. (2020). Industrins omställning – möjligheter och utmaningar. IF Metall.

Bjerkesjö, P. (2021). Grön omställning och arbetsliv – Kunskapsläge och fortsatta forskningsbehov.

Chu, C., Breucker, G., Harris, N., Stitzel, A., Gan, X., Gu, X., & Dwyer, S. (2000). Health-promoting workplaces – international settings development. *Health Promotion International, 15*(2), 155–167. https://doi.org/10.1093/heapro/15.2.155

Crossan, M. M., Lane, H. W., & White, R. E. (1999). An organisational learning framework: From intuition to institution. *Academy of Management Review*, 24(3), 522–537. https://doi.org/10.5465/amr.1999.2202135

Dirani, K. M., Abadi, M., Alizadeh, A., Barhate, B., Garza, R. C., Gunasekara, N., Ibrahim, G., & Majzun, Z. (2020). Leadership competencies and the essential role of human resource development in times of crisis: a response to Covid-19 pandemic. *Human Resource Development International*, 23 (4), 380–394. https://doi.org/10.1080/13678868.2020.1780078

Docherty, P., Forslin, J., & Shani, A. B. (2002). *Creating Sustainable Work Systems: Emerging Perspectives and Practice*. Psychology Press.

Elg, M., Ellström, P. E., Klofsten, M., & Tillmar, M. (2015). *Sustainable Development in Organisations: Studies on Innovative Practices*. Edward Elgar Publishing. https://doi.org/10.4337/9781784716899

Ellström, P.-E. (2001). Integrating learning and work: Problems and prospects. *Human Resource Development Quarterly*, 12(4), 421. https://doi.org/10.1002/hrdq.1006

Fagerlind Ståhl, A.-C., Ståhl, C., & Smith, P. (2018). Longitudinal association between psychological demands and burnout for employees experiencing a high versus a low degree of job resources. *BMC Public Health*, 18(1), 915. https://doi.org/10.1186/s12889-018-5778-x

Garmann-Johnsen, N. F., Helmersen, M., & Eikebrokk, T. R. (2018). Worklife ergonomics in digital co-creation: The "What", the "Why" and the "How". *European Journal of Workplace Innovation*, 4(1). https://doi.org/10.46364/ejwi.v4i1.503

Geary, J., & Trif, A. (2011). Workplace partnership and the balance of advantage: A critical case analysis. *British Journal of Industrial Relations*, 49, s 44–s 69. https://doi.org/10.1111/j.1467-8543.2010.00827.x

Glover, L., Tregaskis, O., & Butler, P. (2014). Mutual gains? The workers' verdict: A longitudinal study. *The International Journal of Human Resource Management*, 25(6), 895–914. https://doi.org/10.1080/09585192.2012.743479

Gregori, F., Papetti, A., Pandolfi, M., Peruzzini, M., & Germani, M. (2017). Digital Manufacturing systems: A framework to improve social sustainability of a production site. *Procedia CIRP*, 63, 436–442. https://doi.org/10.1016/j.procir.2017.03.113

Harlin, U. (2020). A start-up firm's Greenfield Project of building a new state-of-the-art factory in Sweden RISE Rapport; 2020:21.

Harlin, U., & Berglund, M. (2020). Designing for sustainable work during industrial startups – The case of a high-growth entrepreneurial firm. *Small Business Economics*, 1–13. https://doi.org/10.1007/s11187-020-00383-3

Harlin, U., Berglund, M., Skagert, K., & Elg, M. (2021). Stakeholder collaboration inspired by the Nordic model–Towards sustainable work and competitiveness during an industrial startup. *European Journal of Workplace Innovation*, 6(1–2), 198–219. https://doi.org/10.46364/ejwi.v6i2.799

Hasle, P. (2014). Development of sustainable work–is there a future for a Nordic model. Proceedings of the ODAM/NES congress, Ergonomics challenges in new economics, Copenhague, Danemark

Hollnagel, E., Woods, D.D., & Leveson, N. (2006) Resilience engineering: Concepts and precepts. Ashgate Publishing.

Hollnagel, P.E. (2013). Resilience engineering in practice: A guidebook. Ashgate Publishing.

Huzzard, T., & Nilsson, T. (2004). Dancing queen? Partnership, codetermination and strategic unionism in Sweden. *Strategic Unionism and Partnership: Boxing or Dancing*, 86–106.

Kjellberg, A. (2011). *Arbetsmiljön: det arbetssociologiska perspektivet*. Conference paper. Department of sociology. Lund University.

Klofsten, M., MacEachen, E., & Ståhl, C. (2020). New and small firms in a modern working life: How do we make entrepreneurship healthy? *Small Business Economics*, 1–9. https://doi.org/10.1007/s11187-020-00380-6M

Kock, H., Wallo, A., Nilsson, B., & Höglund, C. (2012). Outsourcing HR services: The role of human resource intermediaries. *European Journal of Training and Development*, 36(8), 772–790. https://doi.org/10.1108/03090591211263512

Larsson, S., Harlin, U., Winzenburg, S., & Edström, A. (2020). *Färdplan: Teknik, material och förmågor för hållbar industriell konkurrenskraft* (978-91-89167-28-5 (ISBN)). RISE Rapport 2020:46

McLean, G. N., & Jiantreerangkoo, B. (2020). The role of national HRD in an era of COVID-19. *Human Resource Development International*, 23(4), 418–426. https://doi.org/10.1080/13678868.2020.1780066

Nielsen, K., Nielsen, M. B., Ogbonnaya, C., Känsälä, M., Saari, E., & Isaksson, K. (2017). Workplace resources to improve both employee well-being and performance: A systematic review and meta-analysis. *Work & Stress*, 31(2), 101–120. https://doi.org/10.1080/02678373.2017.1304463

Nilsson, P., Wallo, A., Rönnqvist, D., & Davidson, B. (2018). *Human Resource Development: Att utveckla individer, grupper och organisationer*. Studentlitteratur.

Nordenfelt, L. Y. (1995). *On the Nature of Health: An Action-theoretic Approach*. Springer Science & Business Media.

Patriarca, R., Bergström, J., Di Gravio, G., and Costantino, F. Resilience engineering: Current status of the research and future challenges. *Safety Science*. 2018 February 1; 102:79–100. https://doi.org/10.1016/j.ssci.2017.10.005

Pettigrew, A.M. (1990) Longitudinal field research on change: Theory and practice. *Organization Science*, 1, 267–292. doi:10.1287/orsc.1.3.267

Pham, D. D. T. & Paillé, P. (2019). Green recruitment and selection: An insight into green patterns. *International Journal of Manpower*, 41(3), 258–272. https://doi.org/10.1108/IJM-05-2018-0155

Pot, F., Totterdill, P., & Dhondt, S. (2021). Developing Workplace Innovation Policies in the European Union. *The Palgrave Handbook of Workplace Innovation*, 41. https://doi.org/10.1007/978-3-030-59916-4_3

Romero, D., Stahre, J., & Taisch, M. (2020, January). The Operator 4.0: Towards socially sustainable factories of the future. *Computers & Industrial Engineering*, 139, 106128. https://doi.org/10.1016/j.cie.2019.106128

Sarfati, H. (2014). Review of Nordic lights – Work, management and welfare in Scandinavia, edited by Ake Sandberg, Stockholm: SNS Förlag. ISBN: 978-91-86949-37-2. *Relations Industrielles/Industrial Relations*, 69(1), 229–232.

Sutherland, J. W., Richter, J. S., Hutchins, M. J., Dornfeld, D., Dzombak, R., Mangold, J., Robinson, S., Hauschild, M. Z., Bonou, A., & Schönsleben, P. (2016). The role of manufacturing in affecting the social dimension of sustainability. *CIRP Annals*, 65(2), 689–712. https://doi.org/10.1016/j.cirp.2016.05.003

Svensson, L., & Brulin, G. (2014). Lärande som drivkraft och för utveckling. In K. Henrik (Ed.*), Lärande i arbetslivet : möjligheter och utmaningar : en vänbok till Per-Erik Ellström* (pp. 279–292). Linköpings universitet. http://urn.kb.se/resolve?urn=urn:nbn:se:liu:diva-110874

Wallo, A., Kock, H., Lundqvist, D., & Coetzer, A. (2020). Understanding factors that enable and inhibit assessment of outcomes of competence development. *Human Resource Development Review*, 19(4), 384–421. https://doi.org/10.1177/1534484320943332

Wallo, A., Kock, H., & Nilsson, P. (2016). Setting the stage for innovation: Towards a conceptual model of the HR-innovation link. *International Journal of Human Resources Development and Management*, 16(1/2), 100. https://doi.org/10.1504/IJHRDM.2016.075375

Westgaard, R. H., & Winkel, J. (2011). Occupational musculoskeletal and mental health: Significance of rationalization and opportunities to create sustainable production systems–A systematic review. *Applied Ergonomics*, 42(2), 261–296. https://doi.org/10.1016/j.apergo.2010.07.002

World Health Organisation (WHO) (1986). The Ottawa Charter for Health Promotion. https://intranet.euro.who.int/__data/assets/pdf_file/0004/129532/Ottawa_Charter.pdf (accessed 12 November 2021).

Yawson, R. (2020). Strategic flexibility analysis of HRD research and practice post COVID-19 pandemic. *Human Resource Development International*, 23 (4), 406–417. https://doi.org/10.1080/13678868.2020.1779169

Zink, K. J. (2014). Designing sustainable work systems: The need for a systems approach. *Applied Ergonomics*, 45(1), 126–132. https://doi.org/10.1016/j.apergo.2013.03.023

Cornelia Daheim, Jessica Prendergast, Jörg Rampacher, Annick Starren, Emmanuelle Brun, and Ioannis Anyfantis

Perspectives on the circular economy and its effects for occupational safety and health

Abstract: The European Commission has set Europe on a course towards a green future: its key policy initiative, the 2020 European Green Deal, is primarily focused on making Europe climate neutral by 2050. One of the main building blocks of the European Green Deal is the new Circular Economy Action Plan. Aiming to "close the loop" and keep Europe's resource consumption within planetary boundaries, this plan has many significant policy and regulatory implications that will affect future jobs and have a wide range of consequences for workers' safety and health. What a future "circular economy" could imply for Occupational Safety and Health (OSH), and respective policy and action needs, is the key question of this chapter. Presented here are the results and insights generated to date from EU-OSHA's ongoing foresight project: four scenarios with a 2040 horizon which look at possible alternative futures of the circular economy in Europe and how they would impact on work and OSH. Methodology-wise, the scenarios were developed using a key-factor based approach, drawing from a literature review as well as expert interviews. The scenario portfolio, and the implications identified so far, demonstrate a range of risks and opportunities for OSH which result from the different possible future pathways towards the circular economy paradigm, across various sectors, ranging from e.g. possible synergy effects of increased co-operation between OSH and sustainability initiatives, to a strongly increased need to, e.g., ensure safety of shared, reused, or recycled equipment, tools and materials, or provide better OSH-protection for self-employed and platform workers, etc. In undertaking research for the project, it also became evident that advancing the circular economy offers a window of opportunity to realise OSH improvements simultaneously.

Keywords: occupational safety and health, circular economy, green deal, just transition, emerging risks, waste sector, digitalisation, European Union, sustainable Work

Introduction: The project background and approach

This chapter summarises key insights from EU-OSHA's foresight study on the circular economy and its effects on occupational safety and health (OSH), a project realised by Future Impacts for and with EU-OSHA. Before zooming in on selected findings from the development of four macro-scenarios, including cross-cutting dimensions and key implications for the future of work and OSH from across the scenarios, a brief is provided on the project background and approach.

The project "Foresight Study on the Circular Economy and its effects on Occupational Safety and Health" is being carried out against the background of an EU policy shift towards more environmentally sustainable practices, with several policy initiatives driving efforts in the circular economy arena. The key related policy initiative is the European Commission's European Green Deal initiative, which has the overarching aim of making Europe climate neutral by 2050 (European Commission, 2019a, 2019b). Alongside the Green Deal initiative sits the Commission's 2015 circular economy package, including an EU action plan for the circular economy ("Closing the Loop") with 54 concrete actions to achieve a circular economy, many with significant policy and regulatory implications for the EU's waste and recycling sector (European Commission, 2015).

These initiatives, and indeed the circular economy as a whole, are widely considered to be critical and influential developments that will be beneficial to the action against climate change and will ultimately impact on jobs and OSH. While seen by some as an opportunity to create good-quality jobs (see, for example, WHO, 2018), others point to the rise in hazardous working conditions in the areas of maintenance and repair, disassembly, and recycling (see, for example, EPSU, 2017, 2020). However, it is widely agreed that future jobs will be changed and reshaped as a consequence of adapted processes and the use of different (reused) materials, with impacts felt across all industries explored within this study (including energy; transport; manufacturing; construction; agriculture, forestry, and food; and waste, recycling, and environmental remediation).

The project explores different ways in which future jobs may be impacted by efforts towards implementing a circular economy, and what consequences this may have for OSH in the future. In the first phase of the project, four scenarios were generated by Future Impacts together with the EU-OSHA project team, via a key-factor-based scenario methodology drawing from an extensive literature analysis (which included significant parts of earlier foresight work done by EU-OSHA) and expert interviews.[1]

1 Details on all results, project steps, methodology and especially on the scenarios are available on the EU-OSHA website exploring emerging risks and the circular economy: https://osha.europa.eu/en/emerging-risks/circular-economy. At the time of writing, this encompasses six papers or reports: *Foresight Study on the Circular Economy and its effects on Occupational Safety and Health* (EU-OSHA, 2021a); *Executive Summary – Foresight Study on the Circular Economy and its effects on Occupational Safety and Health* (EU-OSHA, 2021b); *The circular economy and safety*

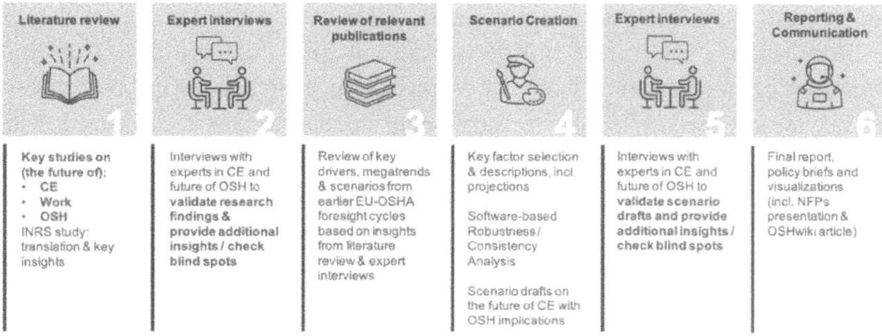

Fig. 11. Overall project approach.

On the methodology: Developing four alternative scenarios

The central foresight methodology followed was the key-factor-based scenario methodology. This methodology uses key factors to capture main developments and changes in the field in question, in this case the future of the circular economy and its potential effects on OSH. This approach was selected principally on account of its ability to integrate existing insights from a variety of sources, e.g., information on trends and drivers, and relevant megatrends. The identification of key factors (as well as later steps in the scenario development) was drawn from two pillars of results: (1) secondary research via a literature review and the review of relevant previous EU-OSHA publications (2) feedback and insights via expert interviews.

With any scenario study it is important to highlight the desired role that the scenarios are created to fulfil, which is to encourage discussion around what these alternative pathways may imply for the future, and what that means for present-day options for action. They are meant to encourage dialogue and reflection with stakeholders around future possibilities, with the aim of informing today's policy- and decision-makers in an anticipatory manner. Thus, it needs to be stressed that these (and indeed any) scenarios are not intended and should not be interpreted as any type of prediction on what the future might or might

and health: project overview and next steps (EU-OSHA, 2021c); *What will the circular economy (CE) mean for occupational safety and health (OSH)?* (EU-OSHA, 2021d); *The circular economy and safety and health: The role of digitalisation in the circular economy and implications for occupational safety and health until 2040* (EU-OSHA, 2021e); *The Circular Economy and Safety and Health: Possible implications for future waste sector workplaces* (EU-OSHA, 2021 f).

not be. Rather, as the growing body of experience of foresight approaches in research and for supporting policy-making has made increasingly clear, they offer tangible insights into what the future could bring, and what these alternative pathways would imply for future and especially present-day options for action. They make discussion and reflection on future possibilities possible, with the aim of informing today's decision-making and making policy more future oriented (following the principle of anticipatory governance).

It is also important to note that these scenarios are not to be taken as the final result of the project. Rather, as a tool for co-operative sense-making, they are to provide an impulse and a basis for further discussion and to encourage in-depth reflection on what the results imply for OSH research, initiatives and policy-making today. The results of these discussions will in turn enrich and deepen the scenarios and all downstream results. Drawing from the specific insights gained from the reviewed literature, alongside the experts' perspectives collected in the interviews, and feedback from EU-OSHA representatives and advisory groups, these findings are condensed into narratives of four possible, imaginable, distinct, and alternative future developments up to 2040, with special emphasis placed on the effects on working conditions, as well as a first look at potential implications for OSH. The core summaries of these four scenarios are outlined below, with a recommendation to explore the final report for further depth of narrative, including how the pathways developed to 2040 in each scenario world, as well as key levers and turning points.

European Circular Economies (and OSH) in 2040: Four Scenarios[2]

The Roaring 40's – Fully Circular and Inclusive	Carbon Neutrality – of a Hazardous Kind	Staying Afloat – Amid Economic and Environmental Crises	Regional Circularities – with European Divides
In 2040, the products that sell best are those that are cradle-to-cradle and 'net-positive' in terms of social and environmental sustainability.	In 2040, Europe has achieved carbon neutrality. But with environmental outcomes taking top priority, job quality and working conditions have suffered – at least in some areas.	In 2040, work is what people want – any job will do. Keeping your head above the water is all that matters, the environment, social rights or job quality come a distant second.	By 2040, work has become a two-tier system: Contracted employees are well looked after, those in non-standard employment are not. Neither is the environment, with circularity being mostly regional.

2 All scenario visualisations were realised by Michelle Winkelsdorf.

Scenario 1: The Roaring 40s: fully circular and inclusive

In 2040, working conditions across all sectors are significantly better than they were two decades ago, pollution has been reduced to a minimum, businesses find that keeping a small footprint is good for the balance sheet, and public trust in policy-makers and national and European leaders is greater than ever. Implementing serious sustainability and realising the principles of "reduce, reuse, recycle" across all sectors takes a lot of collaborative fine-tuning, as does keeping workers safe and secure in a multifaceted labour environment with myriad platforms and forms of employment. But one key difference compared with the situation in 2020 is a palpable sense of optimism: with so many challenges successfully met, the future cannot be anything other than bright.
A glimpse into daily life in 2040, in this scenario:[3]

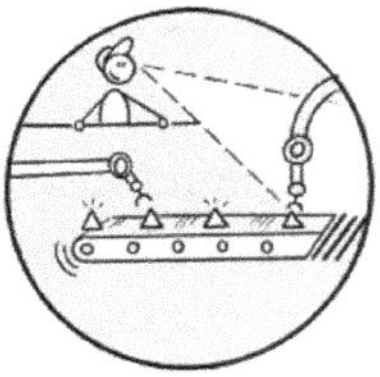

Aurélio Pereira, Urban Miner, Lisbon

"I can honestly say that I like what I do. Urban mining is never not interesting. There are so many positive facets to the job, and with your AI companion to manage risks and procedures (not to mention your schedule) it's a guaranteed safe workplace where you don't have to worry too much! Urban mining is both a hands-on and a desk job. I used to be a surveyor before that work became automated – like so many other professions. I retrained under the Just Transition Mechanism. To be a successful miner you need experience, you have to know how buildings used to be constructed, and you always have to be able to find workarounds. Oh, and you need to be able to read old plans. When was something made? Can it be safely recycled and used? Can you get it out safely, separate it cleanly? Once you've established that, had your samples tested, you move on to the desk part of the work: it's time to find a recycler, a buyer, or a leaser, hire a platform crew, while getting

3 These narrative scenario vignettes illustrate how daily life and work could change by 2040 and have been developed for all four scenarios. For brevity, we have as an example only included the one for the first scenario; for all scenario vignettes see the full report (EU-OSHA, 2021a).

everything done with the builder breathing down your neck because they want to get going NOW with retrofitting and rebuilding. There are other enjoyable parts of the job as well: over the next three months, I'm going to be doing a Material Flow Analysis for a small town near Salamanca to determine their urban metabolism. As I said, it's never boring."

The scenario's key message: "The Roaring 40s" is a best-of-all-worlds scenario: not only do policy-makers and stakeholders (having realised the gravity of the situation) make bold decisions to achieve real, far-reaching sustainability, but worker safety and health is also a key concern and is fully realised. This scenario demonstrates that one does not have to come at the expense of the other, and that both can be achieved in a competitive economy. But, even in this positive situation, OSH will always come up against new challenges, and constant improvement remains necessary.

Scenario 2: Carbon neutrality: of a hazardous kind

In the early 2020s, a warming climate, extreme weather events and habitat loss took centre stage in the public mind. Eco-consciousness reigned, leading to a surge in environmental regulation and environmentally-friendly industry practices. However, with the bulk of funding spent on renewable energy infrastructure and circular economy initiatives, social concerns fell by the wayside. Social infrastructures and services, social rights, inclusion, and job quality have declined for many.

The scenario's key message: "Carbon neutrality" is a "mixed bag" scenario: it demonstrates that, given the right incentives, Europe would be able to kick its addiction to fossil fuels in an incredibly short time span and become a world leader in green technologies, but also that this speed would come at a cost for workers. Unless measures are taken to secure a "just transition" during which workers receive all the (organisational) support and develop all the skills necessary to work new jobs safely, accidents and work-related diseases will increase, even with the use of new, safer technologies. In addition, regional challenges will vary much more widely in a localised economy: areas that sourced much of their employment from fossil fuel energy generation would find themselves faced with rapidly growing unemployment and an exodus of workers with outdated skills, while the OSH-relevant knowledge necessary for the safe dismantling of old energy infrastructures may be lacking. If OSH must take a back seat to a speedy transition to carbon neutrality, the human cost could be considerable, and stakeholders are challenged to not let this happen.

Scenario 3: Staying afloat: amid economic and environmental crises

Recessions, cuts in public spending, environmental crises, and rising unemployment: headlines in 2040 make for grim reading. In the business community, it is a rat race and everyone for themselves; competitiveness and profits are all that count. New technologies, rationalisation and digitalisation have created an ever-growing pool of workers who lack the qualifications, as well as the supporting working conditions, that are necessary to make it in this new, cut-throat economy. Platform work brings rewards to only a few, and, even in the sectors where it is booming, the "Russian doll effect" of sub-contracts within sub-contracts means that workers never see their fair share. The circular economy remains a distant dream, and the transition everyone went through was neither green nor just.

The scenario's key message: in "Staying afloat", the millennium's second decade never delivered on its promises. Policy-makers and stakeholders never dared to make the "big jump" and failed to grasp the opportunity offered by public support for a green transition and the shake-up provided by the COVID-19 pandemic. Now, economic success often comes at the expense of both worker safety and health and the environment, putting OSH institutions and other actors in the OSH field (policy-makers, etc.) under enormous pressure to improve the situation workers find themselves in, and they become less and less able to address core issues comprehensively.

Scenario 4: Regional circularities: with European divides

For both policy-makers and the public, a safe, growing economy was the overriding concern of recent decades. The environment fell by the wayside, but not everywhere. Richer European regions could afford to outsource disposal of waste and pollution to other world regions or poorer EU Member States, and now boast some sort of localised circular economies, but the loops are never fully closed: gaps are simply offshored. Social inclusion was also neglected. With good jobs available to only a minority of well-trained, highly skilled individuals, a growing number of workers are driven towards the informal economy and to unregulated, underpaid and increasingly precarious employment.

The scenario's key message: "Regional circularities" emphasises the dangers inherent in regional and social disparities. Not only is responsibility for waste disposal and polluting practices shifted from the rich to the poorer regions, but the working population is also divided between those who enjoy safe working conditions and good social protection and others who must make do with very little in both respects. In this environment, realising high OSH standards for everyone will be challenging and require broad political coalitions, forcing OSH institutions to reach out and encourage other stakeholders to increase pressure on decision-makers.

Scenario implications and cross-cutting dimensions

In the scenario development process, it became clear that the two dimensions of digitalisation and waste management play a critical role in how the circular economy and OSH might develop until 2040, across all four scenarios. These two dimensions are explored in more detail in the section below.[4] In a subsequent section, key implications from across the scenario portfolio are highlighted.

Digitalisation in the circular economy

The political path towards the circular economy

In the 2015 United Nations Agenda 2030, the move towards more sustainable patterns of production and consumption was globally agreed: 12 of the 17 Sustainable Development Goals (SDGs) (UN, 2020a) adopted by all UN Member States depend directly on increasing resource efficiency to make resource use more sustainable (UNEP, 2017). Most directly connected to the concept of a circular economy are Targets 12.4 and 12.5 (UN, 2020b), which aim to "achieve the environmentally sound management of chemicals and all wastes throughout their lifecycle" and to "substantially reduce waste generation through prevention, reduction, recycling and reuse". At the same time, the EU adopted the Circular Economy Package (European Commission, 2015), its first plan to implement a circular economy. After adding plans for a second major transformation, the achievement of climate neutrality, four years later (European Commission, 2019b), the package was updated in 2020 (European Commission, 2020c, d).

These sustainability visions are supported by a digitalisation policy programme specifically intended to "[s]upport the circular economy" by, among other things, launching a "circular electronics initiative" and improving communication on the origin, composition (including hazardous and rare materials), end-of-life handling and recycling of products (European Commission, 2020f). The New Industrial Strategy for Europe, released in March 2020, stressed the

4 For a more in-depth exploration of these cross-cutting dimensions and the role they play for the future of the circular economy and OSH, see the respective policy briefs: *The circular economy and safety and health: The role of digitalisation in the circular economy and implications for occupational safety and health until 2040* (EU-OSHA, 2021e); *The Circular Economy and Safety and Health: Possible implications for future waste sector workplaces* (EU-OSHA, 2021 f).

role that European industry must play in this process (European Commission, 2020e). Currently, however, only a small number of companies are actively realising smart circular strategies and linking their long-term digital and circular plans, and they lack guidance on how to best leverage digital technologies to maximise resource efficiency (Kristoffersen et al., 2020).

The role of digitalisation in creating a circular economy

To achieve a circular economy, the functionality of materials, processes and products must be optimised and maintained for as long as possible to minimise waste and residues. Here, digitalisation plays a crucial role as a key enabler and accelerator of the circular economy: by providing accurate information on the availability, location and condition of products and materials; by making processes in and between businesses more efficient; and by minimising waste and transaction costs and promoting longer product lives (Antikainen et al., 2018). Closing the material loop: i.e., implementing a circular economy, "is primarily a problem of information" (WI, 2017): without the free flow of huge amounts of data, it is impossible to track resources and resource use over a product's entire life cycle, focus on products-as-a-service business models, improve design, production and recycling, and provide consumers with better, actionable information on the environmental costs of consumption choices.

Today, online platforms, smart devices, AI, the Internet of things (IoT) and blockchain are already used to "improve design, production, consumption, reuse, repair, remanufacturing and waste management, including recycling" (EPC, 2020). But digitalisation does not automatically increase sustainability; unwanted rebound effects are possible. For example, e-commerce can be used to lower resource use (sharing economy) but may also be an enabler of increased consumption with a high material and energy footprint (online purchases). Furthermore, the energy and raw materials required for digitalisation are problematic: if unchecked, the ICT footprint could increase to 14 % of global emissions by 2040 (European Commission, 2020 f).

Digitalisation in the circular economy: effects on OSH[5]

Improved data provision and transfer make it possible to trace products and materials across their entire life cycles, allowing for safer sharing and

5 Note: this section looks only at the general, non-scenario-specific effects digitalisation in the circular economy could have on OSH. For an in-depth, detailed and more task-focused discussion of OSH outcomes, please see an earlier report by EU-OSHA on digitalisation (EU-OSHA, 2018) as well as the final project report (EU-OSHA, 2021a).

recycling of products and safer processing of waste streams. Better informing and empowering of consumers and workers offer the chance for timely safety feedback through digital channels (e.g., on products failing while in use, or suggestions for better OSH practices), while digital tools will improve consumer handling of end-of-life products (no more batteries in household waste, etc.). Digitally enabled increased flexibility of working arrangements (regarding working hours and workplaces) to lower resource use (i.e., reduced need for offices, which stand empty during weekends, better transport use, greater worker autonomy to reduce overheads, etc.) would likely remove some OSH risks (fewer commutes, etc.), but greater worker autonomy could also increase psychosocial stress and lead to unclear OSH responsibilities.

In a circular economy, digital platforms are used to better allocate resources (e.g., to distribute tools, or in Platform as a Service (PaaS) business models) (EPC, 2020). Allocating workers to jobs or tasks using digital platforms can lead to workers taking on jobs despite being unaware of OSH risks, best practices and guidelines, or place workers under increased pressure to ignore OSH regulations, and could result in a highly fragmented OSH landscape, complicating inspections. On the other hand, easier reskilling using online platforms offers the chance to improve overall OSH awareness, in particular regarding a more diverse working population.

Waste management in the circular economy

The political path towards the circular economy

The European Commission is committed to moving Europe towards a sustainable future. This green vision has two cornerstones, achieving climate neutrality (by 2050) (European Commission, 2019b) and creating a circular economy (European Commission, 2020c). A future "closed loop" society will ideally be wasteless or will at least have greatly minimised all potential waste streams. As "take, make, waste" makes way for "refuse, reduce, reuse, recycle", thinking around waste shifts towards understanding waste as a resource as opposed to a burden. This transformation will have considerable impacts on the waste sector in general, and specifically on OSH in the waste sector.

A wasteless future in the circular economy

With the right use of new technologies ("exponential technologies"), we have the opportunity to resolve the problems related to waste management and recycling (Mavropoulos, 2016). The fourth industrial revolution is already a reality in the waste industry, with digital technologies used in monitoring and processing, and new applications currently being tested (e.g., 3D printers in plastic recycling, autonomous collection vehicles, etc.) (ISWA, 2019). Going forward, digital technologies are likely to make waste management regimes more and more effective. Recycling in Europe could improve, use of recyclates ("secondary raw materials") would become easier, and citizens would have the opportunity to make better purchasing and sorting decisions (EEA, 2021). With spatial and temporal patterns of waste generation better understood, green behaviour can be incentivised ("pay-as-you-throw" systems), reducing the risk of unforeseen materials in the waste stream, while the hazardous parts of waste processing (sorting in particular) could be further automated and even remotely managed.

Waste management in the circular economy: Effects on OSH[6]

(Domestic) waste collection and transport by autonomous vehicles could minimise risks for workers, while a greater sensor density could increase awareness of waste stream contents, reducing hazards to workers during handling and sorting. The latter could be increasingly done by learning robots, which are becoming more adept at identifying recyclable components in complex waste streams (PwC, 2018). Human-robot interaction, on the other hand, is likely to become more complex, as workers potentially misestimate robot capabilities and situational awareness. Over-reliance on automation may also lead to deskilling, in particular regarding emergency situations. If workers manage automated processes without contact with other human beings, psychosocial risks may increase. Unless there is regulatory pressure to fully explore recyclability prior to introduction, new materials entering the waste stream may lead to new risks in waste processing. Standardisation of electronics and other complex products could dramatically increase safety in dismantling, however. Continuous reskilling in the waste sector could help workers to better navigate the increased complexity of a more automated environment, reducing the likelihood of OSH events.

6 Note: this section looks only at the general non-scenario-specific or cross-cutting effects the circular economy could have on OSH in the waste sector. For an in-depth, detailed and more task-focused discussion of OSH outcomes and perspectives in the waste sector, please see earlier reports by EU-OSHA on the waste sector (e.g., EU-OSHA, 2007; 2019a; 2019b; 2020c; 2019f; 2020e; 2020f; 2020i) as well as the final project report (EU-OSHA, 2021a).

Key implications for the future of work and OSH across the four scenarios

The four scenarios show that the potential pathways for a circular economy in Europe and their effects on working conditions could vary widely, with a similarly wide-ranging set of first implications for OSH and respective possible future policy areas, among them e.g. increased risks from repeated recycling processes, as well as e.g. opportunities around a socio-ecological transformation approach that includes the integration of OSH considerations from the very first stages of product development and design. From the scenarios and the underlying research, a number of cross-cutting and overarching key messages were identified:

As yet, there is no widely shared or common definition and understanding of what a circular economy is. This contributes to a certain "fuzziness" around existing assumptions and expectations of potential future developments regarding circular economy, and opens the door to the term and its concepts being used for the purpose of greenwashing.

Any reflection on circular economy perspectives in Europe will need to consider global repercussions, as well as value and production chain effects. A paradigm shift towards circular economy principles could be implemented sensibly and ethically, but only if the approach integrates global production chains and elements over the whole life cycle of any product and material.

The European waste sector will need to play a pivotal role in the development of any future circular economy. The integration of new technologies while meeting new challenges will be a complex undertaking, but the necessary reskilling offensive offers opportunities to considerably improve OSH practices and outcomes for workers: if OSH considerations are made an inherent part of this process from the beginning.

Digitalisation is a key enabler and accelerator for the circular economy. A high standard of OSH in a circular economy will be achieved only if digitalisation processes, such as building a universal information ecosystem (a safe data space that minimises manipulation risks) or creating a monitoring system to prevent illegal imports of products that may be hazardous during recycling, are well managed. Accordingly, OSH measures will need to keep pace with these rapid digital changes.

A fundamental shift towards a circular economy seems possible only if driven by robust regulatory efforts and policy mechanisms. Circularity can be achieved only if life-cycle responsibility rests with the manufacturer, and measures are taken to internalise external costs of any material and product life cycle.

Any fundamental shift towards a circular economy would probably have to involve the far-reaching reorganisation of the value chain and the emergence of new actors. This would probably lead to second- and third-order effects on infrastructure to accommodate new feedback loops and more collaborative material streams.

Thus, the large-scale implementation of a circular economy would: based on the principle of a "just transition", come with a significant opportunity to advance OSH conditions but could also lead to the emergence of new risks and undesired side effects (especially around repeated recycling). From another perspective, emerging risks also have the potential to be used as (growth) opportunities: but only if there are clear cost incentives and suitable markets.

Furthermore, the range of progress in the circular economy and the integration of OSH measures could differ widely between regions, EU Member States and sectors, and the risks as well as opportunities for OSH could similarly vary widely. Making sure that there is sufficient support for all regions, sectors, and countries, especially those with comparatively fewer resources, will be a major factor in ensuring that OSH is advanced alongside any kind of progress towards a circular economy.

Concluding remarks and outlook towards next steps

The current decade will be crucial for Europe's future: How can we achieve a future in which the speedy transition to carbon neutrality and a circular economy is successfully managed, where changes also contribute to increased safety and health of workers?

The four scenarios and the underlying research showed that the potential pathways for the circular economy in Europe and their effects on working conditions could vary widely, with a similarly wide-ranging set of first implications and opportunities for OSH and associated future policy. Notably, the study also showed that a window of opportunity currently presents itself for advancing the circular economy and realising OSH improvements simultaneously. This is attributable to several factors, among them a recently increased focus on the interconnectedness of the social and environmental pillars of sustainability, and a growing awareness that an integrated view of efforts in those areas will clearly benefit the third pillar of sustainability, the economic sphere (a "just transition"). Ensuring that OSH perspectives and solutions are included or even pushed within the context of these transformation efforts could be a lever to bring about fundamental progress along the lines of both the circular economy and OSH goals.

In the follow-up phase to this project, the focus centres on stakeholder engagement, i.e., on involving a variety of actors in developing more in-depth insights, and co-creatively reflecting on future action needs and options, with the overall aim of informing today's decision-making towards making policy more future-oriented and making tomorrow's work healthier and safer.

References

Antikainen, Maria, Uusitalo, Teuve, and Kivikytö-Reponen, Päivi (2018). Digitalisation as an enabler of circular economy. *Procedia CIRP* 73, pp. 45–49. https://doi.org/10.1016/j.procir.2018.04.027

EEA – European Environmental Agency (2021). Digital technologies will deliver more efficient waste management in Europe. https://www.eea.europa.eu/themes/waste/waste-management/digital-technologies-will-deliver-more

EPC – European Policy Centre (2020). The circular economy: Going digital. https://circulareconomy.europa.eu/platform/sites/default/files/drce_final.pdf

EPSU – European Federation of Public Service Unions (2017). Waste management in Europe. Good jobs in the circular economy? https://circulareconomy.europa.eu/platform/en/knowledge/waste-management-europe-good-jobs-circular-economy

EPSU – European Federation of Public Service Unions (2020). Safe jobs in the circular economy. Health and Safety in Waste and Wastewater Management. https://www.epsu.org/sites/default/files/article/files/FINAL_Safe%20Jobs%20in%20the%20Circular%20Economy_EN.pdf

EU-OSHA – European Agency for Safety and Health at Work (2007). Expert forecast on emerging biological risks related to occupational safety and health. https://osha.europa.eu/de/publications/report-expert-forecast-emerging-biological-risks-related-occupational-safety-and-health/view

EU-OSHA – European Agency for Safety and Health at Work (2018). Foresight on new and emerging occupational safety and health risks associated with digitalisation by 2025. https://osha.europa.eu/en/publications/foresight-new-and-emerging-occupational-safety-and-health-risks-associated-digitalisation-2025/view

EU-OSHA – European Agency for Safety and Health at Work (2019a). Exposure to biological agents and related health effects in the waste management and wastewater treatment sectors. https://osha.europa.eu/en/publications/exposure-biological-agents-and-related-health-effects-waste-management-and-wastewater/view

EU-OSHA – European Agency for Safety and Health at Work (2019b). Biological agents and work-related diseases: results of a literature review, expert survey and analysis of monitoring systems. https://osha.europa.eu/en/publications/biological-agents-and-work-related-diseases-results-literature-review-expert-survey-and/view

EU-OSHA – European Agency for Safety and Health at Work (2020a). Accidents and injuries in the waste management sector. https://oshwiki.eu/wiki/Accidents_and_injuries_in_the_waste_management_sector

EU-OSHA – European Agency for Safety and Health at Work (2020b). Exposure to dangerous substances in the waste management sector. https://oshwiki.eu/wiki/Exposure_to_dangerous_substances_in_the_waste_management_sector

EU-OSHA – European Agency for Safety and Health at Work (2020c). Waste management. https://oshwiki.eu/wiki/Waste_management

EU-OSHA – European Agency for Safety and Health at Work (2021a). Foresight study on the circular economy and its effects on OSH. https://osha.europa.eu/en/publications/foresight-study-circular-economy-and-its-effects-occupational-safety-and-health/view

EU-OSHA – European Agency for Safety and Health at Work (2021b). Executive summary – Foresight study on the circular economy and its effects on occupational safety and health. https://osha.europa.eu/en/publications/executive-summary-foresight-study-circular-economy-and-its-effects-occupational-safety-and-health

EU-OSHA – European Agency for Safety and Health at Work (2021c). The circular economy and safety and health: project overview and next steps. https://osha.europa.eu/en/publications/circular-economy-and-safety-and-health-project-overview-and-next-steps

EU-OSHA – European Agency for Safety and Health at Work (2021d). What will the circular economy (CE) mean for occupational safety and health (OSH)? https://osha.europa.eu/en/publications/what-will-circular-economy-ce-mean-occupational-safety-and-health-osh

EU-OSHA – European Agency for Safety and Health at Work (2021e). The circular economy and safety and health: The role of digitalisation in the circular economy and implications for occupational safety and health until 2040. https://osha.europa.eu/en/publications/circular-economy-and-safety-and-health-role-digitalisation-circular-economy-and-implications-occupational-safety-and-health-until-2040

EU-OSHA – European Agency for Safety and Health at Work (2021f). The Circular Economy and Safety and Health: Possible implications for future waste sector workplaces. https://osha.europa.eu/en/publications/circular-economy-and-safety-and-health-possible-implications-future-waste-sector-workplaces

European Commission (2015). Closing the loop – An EU action plan for the Circular Economy. COM/2015/0614 final of 2 December 2015. https://eur-lex.europa.eu/legal-content/EN/TXT/?uri=CELEX%3A52015DC0614

European Commission (2019a). A European Green Deal. https://ec.europa.eu/info/strategy/priorities-2019-2024/european-green-deal_en

European Commission (2019b). The European Green Deal. COM/2019/640 final of 11 December 2019. https://eur-lex.europa.eu/legal-content/EN/ALL/?uri=CELEX%3A52019DC0640

European Commission (2020c). A new Circular Economy Action Plan for a cleaner and more competitive Europe. COM/2020/98 final of 11 March 2020. https://eur-lex.europa.eu/legal-content/EN/TXT/?uri=COM:2020:98:FIN

European Commission (2020d). In focus: renewable energy in Europe. https://ec.europa.eu/info/news/focus-renewable-energy-europe-2020-mar-18_en

European Commission (2020e). White paper. On artificial intelligence – A European approach to excellence and trust. COM/2020/65 final of 19 February 2020. https://ec.europa.eu/info/sites/info/files/commission-white-paper-artificial-intelligence-feb2020_en.pdf

European Commission (2020f). Supporting the Green Transition. Shaping Europe's digital future. https://ec.europa.eu/commission/presscorner/api/files/attachment/862091/Supporting_the_green_transition_en.pdf.pdf

ISWA – International Solid Waste Association (2019). How Industry 4.0 transforms the waste sector. Key messages. https://www.iswa.org/knowledge-base/how-industry-4-0-transforms-the-waste-sector-key-messages/?v=3a52f3c22ed6

Kristoffersen, Eivind; Blomsma, Fenna; Mikalef, Patrick; and Li, Jingyue (2020). The smart circular economy: a Digital-enabled circular strategies framework for manufacturing companies. *Journal of Business Research*, 120, pp. 241–261. https://doi.org/10.1016/j.jbusres.2020.07.044

Mavropoulos, Antonis (2016). Vision for a wasteless future. http://wastelessfuture.com/pdf/Vision_for_a_Wastelessfuture.pdf

PwC – PricewaterhouseCoopers (2018). Closing the loop. The circular economy, what it means and what it can do for you. https://www.pwc.com/hu/en/kiadvanyok/assets/pdf/Closing-the-loop-the-circular-economy.pdf

UN – United Nations (2020a). The Sustainable Development Agenda. https://www.un.org/sustainabledevelopment/development-agenda/

UN – United Nations (2020b). Goal 12: Ensure sustainable consumption. https://www.un.org/sustainabledevelopment/sustainable-consumption-production/

UNEP – United Nations Environment Programme (2017). Resource efficiency: Potential and economic implications. http://www.resourcepanel.org/sites/default/files/documents/document/media/resource_efficiency_report_march_2017_web_res.pdf

WHO – World Health Organisation, Regional Office for Europe (2018). Circular economy and health: opportunities and risks. https://www.euro.who.int/en/publications/abstracts/circular-economy-and-health-opportunities-and-risks-2018

WI – Wuppertal Institute (2017). The digital circular economy: can the digital transformation pave the way for resource-efficient materials cycles? https://epub.wupperinst.org/frontdoor/deliver/index/docId/6978/file/6978_Wilts.pdf

III From policy to practice: Channels of implementation

Peter Totterdill[1] and Rosemary Exton[1]

Workplace innovation: Are we serious?

Abstract: Since its first formulation in the early years of the present century, the concept of workplace innovation has gained increasing attention amongst European policymakers and researchers. The chapter demonstrates workplace innovation as a generative, dialogical framework for stimulating and resourcing sustained organisational change in ways which are non-prescriptive and non-linear, leading to positive outcomes for staff and business performance alike.

Surveys, however, show that the adoption of workplace innovation practices at enterprise level remains limited across Europe, and that this should be a matter of concern for policymakers at EU, national and local levels. We argue that to make workplace innovation accessible to enterprise-level decision-makers and employees, it must evolve into a grounded, practice-focused framework. The chapter discusses one such approach, *The Essential Fifth Element*, as a means of addressing the limited adoption of workplace innovation practices and thereby realising key public policy goals.

Keywords: EUWIN, social dialogue, employee-driven innovation, productivity, public policy, workplace innovation

Introduction

This chapter draws on the experience of the authors as co-leaders of Workplace Innovation Europe CLG, a not-for-profit organisation created to promote the concept and practice of workplace innovation through research, consultancy, workforce development and policy advocacy. It also reflects the authors' close involvement in EUWIN (the European Workplace Innovation Network) since its creation in 2013 as a community of researchers, policymakers, social partners and enterprises.

Since its first formulation in the early years of the present century (Totterdill et al., 2002), workplace innovation has gained increasing attention in Europe as a focus for research, generating a growing body of evidence on its efficacy in achieving the simultaneous enhancement of business performance and employee wellbeing (for example, McMurray et al., 2021; Oeij et al., 2017), though case studies of workplace innovation as a participative process are only just beginning to emerge.

We also know from successive EU-wide surveys (most recently the 2019 European Company Survey) that less than 20 % of European companies use

1 Workplace Innovation Europe CLG, Cork, Exeter & Glasgow.

workplace innovation practices systematically throughout their organisations, resulting in the large-scale loss of potential gains in business performance, workforce skills and wellbeing (Eurofound and Cedefop, 2020). Is workplace innovation one of Europe's biggest wasted resources?

Partly in response to the substantial lag between evidence and practice, workplace innovation has gained the attention of policymakers both in the European Commission and in a growing number of national governments, boosted by the creation of EUWIN (Pot et al., 2021). Yet whilst current EU and national level policy commitments to workplace innovation are most welcome, the scale of resources allocated to supporting change on the ground is not sufficient to the challenge of closing the gap between the most and the least advanced companies in Europe. Likewise the design of funding mechanisms is often flawed, focusing on short-term instrumental outcomes rather than realising the full transformative potential of workplace innovation (Johnsen et al., 2021; Totterdill, 2020).

We argue that to make workplace innovation accessible to enterprise-level decision-makers, it must evolve into a grounded, practice-focused framework. One such approach, *The Essential Fifth Element* (Exton & Totterdill, 2019; Totterdill, 2015) is grounded in tangible workplace practices associated with high performance and high quality of working life. Generic principles and exemplary case examples associated with these practices act as a generative resource for questioning and reinventing current ways of working through participative dialogue and the deployment of tacit knowledge. This chapter discusses the potential of *The Essential Fifth Element* both as a means of addressing the limited adoption of workplace innovation practices and of addressing key public policy goals in Europe and beyond.

Workplace innovation as a bridge between theory and practice

How should company decision-makers and change leaders navigate a vast and growing body of research, dating back at least as far as the iconic Tavistock Institute studies of the 1950s? And how should they learn from the experiences of European companies that had succeeded in achieving exemplary performance and enhanced capacity for product and service innovation at the same time as creating high quality working lives for their employees?

In 2001, the European Commission requested a study designed to analyse evidence both from existing literature and from an international sample of more than one hundred private and public sector organisations, each characterised by high performance and high quality of working life. The aim of the Hi-Res study (Totterdill et al., 2002), involving collaboration across eight EU countries, was to elaborate the "high road" of win-win outcomes for organisations and their employees, as previously articulated by the Commission-sponsored European Work & Technology Consortium (1998).

Many different terms were in use to describe these high road approaches including high performance workplaces, high involvement workplaces and innovative work organisation. Although terminologies might differ, all these approaches placed a premium on employee participation and a better utilisation of existing human talent within organisations, primarily by (re)designing the organisation of work and tasks to enable people to be more effective and creative. The shared objective was to improve quality of working life and organisational performance simultaneously (Pot et al., 2016). Yet these proliferating vocabularies were doing much to obscure the real choices available to company decision-makers.

The Hi-Res study sought to establish "workplace innovation" as a conceptual framework that is coherent, grounded in research evidence, yet action-oriented and aimed at company decision-makers and policymakers as well as researchers. Whilst references to "workplace innovation(s)" can be found in literature from the 1990s, they only loosely described the introduction of new forms of work organisation or direct participation. The Hi-Res report represents the first known attempt in Europe to define "workplace innovation" in detail, focusing on the adoption and contextualisation of specific organisational practices associated with high performance simultaneously with high quality of working life.

In broad terms, workplace innovation has been described as "new and combined interventions in work organisation, human resource management, labour relations and supportive technologies" (Pot, 2011). This broad term describes the participatory process of innovation which leads to empowering workplace practices and which, in turn, sustain continuing learning, reflection and innovation. (Totterdill et al, 2013).

The workplace innovation literature rejects prescriptive blueprints; rather it understands global concepts and practices as generative resources which organisational actors contextualise as "local theories" to fit their specific circumstances, resulting in tangible changes to workplace practice (Johnsen et al., 2021). Most importantly workplace innovation is an inherently social process, building skills and competence through creative collaboration.

Drawing on Scandinavian approaches to democratic dialogue (Gustavsen, 1992), workplace innovation seeks to engage all stakeholders in ways which enable the force of the better argument to prevail, building bridges between the strategic knowledge of business leaders, the professional and tacit knowledge of frontline employees and the organisational design knowledge of experts. It works towards "win-win" outcomes based on creatively forged convergence between enhanced organisational performance and quality of working life, leading to self-sustaining processes of participative organisational development fuelled by continuing learning and experimentation.

Workplace innovation is also a systemic approach, influenced both by studies of failed organisational change (for example, Business Decisions Limited, 2002) and by the European sociotechnical design tradition in recognising the interdependence of organisational practice;(Mohr& Van Amelsvoort, 2015) likewise it reflects other bodies of research which emphasise the combination of representative and direct participation in achieving superior outcomes for organisations and their employees (Boxall & Purcell, 2003; Teague, 2005).

EUWIN has recently gone further in attempting to identify the distinctiveness of workplace innovation as a theoretically robust yet practically focused approach to organisational transformation. Its Manifesto (EUWIN, 2021) identifies nine defining characteristics:

"Workplace innovation is:

1. Part of a strategic choice, running through the organisation's entire business model and underpinned by a long-term vision and perspectives, sustainability and ethics.
2. Strongly associated with the *simultaneous* achievement of high performance and high quality of working life – and contributing to wider society.
3. Separate from – but builds on – "fair work" principles such as job security, living wage, equality & diversity, and opportunities for training and education.
4. Promoting occupational safety & health primarily, but not exclusively, through job content (e.g. decision latitude, skill discretion), stress prevention, wellbeing and sustainable employability
5. Focused on workplace practices grounded in substantial research and case study evidence.
6. Based on high levels of employee involvement and empowerment, combining direct and representative participation.
7. A *systemic* approach recognising the interdependence of work organisation, technologies, control structure and labour relations.
8. Not a blueprint. Generic principles and experience are generative resources contextualised within each organisation through inclusive dialogue, experimentation and learning.
9. Not just about changing organisations – it changes and develops the people who work in them. It is strongly associated with trust, accountability, curiosity, creativity, coaching behaviours & emotional intelligence, all of which grow with the workplace innovation journey."

In parallel with its role as a focal point for research and policy advocacy, workplace innovation has emerged as a practice-based framework in the form of "*The Essential Fifth Element*" (Totterdill, 2015). This was initially devised to help communicate the essence of workplace innovation for EUWIN, and in particular to provide a practical framework to stimulate and resource the adoption of workplace innovation practices by enterprises.

Expanding the original Hi-Res framework, and based on a further analysis of published research and case study evidence, *The Essential Fifth Element* identified four bundles (or "Elements") of working practices with a strong association between high performance and high quality of working life (see Tab. 15). Whilst

Tab. 15. The Essential Fifth Element

Element	**Indicative practices**	**Associated outcomes**
Jobs, teams & technology	Individual discretion Job variety Constructive challenges Self-managed teams Collaboration within the team Reflective team practices People-centred technologies	Improved workflow Enhanced quality Better productivity Cost reduction Engagement and retention Improved workforce health
Organisational structures, management and procedures	Reduced hierarchies and silos Strengths-based career structure Coaching style line management Appraisals focused on learning and innovation Simplified procedures	Improved workflow Cost reduction Better productivity Engagement & retention Improved workforce health
Employee-driven innovation & improvement	Productive reflection in teams Cross-team improvement groups Permission to experiment Company-wide innovation events	Enhanced capacity for innovation & improvement Enterprising behaviour Enhanced quality & performance Learning & development Engagement & retention Intrinsic job satisfaction
Co-Created leadership & employee voice	Openness and transparency Emotionally intelligent behaviours Visible leadership Delegated decision-making Representative participation	Strategic alignment Better decision-making Engagement and retention
The fifth element	A self-sustaining culture of empowerment and innovation	Win-win outcomes for the organisation and its employees

each of these Elements bundles together closely interrelated workplace practices, they are also strongly interdependent. Alignment between the Elements creates a synergy in the "Fifth Element", a system of mutually interdependent parts which leads to a sustainable culture of innovation and empowerment embedded throughout the organisation

In short, *The Essential Fifth Element* provides a structured evidential framework to stimulate and inform participative "productive reflection" (Boud et al., 2006; Cressey et al., 2013) and dialogue, leading to the introduction of innovative or improved workplace practices.

An evolving portfolio of practical resources were developed by Workplace Innovation Europe (WIE) to support change at enterprise level in line with *The Essential Fifth Element.* For example, the Workplace Innovation Diagnostic® survey instrument asks employees questions relating to 49 specific workplace practices described by *The Essential Fifth Element.* Following the Diagnostic results, the Workplace Innovation Practitioner Programme provides in-company change facilitators with the actionable knowledge, skills and practical resources required to address the resulting challenges and opportunities in a highly participative manner, supported by peer-to-peer knowledge exchange and shared problem solving.

The following case illustrates the process of contextualising the generic concepts and practices described by *The Essential Fifth Element* within a specific organisational setting. It begins within a national programme funded by Scottish Enterprise (Scotland's national economic development agency), and delivered by WIE. The programme was designed to stimulate the adoption of workplace innovation in Scotland by combining learning and development of individual change leaders with the deployment of their newly acquired knowledge and skills in the facilitation of participative organisational change. Cohorts of nine or ten companies took part in a programme that blended the Workplace Innovation Diagnostic® with semi-structured workshops, interactive e-learning, peer-to-peer action learning, and on-site facilitation (Exton & Totterdill, 2019).

The Essential Fifth Element and the case of Booth Welsh

Booth Welsh is a specialist engineering services company located in Scotland. Previously a family-owned business, Booth Welsh is now part of the Australian Clough Group, which nonetheless affords the company a high level of autonomy in managing its operations. Two members of staff were the company's lead representatives in the Scottish Enterprise programme during 2017–2018 – Aimee (Marketing and Communications) and Gordon (Senior Engineer), assuming the role of principal change agents.

Booth Welsh surveyed its entire workforce using the Workplace Innovation Diagnostic®, and the results confirmed earlier suspicions that, whilst employees were committed to their own areas of work, they were disengaged from the wider company and its strategic direction to a significant extent. They also reported few opportunities to take part in improvement and innovation, and often worked in functional silos with little interaction with the rest of the business.

The findings were of particular concern to the company's senior leadership, which recognised the importance of harnessing staff engagement and innovation potential in order to give Booth Welsh a competitive lead, particularly in respect of emerging digital technologies.

The Diagnostic results provided the framework for a medium-term plan for change, instigating innovations relating to each of the workplace practices summarised in Tab. 15, in every case shaped by dialogue with staff in a range of participative events. With broad workforce participation and active support from WIE's advisers, Booth Welsh was able to translate its Diagnostic results into a clear plan of action, leading to targeted changes from the senior team to the frontline.

One of the initial steps took the form of a facilitated, two-day time out session for a cross-section of managers and staff to analyse the Diagnostic results. The second day was organised as a "Dialogue Conference" (Gustavsen, 1992), and scenario exercises during the session generated a much clearer vision of the company's medium-term direction of travel than had previously been articulated. The vision was one in which innovation (particularly digital innovation) would become the dominant driver for growth, enabled by an empowered and upskilled workforce, while internal policies and practices would be streamlined and enhanced to improve performance and excellence across the organisation. Four "Pillars" were identified (Fig. 12), representing the strategic priorities that would need to be addressed to achieve the vision, and also providing a readily communicable message to stimulate staff involvement.

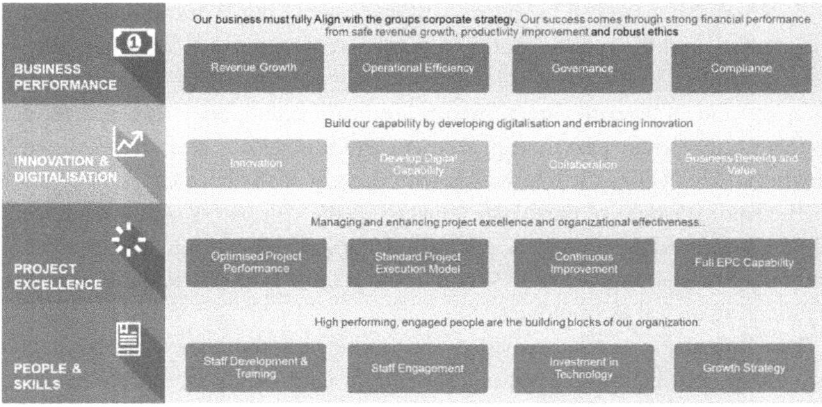

Fig. 12. Booth Welsh's Strategic Pillars.

Company strategy came thus to be seen not just as a means of guiding the business but of harnessing creativity and leadership potential currently underutilised within the workforce. By stimulating broad workforce participation, Booth Welsh sought to translate its Diagnostic results into a clear plan of action, leading to targeted changes from the senior team to the frontline.

The Pillars were communicated to the workforce not as a *fait accompli* but as a challenge. Martin Welsh, the MD, was explicit in his feedback to staff: the company's strategy could not be developed or delivered by the senior team alone but required the knowledge, talent and creativity of everyone. Moreover "strategy" was to be an iterative process based on experimentation and shared learning rather than a one-off effort. In practice, this took the form of an open invitation to all members of staff to lead or to be involved in a working group, project or initiative associated with one or more Pillars. Company-wide dialogue events and forums also ensured alignment across the Pillars.

Staff participation in the Pillars therefore became an important vehicle both for strategy development and workplace innovation. This involved a considerable change in mindset across the senior team and depended on a willingness to embrace more a distributed leadership model based on greater openness, trust and delegation. In essence, whilst ultimate responsibility remains at board level, it means that strategic leadership is no longer the sole prerogative of senior team members.

Initial outcomes

> *The benefits we have seen internally in the business have been quite dramatic in a short space of time. We pinch ourselves and think when we started this and how quickly we have got delivery.*
>
> *Martin Welsh, MD, Booth Welsh (June 2018)*

For Booth Welsh, the result has been a surge of employee creativity and initiative, ranging from minor incremental improvements to strategically significant innovations.

More than half the workforce volunteered to help develop and deliver the company's strategic objectives through their involvement in the Pillars – as well as undertaking their day-to-day tasks. Alongside this, "Co-Lab" events provided each team and department the opportunity to display their own areas of work and current projects to everyone else in the workforce, creating a greater sense of cohesion, promoting shared learning and stimulating cross-functional collaboration and innovation. A dedicated innovation space was created as a resource available to all members of staff, and including AR/VR resources to stimulate creative thinking. The importance of informal interaction was also acknowledged by the creation of "Café Zero" in the reception area for staff and visitors.

Over 60 ideas for innovation and improvement were generated by staff at the outset, and work subsequently continued to ensure that opportunities for productive reflection (Cressey et al., 2013) and creative thinking are embedded in day-to-day working life.

Critically, this new climate of innovation has encouraged and enabled both senior team members and the wider workforce to explore and embrace digital technologies, both to enhance performance at Booth Welsh and as an enhanced offer for the company's clients. Finding opportunities to introduce improved and innovative services through digitalisation is gradually becoming part of the narrative running through day-to-day discourse within the company, particularly through the Pillar groups.

Progress was reflected in significantly improved results when the Workplace Innovation Diagnostic® was re-run in 2018, though several remaining red and amber scores provided plenty of targets for the next stage of the transformation process.

Towards a sustainable momentum of workplace innovation

Booth Welsh recognised that the process of transformation required longer-term commitment than that offered by the Scottish Enterprise programme, moving beyond the provision of opportunities for staff engagement in strategy and innovation into organisational redesign. The WIE team were retained by the company to provide continuing, bespoke support.

Following a series of participative workshops facilitated by WIE during 2019, a renewed vision was expressed in terms of a "Pillar Refresh" (Tab. 16). The table shows how the redesign of workplace practices represented by *The Essential Fifth Element* helps to realise the achievement of Booth Welsh's four strategic Pillars.

During this period, the role of the WIE team shifted towards a greater emphasis on participative dialogue and creating opportunities for productive reflection and action planning. At the same time, Aimee and Gordon joined WIE's Senior Practitioner Programme, providing them with advanced knowledge and insights into workplace innovation, as well as developing enhanced facilitation and coaching skills. Accreditation enables Senior Practitioners to coach and mentor their colleagues within the company on the Practitioner Programme.

Martin, Aimee, Gordon and their colleagues are focusing on creating a flatter organisation based on self-organised teamworking to meet the innovation challenges of the post-COVID, digital world. A further nineteen people from across the company were recruited as change facilitators and are undertaking the Workplace Innovation Practitioner Programme, mentored by Aimee and Gordon as well as by the WIE team. At the same time, Martin Welsh and twelve other members of the senior team are participating in a development programme that includes workplace innovation awareness and building emotionally intelligent leadership competencies. Each of these programmes involves participant involvement in at least one action group, planning and overseeing the implementation of a significant aspect of the company's transformation relating to the "Pillar Refresh" (Tab. 16):

- Self-organised teamworking
- Redesigned ('strengths-based') management roles
- Rethinking performance measurement and improvement
- Emotionally intelligent leadership and culture
- Employee-driven innovation
- Employee voice.

BUSINESS PERFORMANCE	Our business must fully Align with the groups corporate strategy. Our success comes through strong financial performance from safe revenue growth, productivity improvement and robust ethics Revenue Growth · Productivity Improvement · Governance · Compliance
Jobs, Teams, Technology	High performing, self-managing teams improve day-to-day decision-making, task allocation and workflow whilst taking responsibility for compliance.
Structures, Management, Procedures	Removing functional silos improves throughput and workflow. Line managers coach individual & team performance, avoiding micro-management.
Employee-Driven Innovation & Improvement	All staff experience regular opportunities to identify performance improvements as part of their normal routines.
Co-Created Leadership & Employee Voice	Employee Voice brings tacit knowledge and experience to key aspects of governance, e.g. risk assessment.

INNOVATION & DIGITALISATION	Build our capability by developing digitalisation and embracing innovation [illegible] · [illegible] · [illegible] · [illegible]
Jobs, Teams, Technology	Self-managing teams build productive reflection into their working practice, generating ideas for new products, services and processes.
Structures, Management, Procedures	Staff gain wider perspectives without functional silos , facilitating creative thinking. Line managers actively coach and support staff engagement in innovation. Appraisal & performance measurement support involvement in innovation.
Employee-Driven Innovation & Improvement	All staff experience regular opportunities to take part in innovation activities with colleagues from different parts of the company.
Co-Created Leadership & Employee Voice	Leadership visibly champions employee-driven innovation.

PROJECT EXCELLENCE	Managing and enhancing project excellence and organizational effectiveness.. Optimised Project Performance · Standard Project Execution Model · Continuous Improvement · Full EPC Capability
Jobs, Teams, Technology	Self-managing teams build productive reflection and continuous improvement into working practice, taking individual and collective responsibility for overall quality.
Structures, Management, Procedures	Standard Project Execution Model ensures all team members fully understand and engage with the project as a whole, breaking down silo mentality.
Employee-Driven Innovation & Improvement	All staff experience regular opportunities to take part in continuous improvement activities as part of their regular routine.
Co-Created Leadership & Employee Voice	Leadership actively investigates emerging trends and innovative practices globally, and builds capacity for organisational learning.

PEOPLE & SKILLS	High performing, engaged people are the building blocks of our organization. Staff Development & Training · Staff Engagement · Investment in Technology · Growth Strategy
Jobs, Teams, Technology	Individual and team empowerment combined with task variety stimulate continuous learning, development and job satisfaction. Investment in technologies builds on active staff participation.
Structures, Management, Procedures	Removal of silos enhances task variety, multi-disciplinary working and personal development.
Employee-Driven Innovation & Improvement	All staff experience regular opportunities to take part in innovation and improvement activities, enhancing personal development and engagement.
Co-Created Leadership & Employee Voice	Leadership actively champions staff empowerment, learning and development across the company. Employee Voice plays a key role in developing and delivering company strategy.

Tab. 16. Pillar refresh.

Challenges

Whilst Booth Welsh has built a sustained a degree of momentum in its workplace innovation journey, and repeating the Diagnostic in 2020 showed significant gains in practices relating to employee-driven innovation and employee voice. Nonetheless, challenges to realising the vision continue to emerge.

Booth Welsh's transformation takes place in the context of volatile market conditions, a global pandemic, and its acquisition of two additional companies working in related industry fields. Senior management attention has inevitably been stretched in several directions at once, with calls from some quarters to refocus on managing the day-to-day business rather than the vision for change. Reports from current Practitioner Programme participants suggest that several face competing pressures with very busy functional roles and individual/team performance metrics don't always recognise the time commitments required to drive forward change projects.

Overcoming such obstacles to change in this context requires a combination of sensitivity, willingness to experiment, and a consistent emphasis on the centrality of change to Booth Welsh's future from Martin Welsh and other members of the senior team.

Whilst obstacles remain to be overcome, by focusing on competence building through action-based learning, coaching and experimentation, the company is establishing an internal momentum backed by essential knowledge and competencies, and which can be sustained beyond the expectations of a traditional "change initiative".

Post Script: COVID and beyond

Compared with many businesses, Booth Welsh's strategic focus and level of staff engagement appears to have remained remarkably resilient during the pandemic, an outcome which the company attributes to its previous workplace innovation journey – notably its focus on visible leadership, employee voice and employee-driven innovation, maintaining a climate of trust and two-way communication even with the majority of staff working from home for an extended period. This was at least partially validated by a further repeat of the Workplace Innovation Diagnostic® employee survey after the first two months of the 2020 lockdown, indicating an improved score for the overall results. The principal exceptions were slightly reduced scores for employee-driven innovation and for collaboration across functional divisions, likely to be explained by the challenges of remote working.

Innovative methods of communicating such as video blogs, open-ended Q&A sessions with the MD and "virtual community" activities on an online platform helped build and maintain social capital and a sense of connection, helping to overcome the potential isolation and loneliness of remote working. Expert speakers also ran webinars on emotional resilience, mindfulness and how to manage personal finances.

With the majority of the workforce based at home during the pandemic, Aimee, Gordon and Martin saw an opportunity to redesign the Head Office physical environment to align it more effectively with the principles and practice of workplace innovation – specifically to facilitate greater interaction and to minimise the impact of organisational "walls and ceilings" when the post-COVID pattern of hybrid working becomes fully established.

The redesign locates all Head Office staff on the same floor, and directors no longer have separate offices, removing previous "upstairs – downstairs" perceptions and divisions whilst increasing visibility and potential for interaction.

The upper floor has been converted into a series of collaboration spaces where people can take time out from their home or office desks for quiet concentration, or to meet face to face in brainstorming sessions and social catch ups with colleagues. The company's mantra of "people support what they help to create" means that the current cohort of Workplace Innovation Practitioner Programme participants has played a central role in designing these spaces, engaging the ideas and creativity of a wide section of the workforce.

Reflection

Booth Welsh's journey since 2017 demonstrates how the concept of workplace innovation can be operationalised through the improvement and redesign of specific workplace practices associated with superior performance, capacity for innovation and quality of working life, in this case by means of *The Essential Fifth Element*. The case illustrates workplace innovation as a social process with inherent participative and dialogical characteristics, and shows how the individual competence development of in-company change facilitators through structured, action-focused programmes can lead to a sustainable momentum of participative reflection and organisational change. This aspiration has consistently fuelled Booth Welsh's workplace innovation journey rather than an instrumental focus on performance indicators.

For policymakers, social partners and other stakeholders, this conveys important lessons. It is now well understood that workplace innovation has the potential to create landscape change in our economies and societies, reflected in positive outcomes for business performance, innovation, employee health and wellbeing, the retention of older workers, and social inclusion (Oeij et al., 2017). Its product is not a linear shift from one type of workplace innovation to another, but rather the creation of a perpetual, discursive process of external knowledge assimilation, productive reflection, improvement and innovation. This endorses the argument of Johnsen et al. (2021) that policymakers must refrain from programme design based on an instrumentalist fixation with short-term measurables, focusing instead on such factors as the quality of competence development, participation and dialogue as well as the introduction of new workplace practices which support them.

Whilst describing workplace innovation in terms of "new and combined interventions in work organisation, human resource management, labour relations and supportive technologies" (Pot, 2011) remains valid as a high level definition, it makes sense in operational terms only when grounded in specific workplace practices evidenced by research to lead to simultaneous gains for employees and their organisations. *The Essential Fifth Element* is not intended to constrain or rigidify the practice and scope of workplace innovation; rather it blends evidence, dialogue and experimentation.

In Booth Welsh, *The Essential Fifth Element* focused attention on very specific areas of practice highlighted as problematic by the Diagnostic at team, divisional and organisational levels. In addressing these challenges, it brought together the generic knowledge and skills acquired through the programme by Aimee and Gordon, with the tacit knowledge and creativity of Booth Welsh's employees. In short, the case illustrates "local theory" in practice.

References

Boud, D., Cressey, P., & Docherty, P. (2006). *Productive Reflection at Work*. London: Routledge.

Boxall, P. & Purcell, J. (2003). *Strategy and Human Resource Management*. Basingstoke: Palgrave Macmillan.

Business Decisions Ltd (2002). New forms of work organisation: the obstacles to wider diffusion. KE-47-02-115-EN-C, DG Employment and Social Affairs, European Commission, Brussels.

Cressey, P., Totterdill, P., & Exton, R. (2013). Workplace social dialogue as a form of "productive reflection". *International Journal of Action Research*, 2013, 9 (2): 209–245.

Eurofound and Cedefop (2020), *European Company Survey 2019: Workplace Practices Unlocking Employee Potential*, European Company Survey 2019 series, Publications Office of the European Union, Luxembourg.

European Work & Technology Consortium (1998). *Work Organisation, Competitiveness, Employment: The European Approach*. Nottingham: Centre for Work & Technology.

EUWIN (2021) Workplace innovation: Europe's competitive edge A manifesto for enhanced performance and working lives. https://workplaceinnovation.eu/wp-content/uploads/2021/11/EUWIN-MANIFESTO.pdf

Exton, R., and Totterdill, P. (2019). Unleashing workplace innovation in Scotland. *International Journal of Technology Transfer and Commercialisation* 16 (3): 208–227.

Gustavsen B. (1992) Dialogue and development. Assen: van Gorcum.

Johnsen, H. C. G., Hildebrand, C., Aslaksen, H., Ennals, R., & and Knudsen, J. P. (2021). The dialogical approach to workplace innovation. In McMurray, A., Muenjohn, N. and Weerakoon, C. (eds). *The Palgrave Handbook of Workplace Innovation across Developed and Developing Countries*. Cham: Palgrave McMillan.

McMurray, A., Muenjohn, N., & Weerakoon, C. (eds) (2021). *The Palgrave Handbook of Workplace Innovation across Developed and Developing Countries*. Cham: Palgrave McMillan.

Mohr, B.J., & van Amelsvoort, P. (2015) Co-creating humane and innovative communities of work. Evolutions in the practice of socio-technical system design. Portland: Global STS-D Network Press.

Oeij, P., Rus, D., & Pot, F. D. (eds) (2017). *Workplace Innovation*. Cham: Springer International Publishing.

Pot, F.D. (2011). Workplace innovation for better jobs and performance. *International Journal of Productivity and Performance Management* 64 (4): 405–415.

Pot, F., Totterdill, P., & Dhondt, S. (2016) Workplace innovation: European policy and theoretical foundation. *World Review of Entrepreneurship, Management and Sustainable Development* 12 (1): 13–32.

Pot, F., Totterdill, P., & Dhondt, S. (2021). Developing workplace innovation policies in the European Union. In A. McMurray, N. Muenjohn, and C. Weerakoon (eds), *The Palgrave Handbook of Workplace Innovation across Developed and Developing Countries*, pp. 41–56. Cham: Palgrave McMillan.

Teague, P. (2005) What is enterprise partnership? *Organization*, 12 (4): 567–589.

Totterdill, P., Dhondt, S., & Milsome, S. (2002). Partners at work? A report to Europe's policy makers and social partners. Nottingham: The Work Institute.

Totterdill, P. (2015). Closing the gap: 'The Fifth Element' and workplace innovation. *European Journal of Workplace Innovation*, 1 (1): 55–74.

Totterdill, P. (2020) Are we *really* serious about securing enhanced productivity, through our people? Work Foundation Centenary Provocation Paper. Available online at https://www.lancaster.ac.uk/work-foundation/work-foundation-centenary-provocation-papers/

Anders Kjellberg

The shifting role of European unions in the social dialogue: Sweden in a comparative context

Abstract: Industrial relations vary between European countries. For member countries of the European union, the role of European legislation, labour law and other policy measures play a central and co-ordinating role. The current policy development from the European Commission on minimum wages illustrates the tensions between on one hand the Nordic model with collective agreements and a stronger role from social partners and on the other the EU regulation giving a stronger position to European institutions as the European Commission and the European Parliament. This chapter reflects over the Swedish labour market model in a European context by looking at variations in union density, role of social partners and power relations in working life in a more general context.

Keywords: industrial relations, social partners, union density, collective agreements, social dialogue, comparative research

Introduction

A sustainable social dialogue presupposes a relatively even balance of power between trade unions and employers. In several European countries, the actions of employers, states and international institutions have weakened unions so much that the social dialogue is close to collapse. With a wide definition of social dialogue, collective bargaining is included. To examine the differences between the EU/EES countries (including the UK), we will use two indicators of associational and institutional union power of great importance for creating sustainable workplaces: union density and the coverage of collective bargaining. Combining these, Nordic unions are the most powerful in the world, in particular when taking account of the wide right to strike in these countries. This right is absent in the social dialogue as this term is commonly used. In the Central and Eastern European members states (the CEE states),[1] which were part of the former Eastern bloc, social dialogue was often introduced in the form of tripartite talks as a substitute for collective bargaining.

1 Bulgaria, Czech Republic, Croatia, Estonia, Hungary, Latvia, Lithuania, Poland, Romania, Slovakia, and Slovenia.

The social dialogue at EU level does not include wages and industrial action, as they are considered national issues. This has not prevented the EU court from restricting the right to strike in for example the Laval case. Nor has it hindered the European Commission and the European Central Bank from putting pressure on governments to enforce opening clauses in collective agreements.

The bargaining parties in the Nordic countries prefer collective bargaining without the involvement of the state, in other words self-regulation under the auspices of unions and employers' associations. To protect this model, an intense social dialogue at both the national and the EU level has taken place regarding the Laval case and the introduction of a European minimum wage. In a common letter to the European Commission on 22 October 2020, the Nordic ministers of employment stress the importance of fighting social dumping and strengthening the social dialogue, which includes "encouraging higher union density and promoting the possibility for the social partners to find solutions to labour market challenges, many of which require nationally tailored measures." According to the ministers, that means "respect for systems based on collective bargaining" and that future initiatives on minimum wage would "not interfere with labour market models where wages are regulated by collective agreements", that is the Nordic models of self-regulation.

Apart from the industrial relations model of the CEE states, and that of the Nordic countries, the EU/EES also includes the Continental European model, the Southern European and the Anglo-Saxon. The Anglo-Saxon model (United Kingdom and Ireland) was, like the Nordic model, characterised by "voluntarism" (UK), but no longer, and unions are much weaker. In the British private sector, industry agreements are almost absent. Industrial action in the UK is circumscribed by legislated voting rules and bans on sympathy strikes.

The Continental European model comprises Germany, Austria, Belgium, the Netherlands, and Switzerland. Tripartite solutions (social partnership) are common. The German IG Metall, recruiting both blue-collar and white-collar workers, concludes pattern-setting industry agreements. At workplace level employees are represented by works councils. Only Belgium, the birth country of the Ghent system, has a high union density. The density of employers' associations is usually high.

In contrast to the Nordic countries, the employment rate of women is low in both the Continental European model and the Southern European model, in which the union movement is divided along political and religious lines. Apart from Italy, union density is low, but this is partly compensated by a high mobilisation capacity. aimed at influencing political decisions. Due to state extension,

France and Spain have a very high coverage of collective agreements. French state regulation is the opposite to Nordic self-regulation.

In the Central and Eastern European model (the CEE states), the coverage of collective agreements is low or very low, despite EU efforts to introduce social dialogue. The employers, including foreign multinational companies, are reluctant to bargain industry agreements. Where collective bargaining exists, it is usually decentralised to company level. The governments' neoliberal economic and social policy has further weakened already weak union movements.

This typology of five European industrial relations models should not be taken as absolute. Changes may occur by time and the emphasis can be on different aspects. Eurofound (2020) places Germany in the Nordic model, due to the higher autonomy of collective bargaining, and less extensive state intervention, than in other Continental European countries.

Considering the degree of self-regulation and bargaining power of unions and employers, the Nordic and Continental models surpass the CEE model, the Southern European model, and the Anglo-Saxon model (Eurofound, 2020, p. 40). The same applies to the degree of co-ordination and centralisation of collective bargaining.

The Nordic model stands out compared to all the others, by the strength of unions at both industry and workplace level. Consequently, the capacity to deal with economic and other challenges, and to maintain their position vis-à-vis the employers can be expected to be greater than in other European countries. We will see whether this has been true in the last twenty years.

The Nordic model of industrial relations

Nordic industrial relations are distinguished by a high degree of self-regulation, which means that collective agreements concluded by well-organised labour market parties have a prominent position in regulating wages and other employment conditions. None of the Nordic countries have legislated for minimum wages, which does not mean that the state is without influence. The Nordic model includes "social democratic" welfare states strengthening the position of workers vis-à-vis employers. The Ghent systems in Denmark, Finland and Sweden represent a mix of state regulation (state-subsidised unemployment funds regulated by law) and self-regulation (almost all funds are union-led). The government is also responsible for an active labour market policy.

The Swedish model of industrial relations is the closest to a Nordic ideal type, as regards degree of self-regulation. The government is much less involved in wage formation than in Denmark (mediation proposals not seldom transformed into law), Finland (a tradition of tripartite bargaining) and Norway (compulsory arbitration). In contrast to Finland and Norway, Sweden has no state extension mechanisms of collective agreements. Furthermore, Sweden is in a class of itself by its extremely low frequency of labour market conflicts. The socially segregated Nordic model of separate unions and union confederations for blue-collar workers ("the LOs"), academic professionals and other white-collar workers is most evident in Sweden, in particular since LO-Denmark merged with the largest white-collar confederation.

In addition, the Swedish white-collar unions are considerably stronger than their Nordic equivalents. The Danish private sector employer confederation even refuses to conclude collective agreements with the academic confederation Akademikerne and its affiliates.

Sweden is also the only Nordic country in which blue-collar and white-collar unions across confederations set the "mark" (the industry norm) for wage increases throughout the labour market. In the autumn 2020, the former bargaining cartel PTK, representing the large majority of private sector white-collar union members, concluded a basic agreement with the Confederation of Swedish Enterprise. After some adjustments, the two largest blue-collar LO unions, IF Metall and the Municipal Workers' Unions, joined the agreement, but due to internal conflicts LO-Sweden did not join until the autumn 2021. That marks a substantial power shift within the union movement since 1938, when LO alone signed the basic agreement, the Saltsjöbaden Agreement. Both these basic agreements were negotiated after pressure from social democratic governments. As the government this time was dependent upon two neoliberal parties, the employers had a very strong negotiating position. Although the agreement will be implemented through a social dialogue between the signatories and the government, it is considered a victory for the Swedish model of self-regulation. There will be tripartite deliberations about changes of the Law on employment protection, the implementation of the new transition agreement, and a collectively agreed unemployment insurance, in which the current unemployment funds will remain. The revised law will increase the employers' freedom to select individuals in case of layoffs. In the two other issues, the participation of the government is necessary for financial reasons.

Another tripartite reform in 2020 was the introduction of short-term work. In contrast to the 2009 Crisis Agreement between IF Metall and employers' associations, the government this time was involved by providing state subsidies. Very soon, a large number of collective agreements on short-term work were signed. As these allowed greater flexibility for both employees and employers than short-term work without an agreement, they received a largescale application.

Despite their outstanding strength, Nordic unions face a multitude of challenges. Sweden is chosen as an illustration, as the Swedish variant of the Nordic model includes the most far-reaching self-regulation, together with Denmark the highest union density, the highest density of employers' associations, and the longest record of social democratic government influence on the welfare state and labour market: 1932–1976, 1982–1991, 1994–2006 and since 2014. As in Denmark and Finland, union density has declined considerably since the mid-1990s. Swedish unions are also challenged by a shift of power to large transnational companies expanding their share of employees abroad, a rapid growth of non-unionised posted workers, and the most extensive privatisations of welfare services.

Swedish unions facing challenges

The 1997 Industry Agreement assigns the role of setting the wage "mark" for the whole labour market to unions and employers' associations within the export-dominated manufacturing industry (Kjellberg, 2019b). An important aim is preventing wage increases jeopardising Swedish competitiveness. The Industry Agreement for more than twenty years has been compatible with rising real wages and a very low frequency of labour conflicts. The "wage mark" or "industry norm" is set through negotiations between the employers' associations and unions in manufacturing industry, among them IF Metall (affiliated to the blue-collar Swedish Trade Union Confederation, LO), Unionen (affiliated to the white-collar Swedish Confederation of Professional Employees, TCO) and the Association of Graduate Engineers (affiliated to white-collar Swedish Confederation of Professional Associations, Saco). Unionen is the largest Swedish union, the Association of Graduate Engineers the largest Saco union, and IF Metall the largest private sector LO union. The alternative to this model of self-regulation would have been increased state intervention into wage formation. The new, reinforced Swedish Mediation Office, founded in 2000, instead has a supplementary role of facilitating the implementation of the mark set by the parties behind the Industry Agreement. In the early 1990s the strongest state involvement ever in Swedish wage formation took place through a social dialogue, in which a government commission under pressure persuaded the unions to conclude "stabilisation agreements".

Declining Swedish union density

Swedish union density has declined considerably since 2000, in particular since 2007, creating growing divisions between different categories of employees (Tab. 17):

- In 2006 union density was 77 % among both blue-collar and white-collar workers. In 2020 only 61 % of blue-collar workers were union members compared to 73 % of white-collar workers. The Swedish definition of blue-collar workers is very wide, and includes most sales personnel and restaurant employees. Especially the latter had to pay very high contributions to their unemployment fund, since the centre-right government raised them considerably in 2007 (Kjellberg, 2011). From mid-2008, the contributions were linked more closely to the unemployment among the members of each fund. As unemployment in general is highest among blue-collar workers, the total union and fund fee could be very high for this category of workers. That is the main explanation to the increasing divergence between blue-collar and white-collar union density during the period 2007–2013, when fund contributions were considerably raised.
- Likewise, in 2006 77 % of both domestic-born and foreign-born blue-collar workers were affiliated to a union. In 2020 64 % of domestic-born and only 52 % of foreign-born blue-collar workers were union members.
- Union density has declined most among employees with fixed-term jobs and among young people.

Tab. 17. Union density in Sweden among blue-collar and white-collar workers by country of birth, 2006–2020 (% and percentage points).

	2006	2013	2020	2006–2020	2013–2020
Blue-collar union density					
Foreign-born	77	60	52	−25	−8
Domestic-born	77	67	64	−13	−3
All blue-collar workers	77	66	61	−16	−5
Share of blue-collar workers born abroad	16	21	29	+13	+8
White-collar union density					
Foreign-born	70	67	66	−4	−1
Domestic-born	77	74	75	−2	+1
All white-collar workers	77	73	73	−4	0
Share of white-collar workers born abroad	10	13	16	+6	+3

Remark. Employees aged 16–64 years, excluding full-time students working alongside the studies.
Source: Labour force surveys.

Since 2006, union density among foreign-born blue-collar workers has declined twice as much as among native-born, and three times more if only taking account the period 2013–2019, when refugees in very large numbers arrived in Sweden. In contrast to most other countries, asylum seekers have the right to work during the asylum application process. Contributory to their low rate of unionisation is that most refugees arriving during the past ten-fifteen years are from non-European countries, and therefore with limited knowledge of trade unions and collective agreements. Furthermore, foreign-born blue-collar workers are overrepresented in private services with a low union density, like restaurants and cleaning.

Growing share of foreign-born workers

Sweden received more refugees per capita than almost all other EU countries, and has one of the most liberal regulations in OECD regarding third country labour migrants. In some industries, there are signs of ethnic segmentation and exploitation of low-skilled foreign-born workers. In restaurants, they often have employers with a foreign background (Frödin & Kjellberg, 2018, 2020). A large share of these, often small, companies have no collective agreements. Foreign-born employees to a much higher degree than native Swedes risk falling outside the Swedish labour market model, also because of much higher unemployment (15 % in 2019) compared to native-born employees (4 %).

Sweden is among the European countries with the highest share of foreign-born in the population. This share has increased rapidly among blue-collar workers: from 16 % in 2006 to 29 % in 2020. In the public sector and private services excluding commerce, every third worker is foreign-born.

Few workers posted to Sweden are union members. There is plenty of evidence suggesting a high prevalence of bad working conditions at many sites with posted workers. The government failed in 2020 to give the regional safety representatives access to workplaces with collective agreements but without union members. The parliamentary majority of liberal and conservative parties rejected the proposal, but the Building Workers' Union, after a strike notice, succeeded in obtaining this right. The Swedish Confederation of Enterprise wishes to replace regional safety representatives with non-union representatives assisted by officers from the Work Environment Authority. Obviously, the employers wish to get rid of representatives who, with some authority, can demand improved working environment in companies without local union safety representatives. Non-union safety representatives at such workplaces would hardly be able to effectively represent the workers vis-à-vis the employer, in particular as they often are afraid of being sent home if they contact a union. This is a problem for Swedish unions trying to organise posted workers in construction, where most of them are from Poland, and far from always formally employees. In construction the growing "grey area" of false self-employed, dependent upon a single employer, is closely related to "the frequent use of long subcontracting chains in which self-employed migrant workers are often to be found at the end-point of these supply-chains" (Thörnquist, 2015, p. 419).

Recently the Swedish Work Environment Authority found evidence on excessive working-hours and illegal night work, increasing the risk for accidents, among subcontractor workers at the large construction site for the new Northvolt battery plant in Skellefteå. Several foreign workers did not even have work permits. When finished, the Northvolt plant will be important for the green transition, but it is paradoxically constructed under not fully sustainable working conditions. The problem with unserious subcontractors in the construction industry is widespread and nothing unique for the Northvolt site. The Building Workers' Union demands companies to limit the number of subcontractors and to those with collective agreements. The monitoring of Swedish working environment is made more difficult by the declining number of working environment inspectors and union safety representatives. The former decreased from almost 400 in 2006 to 223 in 2018. Despite an increase to 258 in 2000 or 0.5 per 10,000 employees, that is much less than in Finland (1.3) or Norway and Denmark (both 1.1), and far below the ILO recommendation (at least 1.0).

The Swedish model of self-regulation was for many years curtailed by the EU directive on posted workers, as industrial action for terms of employment in accordance with Swedish collective agreements became illegal after the 2007 Laval sentence. Consequently, the closest Swedish equivalent to extension mechanisms, the right to take action to get a collective agreement, by EU institutions was partly eliminated. When Sweden in 1995 joined the EU, it was promised that the Swedish model of industrial relations would be left intact, but the Laval sentence showed that the principle of free movement of services had priority over the principles of subsidiarity and non-discrimination by nationality.

A shift of power to globalised companies

Another challenge facing Swedish unions is that globalised companies can easily move production across borders. In the 80 largest Swedish-owned manufacturing groups, the share of employees abroad was more than doubled between 1980 and 2019 (Tab. 18). The number of employees in low-wage countries employed by these groups grow by almost four times, and made up 2019 more than twice as many as those in Sweden. Remaining in Sweden was less than every sixth employee in the 80 largest manufacturing groups. In 2018–2019 the expansion in low wage countries seems to have ceased.

Tab. 18. Number of employees in Sweden and abroad in the 80 largest Swedish-owned manufacturing groups, 1980–2019.

Year	Total number of employees	Employed in Sweden	Employed abroad	Of which in low wage countries*
1980	773,100	447,000 (58 %)	326,100 (42 %)	74,300 (23 %)
2000	706,500	220,200 (31 %)	486,200 (69 %)	133,200 (27 %)
2010	672,000	137,100 (20 %)	534,900 (80 %)	237,500 (44 %)
2015:1	870,800	146,000 (17 %)	724,800 (83 %)	349,600 (48 %)
2015:2**	757,800	129,700 (17 %)	628,100 (83 %)	288,000 (46 %)
2017	819,500	131,100 (15 %)	688,400 (85 %)	321,400 (47 %)
2018	819,800	133,400 (16 %)	686,400 (84 %)	319,300 (47 %)
2019	826,000	127,700 (15 %)	698,300 (85 %)	304,400 (44 %)
1980–2015:1	+97,700 (+13 %)	−301,000 (−67 %)	+398,700 (+ 122 %)	+275,300 (+ 371 %)
2015:2–2019	+68,200 (+9 %)	−2,000 (-2 %)	+70,200 (+11 %)	+16,400 (+6 %)

* Share of employes abroad (%).
** Some large groups changed code from manufacturing to services.
Source: Swedish Agency for Growth Policy Analysis.

Above all, the number of *blue-collar* workers in Sweden decreased. In manufacturing, a largescale *migration of jobs* has taken place, many of which were unskilled assembly jobs. The dominant employer response to the intensified international competition is increased flexibility, for example through outsourcing and hiring of personnel. In manufacturing industry, it is easier to hire personnel or move production abroad if the work is standardised and cycle times short. The introduction of lean production promotes such a development. Today the strategy of IF Metall is to co-operate with the companies, in order to design lean production in a way that prevents impoverishment of work while raising productivity. Given the change of the balance of power to the advantage to the employers due to the globalisation process, the union found no other choice.

According to surveys among the IF Metall workplace clubs, the cycle times have successively been shortened (Kjellberg, 2019a). The most negative development occurred along assembly lines and in the largest companies. A dual picture emerged. In some workplaces, all blue-collar workers were covered by development at work. In others, primarily skilled workers got the opportunity to develop in their work, while other workers were not included at all, or experienced negative development. Much higher unemployment than in the 1970s and 1980s, and the hiring of personnel, restrain the companies' interest in creating developing jobs. The contrast is sharp to the 1980s, when the Metalworkers' Union launched the concept of "good work" and some large manufacturing companies showed great interest for this, in order to solve problems of quality and high labour turnover. In the 1990s, rapidly rising unemployment and the introduction of new production concepts fundamentally changed this. As a result, "simple jobs" have far from disappeared in manufacturing industry. Ericsson and Electrolux have moved almost all production abroad, but the vehicle manufacturers Scania, AB Volvo and Volvo Cars have still a significant production in Sweden, primarily based on assembly lines.

The main reason for IF Metall joining the new 2020 basic agreement was gaining access to the transition scheme. This includes very generous opportunities to competence development at a time when many jobs are threatened in connection with the introduction of new technology such as digitalisation and the replacement of internal combustion engines with electric motors in the large Swedish automotive industry. Also employees not risking losing their jobs: for example those wishing to change occupation, are covered by the agreement.

As we have seen, the globalisation of jobs comprises a twofold process: a migration of jobs from Sweden and a migration of workers to Sweden. Of course, far from all jobs created abroad by Swedish transnationals have moved from Sweden. Conversely, some jobs are created or retained in Sweden due to the expansion abroad. Anyhow, several Swedish manufacturing jobs have moved to other countries, or disappeared because of raised productivity.

A similar employment shift appears also when we look at all Swedish-owned international groups, including services. In 1993, every second employee is these groups worked outside Sweden and in 2019 seven of ten (Tab. 19).

Tab. 19. Number of employees in Sweden and abroad in all Swedish-owned international groups, 1993–2019.

	Groups	Number of employees			
Year	Number	In all	Sweden	Abroad	Of which in low wage countries*
1993	750	1,146,400	611,300 (53 %)	535,100 (47 %)	88,700 (17 %)
2000	913	1,499,900	589,900 (40 %)	910,000 (60 %)	212,700 (23 %)
2010	2 288	1,619,300	488,200 (30 %)	1,131,100 (70 %)	408,800 (36 %)
2015	3 132	1,957,200	560,800 (29 %)	1,396,400 (71 %)	586,300 (42 %)
2017	3 199	2,044,800	588,800 (29 %)	1,456,000 (71 %)	605,300 (42 %)
2018	3 103	2,165,800	659,400 (30 %)	1,506,400 (70 %)	613,000 (41 %)
2019	3 813	2,207,000	690,700 (31 %)	1,516,300 (69 %)	607,400 (40 %)

* Share of employes abroad (%).
Source: Swedish Agency for Growth Policy Analysis.

Another indicator of increasing globalisation is that the number of employees in foreign companies between 1980 and 2019 increased from 114 000 to 683 100, or from 5 % to 21 % of private sector employees. In manufacturing industry, 39 % worked in foreign-owned companies in 2019, and in private services 20 % (Tillväxtanalys, 2020). Being large, former Swedish-owned companies with headquarters in Sweden, Volvo Cars and Scania are well-integrated into the Swedish model. That is far from always the case with recently established American IT or gig giants as Facebook, Google, Amazon Web Services and Uber, with Microsoft as an exception.

Many Swedish-owned IT companies, like Spotify, also prefer not signing collective agreements. At the end of 2018 nine out of ten startup tech companies founded in Sweden had no agreements. In the private sector, Swedish collective bargaining coverage is about 82–83 % of the employees. Anyhow, about a half million employees work in companies without collective agreements. To these should be added several self-employed persons, freelancers, gig-workers etc., who in reality are dependent on a single or a few companies providing them with jobs.

Flexibility for employers: not always sustainable for health care and health care workers

The terms of employment, however, might be worse for some blue-collar workers with collective agreements, than for white-collar workers in some large IT companies without agreements. In the women-dominated health and care sector, there exist large qualification and education gaps between different categories of employees. In health care, the educational level was raised by the replacement of health care assistants (*sjukvårdsbiträden*) by practical nurses (*undersköterskor*), in turn partly replaced by nurses (*sjuksköterskor*). The remaining health care assistants (*vårdbiträden*) are above all found in elderly care and home care, where also the majority of practical nurses are employed. A substantial and growing proportion of the health care assistants have the most insecure forms of temporary work, such as employment on time or call basis. In 2010 37 % of the health care assistants were hourly employed and in 2019 50 %.[2] During the corona pandemic, it became obvious that their lack of education and insecure employment facilitated the spread of the disease. Those employed per hour without guaranties for additional work are in reality self-employed day labourers. Would they, because of sickness, stay at home, they risk not being called in more times. Nor do they have the right to sickness benefits. In the first half of 2020, the number of registered work-related diseases increased dramatically (by 60 %), and most in health and elderly care, wh\\ere the increase was no less than 219 % (Swedish Work Environment Authority, 13 October 2020).

Employer demands for increased flexibility, which the centre-right government met by the introduction of "general fixed-term employment" in 2007, explains the growing share of health care assistants with the most insecure forms of employment. Temporary employment is common in public sector and private sector elderly care, but most frequent in the latter (Kommunal, 2016). The Municipal Workers' Union, which recruits members in both the public and the private sector, signed the 2020 basic agreement after negotiations, resulting in improved terms of employment for the most insecure forms of fix-term employees.

Both practical nurses and health care assistants are in Sweden classified as blue-collar workers (*arbetare*) and are organised by the Municipal Workers' Union (LO), nurses by the Swedish Association of Health Professionals (TCO) and doctors by the Swedish Medical Association (Saco). The rate of unionisation varies strongly between these categories of personnel: from circa 50 % among health care assistants to almost 80 % among practical nurses and nurses, and just

2 Since 2010 the health care assistants' share of the employees in health and long-term care, however, has declined somewhat, while the share of practical nurses has increased. In 2019 the latter was almost twice as many as the former. Email 25 June 2020 from the Swedish Association of Local Authorities and Regions.

above 80 % among doctors (Kjellberg, 2020). Private sector health care assistants have a lower union density (about 40 %) than those in the public sector (about 50–55 %). In the years 2001–2003, about 80 % of health care assistants at public employers were union members, consequently a remarkable drop in union density. To sum up: low union density, low wages, a growing share on insecure jobs and insufficient education motivates to label many health care assistants in elderly care and home care as precarious workers: despite a very high coverage of collective agreements.

That does not prevent the general level of education in the health care sector from increasing considerably, especially in the hospitals, as the health care assistants there have almost disappeared. Many of them studied as practical nurses in municipal upper secondary level courses (*Komvux*).[3] The number of skilled workers in health care and other services has increased to such a degree that the job polarisation thesis for Sweden has been rejected (Tåhlin, 2019). There might be a polarisation of wages, but this has to be distinguished from job polarisation. Low-paid workers is not always the same as unskilled workers, particularly not in woman-dominated sectors like health care. Women wages are lagging behind those of male workers with comparable qualifications in other sectors. According to Tåhlin (2019), the growth of women-dominated skilled jobs, in for example health care, has compensated for the decrease of men-dominated manufacturing jobs.

In Sweden, a relatively large proportion of the employees in welfare occupations today work in the private sector.[4] This share is highest in elderly and home care, and not without consequences for the balance of power between unions and employers. As we have seen, union density is considerably lower among health care assistants in the private compared to the public sector. The same applies to primary school teachers, nurses, and practical nurses. Deregulation of railways, telecom, taxi etc., like outsourcing of IT, cleaning etc. from manufacturing companies, has similar effects. Today only 40 % of taxi drivers are union members (lower among foreign-born).

Already at the beginning of the pandemic the Municipal Workers' Union considered that wearing a face shield together with a face mask (not including the nose) in home and elderly care was insufficient, and demanded access to breathing masks. In several places the safety representatives used their right to

3 In 2018 the number of nurses in Sweden was 106,100, practical nurses 183,100 and health care assistants 76,700 (Swedish Occupational Register).

4 In 2018 12 % of teachers, 13 % of practical nurses, 15 % of nurses and 25 % of health care assistants (Swedish Occupational Register).

stop dangerous work, but the Swedish Work Environment Authority repealed the stops as it lacked evidence that Covid-19 was airborne, but infected only by contagion. More than a year later the Work Environment Authority, however, issued new guidelines as research now showed that the virus is also airborne. Breathing masks were required in home care service in case of Covid-19 or suspicion of the disease and in elderly care after risk assessment after taking into account the state of knowledge. This course of events illustrates that the social dialogue, even in Sweden, does not always work, in this case between the Municipal Workers' Union, the employers and the authorities. The union was rewarded for its struggle to protect the care personnel by a substantial membership growth in 2020. Another example of a proactive union, but coupled with a successful social dialogue, we will find below regarding the green transformation of the Volvo Cars' engine factory in Skövde.

How to check terms of employment in companies without collective agreements

Municipal procurements usually go to companies offering the lowest prices, and often without collective agreements. Companies affiliated to employers' associations often abstain from participation in procurements, as they consider the chances as too small, and the terms of competition as distorted (Kjellberg, 2020). Also, state-subsidised jobs for long-term unemployed, recently arrived immigrants and disabled persons tend to have such effects. From June 2017 the law on public procurements requires that wage, working-time and vacation must not be below the minimum level of the collective agreement, but insurances were not included, and without a collective agreement unions are not able to sue employers for breach of contract.

EU plans to introduce legislated minimum wages in all member states. One of several questions is who should control that these wages are implemented also at workplaces without collective agreements. If legislated wages are introduced, the interests of joining unions might decline, together with the capacity of unions to enforce agreements at workplaces without agreements. In Sweden the Nordic model of collective agreements is widely considered as superior to legislation, as it allows greater flexibility, for example when implementing the EU directive on working-time. Minimum wages set by the state will not be adapted to the concrete circumstances in each industry. Above all, they will prevent the labour market parties from influencing an essential aspect of wage formation. Furthermore, according to the EU proposal, the minimum wage will be 60 % of the median wage in each country. If applied, for almost all Swedish employees this would result in considerably reduced minimum wages (Hällberg and Kjellström, 2020). Legislated minimum wages will prevent the labour market parties from influencing an essential aspect of wage formation, and will be dependent upon the colour of the government in office.

Declining union density, but not converging except in CEE states

Since the year 2000, union density has declined considerably in almost all EU/EES countries, particularly in the new member states in Central and Eastern Europe (the CEE states). In three of these (Slovenia, Romania, and Croatia), the share of workers affiliated to trade unions decreased from a relatively high level (40–44 %) to 20–24 %, which means a halved union density (Tab. 20). The CEE states, already having a low density, also experienced considerable drops measured in percentage points and far more in relative terms, that is in per cent. In Lithuania, for example, union density declined by 12 percentage points (from 19 % to 7 %), which means a fall of almost 70 %.

Among the old EU states, the Nordic countries Sweden, Finland, and Denmark are distinguished by the largest declines in percentage points. In all these three cases, a substantial part of the massive membership losses was a result of the remodelling of the Ghent systems (state-subsidised union unemployment funds; Kjellberg & Ibsen, 2016). In Sweden, the contributions to the unemployment funds were considerably raised in the period 2007–2013. Union density declined from 77 % in 2006 to 71 % in 2008. A decline of six percentage points in the course of two years is remarkable also from an international perspective. In Finland an independent unemployment fund, which attracted large numbers of employees, came about in the 1990s.

In Denmark, cross-occupational unemployment funds in 2002 were introduced as an alternative to the traditional union-run funds. Many of them stand close to so-called alternative, "yellow" unions with low membership fees, and which are not involved in collective bargaining. If these unions are excluded from the calculation, the Danish union density declined from 72 % in 2000 to 52 % in 2019, that is a drop by no less than 20 percentage points. Excepting the four CEE states Romania, Slovakia, Slovenia, and Croatia this is the largest fall registered in Tab. 20.

The Nordic high-density countries Sweden, Finland and Denmark were exposed to considerable declines in percentage points (about 12–15 points), but compared to Slovakia, Hungary, Lithuania, the Czech Republic, Estonia, Romania, Poland, Bulgaria, Latvia, And Slovenia there was a much smaller decline in relative terms, and therefore not so serious consequences. In the latest available year, no more than every fifth worker belonged to a union in three CEE states (Slovenia, Romania, and Croatia), in five density was down to 11–13 % (Slovakia, Czech Republic, Poland, Bulgaria and Latvia) and in another three just 6–8 % (Hungary, Lithuania and Estonia).

To illustrate the significance of different ways of measuring union decline, it could be mentioned that the Swedish union density since 2000 has decreased more in percentage points (minus twelve points) than the Estonian one (minus eight points). While the Estonian relative decline, however, was as large as 57 %, the Swedish decline was limited to 15 %.

In a few countries, the fall in union density was modest or absent. Italy had 33–35 % unionised workers in both 2000 and 2019. Norway showed a small decline (from 53 % to 50 %) like France (from 10 % to 9 %).

Like twenty years ago, the share of workers affiliated to unions differs greatly between countries and country groups. Among the old EU member states, varies union density considerably between South and North: from 9 % in France and 13–15 % in Spain and Portugal to 69 % in Sweden, with Italy in a middle position on 33 %. It is remarkable that only every sixth worker in a Continental European country like Germany is a union member, a country known for strong unions like IG Metall, but now adhering to the large group of member states with a statutory minimum wage, introduced on the initiative of the weakened German union movement.

Tab. 20. Union density in 27 EU/EES countries, 2000–2020 (%).

	2000	2005	2006	2010	2015	2016	2017	2018	2019	2020	2000–*	2000–**
Nordic												
Sweden	81	78	77	71	69	69	69	68	68	69	−12	−15
Finland	74	73	72	71	68	66	63	60	59		−15	−20
Denmark (1)	75	72	69	69	/64	63	63	64	63		−12	−16
Denmark (2)	72	68	65	62	/55	53	53	53	52		−20	−28
Norway	53	51	51	51	50	50	50	50	50	51	−2	−4
Continental												
Belgium	57	55	54	53	52	52	51	50	49		−8	−14
Austria	37	34	32	29	27	27	27	26	26		−11	−30
Germany	25	22	22	19	18	17	17	17	16		−9	−36
Netherlands	22	22	21	20	18	17	17	17	15		−7	−30
Switzerland	21	20	19	18	16	15	15	14			−7	−33
Anglo-Saxon												
Ireland	36	32	32	32	25	23	24	24	25	26	−10	−28
UK	30	29	28	27	25	24	23	23	24	24	−6	−20
Southern												
Italy	35	34	34	35	34	34	33	33	33		−2	−6
Greece	25	24		22		19					−6	−24
Portugal	21		21	20	16	15					−6	−29
Spain	18	16	16	18	14	14	13	13	13		−5	−28
France	10	9	9	9	9	9	9	9			−1	−10
CEE												
Slovenia	44	38	32	33	24						−20	−45
Romania	44	32	32			20					−24	−55
Croatia	40	38			23	22	21	20			−20	−50
Slovakia	34	24	21	16	13	12	12	11			−23	−68
Czech Rep	27	19	18	16	12	12	12	11			−16	−59
Poland	24	24	18	17		14	13				−11	−46
Hungary	24	17		15		9		8			−16	−67
Bulgaria	23	19		15	14	14	13				−10	−43
Latvia	21		18	15	13	12	12	12			−9	−43
Lithuania	19		10	10	8	8	8	7			−12	−63
Estonia	14	9	8	8	5	5	5	6	6		−8	−57

Remark. United Kingdom (UK) included in the table as it was EU member most of the period. Three small EU states (Cyprus, Luxembourg, and Malta) excluded. Denmark including unemployed. Denmark (2) excluding "alternative" or "yellow" unions.
* Change in percentage points between 2000 and latest available year.
** Change %.
Source: Kjellberg (2021).

Despite declining union density in almost all EU/EES states, there are no clear signs of convergence between East and West, or between North and South. The same applies within the group of old member states. The only clear convergence appears among the new CEE member states, none of whom today has a union density exceeding 24 %. In 2000 there was a span of 30 percentage points in this group (from 14 % in Estonia to 44 % in Slovenia and Romania) compared to 18 points in recent years (from 6 % in Estonia to 24 % in Slovenia).

Declining coverage of collective bargaining

Another development also tending to undermine the social dialogue, likewise manifested strongest in the CEE states, is the declining coverage of collective bargaining. This is particularly evident in Bulgaria, Estonia, Romania, Slovakia, and Poland. In all these countries, the coverage rate has since 2000 been halved or reduced even more (Tab. 21). Greece is another example of a massive decline. The 100 % collective bargaining coverage in 2000 dwindled to 14 % in 2017.

Two contrasting models of industrial relations are associated with a high or very high coverage of collective agreements. One of them is distinguished by a strong tradition of collective bargaining, the other by state extension mechanisms to secure a high coverage of collective agreements. In the first model, the Nordic model, well-organised labour market parties by themselves regulate the terms of employment for most workers. In contrast to this model of "self-regulation" (Kjellberg, 2017), the other is a model of "state regulation", most common in Southern Europe, whereby the state ensures that the agreements do not just cover a small minority of the workers, but sometimes even almost all of them.

Tab. 21. Coverage of collective agreements in the EU/EES countries, 2000–2020.

Eurozone states in italics	**2000**	**2005**	**2017**	**2018**	**2019**	**2020**	**2000–**	**Extension mechanism by law**	**Statutory minimum wages**	**Dominant bargaining level**
Nordic										
Sweden	88	89	89	90	90	90	+2			Industry
Finland	85	91	89				+4	X		Industry
Denmark	85	85		82			–3			Industry
Norway	77	73	69				–8	X		Industry
Continental										
Belgium	96	96	96	96	96		0	X	X	Industry
Austria	98	98	98	98	98		0			Industry
Germany	68	65	55	54			–14	(X)	X	Industry
Netherlands	82	91	79	77	77	76	–6	X	X	Industry
Switzerland	41	41		45			+4	X		Industry
Anglo-Saxon										
Ireland	44	42	34				–10		X	Ind/comp
UK	36	35	26	26	27		–9		X	Ind/comp
Southern										
Italy	100	100	100	100	100	100	0			Industry
Greece	100	100	14				–86	–2011	X	Company
Portugal	78	83	73	74			–4	X	X	Industry
Spain	85	77	79	80			–5	X	X	Industry
France		98		98			0	X	X	Industry
CEE										
Slovenia	100	100	79				–21	X	X	Industry
Romania		85	25				–60	–2011	X	Ind/comp
Croatia	71	63	54				–17	X	X	Ind/comp
Slovakia	52	40	24				–28	(X)	X	Industry
Czech Rep	42	38	34	34	35		–7	(X)	X	Company
Poland	25			13			–12		X	Company
Hungary	38	25	23	21	22		–16	(X)	X	Company
Bulgaria	56	35	12				–44	(X)	X	Ind/comp
Latvia	18	15		27			+9	(X)	X	Company
Lithuania	12.5	10	8	8	8		–4		X	Company
Estonia	31.5	16		6			–26	(X)	X	Company

Finland 2005 refers to 2004, Norway 2000 refers to 1998, Switzerland 2000 refers to 2001, France 2005 refers to 2004, Romania 2017 refers to 2017, Croatia 2017 refers to 2016, Slovakia 2017 refers to 2015, Bulgaria 2000 refers to 2002, 2005 to 2006 and 2017 to 2016, Lithuania 2005 refers to 2006. Estonia 2000 refers to 2001.

Source: Sverige Kjellberg (2022), Norge Nergaard (2020), and all other countries OECD. Dominant bargaining level: Müller et al. 2019, volume III, Table 30.1.

French state regulation contra Swedish self-regulation

Among the old EU member states, Sweden and France form the extremes, representing the Nordic and the Southern European model respectively (Tab. 22). Despite a very low union density, French collective agreements cover 98 % of the employees, due to the very frequent use of extension by the Ministry of Labour. Sweden has an almost equally high coverage rate without extension mechanisms, and exclusively by negotiations between unions and employers' associations, each of which covers the large majority of employees.

French state regulation, however, does not stop at extending collective agreements to almost all employees. It has also a direct impact on wages by the statutory minimum wage, which more or less sets the pace for wage agreements at industry level (Vincent, 2019). In Sweden, minimum wages are exclusively a matter for collective bargaining. Common for both countries is that industry is the dominant bargaining level, a prerequisite for the high coverage rate in these countries.

Tab. 22. France and Sweden compared.

	France	**Sweden**
Union density	9 %	69 %
Density of employers' associations	75 %	89 %
Coverage of collective agreements	98 %	90 %
Extension mechanism	Yes	No
Statutory minimum wage	Yes	No
Dominant bargaining level	Industry	Industry

Remark. Density of employers' associations refers to the share of workers in firms and public authorities affiliated to employers' associations.

At workplace level, Swedish industrial relations are distinguished by dialogue, rather than confrontation as often is the case in France. A recent Swedish example of proactive unions promoting new technology to secure the jobs for green production is the success of the workplace unions at Volvo Cars' engine plant in Skövde to persuade the company to invest €70 million to transform the factory for production of electric engines. The blue-collar union IF Metall and white-collar Unionen, and the Association of Graduate Engineers in the plant co-operated closely, and raised the issue in the group union. Also the union representatives in the company board pushed the issue. An employee consultant produced factual evidence that supported the unions' views. The chairman of the group union was also the IF Metall representative in the company board. There was a dialogue between the group union, the CEO and the HR manager during "countless meetings". The Chinese-owned company was open for arguments and prepared to change the preliminary decision not to produce electric engines in Skövde.

The contrast between Swedish dialogue and French confrontation dealing with such issues is obvious when referring to the French praxis locking-in top managers to prevent layoffs or closing of plants. Such a "bossnapping" occurred in 2021 at a Renault-owned vehicle component plant in North-Western France.

The relatively large decline in Swedish union density since 2006 has not yet become a threat to the Swedish model of collective bargaining as the continuously high share of workers covered by employers' associations compensate for the fall in unionisation. The German development is quite different, as many firms have abandoned their organisations, union density decreased from 25 % to 16 % and the coverage of collective agreements from 68 % to 54 %. These fissures in the German industrial relations model ended in increased state regulation by the introduction of statutory minimum wages. The German union movement changed its attitude from a negative stance to a driving force for such a reform.

As appears from Tab. 21, an overwhelming majority of the countries (20 out of 27) have statutory minimum wages. Sixteen countries more or less frequently extend collective agreements to enterprises not affiliated to employers' associations. Only Austria, Sweden, Denmark, and Italy practice none of these two forms of state regulation. In Austria collective bargaining is, however, de facto extended to almost all employees as membership in the national employers' association (the Chamber of the Economy) is compulsory. Until 2006, Slovenia had a similar chamber system with compulsory membership for employers.

Although Italy has no formal extension mechanism, there is a constitutional obligation to pay "a fair wage", which by juridical practice is the same as the minimum wage in the relevant collective agreement. Consequently, only Sweden and Denmark, in reality, remain in the group of countries with neither statutory minimum wages, nor extension mechanisms.

In Sweden, the unions' right to take actions against unorganised employers is the closest Swedish equivalent to extension mechanisms, and is of central importance for maintaining the model of self-regulation. Although very few conflicts to force employers concluding collective agreements take place per year, the right to sympathy conflicts (strikes, blockades etc.) is here of central importance. The right to sympathy conflicts, of course, is important also at industry level in the regular bargaining rounds, but also in this respect Sweden has a very low frequency of strikes and lockouts. In the UK, sympathy actions are illegal (restricted from 1980 and outlawed entirely since 1990). The leading Swedish private sector employer organisation, Confederation of Swedish Enterprise, demands a ban on sympathy conflicts.

In two countries: Greece and Romania, extension of collective agreements was very common before 2011, but since then not in use. As a result, the coverage rates have fallen dramatically: in Greece from 82 % to 10 % cent and in Romania from 85 % to 35 %. Beginning in May 2010 the Greek government signed loan agreements with the EU/IMF institutions, which required far-reaching decentralisation, individualisation, and deregulation of industrial relations (Katsaroumpas & Koukiadaki, 2019, pp. 269, 272–274). Minimum wages set by collective bargaining were replaced by statutory minimum wages, which later were cut down. All these measures discouraged the employers to continue with industry-level bargaining and resulted in a collapse of bargaining coverage.

Company bargaining dominates in the CEE states

Greece is the only Western European country among the seven in which company level bargaining dominates. Considering only the private sector, company bargaining dominates also in the UK and Croatia, although not so clear in Croatia as in the UK. Consequently, company bargaining dominates in every third of the 27 countries in Tab. 21 if only the private sector is considered. Still the CEE states make up a clear centre of gravity in decentralised bargaining: seven out of the nine countries in question (seven out of the eleven CEE states). As the coverage of collective agreements in most of these countries is very low, unilateral employer wage setting and not company bargaining involving unions characterises these countries, excepting Croatia in which collective bargaining coverage due to extension was 54 % in 2016.

Similarly, the 2008 financial crisis caused the Romanian centre-right government to take a series of actions to liberalise the labour market: prohibit cross-industry bargaining (important in Romania until then), de facto abolish extension of collective agreements, restrict union rights, and make it easier to dismiss employees. The result was a massive decline in bargaining coverage and union density (Trif & Paolucci, 2019).

In several new CEE member states, the low coverage rates of collective agreements, hardly by accident, coincide with the company being the dominant bargaining level. Furthermore, these countries are distinguished not only by a low union density, but in some cases also by a low density of employers' associations. These cover 14 % of employees in Lithuania, 20 % in Poland and 25 % in Estonia (Müller et al., 2019, vol. IV, p. 676). Considering all countries in Tabs 20 and 21, the density of employers' associations on the whole, however, appears more important than union density for determining bargaining coverage (Müller, Vandaele & Waddington, 2019, p. 646). Their weakness, fragmentation and negative attitude negotiating industry agreements in many CEE members states play an important role for the low coverage of collective agreements. In Germany and other Western European countries, the employers' preference for local flexibility has weakened the significance of industry agreements and contributed to their declining coverage. The UK is an extreme example of this tendency.

Without support from industry agreements, it is hard for unions at company/workplace level to conclude advantageous local agreements or any agreements at all. Among the six CEE states listed in Tab. 21 where the company is the dominant bargaining level, the coverage rate varies from 7 % in Latvia and Lithuania to 30 % in Czech Republic with Poland, Estonia, and Hungary in between. In none of these states does union density exceed 13 %. With union density and collective bargaining coverage in decline, the prospects for a developed social dialogue appear problematic.

Similarly, in the former member state UK, industry agreements are today almost absent in the private sector, in which collective bargaining coverage in 2011 was as low as 16 % of the employees. In the UK private sector, "unilateral management pay setting has largely replaced collective bargaining" (ibid, p. 611), a situation reminding us of the state of affairs in several of the new members states. The far-reaching legislation introduced in the UK 1980–1993 did not accept "the legitimacy of collective labour power" (ibid, p. 605) and played a crucial role for the dismantling of the industry agreements, and by that promoting the overall decline of collective bargaining coverage. Neoliberal ideas introduced under the Thatcher governments in this way had a major impact in transforming the British labour market.

Trade unions viewed as sources of rigidity

Many employers and governments view trade unions and collective bargaining as sources of rigidity obstructing economic growth. In the Southern EU member states Greece and Portugal, as in Ireland did the governments after pressure from "the Troika" (the European Commission, the European Central Bank, and the International Monetary Fund) introduce "structural reforms" aimed to promote labour market flexibility. In Greece, it became more difficult for national unions to strike, and non-union "associations of persons" got larger rights concluding company agreements. During the Troika period in Portugal, opening clauses in collective agreements were introduced, and collective bargaining blocked in the public sector. Also, in Romania, measures to increase labour market flexibility were among the conditions for getting financial assistance from the Troika (Trif & Paolucci, 2019, pp. 507, 519).

In Hungary, the successive changes of the Labour Code, motivated as flexibility reforms, had the effect to weaken unions in favour of unilateral management (Borbély & Naumann, 2019). Collective agreements are mainly concluded at company level. Industry agreements cover just every tenth employee. Also, in Poland, company/workplace agreements dominate, but low union density and employer hostility hamper collective bargaining at this level.

In a growing number of countries in which the industry level still dominates, the favourability principle, according to which agreements at lower levels must not be less favourable than those at industry level, has been undermined by new legislation. In some cases: Greece, Portugal, Spain and partly Romania, this occurred under strong pressure from European and international institutions as a condition for financial support (Müller et al., 2019, pp. 633–634). The French government's efforts to give company agreements a leading role in small and middle-sized companies have led to a removal of the favourability principle and facilitated collective bargaining without unions (Vincent, 2019).

Increased state intervention, not seldom under international pressure

To conclude, the dominant tendency in the 27 EU/EES countries listed in Tabs. 20 and 21 is declining union density, shrinking coverage of collective agreements, increased decentralisation of bargaining and growing state regulation in the form of statutory minimum wages (Germany from 2015). Other forms of state intervention were carried out from a neoliberal agenda, not seldom under pressure from international organisations and financiers. In several cases, the absence of national currencies pressed for "internal devaluation" to restore international competitiveness and public finances, for example in Greece, Ireland, Portugal, and Spain. As in other countries special attention was given to, what was labelled as labour market "rigidities".

Although many of these processes characterise most countries, the pace and forms of the changes indicate divergence rather than convergence among the studied 27 countries. In the CEE states the industrial relations systems, however, appear to become more and more similar, as the weakening of collective bargaining and social dialogue progress.

As we have seen, the Nordic Ghent countries were also subject to state intervention into industrial relations, in this case by the remodelling of unemployment funds, in a way that caused large losses of union members. Among the Nordic countries, the deep economic crisis in Finland and Sweden in the 1990s resulted in a much higher share of employees with fix-termed contracts than in Denmark and Norway (Rasmussen et al., 2019). In addition, Sweden is the only Nordic country with gradually weakened employment protection, for example by legislation in 2007 promoting fix-term employment. Under the threat of further legislative changes, Swedish unions, and employers' associations in 2020 concluded a new basic agreement to satisfy the political demands on increased labour market flexibility. It will be followed up by changed legislation.

"Internal devaluation": An option also for Eurozone core countries

The pressure for "internal devaluation", that is downwards adjustments of wages and increased labour market flexibility, is not concentrated in "peripheral" Eurozone states or to the years of financial crises and sovereign debt crisis. Already in the early 2000s, the red-green Schröder government introduced a series of reforms to improve German competitiveness relative to other Eurozone countries, and fight high unemployment as well as preventing further jobs moving abroad. For several years, German real wages either declined (2002, 2004–2008) or were unchanged (2001, 2009): see Müller, Vandaele & Waddington 2019, p. 672. Due to rising employment and regained German competitiveness, the unions strengthened their position vis-a-vis the employers and the government, despite continued decreasing union density and falling collective bargaining coverage. The conservative-led grand coalition from 2013 reregulated temporary agency work, introduced a statutory minimum wage, and made other concessions to unions (Rathgeb & Tassinari, 2020). The degree of union influence stood in inverse relation to the competitive pressure on German economy. Already before that, however tripartite consultation experienced a revival during the crisis years 2008–2009 when short-time work to fight unemployment was introduced (in Sweden the same measure was taken during the 2020 corona crisis).

Another Eurozone core country, Finland, also fits into a pattern of union influence varying with the competitive pressure on the economy. Despite a very high union density, and a tradition of tripartite centralised wage formation, the Finnish unions after a general strike had to accept a "Competitiveness Pact" including a wage freeze for 2017, reduced public sector wages, and increased social security contributions paid by the employees (Rathgeb & Tassinari, 2020). Furthermore, this tripartite pact also meant that collective bargaining at peak (confederal) level was abolished and opening clauses introduced. The unions received no concessions from the centre-right government, which had threatened with unilateral intervention. Against union protests the government in 2018 continued with liberalising labour market reforms. As currency devaluation was no option, Finland resorted to "internal devaluation" to restore its strongly impaired competitiveness after other Eurozone countries had taken such steps. Furthermore, the important Finnish forestry industry had, and has, a severe disadvantage by its Swedish competitor being outside the Eurozone.

Also, in the second-largest Eurozone core country, France, which since the 2010s has experienced a gradually deteriorating competitiveness vis-à-vis Germany, trade unions are facing governments prioritising reduced labour costs and "rigidities". The result of the dialogue between the socialist Hollande government and some union confederations by the employers and the EU Commission were considered insufficient. The government in 2015 and 2016 therefore embarked on a strategy of unilateral liberalisation. This was implemented against joint union opposition laws on reduced employment protection, and increased scope for company agreements to derogate downwards from sectoral agreements and labour law (Rathgeb & Tassinari, 2020). The centrist Macron government from 2017 further undermined the favourability principle by encouraging non-union company agreements with even stronger derogations downwards.

Conclusion

The declining share of employees covered by collective agreements reflects the erosion of collective bargaining in Europe. In several countries sectoral (industry) agreements are undermined by downwards derogations at workplace level. This is possible by the abolishment of the "favourability principle", which still prevents such practices in for example Sweden, but not in Germany with its "opening clauses". In six CEE states and Greece, sectoral agreements are rare and collective bargaining is more or less concentrated at company level (Tab. 21). For the large majority of employees in these countries, unilateral (employer) wage setting is the rule. The same applies to the UK private sector. Consequently, the social dialogue has a modest role in these eight countries, particularly in the private sector.

Variations between countries are large in almost all respects: union density, density of employers' associations, coverage of collective bargaining, degree of centralisation/decentralisation of industrial relations, co-operative versus hostile relations between trade unions and employers' associations, and macroeconomic indicators (competitiveness, unemployment, national debt, etc.).

Another dimension is self-regulation versus state regulation. Here Sweden stands in sharp contrast to France, but also to other countries with state extension of collective agreements, statutory minimum wages, etc. Sweden and France represent the most far-reaching variants of the Nordic and Southern European models respectively.

There are also large variations over time. Particularly in the CEE group of new member states, the share of employees covered by unions and collective agreements has declined considerably in the last few decades. In the UK, the decisive change occurred much earlier with legislation introduced by conservative governments depriving the British unions of their former impressive workplace strength. The German Schröder reforms in the early 2000s illustrates that also a social democratic government can radically liberalise the labour market.

The Swedish case illustrates that the Swedish model is also exposed to pressure by considerably declining union density, and increasing power of transnational companies that do not attach much importance to developing work. As in Denmark and Finland, centre-right governments' change of the Ghent system caused large losses of union members. In Sweden, the result was also a rapidly growing divergence between white-collar and blue-collar union density (73 % and 61 % respectively in 2020), causing a power shift within the union movement, clearly manifested in the 2020 basic agreement signed by the white-collar private sector cartel PTK, and not the blue-collar confederation LO (until the end of 2021), which was weakened by internal conflicts. The two largest LO unions soon, however, joined the agreement, labelled a victory for the Swedish model of self-regulation, although it will be followed up by tripartite social dialogue including the social democratic government. The agreement can be interpreted as a step towards Swedish flexicurity, as it contains both increased space for employers to make derogations from the rule last in, first out in case of layoffs, and improved transition arrangements for employees whose skills need to be developed when new technology is introduced.

The Swedish model shows a great capacity for renewal, manifested in the 2020 basic agreement and the 1997 Industry agreement. For Swedish wage formation, the 1997 Industry Agreement played a decisive role. This institutional innovation, reminding of the classical 1938 Saltsjöbaden Agreement, came about by the labour market parties themselves although under pressure from the social democratic government. Ahead of the planned accession to the EMU, there was a great consensus about the wage leading role of the manufacturing sector in a small, heavily export-dependent country like Sweden. Besides limiting the role of the state, an important union motive was restoring the centralised component of the Swedish model. Since then, different types of co-ordinated bargaining, supported by the new National Mediation Office, is a prerequisite for the implementation of the "industry norm". Some white-collar unions, particularly in the public sector, have "figureless agreements", but the employers in general make sure that they do not result in wage increases exceeding the norm too much, although such deviations sometimes enable changed wages relative to other groups. With this renewed version of the Swedish model, the position outside the Eurozone, the floating krona and the up to the corona crisis declining sovereign debt, there has been no international pressure for internal devaluation.

In contrast, internal devaluation in many countries became the main instrument for restoring competitiveness during the financial and sovereign debt crisis, and in the post-crisis period even in core Eurozone countries like Finland and France. Neither high union density (Finland) nor high mobilisation capacity (France) could prevent governments from forcing through such a policy. Conversely, German trade unions in the same period had a much better dialogue with the government. That clearly demonstrates that the balance of power on the labour market is closely dependent upon the economic performance of a country. Not even in Sweden did the unions succeed in convincing employers to continue investing in "developing work" when unemployment reached quite other levels than in the 1980s and new international production concepts such as lean were adopted by the increasingly globalised companies. During the corona crisis, similar work organisations in Swedish elderly care proved to be highly inappropriate.

References

Borbély, S. & Naumann, L. (2019). Neglected by the state: The Hungarian experience of collective bargaining. In Müller et al. Volume II, pp. 2955–314.

Eurofound (2020). Industrial relations: Developments 2015–2019. Publication Office of the European Union, Luxembourg.

Frödin, O. & Kjellberg, A. (2018). Labor migration from third countries to Swedish low-wage jobs. *Nordic Journal of Working Life Studies*, 8(1), 65–85. https://portal.research.lu.se/sv/publications/labor-migration-from-third-countries-to-swedish-low-wage-jobs

Hällberg, P. & Kjellström, C. (2020) Collective agreements and minimum wages. A report from the Swedish National Mediation Office. Stockholm, Swedish National Office Mediation. https://www.mi.se/app/uploads/Minimum_wages_eng_2.pdf

Katsaroumpas, I. & Koukiadaki, A. (2019). Greece: "contesting" collective bargaining". In Müller et al., 2019. Volume II, pp. 267–293.

Kjellberg, A. (2011). The Decline in Swedish Union Density since 2007. *Nordic Journal of Working Life Studies*, 1(1), 67–93. https://portal.research.lu.se/sv/publications/the-decline-in-swedish-union-density-since-2007

Kjellberg, A. & Lyhne Ibsen, C. (2016). Attacks on union organizing: Reversible and irreversible changes to the Ghent-systems in Sweden and Denmark. In Larsen, T. P. & Ilsøe, A. (eds) Den danske model set udefra – komparative perspektiver på dansk arbejdsmarkedsregulering. København, Jurist- og Økonomforbundets Forlag, pp. 279–302. https://portal.research.lu.se/sv/publications/attacks-on-union-organizing-reversible-and-irreversible-changes-t

Kjellberg, A. (2017). Self-regulation versus State Regulation in Swedish Industrial Relations. In Rönmar, M. &. Julén Votinius, J. (eds) Festskrift till Ann Numhauser-Henning. Lund, Juristförlaget, pp. 357–383. https://portal.research.lu.se/sv/publications/self-regulation-versus-state-regulation-in-swedish-industrial-rel

Kjellberg, A. (2019a.). Den svenska partsmodellen – facket, arbetsgivarna och lönebildningen. In Sandberg, Å. (ed.) Arbete & Välfärd. Ledning, personal och organisationsmodeller i Sverige. Lund, Studentlitteratur, pp. 119–147.

Kjellberg, A. (2019b). Sweden: collective bargaining under the industry norm". In Müller et al., Volume III, pp. 583–604. https://portal.research.lu.se/sv/publications/sweden-collective-bargaining-under-the-industry-norm

Kjellberg, A. (2020). Den svenska modellen i en oviss tid. Stockholm, Arena Idé. https://portal.research.lu.se/sv/publications/den-svenska-modellen-i-en-oviss-tid-fack-arbetsgivare-och-kollekt

Kjellberg, A. (2021). Kollektivavtalens täckningsgrad samt organisationsgraden hos arbetsgivarförbund och fackförbund. Department of Sociology, Lund University, Studies in Social Policy, Industrial Relations, Working Life and Mobility. https://portal.research.lu.se/sv/publications/kollektivavtalens-t%C3%A4ckningsgrad-samt-organisationsgraden-hos-arbe-2

Kjellberg (2022). Parternas organisationsgrad och kollektivavtalens utbredning. In Medlingsinstitutets årsrapport 2021. Stockholm, Swedish National Mediation Office.

Kommunal (2016). Vad du behöver veta om otrygga anställningar. Stockholm, Kommunal.

Müller, T., Vandaele, K., & Waddington, J. (2019). *Collective Bargaining in Europe: Towards an Endgame*. Volume I–IV. Brussels, European Trade Union Institute.

Müller, T., Vandaele, K., & Waddington, J. (2019). Conclusion: Towards an endgame. In Müller et al. Volume III, pp. 625–668.

Nergaard, K. (2020). Organisasjonsgrader, tariffavtaledekning og arbeidskonflikter 2018/2019. Fafo-notat 2020:12. Oslo, Fafo.

Rasmussen, S., Nätti, J., Larsen, T. P., Ilsøe, A., & Garde, A. H. (2019). Non-standard Employment in the Nordics – toward precarious work? *Nordic Journal of Working Life Studies* 9 (56), 7–32.

Rathgeb, P. & Tassinari, A. (2020). How the Eurozone disempowers trade unions: the political economy of competitive internal devaluation. *Socio-Economic Review* [Online].

Tåhlin, M. (2019). Polariseringsmyten: försvinner verkligen de medelkvalificerade jobben? Stockholm, Arena idé.

Thörnquist, A. (2015). False self-employment and other precarious forms of employment in the "grey area" of the labour market. *International Journal of Comparative Labour Law and Industrial Relations*. 31(4), 411–429. http://liu.diva-portal.org/smash/get/diva2:894030/FULLTEXT01.pdf

Tillväxtanalys (2020). Utländska företag 2019. Stockholm, Tillväxtanalys.

Trif, A. & Paolucci, V. (2019). Romania: from legal support to frontal assault. In Müller et al., Volume III, pp. 505–523.

Vincent, C. (2019). France: The rush towards prioritising the enterprise level. In Müller et al., Volume I, pp. 217–238.

Mary Trainor, Louis Laurent, Jan Michiel Meeuwsen,
and Paulien Bongers

Promoting health and safety for sustainable workplaces: A PEROSH perspective

Abstract: PEROSH is the Partnership for European Research in Occupational Safety and Health (OSH). The PEROSH vision is that policymakers, workplaces and other stakeholders across Europe are inspired by, and use, knowledge generated by PEROSH in their efforts to develop innovative and sustainable workplaces which are healthy and safe. PEROSH comprises 14 national research institutes from 13 countries on the continent of Europe. Each institute plays a key national role through their affiliation to government, health and accident insurance systems, or industry and trade unions. The partnership acts collectively to: strengthen co-operation on OSH research and accelerate the generation of knowledge in key areas of OSH; and disseminate and exchange knowledge and information on OSH issues. In 2019, The International Labour Organisation identified that PEROSH has "strong national and regional [European] policy impact". This chapter gives an overview of PEROSH: an introduction to its history and strategy; governance and core activities including the PEROSH Joint Research Programme and the PEROSH international Wellbeing at Work conference series. It summarises PEROSH outreach and networking activities at national, European and global level. The chapter concludes with reflections on the importance of robust scientific evidence to underpin and inform the actions of stakeholders for a sustainable world of work which is healthy and safe. It also reflects on PEROSH activities in the light of the ongoing pandemic.

Keywords: sustainable workplace, workplace innovation, occupational safety, occupational health, wellbeing at work, working conditions, PEROSH, international network, OSH

Introduction: PEROSH history and strategy

In an ever-changing world of work, the promotion of the health and safety of the present and future workforce is crucial for guaranteeing a healthier, longer and more productive working life. National institutes for occupational health and safety (OSH) research in Europe play a distinctive role in anticipating, creating, and synthesising the evidence needed to underpin and inform the actions of: national policymakers; regulators; health and insurance systems; and industry and trade unions. However, workplace challenges transcend national borders. Recognising the opportunity in Europe to exploit synergies in their roles and research activities and to gear national funding through collaboration, in 2003 a group of these national institutes founded The Partnership for European Research in Occupational Safety and Health, PEROSH. The partnership operates through a formal Agreement (PEROSH, 2018). Today, PEROSH has 14 partner institutes from 13 countries on the continent of Europe (PEROSH, Online-f). Each institute plays a key national role through their affiliation to government, health and accident insurance systems, or industry and trade unions ("social partners").

The partnership acts collectively to: strengthen European co-operation on OSH research and accelerate the generation of knowledge in key areas of OSH; and disseminate and exchange knowledge and information on OSH issues. PEROSH builds on the success of the international "Sheffield Group: an informal network of directors of national research institutes for occupational OSH institutes. The network first met in 1989 at the laboratory of the UK Health and Safety Executive, HSE (at that time based in Sheffield). Its members span four continents: North America (IRSST – Canada and NIOSH-USA); Oceania (NIOH-New Zealand); Asia (IIOSH-Israel, JNIOSH-Japan, KOSHA-South Korea and WSHI-Singapore); and Europe. Information on these institutes is at: www.irsst.qc.ca; https://www.cdc.gov/niosh/; www.nioh.ac.za; www.osh.org.il; www.jniosh.johas.go.jp; www.kosha.or.kr; www.wshi.gov.sg. The annual meetings are hosted by one of the institutes on a rotating basis, and continue to be chaired by HSE. PEROSH maintains strong links with the Sheffield Group, including biennial joint meetings of the institute directors.

The PEROSH Strategy 2019–2023, Research co-operation to promote a healthy, productive and innovative workforce (PEROSH, 2019a), sets out the mission, vision, activities, outreach and ambition for the partnership. The mission of PEROSH is to create and exchange new knowledge and practice on occupational safety and health, and make it accessible to policymakers, workplaces and other stakeholders in Europe. The PEROSH vision is that policymakers, workplaces and other stakeholders across Europe are inspired by, and use, knowledge generated by PEROSH in their efforts to develop innovative and sustainable workplaces which are healthy and safe. PEROSH seeks impact and adds value through the exchange of knowledge and good practices across Europe to the benefit of all. The PEROSH strategy sets out the following activities through which the mission and vision are fulfilled: (1) We pool resources and create new knowledge through joint activities. (2) We disseminate share and exchange knowledge on OSH issues between members and within Europe to all relevant stakeholders. (3) We provide the evidence base that informs and underpins decisions by national and European policymakers on healthy and safe working lives. (4) We identify new research challenges in the field of OSH.

The generation and exchange of knowledge for use to develop innovative and sustainable workplaces that are healthy and safe is a "golden thread", aligning the activities of PEROSH to its vision. These activities span the ongoing challenges to health and safety in today's workplaces, and anticipating and meeting the new challenges and opportunities from technological change, disruptive innovation and the changing world of work. They include research activities in relation to: technologies, materials and equipment in the work environment; demographic change and changing employment practices; and effective work organisation and leadership to reduce occupational accidents and ill-health, while promoting wellbeing at work.

This paper gives an overview of the partnership's: structure and governance; core activities including the Joint Research Programme, researcher exchange visits, biennial member research conferences, and the PEROSH international Wellbeing at Work conference series; and outreach activities at national, European and global level.

Governance and Structure

PEROSH is governed by its Steering Committee (SC) which comprises the director general or research director of each member institute. The SC is responsible for the strategic direction and management of PEROSH, its finances, and decisions on admitting new member institutes. The SC currently meets twice yearly. The PEROSH website gives an overview of the current 14 member institutes. Each member institute plays a key national research role, through their affiliation to government, health and accident insurance systems, or industry and trade unions. Some national organisations are members through their OSH science and research institute or function (for instance AUVA, BAuA, HSE, TNO and Unisanté): these are represented on the SC by their OSH research director or equivalent. Decisions on new members consider, for instance, alignment to the PEROSH mission and vision, research quality, and commitment to research ethics.

The governance of PEROSH is managed by the Steering Committee which is supported by a Scientific Steering Group managing all joint research activities and events. Each member institute pays an equal annual PEROSH subscription. This subscription is used to support the core PEROSH activities, in particular through: the appointment of part time paid officials, the Manager of International Affairs (MIA) and the secretariat; and the operation of its website (including the online repository of PEROSH publications), the PEROSH e-newsletter, and other media channels in line with the outreach ambitions in the PEROSH Strategy.

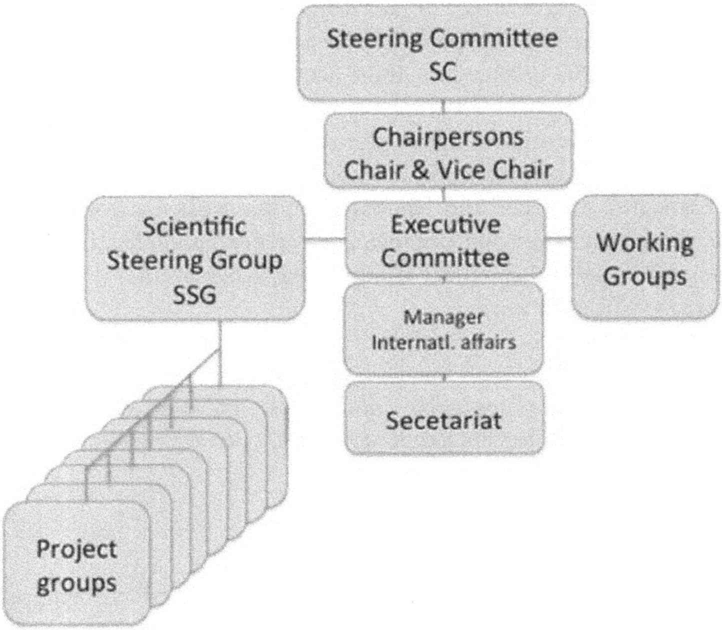

Fig. 13. Structure of PEROSH under the Steering Committee of institute directors.

The main objective of PEROSH is to provide evidence-based knowledge and information about occupational health and safety in a European context. PEROSH provides also services to its members with the purpose of exchanging information, sharing good research practices or current research reviews in OSH fields. It is important to underline that PEROSH does not interfer in national policies or ways of implementation. Key is its role as a knowledge and learning community rather than a policy community. The PEROSH network aso engages to share its research activities. with EU-OSHA or follows their activities.

The International Labour Organisation, ILO (www.ilo.org) included PEROSH in a study of six OSH networks from different regions of the world: Europe, Latin America, Asia and Africa. The study aimed to understand how and why OSH agencies institutions, organisations and experts collaborate. Some of the characteristics of a successful network which ILO developed from this study comprise:

- Limited number of members sharing the same vision (social capital), or membership determined by special criteria such as research area or institutional or professional status

- Practice of inviting members to draw up interest, competence, or activity profiles
- Well-identified co-ordinating body and focal point for speaking in the collective voice of the network
- Co-ordinator or "leader" with competencies and capacities to lead the network's activities
- Annual meetings in vivo and publishing of a network newsletter or e-newsletter are considered important instruments for both cohesion and the functions of the network
- Growing emphasis given to behavioural and ethical principles in networking

The ILO study report identifies that PEROSH has "strong national and regional policy impact" (Rantanen, 2018; ILO, 2019) and includes a detailed profile of PEROSH (*op. cit.*, p. 151).

PEROSH core partner activities

The core activities of the PEROSH partnership members include: identification of key research needs; the Joint Research Programme; a wide range of activities to share scientific knowledge and provide developmental opportunities for upcoming researchers; and the PEROSH international *Wellbeing at Work* conference series. These activities have developed since PEROSH began in 2003, building on the approaches found most effective to realise the partnership's mission and vision. The activities continue to grow and evolve, most recently with the first PEROSH international conference on *Prolonging Working Life*, hosted online in May 2020 by NFA (PEROSH, Online-a).

(A) PEROSH Identification of Key Research Needs

Joint identification of key OSH research needs is a core partner activity. It supports: identification of synergies in existing and planned member institute research programmes; opportunities to leverage institutes' national funding through collaborative, co-funded research to meet common needs; awareness among policymakers and the wider research community in Europe and other stakeholders, of knowledge and evidence gaps to enable innovative and sustainable workplaces; and global research networking and activity. The distinctive research needs for each member institute are defined and agreed at national level, according to the institute's statute and role; for instance, some institutes focus on occupational ill health and accident prevention, and others on supporting return to work after injury or ill-health.

A review of European research priorities (Gagliardi et al., 2017) was carried out by an interdisciplinary group of PEROSH researchers from member institutes, including foresight specialists, using a modified Delphi study. The authors note that it is the first published study providing, "a reliable expression of the perspective of the European OSH Research Community together with an analysis of differences between European geographical areas." The highest priorities identified include new issues such as: "OSH management in new forms of employment (eg, crowdsourcing, internships, zero hours contracts); impacts of innovation and new ways of working (ie, telework, e-work, boundary less work); health and safety in human–computer interaction and the introduction of unsafe and unhealthy work equipment following the reduction of barriers to the free movement of goods." The researchers also note the high importance attributed to two transversal priorities: translation of research results into practical and effective tools; and support for OSH implementation in micro, small and medium enterprises. Figure 14 illustrates the differences in priorities by geographical area.

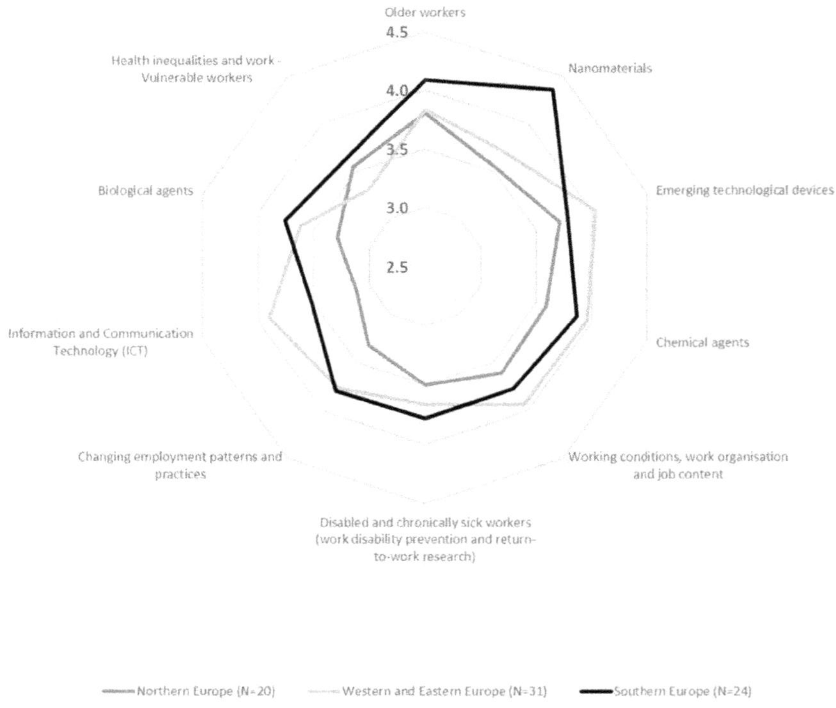

Fig. 14. Research priorities by European geographical area on a scale of 5 (high) to 1 (low) from PEROSH study (Gagliardi et al., 2016).

(B) PEROSH Researcher Exchange Programme

PEROSH has an active programme of researcher exchange visits. These are short visits between institutes, typically one- or two-weeks' duration, often on a reciprocal basis. The benefits include: exchange of practical knowledge on laboratory techniques; support for current research through discussion with experts at another institute; introducing the upcoming generation of researchers to how evidence from another institute is used to inform and underpin the work of national stakeholders; and promoting new collaborative projects, either bilateral or within the PEROSH Joint Research Programme. Examples of researcher exchanges that facilitated or led to collaborative research on common evidence needs are: between FIOH and BAuA on the impact of working times on well-being for healthcare professionals (Karhula et al., 2020); and between TNO and HSE on insights into effective interventions for occupational asthma among bakery workers (Meijester et al., 2011). An example exchange that provided support and insights from host institute experts to an upcoming researcher is a visit to NFA by a new HSE researcher, to support a review of occupational asthma in wood and furniture manufacturing (Wiggans et al., 2016)

(C) PEROSH Member Research Conferences

Since PEROSH was formed in 2003, it has continued to evolve, and introduced new approaches to strengthen knowledge exchange and networking between member institutes. In 2015, the inaugural PEROSH Member Research Conference was held. These biennial conferences bring together upcoming and experienced researchers from member institutes, and include a tour of the host institute's facilities. Speakers are from PEROSH with additional invited keynote presentations including from European industry and from OSH national research institutes outside Europe. On average there are 70 delegates and 25 speakers per conference. Common to each conference is a focus on OSH impact. This covers both: multidisciplinary solution-focused, translational research by PEROSH institutes that is taken up by policymakers, regulators, industry and other stakeholders to improve occupational safety and health; and measurement and evaluation of the impact of OSH interventions and campaigns at national level. To support outreach activities, PEROSH publishes a conference overview, for instance videos of panel discussions and keynote speakers, or a "Book of Abstracts" (PEROSH, Online-b,c,d). Each conference focuses on three key research topics aligned to the PEROSH vision for innovative and sustainable workplaces which are healthy and safe. The conferences facilitate: *"exchange of information between our young researchers and experienced researchers around many of the important topics that are facing the OSH research community like additive manufacturing; the ageing workforce; and respiratory health,"* PEROSH SC member Professor Andrew Curran (PEROSH, 2016).

(D) PEROSH Joint Research Programme

PEROSH has an active Joint Research Programme consisting of a set of collaborative projects between member institutes. Around six to ten projects are ongoing at any given time, most of them with more than six partners and sometimes external partners bringing their own expertise. When PEROSH was formed in 2003, member institutes were already collaborating through a range of ad-hoc opportunities and networking. The Joint Research Programme was introduced in 2009 to realise the opportunities to exploit synergies in distinctive research needs that transcend national boundaries across the European institutes that form the PEROSH partnership.

There is no external funding; each institute within a project team arranges its own funding. The PEROSH benefits in such activity are threefold. First, institutes *join forces* and reach a critical mass to undertake action they could not perform individually. Second, the group has an easier *access to national information* such as regulations, prevention measures, grey literature, rendering benchmarking activity easier. Finally, the *diversity of approaches and culture* leads to a mutual enrichment. The administrative burden at the PEROSH level is made as low as possible to ease these collaborations.

Many projects address the need to both facilitate and undertake the synthesis of research evidence. The common driver across PEROSH is the importance of robust evidence to underpin and inform decision-making and advice to workplaces by national policymakers, regulators, and other stakeholders. The aim of these projects are most of the time (1) international comparisons of practices, research activity, regulations, (2) collective development of tools, guidance documents, methodology development, (3) data frame work or shared data base, (4) synthesis of research evidence through literature review. The following projects illustrate this diversity:

1. *PEROSH recommendations for procedures to measure occupational physical activity and workload.* Ten institutes and external partners have run this project between 2014 and 2018. A PEROSH research team developed evidence to support actions by stakeholders to reduce work-related MSDs. They aimed to unleash the potential for knowledge exchange between institutes by generating a common framework for technical measures of physical work demands. They developed specialist technical information on assessing sedentary behaviour (Holtermann et al., 2017a, b) and arm elevation (Weber

et al., 2017). An indication of the outreach of this work is the "Best Paper Award 2017" given by the Journal for Applied Ergonomics for the team's practical technical guide for researchers and OSH practitioners on assessing occupational sedentary behaviour (Holtermann et al., 2017a). It is intended that the outcome can be used to inform and support the development of national-level tools, guides and interventions. For instance, the results of this work informed the decision by the Danish Ministry of Labour to request the development and evaluation of a new technical system for measuring ergonomic work demands for use in national workplace surveillance (work now underway at NFA). This project has been followed by the *PEPPA* project (*PEROSH Exchange Platform for Measurements of Occupational Physical Activity and Physical Workload – a Feasibility Study*) run by eleven partners between 2019 and 2021. Its aim is to analyse the feasibility of a data exchange platform for workload data allowing to perform analysis on larger data sets

2. *Exposure of workers to indirect UV- and IR-radiation emitted by arcs, flames and thermal radiators IndIR-UV.* This project was run by six partners between 2015 and 2017 and it developed evidence to help protect workers exposed to UV and IR radiation emitted by arcs, flames and thermal radiators. Exposure of workers can damage the eyes and skin. Simple, practical, risk assessments by companies are important to decide what protective control measures are needed. However, there was a lack of scientific evidence as a basis for risk assessment for *indirect* exposures, for instance a worker in the vicinity of a welder. The outcome of the project (Bauer et al 2015) can be used as a basis to develop advice and tools tailored to national needs. For instance, in Austria it has been used to underpin a simple online risk assessment tool for companies (AUVA, Online).
3. *Assessment of comfort and ergonomics of protective clothing for firefighters vs. normative requirements in various European countries (ERGO FIREFIGHTER).* This project with three partners took place between 2018 and 2019. It consisted mainly in a review of the European research literature on ergonomics of protective clothing for firefighters, including the potential benefits of smart wearable devices. The national regulations in the three countries of the partners were also compared. The research produced evidence that can be used to inform updates on national standards to better protect firefighters (Młynarczyk *et al.*, 2019).
4. *Dose-Response Relationships (DRR).* Seven Institutes have carried out this project between 2016 and 2020. They developed a methodology for the hazard assessment for chemical substances from an analysis of literature. Both toxicological and epidemiological studies have been considered and

analysed separately since they cannot be easily compared (human/animal, type of exposure). For a given chemical, the method includes (1) the systematic review of the literature and selection of eligible publications, (2) the reliability assessment for each identified paper according to well defined quality criteria. Care has also been taken to avoid redundancies of epidemiological studies on the same cohort, (3) the derivation of the Lowest Observed Effect Levels (toxicological studies) or dose response relationships (epidemiological studies) sorted by health outcome. Then the method has been tested on the 1,3-butadiene. 75 toxicological for five health outcomes (e.g. local effects on skin and mucous membranes or genotoxicity) have been investigated and 5 epidemiological studies have been selected. The outcome of this work is a global picture of the findings of these studies sorted by quality level. The results are summarized in a report (Nold et al. 2021)

5. *Waste workers.* Between 2018 and 2021, nine institutes participated to this project, which addressed the topic of the biological risk related to the collection of waste. The project analysed first how waste is collected in Europe. A significant part of the work consisted in a review of the literature. A first topic is the waste workers exposure to dust and various biological agents (endotoxins, bacteria, funghi) for various types of waste. The factors modulating the exposure were also discussed, such as the worktask (driver, loader), the type of waste, temperature and humidity, technical parameters (type of truck, waste container or bag, ventilation, robotic arm, etc) and prevention measures. The project also reviewed the acute health effects on waste workers using various methods (spirometry, biomarkers of inflammation, and questionnaires about respiratory and gastrointestinal symptoms) and long-term effects. The prevention measures in five European countries have been analysed. The main outcome of this project is a review paper which has been published in Science of the total Environment (Madsen, 2021).(Madsen et al., 2021).
6. *European harmonization of exposure assessment for asbestos in the workplace.* This project with nine partners will run in 2021 and 2022. It is motivated by the variety of sampling and analytical methods in Europe to assess exposure to asbestos. In addition, the European commission plans to propose a new protective occupational exposure limit value on asbestos. The aim of this project is to compare the outcomes of different existing exposure assessment methods and propose a harmonized approach for new data collection in order to make it possible to share the results of exposure measurements at European level.

Details of new, ongoing and completed projects in the Joint Research Programme are at (PEROSH, Online-e). Through these exchange activities, the European learning community on OSH problems and challenges is further widened. PEROSH members collaborate together and strive for further collaboration with others to underpin the importance of OSH in many of the challenges Europe faces.

(E) PEROSH "Wellbeing at Work" Group and International Conference Series

The importance of wellbeing at work has become an increasing focus for policymakers and industry within many European nations and globally. In 2009, nine PEROSH member institutes held a workshop at HSE to share information and identify common research needs (Fishwick et al., 2010). Participants suggested that drivers for research include: "societal costs, governmental policy, legislative positions, altruism and moral arguments within civilised societies." They identified that: "At the heart of the well-being debate is the paradox that 'good work is good for you, but work can also harm your health.'" They discussed the differences in the way "wellbeing at work" as a concept is understood and identified various themes. These include that, "wellbeing is not defined as only the lack of mental ill health, but incorporates social and physical functioning. Well-being has to be a positive, sustainable concept of optimal functioning … with the emphasis on positive consequences for work ability and creativity."

The research needs discussed were in five categories: "(i) defining the rationale for improving well-being, (ii) developing evidence-based approaches that facilitate improved well-being and the prevention of negative influences, (iii) developing communications systems to improve the ongoing debate on these issues; (iv) using case studies to facilitate engagement with stakeholders on the benefits of the well-being concept, and (v) filling the evidence gaps and how to share these research findings." At the workshop, FIOH explained the plans they already had for a conference to bring together international thinking on this important emerging workplace need. Jointly, these activities led to what became the first in the series of PEROSH international Wellbeing at Work conferences (see our website for an overview) and the formation in 2010 of the multidisciplinary PEROSH Wellbeing Group, which continues today as the central focus of co-ordination for the series.

An early activity by the PEROSH Wellbeing Group was to develop the PEROSH Wellbeing Tree, to help visualise and communicate about the different factors that feed into wellbeing at work. There are two versions, one for employers (see Fig. 15) and one which uses more specialist language for researchers. Wellbeing Group members have used the tree in national-level engagement and articles; for instance (Lunt et al., 2014 a, b). Lunt et al., 2014a, note that: "The Wellbeing Tree is not intended to be an empirical, testable model: rather, it shows in an intuitive way the great variety of factors that can affect wellbeing … The many different factors that contribute to workplace wellbeing are the roots of the tree, implying a clear relationship between investing in workforce wellbeing, and the benefits of doing so: the 'growth' of the tree, and the fruit it produces. The tree image also helps to show the interdependence between the worker and the context of their work, in relation to wellbeing. The interaction of the individual and wider society can be made clear."

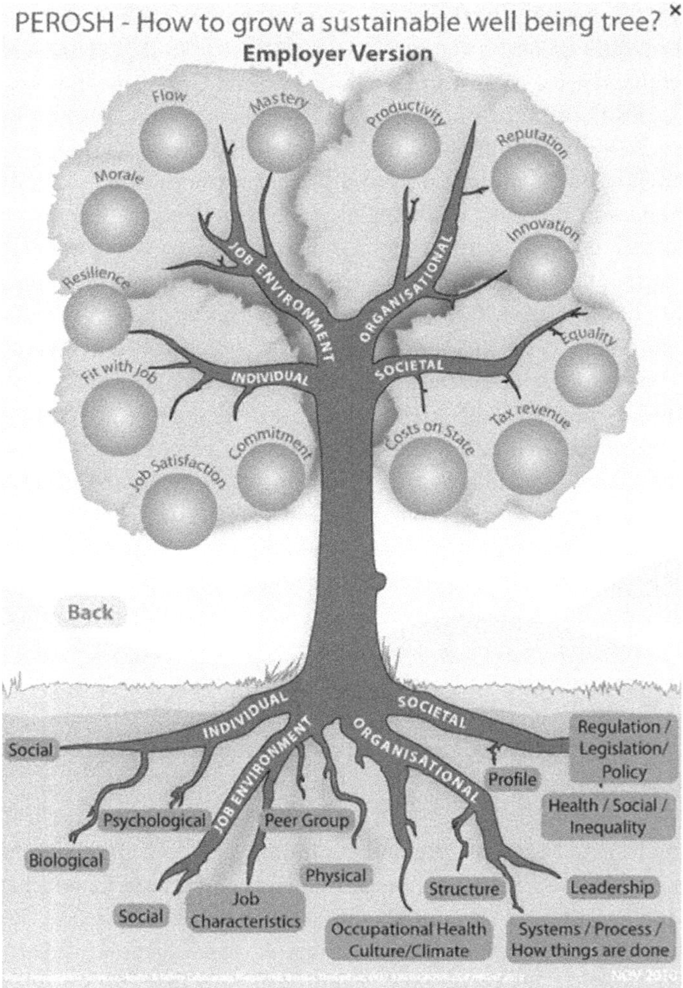

Fig. 15. The PEROSH Wellbeing Tree: Employer version.

Activities by the Wellbeing Group have included considering the impact of the changing world of work (Lunt et al., 2015), including transient working and greater flux in the job market. This identified that, "trends towards increased globalisation and technological advances could make it increasingly more difficult to maintain the classical attributes of a 'good job.'" The group has also investigated factors associated with job satisfaction in the general working population. This study used the Danish Work Environment Cohort Study with replies from 10,000 workers. In a paper called "Job satisfaction is more than a fruit basket, health checks and free exercise" (Andersen et al., 2017), the researchers identify that: "While psychosocial work factors and to some extent physical work demands are important for job satisfaction, workplace health-promotion offers appear to play a minor role." The researchers note, as the driver for their study, that: "Workers who are satisfied with their job are the cornerstones of healthy and productive companies." The group has also published a Good Practice Checklist "for workplaces that wish to do more to support everyone at work to be physically active and to reduce sedentary behavior" (Fishwick et al., 2014). The checklist's introduction for workplaces notes that: "In addition to the health benefits of increasing physical exercise, there is increasing evidence that regular sedentary behaviour can be harmful to health. Sedentary behaviour is a term used to describe prolonged sitting at work without regular active breaks."

The Wellbeing at Work conference series is providing an international platform that is building evidence to meet these research needs and facilitating cross-fertilisation of ideas and approaches globally. Global research trends have been evident through the presentations given in the decade from the first to the most recent fifth conference. "We see a movement from very early understanding of wellbeing, pretty much risk factors … Now we're dealing with intervention studies in workplaces… We hope that as we continue to host these conferences, we start to develop solutions which are evidence based," David Fishwick, Chair of the PEROSH Wellbeing Group (PEROSH, 2019b).

(F) PEROSH Information Sharing Workshops

Short, topic-based, Information Sharing Workshops are used by PEROSH members to exchange knowledge about priority research areas and evidence needs. In line with common priorities for PEROSH institutes, see above and (Gagliardi et al. 2017; PEROSH, 2012), topics include: transversal (translation of research to give impact;) sector or technology specific; specific diseases or ill-health with a high burden on workers; and cross-cutting OSH priorities spanning multiple workplaces. The topics span both current and emerging challenges to health and safety. These last three years, six workshops have been organized with a move to the online format due to the pandemic:

"Work-related stress and related mental-health issues" hosted at HSE, Buxton, UK, 2019;
"Metalworking fluid and respiratory ill-health" hosted at INRS, Paris, France, 2020;
"PEROSH workshop on safe working with asbestos" hosted by TNO, The Netherlands, 2020
"Health and Safety Guidelines for Intelligent Robots" organized by TNO, online, 2020.
"Innovating with VR and AR in Safety", organized by TNO, online, 2021.
"Metalworking fluid and respiratory ill-health-2" organized by HSE and AUVA, online, 2021;

While the primary goal of each workshop is to share information, some lead to projects in the Joint Research Programme, or other activities. The example is the birth of the "Well being and work group". For instance, as noted above, the ongoing activities following the 2009 Information Sharing Workshop on "Wellbeing and Work" include the PEROSH international Wellbeing at Work conference series. All workshop topics align to the PEROSH vision for innovative and sustainable workplaces. The last example is the workshop on asbestos in 2020, which has been followed by the above-mentioned research project.

PEROSH Outreach Activities

The PEROSH strategy (PEROSH, 2019a) has five pillars. The first three focus on European and national outreach. The first pillar is: "*Outreach and visibility of PEROSH to European stakeholders.* PEROSH will take initiatives to reach out and contact on a regular base stakeholders in Europe. The ambition is to further raise the profile of its robust scientific evidence and foresight activities on important OSH issues in Europe." These activities include proactive dialogue with European Union institutions including EU-OSHA (www.osha.europa.eu) and EUROFOUND (www.eurofound.europa.eu). For instance, EU-OSHA used the PEROSH articulation of common research needs (PEROSH, 2012) to inform their identification of research needs (EU-OSHA, 2013). EU-OSHA has also requested to use the 2020 PEROSH Prolonging Working Life international conference as an example of good practice in its OSH Campaign Toolkit (EU-OSHA, online).

The second pillar is: "*Visibility of PEROSH at the National level.* Each member will provide knowledge and experience to PEROSH, and take home to its own national level the enriched knowledge produced by this partnership. The enrichment will be based on information from joint trend analyses, joint research projects and information sharing events, and joint identification of key research needs. All members have their specific national dissemination channels, and will use these effectively." These activities are specific to each institute, according to their national statute, mission and key stakeholders. The host institute of PEROSH events has the opportunity to invite key national stakeholders. For instance, the 2019 PEROSH Information Sharing workshop on work-related stress was attended by two HSE policymakers in an observer capacity. (HSE is a government agency and the regulator for workplace health and safety in Great Britain.)

The third pillar is: "*PEROSH in Europe*. PEROSH was founded because workplace challenges in a globalised world transcend national borders. Sharing of knowledge and joint research activities by PEROSH members realises significant benefits. Therefore, research institutes in other European countries will actively be offered membership, if they have a national role and are willing to commit to the PEROSH mission, vision, activities and ambitions." Recent PEROSH outreach in Europe has included activities from 2016 to connect with the Swedish OSH research community, through attendance at meetings and conferences. In parallel with these activities, some individual PEROSH member institutes collaborated with the "Swedish Platform for sustainable work as a resource for health, innovation and growth in EU's Horizon 2020" (Sustainable Work 2020, Online). Although this collaboration was not a PEROSH activity, it was facilitated by the existing networking between PEROSH member institutes. In 2018, The Swedish Agency for Work Environment Expertise, SAWEE (MYNAK), was formed under the Ministry of Labour and Employment. Sweden does not have a national research institute. Therefore in 2020, building on the earlier outreach activities, SAWEE became a PEROSH member, to explore a research partnership model in the Swedish context.

The fourth PEROSH outreach pillar moves beyond Europe: "*PEROSH in the world*. PEROSH is willing to share its knowledge, good practice and lessons-learned with similar OSH research organisations and networks across the globe. PEROSH maintains contacts with global players in the world of OSH research." Contact with global players encompasses a wide range of activities led by the members of the PEROSH Steering Committee, SC. These include: biennial joint meetings with the international Sheffield Group; engagement with the International Labour Organisation, ILO, the International Social Security Association, ISSA, and the World Health Organisation, WHO; an invitation to the newly formed OSHAfrica (www.oshafrica.africa) to attend an SC meeting hosted by IFA; and engagement with the International Commission on Occupational Health, ICOH (www.icohweb.org). The ICOH engagement is facilitated through PEROSH SC members who are, or have been, ICOH officials or board members. Similarly, the WHO engagement is facilitated through PEROSH member institutes that are WHO Collaborating Centres.

The fifth pillar is: "*PEROSH impact*. PEROSH will focus on the societal impact of its research results. The ambition is to demonstrate the added value of PEROSH research on occupational safety and health carried out by its members. PEROSH will endeavour to develop methodologies, and share approaches to measure and evaluate the benefits of OSH research results for policymakers, workplaces, insurance systems, and other stakeholders." This is an ongoing strategic activity for PEROSH. The most recent PEROSH member research conference took this as a key topic and further sharing of approaches and good practice from across the partnership is planned.

In 2021 PEROSH organized special sessions with PEROSH researchers sharing their outcomes at the XXII World Congress on Safety & Health at Work 2021 and IETOX2021 (3rd International Industrial and Environmental Toxicology Congress). Furthermore, preparations have been made for a special session of PEROSH contributions for the upcoming ICOH2022 conference.

PEROSH and the pandemic

Today, the COVID-19 pandemic is fundamentally affecting work and society. Multitudes of scientists globally are developing evidence to combat the impact of the virus. Among them are scientists from PEROSH institutes, working according to their institute's national role or as part of national task forces. For instance they are: providing advice on suitability of personal protective equipment (PPE) for healthcare workers; investigating methods for PPE decontamination and reuse as a last resort if supplies fail; developing evidence to inform effective measures to control the risk of workplace transmission, and to identify its contribution to total transmission; and informing advice by government ministries to support the health of those working from home (see for instance CIOP, 2020; Marinaccio et al., 2020; MvSZW, 2020; SAGE-EMG, 2020; Vernez et al., in press). Foresight specialists are developing possible futures scenarios to support debate and decision making (Héry and Malenfer, 2020). During the PEROSH 4th Research Conference in Madrid many PEROSH researchers presented their approaches and publications. The presentations during this session can be found in the PEROSH on line repository.

Obviously the PEROSH institutes had to cope with similar issues. Soon after the beginning of the lock-down the 24 March 2020, 12 Perosh members met through a telephone conference to share questions they had to answer in their countries, identify knowledge gaps, and envisage co-ordinated actions. Tools to foster collaborations (platforms to share information, on line conference, translation tools) were also discussed. The 25 March a common Internet platform had been set up by AUVA (the Austrian member) to exchange information about national activities and research results. It has been used intensively more than one year by 84 participants (86 % from PEROSH plus a few guests in particular from the US NIOSH).

In 2021, the topics addressed by PEROSH are rather related to what we have learned during the pandemic and lessons for the future. One of the topics of the PEROSH conference in Madrid (30-09-2021) was "pandemic and post pandemic challenges" (PEROSH, Online-g). One of the keynote lectures was dedicated to the management of the "PPE crisis" by the Spanish institute. Then seventeen talks given by authors from 11 different institutes, addressed questions related to the pandemic: exposure to SARS-COV2 at the workplace, psychosocial risks at the workplace, prevention at the workplace, effect of telework (Laurent, 2021)

It is likely that this collaborative action will last in 2022, with new initiatives prolonging the activity of the two last years.

Discussion and outlook

The ongoing challenge for health and safety systems in Europe is to tackle the burden on workers, their families and society of life-changing workplace injuries, occupational diseases and ill health, and deaths at work: the loved ones who will never again come home at the end of the working day. The world of work continues to change. There are potential benefits and risks to workers from new technologies, materials and equipment, and disruptive innovation. Net Zero technologies, advanced manufacturing, smart sensors and the Internet of Things, cobotics and machine learning ("AI") are among the drivers for change. There are challenges and opportunities from demographic change and longer working lives, globalisation, deglobalisation, and changing employment practices including the gig economy and digitalisation. Recently some, PEROSH members responded to a consultation from the Commission DG Research & Innovation on a Strategic Research and Innovation plan (SRIP) for chemicals related to the new Green Deal. Robust work organisation and leadership is important to effectively control risks to health and safety while promoting wellbeing at work.

The ongoing challenge for national occupational safety and health research institutes is to develop, synthesise and translate robust evidence on current and emerging challenges, to anticipate future evidence needs for the changing world of work, and to transfer this knowledge to the health and safety system. Through

PEROSH, 14 national institutes in 13 European countries are acting collectively to: strengthen co-operation on research, accelerate the generation of knowledge in key areas; and disseminate and exchange knowledge and information. Their common vision is that policymakers, workplaces and other stakeholders across Europe are inspired by and use knowledge generated by PEROSH in their efforts to develop innovative and sustainable workplaces which are healthy and safe. Since its inception in 2003, the partnership has continued to develop and strengthen its activities and outreach.

The new 2021–2027 OSH framework, announced in the European Pillar of Social Rights action plan, sets out the key priorities and actions necessary for improving workers' health and safety over the coming years in the context of the post-pandemic world, marked with green and digital transitions, economic and demographic challenges and the changing notion of a traditional workplace environment. Healthy and safe working conditions are a prerequisite for a healthy and productive workforce. Nobody should suffer from job related diseases or accidents. It is also an important aspect of both the sustainability and competitiveness of the EU economy. Some members of PEROSH responded to an earlier consultation on this new OSH framework and are glad to see that it reflects many of the aspects PEROSH members strive for.

Acknowledgements and Disclaimer

This paper was prepared on behalf of PEROSH. The authors thank the dedicated researchers throughout the member institutes, whose activities are contributing to the development of innovative and sustainable workplaces which are healthy and safe. The paper is written, from the perspective of PEROSH activities, by the research function of the PEROSH member institutes. Its contents, including any opinions and/or conclusions expressed, are those of the authors alone, and do not necessarily reflect policy for any PEROSH member institute including the UK Health and Safety Executive.

References

Andersen, L. L., Fishwick, D., Robinson, E., Wiezer, N. M., Mockałło, Z., & Grosjean, V. 2017. "Job satisfaction is more than a fruit basket, health checks and free exercise: Cross-sectional study among 10,000 wage earners." *Scandinavian Journal of Public Health*, 45(5), 476–484.

AUVA. Online. "Modell zur Evaluierung von Schweißumgebungen (Model for evaluating welding environments)." AUVA. https://www.eval.at/spezielle-evaluierung-nach-vopst/evaluierung-schweißumgebung (Accessed 24 December 2021).

Bauer, S et al (2018) Ultraviolet spectral irradiance measurements: an intercomparison of spectroradiometers in laboratory combined with a workplace field test. Journal of Physics Communications.

CIOP-PIB. 2020. "Numer Poświęcony Pandemii SARS-CoV-2 [Special Issue SARS-CoV-2 Pandemic]." Bezpieczeństwo Pracy: Nauka i Praktyka [*Occupational Safety: Science and Practice*] [online] 4/2020 ISSN 0137-7043. (Accessed 24 December 2021).

EU-OSHA. Online. "OSH Campaign Toolkit". EU-OSHA. https://osha.europa.eu/en/tools-and-resources/osh-campaign-toolkit. (Accessed 24 December 2021).

EU-OSHA. 2013. "Priorities for occupational safety and health research in Europe: 2013–2020." EU-OSHA. [online] https://doi.org/10.2802/25457. (Accessed 24 December 2021).

Fishwick, D., Till, S., Lunt, J. et al. 2014. "PEROSH workplace exercise guide. Physical exercise and sedentary behaviours: Good practice checklist." PEROSH. [online] DOI 10.23775/20201013 (Accessed 24 December 2021)

Fishwick, D., Lunt, J., Curran, A., Trainor, M. 2010. "Well-being and work: A perspective from eight European Countries on common areas of understanding, national drivers for progress, and research needs." Towards Better Work and Wellbeing. International Conference, Helskinki, 12–12 February 2010, 118. Helsinki, Edita Publishing Oy. ISBN [print] 978-952-261-036-2. DOI: 10.23775/20201016 (Accessed 24 December 2021).

Gagliardi, D., Rondinone, B.M., Mirabile, M. et al. 2016. "Futures: Foresight and priority setting in OSH." PEROSH [online] DOI: 10.23775/20201015 (Accessed 24 December 2021).

Gagliardi, D., Rondinone, B.M., Mirabile, M. et al. 2017. "The perspective of European researchers of national occupational safety and health institutes for contributing to a European research agenda: A modified Delphi study". BMJ Open [online] doi: 10.1136/bmjopen-2016-015336 (Accessed 24 December 2021).

Héry, M., Malenfer, M. 2020. *Occupational Hazards in a Post-pandemic World.* INRS, Paris, France.

Holtermann, A., Schellewald, V., Mathiassen, S.E. et al. 2017a. "A practical guidance for assessments of sedentary behavior at work: A PEROSH initiative." *Applied Ergonomics*, 63, 41–52.

Holtermann, A., Mathiassen, S.E., Pinder A. et al. 2017b. "Assessing sedentary behaviour at work with technical assessment systems." [online] PEROSH. DOI:10.23775/20170701. (Accessed 24 December 2021).

ILO. 2019. "Working paper: Multiple case study on six regional occupational health and safety networks." *ILO* [online] ISBN 978-92-2-133491-0 https://www.ilo.org/wcmsp5/groups/public/---ed_dialogue/---lab_admin/documents/publication/wcms_710903.pdf (Accessed 24 December 2021).

Karhula, K., Wöhrmann, A.M., Brauner, C. et al. 2020. "Working time dimensions and well-being: a cross-national study of Finnish and German health care employees." *Chronobiology International* [online] doi:10.1080/07420528.2020.1778716 (Accessed 24 December 2021).

Laurent, L. 2021. "PEROSH 2021 conference. Summary of the COVID talks." [0nline] https://perosh.eu/wp-content/uploads/2021/12/COVID-SESSION-V10_final-1.pdf (Accessed 28 December 2021)

Lunt, J.A., Fishwick, D.F., Robinson, E. et al. 2015. "Work-life balance: Time for a change." *Occupational Medicine & Health Affairs*. [online] doi: 10.4172/2329-6879.1000e111 (Accessed 24 December 2021).

Lunt, J., Fishwick, D., Curran, A. 2014a. "Health and wellbeing: taking root". *Safety Health Practioner* [online] May 2014, 43–45. https://www.shponline.co.uk/wellbeing/health-and-wellbeing-taking-root/ (Accessed 24 December 2021).

Lunt, J., Fishwick, D., Curran, A. 2014b. "Wellbeing Tree: European tool for workplace health bears fruit". *Personnel Today*. 26 September [online] https://www.personneltoday.com/hr/wellbeing-tree-european-tool-workplace-health-bears-fruit/ (Accessed 24 December 2021).

Madsen, A.M., Raulf, M., Duquenne, P., Graff, P., Cyprowski, M., Beswick, A., Laitinen, S., Rasmussen, P.U., Hinker, M., Kolk, A., Górny, R.L., Oppliger, A., & Crook, B. "Review of biological risks associated with the collection of municipal wastes." *Science of the Total Environment* 2021:148287. https://doi.org/10.1016/j.scitotenv.2021.148287 (Accessed 27 December 2021)

Marinaccio, A., Boccuni, F., Rondinone, B.M., et al. 2020 "Occupational factors in the COVID-19 pandemic in Italy: Compensation claims applications support establishing an occupational surveillance system." *Occupational and Environmental Medicine* [online] doi: 10.1136/oemed-2020-106844 (Accessed 24 December 2021).

Meijester, T., Warren, N., Heederik, D., & Tielemans, E. 2011. "What is the best strategy to reduce the burden of occupational asthma and allergy in bakeries?" Occupational and Environmental Medicine, 68(3), 176–182.

Młynarczyk, M., Rissanen S., Jussila, K. et al. 2019. "Assessment of comfort and ergonomics of protective clothing for firefighters vs. normative requirements in various European countries." PEROSH [online] DOI: 10.23775/20200722. (Accessed 24 December 2021).

MvSZW. 2020. "Hoe behoud je een goede balans tussen werk en privé? [How do you keep a good work-life balance?]." Ministerie van Sociale Zaken en Werkgelegenheid, MvSZW [online] https://www.arboportaal.nl/documenten/brochure/2020/9/1/factsheet-vitaal-thuiswerken (Accessed 24 December 2021).

Nold, A., Bochmann, F., Tranfo, G., Gherardi, M., Cabella, R., Marinaccio, A., Hougaard, K.S., Jimenez Saavedra, R., Mahiout, S., Johnsen, H., Zapor, L., & Miranowicz-Dzierzawska, K. 2021. Dose-Response Relationship of 1,3-butadiene: A Systematic Review with Quality Assessment of Study Results. Partnership for European Research in Occupational Safety and Health – PEROSH. DOI: 10.23775/20210523. (Accessed 27 December 2021)

PEROSH. Online-a. "1st International PEROSH Conference on Prolonging Working Life, May 2020." PEROSH. https://perosh.eu/event/1st-international-perosh-conference-on-prolonging-working-life/ (Accessed 24 December 2021).

PEROSH. Online-b. "1st PEROSH Research Conference, Warsaw 2015." PEROSH. https://perosh.eu/1st-international-perosh-conference-translational-research/ (Accessed 24 December 2021).

PEROSH. Online-c. "2nd PEROSH Research Conference, Sankt Augustin 2017." PEROSH. https://perosh.eu/2nd-perosh-research-exchange-meeting-on-14th-september-2017/ (Accessed 24 December 2021).

PEROSH. Online-d. "3rd PEROSH Research Conference, Copenhagen 2019." *PEROSH*. https://perosh.eu/3rd-perosh-research-conference-in-copenhagen/ (Accessed 24 December 2021).

PEROSH. Online-e. "Overview: Projects". PEROSH. https://perosh.eu/project/ (Accessed 24 December 2021).

PEROSH. Online-f. "Members overview". PEROSH. https://perosh.eu/member/ (Accessed 24 December 2021)

PEROSH. Online-g. "4th PEROSH research conference, Madrid, 2021." PEROSH. https://perosh.eu/4th-perosh-research-conference-in-madrid/ (Accessed 24 December 2021)

PEROSH. 2012. "Sustainable workplaces of the future – European Research Challenges for occupational safety and health." PEROSH [online] http://www.perosh.eu/wp-content/uploads/2013/05/Perosh-Research-Challenges_lowres.pdf (Accessed 24 December 2021).

PEROSH. 2016. "Andrew Curran: Seminar 1st PEROSH Research Exchange Warsaw." PEROSH [online]. https://youtu.be/pABDmBnWzN4 (Accessed 24 December 2021).

PEROSH. 2018. "Agreement of the Partnership for European Research in Occupational Safety and Health." PEROSH [online] https://perosh.eu/wp-content/uploads/2020/03/PEROSH-agreement-2018-to-2022_signed.pdf (Accessed 24 December 2021)

PEROSH. 2019a. "PEROSH strategy 2019–2023." PEROSH. [online] https://perosh.eu/wp-content/uploads/2020/03/Strategy-flyer-Perosh-2019-2023.pdf (Accessed 24 December 2021).

PEROSH. 2019b. "David Fishwick, coordinator of the PEROSH Wellbeing Group, describes his ideas for the future work of this group." PEROSH [online] https://youtu.be/8Wq7CU2egfc (Accessed 24 December 2021).

Rantanen, J. 2018. "Multiple case study on regional OSH networks." *Newsletter on Occupational Health and Safety. ILO*. Special Issue: 22–25.

SAGE-EMG, Scientific Advisory Group for Emergencies – Environment and Modelling Group. (List of members) 2020. "Environmental influence on transmission of COVID-19." UK Government Publications [online] 28 April 2020. https://www.gov.uk/government/publications/environmental-influence-on-transmission-of-covid-19-28-april-2020 (Accessed 24 December 2021).

Sustainable Work 2020. Online. "Platform for sustainable work as a resource for health, innovation and growth in EU's Horizon 2020." Sustainable Work 2020. http://sustainablework2020.se/about (Accessed 24 December 2021).

Vernez, D., Save, J., Oppliger, A., et al. In Press. "Reusability of filtering facepiece respirators after decontamination through drying and germicidal UV." *BMJ Global Health* [online]. https://gh.bmj.com/content/5/10/e003110 (Accessed 24 Decemer 2021)

Weber, B., Douwes, M., Forsman, M. et al. 2017. "Assessing arm elevation at work with technical assessment systems." PEROSH [online] DOI: 10.23775/20181201 (Accessed 24 December 2021).

Wiggans, R., Evans, G., Fishwick, D., & Barber, C. 2016. "Asthma in furniture and wood processing workers: a systematic review." *Occupational Medicine*, 66 (3), 193–201.

Lennart Levi

Stressors at work and elsewhere: a global survival approach

Abstract: The United Nations´ "Agenda 2030" aims, in an integrated manner, to address the entire multitude of major global risks: e.g., to end poverty and hunger, realise the human rights of all, and ensure the lasting protection of the planet and its natural resources. However, recent political changes put this bold initiative at risk. To increase the likelihood of success, higher education institutions worldwide should teach and train today´s students: – tomorrow´s decision makers, to think both critically and ethically, to learn to cope with ethical dilemmas, and to apply systems-thinking approaches to serious and complex societal problems. The Covid-19 pandemic provides just one example of a complex and serious challenge necessitating such approaches. Promoting decent work, full employment and economic growth are other major challenges. None of them can be successfully dealt with in a piecemeal manner.

Political scientist Professor Bo Rothstein and I have for a number of years argued for the implementation of the entire Agenda through Higher Education, in Sweden, in Europe, and globally (Levi&Rothstein, 2018). One of the Agenda´s 17 Sustainable Development Goals – Decent work – is a universal objective and has been included in major human rights declarations, UN resolutions and outcome documents from major conferences – ranging from Article 23 of the Universal Declaration of Human Rights (1948), to the UN´s 2030 Agenda for Sustainable Development (2015).

On 3 June 2022, a crucial international environmental meeting will be held in Stockholm, Sweden. It will commemorate the 1972 United Nations Conference on the Environment. Anchored in the Decade of Action, under the theme "Stockholm+50: a healthy planet for the prosperity of all – our responsibility, our opportunity", it recognizes that:- It´s time for bold choices! It´s time for urgent and co-ordinated action! It´s time for a better future, on a healthy planet! And – words do not cook rice!

Keywords: Agenda 2030, sustainable development, critical-ethical, systems approach, higher education

According to Ban Ki-Moon, former UN-Secretary-General, "We are the first generation to eradicate poverty, and the last to combat climate change".

Antònio Guterres (2020), the present Secretary-General of the United Nations, emphasises that the "17 Agenda 2030 Sustainable Development Goals (SDGs) demand nothing short of a transformation of the financial, economic and political systems that govern our societies" and further that "global efforts to date have been insufficient to deliver the change we need, jeopardising the Agenda´s promise to current and future generations."

Mentioning the Covid-19 impact, he points out that "the livelihood of half the global workforce has been severely affected." Absence of decent work, full employment and economic growth is similarly likely to affect the livelihood, health, and wellbeing of humanity.

The world is not on track

In its Sustainable Development Goals Report 2020, the United Nations Department of Economic and Social Affairs (2020), in collaboration with over 200 experts from more than 40 international agencies, concludes that one third of the way into our SDG journey, the world is not on track to achieve the global Goals by 2030. … Forecasts indicate that the (Covid-19) pandemic will push 71 million people back into extreme poverty in 2020 … Many of these people are workers in the informal economy, whose incomes dropped by 60 % in the first month of the crisis. Half of the workforce: 1.6 billion people, support themselves and their families through insecure and often unsafe jobs in the informal economy, and they have been significantly affected. The impacts of COVID-19 are also increasing the vulnerability of the world´s one billion slum dwellers. "As of April 2020, recommended or required workplace closures around the world affected 81 per cent of employers and 66 % of self employed workers." This has already "led to a sharp increase in unemployment and underemployment, a decline in labour income and job-quality challenges."

The Report further points to the "much greater risk of child labour, child marriage and child trafficking", that "the world is now facing its worst recession in generations" and that "there is no doubt that the COVID-19 pandemic has shaken the 2030 Agenda for Sustainable Development to its very core."

We can, indeed must, cope with the situation and trends described above: by promoting "sustainable development" (SD). SD is usually defined as "a development that satisfies *today´s* needs: without jeopardising the ability of *future* generations to satisfy their needs" (my italics) according to the Brundtland Commission (WCED, 1987).

The question of what actually constitutes SD is an entrance both to an improvement of living and working conditions, to poverty reduction through economic growth: and to protection of the environment.

In the question of method choice, however, opinions differ greatly. Some believe that it requires a return to a simpler life, where people approach nature, live self-sufficiently and locally, and where economic growth stops.

Others argue that SD requires stronger economic growth, where an explosion of technological innovations solves environmental as well as economic and social problems.

I have devoted almost my entire professional life to psychosocial environmental medicine, with a focus on occupational medicine. My intention has been to find ways to prevent noxious stress and disease resulting from it, and to promote health and wellbeing (Cohen, et al., 1986; Kompier & Levi, 1994; Levi, 1959, 1971, 1972, 1979, 1981, 1984, 2000; Levi & Andersson, 1974), in line with what is now referred to as many of the 17 Sustainable Development Goals.

One source of inspiration has been one of our world´s leading social epidemiologists, Michael Marmot. In his search for the causes for disease as well as for health, his plea was to "look for (and subsequently target) the causes behind the causes"; i.e., the root causes. Marmot´s classical study (2004) of the significance of socioeconomic status, social protection and occupational health, provides convincing arguments for such an approach.

A series of recent and most impressive searches for such causes is provided by the World Economic Forum´s annual reports on "Global Risks". They demonstrate that many risks at work and elsewhere are indeed real, powerful and likely to materialise. In addition, they usually are very complex, and highly *interconnected,* cf. Fig. 16.

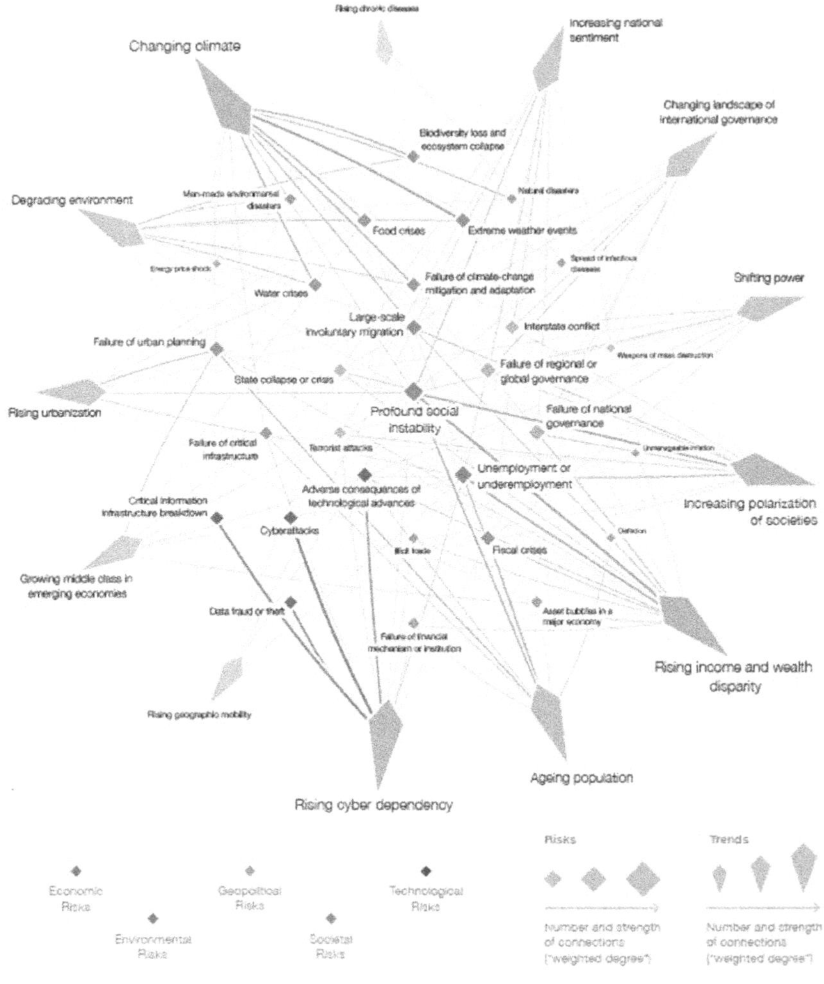

Fig. 16. The Risks-Trends Interconnections Map 2018.
Source: The Global Risks Report 2018 13th Edition, WEF

Contrary to what is true for much of today´s political practice, they cannot be ticked off one by one, or dealt with effectively with any quick fixes.

I have also been inspired by the discoverer of the biological stress concept, the late Hans Selye. Discussing the foundation for a good life, Selye disagreed with the Bible´s command "Love thy neighbour as thyself". In its place, he proposed

"Earn thy neighbour's love". To work for a more humane future for humankind and its planet may be such a way (Karasek & Theorell, 1990).

To counteract the global risks described by the World Economic Forum, as well as the present mounting disaffection and disruption across the world, partly due to short-term and silo thinking by many elites, all 193 member states of the United Nations have agreed on an Agenda 2030, comprising 17 very ambitious Sustainable Development Goals (SDGs), and 169 targets. The President of the International Association of Universities (IAU), Professor Pam Fredman, has inspired me to try to integrate the latter approach with what Bo Rothstein and I initiated, promoting critical-ethical and systems thinking in all higher education (Poznan Declaration, 2014).

Focusing on the causes behind the causes: Agenda 2030

The SDGs are concerned with a wide variety of stressors, and accordingly intend to reach an entire package of interacting goals: end poverty; end hunger; encourage good health and well-being; provide quality education; promote gender equality; provide clean water and sanitation; promote affordable and clean energy; provide decent work and economic growth; address industry, innovation and infrastructure; reduce inequalities; develop sustainable cities and communities; encourage responsible consumption and production; take action on climate change; promote life below water; promote life on land; work towards peace, justice and strong institutions; and create partnerships to achieve these goals.

However, recent political changes put these ambitions at risk. To increase the likelihood of success for these 17 SDGs, higher education institutions worldwide must teach and train today's students: tomorrow's decision-makers, to think both critically and ethically, to learn to cope with ethical dilemmas and apply systems-thinking approaches to serious and complex societal problems (Levi & Rothstein, 2018; Hedenus et al., 2018). This concerns professionals belonging to the health, economy, technology, law and many other sectors.

Needless to say, the resulting stress and pathogenic effects of noxious exposures *also* depend on our individual and collective resilience and coping ability. Such aspects remain important targets for disease prevention and health promotion.

Adjusting the "foot" and/or the "shoe"

However, they can never *replace* the situational factors focused on in this chapter.

True causality may imply a range of relationships. It can mean that a certain exposure or characteristic is *necessary:* enough for a certain disease to develop (such as exposure to lead causing lead poisoning). An exposure may also be *sufficient:* no additional influences or vulnerabilities are necessary. Or exposure may be *contributory*, and neither necessary nor sufficient. The question also remains about whether an exposure really causes a specific disease: or if it "just" aggravates it, accelerates its course, or triggers its symptoms. If we keep all these options in mind, it becomes clear that work-related exposures may very often be a prerequisite for the development of specific diseases, as a sine qua non. On the other hand, it becomes equally clear that they may contribute to a wide variety of morbidity and mortality, a much wider spectrum than is usually realised.

As pointed out in the European Commission´s Guidance on Work-Related Stress (Levi, 2000), work-related disease prevention programmes can aim at a variety of targets, and be based on various philosophies. If the conditions at work: the "shoe", do not fit the worker: the "foot", one approach may be to urge the "shoe factories" to manufacture a wider variety of shoes in different sizes and configurations to fit every, or almost every, conceivable foot.

Whenever possible, such instructions to the "shoe factories" should be evidence-based: in other words, based on measurements of a random sample of all feet, all shoes, and of the existing fit. This is a first, diagnostic, step in a primary prevention approach on a population level.

Another approach, again based on primary prevention, aims at finding the right "shoe" for each individual "foot": promoting "the right person in the right place."

A third, complementary approach is to provide the owner of each foot with a "lasting device" to adjust available shoes to fit his or her feet.

A fourth, very important approach can address the inequity of various feet in various shoes (Marmot, 2004, 2015).

Examples of such amendments would be avoiding, e.g., overemployment, unemployment, exposure to noxious physical, chemical, and biological agents, organisational inadequacies, bullying, and insufficient training and instruction.

Developing critical and ethical leaders of the future

Students need to be made aware of the local, regional and global contexts in which they live and make decisions. Many of today's students do not grasp their role in, and responsibility to, the world, and large numbers do not seem to care.

A single course at college can only ever be a beginning. Families, media, religious bodies, primary and secondary schools and workplaces as well as higher education institutions *must* be educated and recruited to play their part.

The 2030 Agenda for Sustainable Development aims to promote the entire cluster of 17 SDGs and 169 targets. The critical,-ethical, analytical skills, and systems-based approaches mentioned above are indispensable prerequisites to achieving this.

By "critical" we may refer to the application of careful, exact evaluation and judgement. By "ethical" we may refer to a set of principles about the right way to behave. By "systems" we may refer to a group of interacting, interrelated or interdependent elements forming a complex whole.

All this could and should be organised and implemented in collaboration with the social partners.

Universities need to start to become ethical leaders by looking first at themselves and lead by example. The Council for Higher Education Accreditation/ International Quality Group and UNESCO's International Institute for Educational Planning have issued an advisory statement on combating 'corruption" in higher education internationally (CHEA/CIQG IIEP-UNESCO, 2016).

The statement, however, uses "corruption" as a general term to designate a *broad variety* of malpractice in institutions of higher education, such as appropriation, bribery, cheating, corruption, deceit, embezzlement, extortion, favouritism, fraud, graft, harassment, nepotism, etc.: an ABC of misconduct.

To deliver the badly needed SDGs and targets, we need trustworthy, ethical, honest and impartial government institutions that exercise public power, oversee policies fairly and take into account their range, complexity and occasional incompatibility. These institutions are much more likely to promote trust and social capital which in turn improves health and well-being. Tackling corruption is vital (Levi & Rothstein, 2018).

It may also be noted that as early as in the mid-to-late 1800s, major companies have tried to give back to society while bolstering brand reputation. American economist Howard Bowen (1953) introduced the term "Corporate Social Responsibility", and the US Committee for Economic Development (1971) coined the concept of the "Social Contract" between businesses and society.

Over 2,000 universities and colleges world-wide

The International Association of Universities (IAU) with its over 640 member universities world-wide, has engaged itself for Agenda 2030 and its implementation, in collaboration with the Association of Commonwealth Universities and the Agence Universitaire de Francophonie. These three global university networks, with their *over 2,000 institutions*, have called on the higher education sector to adopt policies which maximise their contribution to the Agenda

2030 across teaching, research and community engagement, and to incorporate education about and for sustainable development into undergraduate curricula. IAU has designated 16 universities, each taking on one of the first 16 SDGs, and each in collaboration with a dozen or so allies for its specific purpose, but with an awareness of the dynamic interaction between all ingredients of the system.

Work on goal 17, which will consist of multiple organisations working together, is led by IAU. Gradually, additional institutions will be invited on board. The Cluster will be supported, monitored and steered by an IAU Working Group.

The European network occupational safety and health

SDG 8 aims at "promoting sustained, inclusive and sustainable economic growth, full and productive employment and decent work for all". This contrasts sharply with our current world´s labour market reality. Un- and underemployment remains high (ILO, 2019; UN, 2020) Working conditions are often precarious and pathogenic, and in some countries child labour and slavery are not yet under control. As summarised by ILO, "*unemployment and decent work deficits remain high*" (ILO, 2019).

The resulting cluster of challenges to higher education inspired a major Conference on "Rethinking Higher Education, Inspired by the Sustainable Development Goals", organised by the Karolinska institute in collaboration with University of Gothenburg, Chalmers University of Technology and Royal Swedish Academy of Sciences (Karolinska institutet, 2019).

One of the Conference´s Workshops, "Decent work and economic development", subsequently developed into a Task Group: "SDG 8 – Promoting decent work and productive employment through Higher Education", recently endorsed by the ILO-led "Global Occupational Safety and Health Coalition". This task group comprises a dozen international experts and is managed by *Johannes Siegrist* (University of Duesseldorf) and the *ENETOSH* Group "Mainstreaming OSH into Education", co-ordinated by Dr. Ulrike Bollmann (Dresden).

The Task Group aims to collect and analyse examples of the implementation of SDG 8 in higher education, establishing links to SDG 3 and focusing on the quality of education SDG 4.

Involvement of the World Health Organization (WHO)

The adoption of the 2030 Agenda for Sustainable Development and the Sustainable Development Goals have provided a framework within which to strengthen actions to improve health and well-being for all, and to ensure that no one is left behind. Despite overall improvements in health and well-being in the WHO European Region, inequities within countries persist (WHO, 2019).

The WHO report identifies five essential conditions needed to create and sustain a healthy life for all: good quality and accessible health services; income security and social protection; decent living conditions; social and human capital and decent work and employment conditions. Policy actions are needed to address all five conditions. WHO´s Health Equity Status Report also considers the drivers of health equity, namely the factors fundamental to creating more equitable societies: policy coherence, accountability, social participation and empowerment.

Based on the above, WHO´s Regional Committee for Europe (2019) in its resolution on "Healthy, Prosperous Lives for All", requested its Regional Director:

- To support Member States in placing health equity at the centre of sustainable development and inclusive economies.
- To take the lead in exploring ways of bringing together policymakers from other sectors responsible for the determinants of health, including education, housing, employment, the environment, and poverty reduction, in order to develop a systematic approach to taking action.

What is the IAU global cluster on HESD?

Launched in 2018, the IAU Cluster on HESD promotes the role of higher education institutions in building more sustainable societies. It is a consortium of IAU Member universities from all parts of the world, working in collaboration to develop existing and new exciting initiatives to achieve the goals Sustainable Development Goals (SDGs) adopted by all United Nations Member States in the framework of the Sustainable Development Goals. 2030 Agenda for Sustainable Development.

The Cluster encourages a holistic approach to the SDGs, promoting the whole institution approach, where institutions aim to embed sustainable development in their strategic planning, academic and organisational work.

How does the IAU global cluster on HESD work?

Each of the 17 Sustainable Development Goals is assigned an *institutional team leader*, joined by a group of up to *8 Satellite Universities*. IAU is responsible for leading the work on SDG 17 – Partnerships for the goals.

IAU and the 16 lead institutions, together with their satellite universities are acting as *the voice for higher education*United Nations' High Level Political Forum. Through this international co-operation, the project has greater global outreach than any other project in the field.

Words do not cook rice: Next steps

According to the Agenda 2030´s Target 4.7, it should be ensured that "by 2030 all learners (should have acquired) knowledge and skills needed to promote sustainable development". The European Commission´s Strategy on CSR aims at "integration of CSR into education, training and research." It is obvious that such targets fit exceedingly well into the aim of the *European Journal for Workplace Innovation* (see EJWI special issue 6.1–2, 2021).

However, as a Chinese proverb formulates it: "words do not cook rice." There is a very considerable gap between what we know, and what we implement (cf. Levi, 2017).

Recognising the university sector's potential and responsibility to help shape the moral contours of society for the better, and given the societal benefits from increased social capital, universities and institutions of higher education should shoulder their role as key agents of change, as stated in the Compostela Group of Universities' Poznan Declaration (2014). They should, inter Alia:

- Endorse a cross-faculty approach to broaden the curricula to include components of critical-ethical analysis and systems thinking (and, of course, Agenda 2030 based thinking, my addition).
- Appreciate the unique opportunity they have to shape professional identities. At universities, the norms and boundaries of acceptable behaviour are to a large extent set for a number of professions. Universities have a possibility as well as a responsibility to help shape the normative contours of society for the better.
- Teach the teachers through the provision of pedagogical resources and training to a wide range of faculty.
- Develop partnerships with other universities, networks, national authorities for higher education and civil society organisations championing the critical-ethical agenda.
- Co-ordinate with national education authorities and social partners with regard to fulfilling the state's obligation under the UN Agenda 2030 SDGs.
- Talk the talk and walk the walk. In addition to teaching critical-ethical behaviour and promoting systems thinking, it is crucial that higher education

institutions: as agents providing public goods, act accordingly, ensuring impartiality in teaching, student assessment and research and that matters regarding awards of degrees, employment and promotions are based on legitimate, transparent and objective criteria.

The Poznan Declaration was issued in 2014, i.e. one year before Agenda 2030. As mentioned above, an important addition to the declaration would be the Agenda´s Target 4.7: "By 2030, ensure that all learners acquire the knowledge and skills needed to promote sustainable development, including, among others, through education for sustainable development and sustainable lifestyles, human rights, gender equality, promotion of a culture of peace and non-violence, global citizenship."

Low costs, high gain

Considering the relatively low costs of implementation, and the possible very considerable societal gains if these proposals are implemented broadly, this initiative has the potential to be extremely cost efficient in the long term. More important, however, is that, ethically, it is the right thing to do.

This is why we propose additional high-level conferences on such issues, with a focus on the implementation of Agenda 2030 (what should be taught, and how). Based on the outcomes of these, recommendations should be made regarding the necessary redesign of all higher education: and for its subsequent and urgent implementation.

Acknowledgement

This article is based on contributions by Professor Bo Rothstein and the author to the World Academy of Art and Science and Roma Tre University's International Conference in Rome on "Future Education" in November 2017, the European Commission's Working Group Meeting in Brussels in December 2017, an article for the University World News on November 9., 2018 and on Levi, L.: Stressors at Work and Elsewhere – A Global Survival Report. Contentment. New York: The American Institute of Stress, 2020 (pp. 46–51).

References

Bowen, H.R. (1953). *Social Responsibilities of the Businessman*. New York: Harper.

Cohen, A., Levi, L. et al. (1986). *Psychosocial Factors at Work. Recognition and Control*. Geneva: International Labour Office.

Committee for Economic Development (US) (1971). Social Responsibilities of Business Corporations. Committee for Economic Development. A Statement by the Research and Policy Committee. New York. https://www.ced.org/pdf/Social_Responsibilities_of_Business_Corporations.pdf

Guterres, A. (2020). Foreword. In: United Nations: The Sustainable Development Goals Report 2020.

Hedenus, F., Persson, M. & Sprei, F. (2018). *Sustainable Development – Nuances and Perspectives*. Lund: Studentlitteratur.

International Labour Organisation (ILO) (2019). *Time to Act for SDG 8 – Integrating Decent Work, Sustained Growth and Environmental Integrity*. Geneva: ILO.

Karasek, R. &Theorell, T. (1990). *Healthy Work: Stress, Productivity, and the Reconstruction of Working Life*. New York: Basic Books.

Karolinska institutet (2019). Rethinking Higher Education Inspired by the Sustainable Development Goals. Conference report. http://nyheter.ki.se/media/6404/download?Ga=2.13950846.871996580.159825549-1399516327.1593414792

Kompier, M. & Levi, L. (1994). *Stress at Work: Causes, Effects and Prevention. A Guide for Small and Medium-Sized Enterprises*. Dublin: European Foundation for the Improvement of Living and Working Conditions.

Levi, L. (1959). Kropp, själ och sjukdom. En introduktion i psykosomatisk medicin. Stockholm: PA-rådet.

Levi, L. (Ed.). (1971). *Society, Stress and Disease. Vol. 1. The Psychosocial Environment and Psychosomatic Disease*. London: Oxford University Press.

Levi, L. (Ed.). (1972). Stress and distress in response to psychosocial stimuli. *Acta Medica Scandinavica*, Suppl 528.

Levi, L. & Andersson, L. (1974). *Population, Environment and Quality of Life*. Stockholm: Royal Swedish Ministry of Foreign Affairs.

Levi, L. (1979). Psychosocial factors in preventive medicine. In: *Healthy People. The U.S. Surgeon General´s Report on Health Promotion and Disease Prevention*. Background Papers. Washington: U.S. Department of Health, Education and Welfare.

Levi, L. (Ed.). (1981). *Society, Stress and Disease. Vol. 3. Working Life*. Oxford: Oxford University Press.

Levi, L. (1984). *Stress in Industry. Causes, Effects and Prevention*. Geneva: International Labour Office.

Levi, L. (2000). *Guidance on Work-Related Stress. Spice of Life, or Kiss of Death?* Luxembourg: European Commission.

Levi, L. (2017). Bridging the science-policy and policy-implementation gaps – A crucial challenge. In: Cooper, C.L. & Quick, J.C. (eds): *The Handbook of Stress and Health – A Guide to Research and Practice.* Chichester: Wiley-Blackwell.

Levi, L. & Rothstein, B. (2018a). To cope with present and future catastrophic risks higher education must train future decision makers to think critically, ethically and in systems. World Academy of Arts and Sciences Rome Conference Proceedings, 13–15 March 2018. http://worldacademy.org/files/rome2017/papers/RCP-complied-papers.pdf

Levi, L. & Rothstein, B. (2018b). Universities must lead on sustainable development goals. *University World News*, 9 November 2018.

Marmot, M. (2004). *Status Syndrome.* London, Bloomsbury.

Marmot, M. (2015): *The Health Gap.* London: Bloomsbury.

Poznan Declaration (2014): Whole-of-University Promotion of Social Capital, Health and Development. At http://qog.pol.gu.se/digitalAssets/1497/1497769_the-poznan-declaration.pdf

United Nations (2020). *The Sustainable Development Goals 2020.* New York: United Nations, 2020.

WCED (1987). *Report of the World Commission on Environment and Development: Our Common Future.* New York: United Nations.

World Health Organization (2019). Healthy, Prosperous Lives for All: The European Health Equity Report. Copenhagen: WHO Regional Office for Europe, 2019.

Kenneth Abrahamsson

Towards Sustainable Workplace Innovations: Concluding Reflections

Beyond continued efforts to tackle the health dimension, the EU must prioritise the social dimension of Sustainable Work, notably by implementing the European Pillar of Social Rights. We must invest in protecting and creating jobs, and in driving our competitive sustainability, by building a fairer, greener and more digital Europe. We must repair the short-term damage from the current crisis, in a way that also invests in our long-term future. To achieve this, the EU must now show clarity of purpose and certainty of direction through its policies.[1]

Making sustainable work a member of the SDG family

The concept of Sustainable Work has over the years encountered difficulties in being included in the broader Sustainable Development family. This lack of family attention is, however, fundamentally solved in the UN Sustainable Development Goals with DG 8 Decent work and economic growth, with the aim of *promoting sustained, inclusive, and sustainable economic growth, full and productive employment, and decent work for all.* The next challenge is to promote greener and more sustainable jobs.[2] Another major challenge in the global policy of Sustainable Development mission is to integrate ecological, economic, and social goals, with the role of decent and sustainable work, productive labour market regimes, and jobs for all. These challenges need to operate at national, regional, and global levels.

As has been presented elsewhere, in the double issue of EJWI 6.1-2 2021 (Abrahamsson, 2021), one of the inspiring minds of the concept and policies of Sustainable Work was Peter Docherty (Docherty et al., 2009), previously

---

1 https://eur-lex.europa.eu/legal-content/EN/TXT/PDF/?uri=CELEX:52020DC0456&from=EN. Europe's moment: Repair and Prepare for the Next Generation. COM (2020) 456 final. Downloaded 9 February 2021.

2 https://www.undp.org/content/undp/en/home/sustainable-development-goals/goal-8-decent-work-and-economic-growth.html. Downloaded 9 February 2021.

employed at the Swedish National Institute for Working Life. Good working conditions and the regeneration of resources and environmental considerations were part of the concept. Policies and research on sustainable work in Sweden have over the years been a significant field in the Swedish research tradition (Abrahamsson 2017, Håkansta 2014 and Lagerlöf&Albin, 2021). In 2007, the National Institute for Working Life, NIWL was abolished, which created some backlash in the collaboration with the European and international research community and the current situation cannot be compared with the level of collaboration at the turn of the millennium (Ennals 1999, 2000, 2001a and 2001b).

Over the years, various approaches to quality of work have been designed in the European policy community and on the research frontiers. Quality of work, decent work, and flexicurity have been signalled in the policy development. The Lisbon Strategy focussed on economic growth, job creation and more and, better jobs, while the Europe 2020 Strategy had the basic goals to stimulate *smart, sustainable, and inclusive growth*. The new strategy also contained convergence policies, macro-economic stability, and sound public budgets as prerequisites for growth. Future working life strategies cannot only be built on sustainable work. It is now becoming more and more crucial to focus on sustainable employment and forms of job transitions, as well as sustainable welfare.

The launching of the consultation on the European Pillar of Social Rights in 2017 highlights the importance of the future of work and welfare systems in Europe (EU 2017). The challenges of global competition, digitalisation and demographic change demonstrate the need for new research and innovation in sustainable work systems and innovative workplaces (EU 2019). Longer and healthier working lives are a key issue for Europe's future prosperity. The new triple challenges, Covid-19, Green Deal, and digitalisation open the way for new European research programmes. The EU Commission has also launched an Action Plan for the European Pillar of Social Rights, focusing on EU Targets by 2030: on employment levels, adult learning participation and reduction of citizen living in extreme poverty.[3]

New technology, innovation, and skills development

New technology can be perceived as scary, but the alternative can be even more threatening. The Swedish Trade Union Confederation, LO and the Swedish

---

3 https://ec.europa.eu/info/strategy/priorities-2019-2024/economy-works-people/jobs-growth-and-investment/european-pillar-social-rights/european-pillar-social-rights-action-plan_en

Metal Worker's Frederation, IF Metall, described it this way: "We are not afraid of the new technology, but of the old". The effort to protect old jobs and old technology, can in the long run mean a loss of new jobs. The processes of job retention, job destruction and job creation are an ongoing transformation that has been well documented over centuries by economic historians, economists, and sociologists. The study of influence and control of technology from a human factor point of view is a recurrent challenge.

The social dimension must have a prominent place in designing the technology. The design of the interface between man and machine is a delicate task, that requires reflection and consideration, so that we do not create more problems than we solve. Research has an important role to play, when new technology should be evaluated and introduced, but that role is not being pregiven; we must mark our position by highlighting issues that are perceived as important and relevant

Another field is skill development and technology change. There is an urgent need to deal proactively through skill-development, and especially in-work training, to counteract the inequalities and labour market dislocation that innovation tends to generate. This means targeting innovation support to firms and organisations that seek to boost innovation, by experimenting with improving innovation capacity, by improving job quality and social inclusion, rather than solely targeting support to specific innovations for profit. European policies and the social dialogue for sustainable and greener jobs need to cope with the challenges of digitalization, fossil-free solutions and new energy systems and a post-pandemic world. Its impact is a more intensified and far-reaching structural transformation as well as job shift, upskilling and changing working conditions for the employees (Figure 17).

Fig. 17. Circles of change shaping the context for the social dialogue on sustainable and greener jobs.

It is also important to encourage firms to undertake "innovation impact assessments" to analyse the impacts that larger innovations are expected to have (prospective) and have resulted in (retrospective) to improve firms' abilities to increase the beneficial, and minimise the detrimental, effects of innovations. We should promote the use of qualitative case-study research to understand the complexity of and mechanisms behind the interaction of innovation and job quality across industries, especially in the services, is also important.

Whether it is climate change, globalisation or digitalisation, there is no holding back the impact of the megatrends described. As a society, we must adapt while preserving the values and standards we hold dear. Technological advances, such as the use of artificial intelligence in human resource tools, or in "intelligent cobots", are not necessarily a threat to OSH. However, it is essential that the design, implementation and roll-out of new technology follows established principles, such as worker participation, or "prevention through design" and others yet to be consolidated, such as an ethical framework for digitalisation, codes of conduct and proper governance. Digitalisation will bring challenges, but also opportunities.

Automation allows the design of better jobs; data analytics can improve risk assessment, and access to data can help inspection and enforcement. Fortunately, these challenges and opportunities are not country specific, and there is much to be gained from sharing knowledge and experience of different approaches. EU-OSHA is a networking organisation that aims to act as a catalyst and facilitator for exchange among the EU 27 member states, and initiatives such as the ILO led Global Coalition are essential to exchange knowledge and experience at a global level.[4]

Social dialogue and social partners need to be driving forces for green transition. Early co-operation between a new firm and trade unions has the potential to proactively address prerequisites for sustainable work in design phases of new factories, but also to strengthen attention to other dimensions of social sustainability that are vital for start-ups. Building a stakeholder chain, inspired by the Nordic model, emphasises the dimensions of social sustainability needed in work processes in the early development phases, which is also beneficial from a society perspective. However, a systematic approach with anchoring activities, both within and between the stakeholders at different levels, is needed. These findings are reflected upon in the case study carried out in early phases of a major greenfield project aiming at establishing a new industrial domain in a Nordic context.

The policies to support low carbon use and reduction of CO2 omissions are using various instruments. *Fossil Free Sweden* was started at the initiative of the Swedish Government in 2015, ahead of the major UN climate conference in Paris. Its purpose is to increase the pace of the climate transition. The goal is to build a strong industrial sector and to create more jobs and export opportunities by going fossil free.[5] There is a wave of new industrial settings in green industries established in northern Sweden: the region can become a leader in the climate change adaptation by supporting new energy systems, and increasing the capacity of electrification. In addition, there is an investment in community service, with new housing and communities that are attractive to live in.[6]

---

4 Cockburn, W. (2021) OSH in the future – Where next? EU OSHA, European Agency for Safety&Health at Work. EJWI.

5 https://fossilfrittsverige.se/en/about-us/

6 https://ec.europa.eu/info/strategy/priorities-2019-2024/economy-works-people/jobs-growth-and-investment/european-pillar-social-rights/european-pillar-social-rights-action-plan_en

Equality, sustainable work, and economic growth

The opposite to sustainable work is the lack of good job qualities, such as an unhealthy work environment, lack of influence and co-determination, low work dignity and job enjoyment, and weak employment relations or none. Inequalities, gender gaps and discrimination of migrants are other signs of the bad side of the coin. To combat inequalities in working life is not just an issue of social justice and respect. Equality is a goal that also has a productive mission, and it is beneficial for economic development and growth. In this context, it is worrying that inequalities of income, social standard and living conditions are increasing in many countries; Sweden is not an exception (OECD 2015b).[7] A crucial dimension of increasing inequalities is the gender gap on the labour market and the role of welfare regimes providing social protection, daycare and ageing care. The greying of European countries can also be characterised as a transition to a four-generation society, which has a far-reaching impact on social system, organisatyion of work and work-life balance. "More years – better lives" have been a slogan for European societies and a major research initiative.[8]

"How can economic and social production be maintained across the extended lifespan in ways that are sustainable, equitable, and efficient in the use of human and technical resources?"

The MYBL-programme highlights the demographic change which have repercussions of living and working contions in Europe and takes the step from sustainable work to a sustainable life context over the whole lifespan.[9]

> Demographic change provides a great opportunity: for all of us to live longer, more active and rewarding lives, to fulfil ambitions, to see grandchildren grow and to contribute to society through informal activities and voluntary work. However, it also presents us with significant challenges. Are social, economic and political structures created when 40 years of employment was sufficient to pay for the care of the young and old, still sustainable when "retirement" grows from five years to twenty or even thirty?

Sustainable work over the life-course and career longevity are not goals in themselves, but missions for good living and working conditions. In Sweden

7 OECD (2015b), In It Together: Why Less Inequality Benefits All, OECD Publishing, Paris, https://doi.org/10.1787/9789264235120-en. Downloaded 9 February 2021.

8 https://jp-demographic.eu/. Downloaded 26 January 2022.

9 https://jp-demographic.eu/wp-content/uploads/2021/02/Executive-Summary-JPI-MYBL-strategic-research-agenda-on-demographic-change-May-2014.pdf. Downloaded 26 January 2022.

and other countries, the number of post-retirement age or senior workers is increasing, and it is more noticeable for white-collar workers than blue-collar workers. However, career-longevity and postponed retirement could also create new gaps, between employees not being able or healthy enough to work until retirement, and those who continue into their seventies. At the end of the day, Sustainable Work also interacts with institutions supporting sustainable welfare, security, and wellness for all citizens, and not only those who have a strong employment position or contract.

The pandemic has brought a renaissance for occupational health and safety measures, i.e., protective masks being the most visible sign. The interface between occupational health and public health has never been so significant, relevant, and crucial as in the pandemic period. The breadth and depth of the changes that are already affecting the world of work demand a response from the OSH community. Policy makers need to ensure that the regulatory framework is fit for purpose, and that tools and resources are in place to ensure adequate protection is afforded to all workers, while not stifling innovation, or acting as a brake on business.

The Nordic model under scrutiny

There are also several important initiatives taken by the Nordic Council of Ministers. The project "The Future of Work: Opportunities and Challenges for the Nordic Models" 2017–2020, was funded by the Nordic Council of Ministers, and organised by the Fafo Institute for Labour and Social Research, in Oslo. This project was inspired by the Global Future of Work project organised by the International Labour Organisation (ILO) in the context of its 100th Anniversary in 2019.

This research programme consists of seven pillars, covering various aspects of Nordic working life, labour market transformation and quality of work (Dølvik & Røed Steen, 2018, p. 13).[10]

> Whereas Nordic working lives have been privileged by their strong and adaptive institutions, they are now apparently entering a phase where their ability to master the emerging challenges increasingly will depend on the actors' capacity to foster institutional innovation. Be it in the areas of life-long learning, protection for new categories of workers, inclusion of groups with poor or no formal schooling, or prevention of rising inequality, and ensuring that all economic actors contribute to the common good, the preparations needed to become fit for the future of work will entail engagement in

10 http://norden.diva-portal.org/smash/get/diva2:1265618/FULLTEXT01.pdf

> imaginative renewal and reconstruction of the institutions that we once inherited from the pioneers of the Nordic model.

The seven pillars or thematic approaches are: (1) The main drivers of change demographic change: ageing and migration, climate change, and economic and political changes associated with globalisation, European integration, and rising income gaps. (2) The digitalisation of work, new technology, robotics automatisation, industrialisation 4.0, and new platforms. (3) The self-employed, independent, and atypical work and non-standard work, marginal part-time, temporary agency work, fixed-term contracts and self-employed without employees. (4) The new labour market agents as various platforms. (5) The occupational health-consequences and challenges, and new and unforeseen work environment challenges. (6) The labour law and regulations, (7) The core of the Nordic model of labour market governance.

It is important to underline that while this programme was launched before the pandemic, the final report was published during spring 2021.The triple challenge of Covid-19, digitalisation, and the Green Deal, will comprise fundamental challenges to working life and sustainable work in Sweden, the Nordic countries, Europe at large and all continents. The current policy debate and decisions on EU policy on minimum wages, and the Nordic model of collective agreements between social partners, have articulated many voices and viewpoints. In Sweden both unions and employers' organisations are hesitant about the proposal of minimum wages, saying that it has a negative impact on wage setting and other policies in charge of social partners. Industrial relations on the European level varies. The Swedish Trade Union Confederation has recently questioned its membership regarding the policies of the European Trade Union Confederation, ETUC. Social partners in Sweden are in general critical of possible forthcoming EU regulation of the labour market, and are reluctant regarding governmental interventions in the rules and negotiations on the labour market.[11]

> The proposed EU directive on minimum wages now being negotiated is a disaster for Swedish workers. Despite extensive protests from the Swedish labour movement, the European Commission in 2020 presented a legislative proposal that is contrary to the EU Treaty and is a powerful blow against the Swedish collective agreement model. The Swedish model is a cornerstone that has made Sweden one of Europe's most competitive economies.

11 https://www.lo.se/english/news/congress_statement_on_european_minimum_wages. Downloaded 26 January 2022.

Parallel to the tensions between Sweden and EU in labour market regulation, there has been a dynamic political debate and governmentalk task forces on job security, flexibity and labour market transitions. The European Social Model and the Nordic models are commonly discussed with respect to industrial relations. In fact, there is no joint European Social Model, but a European legislation and infrastructure of support and facilitation. Each country or clusters of countries share various models of regulation of work life conditions in various combinations of labour laws and regulation, agreements between social partners or market alliances.

Labour law and the regulation of European labour markets is a growing research field. Climate change, digitalisation, the pandemic, new forms of work, precarious work, discrimination as well as occupational hazards are major challenges for labour law research community. Another dimension is what is meant by fair transition and if, and how, it could be regulated by law or monitored by negotiations between social partners. The book *The New Foundations of Labour Law* (Ahlberg & Bruun, 2017) is a result of a Swedish comparative research programme on labour law in transition. It focusses on if precarious work can be a new normative model for labour law, labour law and new forms labour market mobility, human rights and international labour standards and new development in labour law as such. The concluding remarks point at the risks of migrant workers, temporary and low paid jobs in the margins of the labour market. There is an urgent need of a new European labour law research programme on the impact of the triple challenges of digitalization, climate change and the pandemic.

Another way of describing labour market relations in an international comparative sense is the concept model *Varieties of Capitalism* (Bamber, et al., 2021; Hall and Soskice, 2001). The model aims at explaining similarities and differences between various countries in terms of the labour market's functioning, regulation, and institutional conditions. It distinguishes between Liberal market economies (LMCs) such as the USA, UK, Canada, and Australia and Co-ordinated market economies, (CMEs) with countries such as Denmark, France, Italy, Germany, Sweden and Japan. An overview of discussion and criticism of the Varieties of Capitalism model is presented in the book *International & Comparative Employment Relations, published in the spring of 2021. Global Crises and Institutional Reponses.* (Bamber, G.J. et al. 2021, Seventh Edition, London: SAGE). Thus, the challenge of sustainable work in Europe must be seen through the glasses of industrial relations and the power relations between state, social partners and the market.

Sustainable workplace innovation as job-transitions

In addition to reskilling and up-skilling, the combined impact, the green deal, digitalisation and the pandemic, there are growing needs for new forms of career transition support. Helping employees' transition to new jobs, and to re-orient themselves in the job market, are available to some extent in most countries. They are a means for attaining a fair labour market, as well as being a cog in social protection systems. These efforts come in many forms, and they vary greatly between countries and over time.

Sweden has longstanding experience of Job Transition Funds, and the model bears resemblance to a collective insurance plan, which has proven quite successful. In Sweden: whenever restructuring involves reducing the size of the workforce, displaced persons have two main forms of support. In addition to the Swedish Public Employment Service (*Arbetsförmedlingen)*, there are also several Job Transition Funds (or Job Security Councils) that provide support for new employment. The job security councils are independent of the state, and they are the result of collective bargaining agreements between social partners.

The report "Back to Work: Sweden", from the OECD, notes that "Much of the Swedish success can be attributed to the role of social partners who have developed a solid infrastructure to anticipate economic changes on the one hand, and manage structural change via the so-called Job Security Councils on the other(OECD 2015a)."[12] Although the Swedish system with Transition funds or security councils is applied to uniquely Swedish experiences, and complements a labour model with a high level of representation of both workers and employers, aspects of the models can be translated and adapted to other European countries or social partners' agreements.

Over the last two years there has been an intensive policy debate in Sweden on job security, flexibility, and adaptation to new demands on firms and the public sector. A governmental task force had the mission of modernising Swedish labour law and making it more flexible on behalf of emplyeers' priorities, while unions were more reluctant. The final report reflects the mission of the Inquiry.[13]

> The Inquiry's proposals, taken together, are intended to promote the adaptability of organisations and, by doing so, to promote growth and the level of living standards.

---

12 OECD (2015a), *Back to Work: Sweden: Improving the Re-employment Prospects of Displaced Workers*, Back to Work, OECD Publishing, Paris, https://doi.org/10.1787/9789264246812-en.

13 https://www.regeringen.se/49b76a/contentassets/0f11fafa5dae408c9be5e080d529a9fa/en-moderniserad-arbetsratt-sou-202030.pdf. Summary in English.

> At the same time, workers have to continue to be protected from unfair dismissal, and job security will be based to a greater extent on increased opportunities for skills development, greater chances of finding jobs and increased possibilities of becoming firmly established in the labour market. These are important steps in adapting job security to how the labour market has developed and changed since the introduction of the Employment Protection Act.

There was strong criticism in the final report from unions and other actors. In a way, the task force presented a Danish model by somewhat weaker job protection and stronger transition and career support. This led also to an intensified policy debate between the government and social partners, and caused political påressures in the parliament, the Riksdagen. From the government's side, the mission was given to the social partners to solve the problems and sign new agreements, a process that initially divided the Swedish Trade Union Confederation. New commissions were initiated on labour law and on various forms of transition support.

The result is both a new agreement between the social partners, and a new adult education reform supporting skill upgrading and further education for employees. The innovation in this model is that you can get anticipatory support, without being notified or dismissed. It will be very interesting to see over a longer time, how this new work-related form of adult education and training will develop, supplementing current forms of study assistance in grants. loans and right for study leaves of absence for adults. The bill to the Swedish Riksdag will be launched during spring 2022 and the new system will start from October 2022. This initiative is one of the major adult education reforms in modern times in Sweden. It is built on the infrastructure of several adult education reforms in the Seventies and the knowledge promotion reform (kunskapslyftet) in the Nineties.

One other example from Sweden is that the Government last year launched a new work environment strategy highlighting the purpose and missions of sustainable work, summarised in these four points.[14]

- A sustainable working life: everyone should be able, strong, and willing to work a whole working life.
- A healthy working life: working life must contribute to development and well-being.
- A safe working life: no one should risk life or health because of worked.

14 https://www.regeringen.se/rattsliga-dokument/skrivelse/2021/02/skr.-20202192/

- A labour market without crime and cheating: a deficient work environment must never be a means of competition.

Sustainable Work is today a policy and mission shared by the Swedish government, the social partners, and the research funders, and is also reflected in the research community. The next challenge is to transform and implement these policies into good, healthy, innovative and productive ways of organising work for the future.

The Swedish government is also setting up its own office for Sustainable Working Life. The work of the unit will largely be about identifying needs, proposing measures, consulting and co-ordinating, so that measures and policies for a sustainable working life become a whole. The work will take place in a co-ordinated manner within the Government Offices, and in close dialogue with the social partners. To strengthen the collaboration within the Government's office, a steering group consisting of State Secretaries from the Ministry of Social Affairs, the Ministry of Labour, the Ministry of Education, the Ministry of Trade and Industry and the Ministry of Finance has been established. This co-ordinating unit is a sign that sustainable work policies have a strong position in Sweden, and not only the government's office but among agencies, research funders and social partners.

References

Abrahamsson, K. (2017) Reflections on working life research in Sweden. Institutional transformation, current policies, and new networks. *EUWIN Bulletin 2/2017.*

Abrahamsson, K. (2021) Sustainable work in transition. Policies, practices, and research. *European Journal of Workplace Innovations*, 6 (1–2).

Ahlberg, K. & Bruun, N. (eds) (2017) *The New Foundations of Labour Law.* Frankfurt: Peter Lang

Bamber, G.J. et al. (eds) (2021) *International & Comparative Employment Relations. Global Crises and Institutional Reponses.*, 7th edn. London: SAGE.

Docherty, P., Kira, M., & Rami Shani (2009) *Creating Sustainable Work Systems. Developing Social Sustainability.* 2nd edn. London: Routledge.

Dølvik, J.E. and Røed Steen, J. (2018) The Nordic future of work drivers, institutions, and politics. Tema Nord 2018:555

Ennals, R. (ed.) (1999) *Work Life 2000 Yearbook I: 1999.* London: Springer-Verlag

Ennals, R. (ed.) (2000) *Work Life 2000 Yearbook 2: 2000.* London: Springer-Verlag

Ennals, R. (ed.) (2001a) *Work Life 2000 Yearbook 3: 2001.* London: Springer-Verlag

Ennals, R. (ed.) (2001b) *Work Life 2000 Supplementary Volume.* Centre for Working Life Research Kingston University.

EU (2017) European Pillar of Social Rights. EU Publication Office.

EU (2019) Europe's moment: Repair and prepare for the next generation. *COM* (2020), 456 final (Downloaded 02 September 2021).

Håkansta, C. (2014) Swedish working life research. Formation and conceptual development of a research field in transition. Dissertation. Luleå University of Technology, Sweden.

Lagerlöf, E. & Albin, M. (2021) The Swedish platform for sustainable work in Horizon 2020 – in retrospect. *European Journal of Workplace Innovations.* EJWI Double issue. March 2021.

OECD (2015a) *Back to Work: Sweden: Improving the Re-employment Prospects of Displaced Workers, Back to Work.* OECD Publishing, Paris.

OECD (2015b) *In It Together: Why Less Inequality Benefits All.* OECD Publishing, Paris.

Richard Ennals

Postscript

This invited Postscript provides an opportunity for brief reflection on the Swedish tradition of Working Life Research, in which I have been actively engaged since December 1986, and on Swedish engagement in the European Union.

I have had the privilege of working in Sweden with several remarkable researchers, each of whom has brought distinctive insights. They tend to have focused on their own theory and cases, often resisting inclusion in accounts of a single movement. There have often been tensions between researchers who see themselves as social scientists, and those who feel loyalty to a medical model.

I would argue that there is a common vocabulary employed by Swedish Working Life researchers, but that the meanings of the words and concepts are seen in their use. The late Stephen Toulmin, who, like me, came from the UK, and with a philosophical approach which was heavily influenced by Wittgenstein, provided a unifying overview. He argued that social scientists had much to learn from Action Research, and that they should emulate the clinical model of intervention.

The series of chapters in this book reflects this common vocabulary and diversity of meanings in use. There is no one unified position. Furthermore, we can at times note gaps between theory, practice, and policy. The core team of contributors led a session of the European Workplace Innovation Network (EUWIN) Forum, and as a result some further chapters have been added, setting the Swedish approach in a wider European context.

There is no room for complacency in a practical context of Working Life which is turbulent and rapidly changing. The book is intended to stimulate further research, policy development and workplace innovation in Sweden, across Europe, and beyond.

About the Authors

Abrahamsson, Kenneth, former programme director, Swedish Research Council for Health, Working Life and Welfare, Forte, and Adjunct Professor, Human Work Science, Luleå University of Technology, Sweden
kenneth.abrahamsson1@gmail.com

Abrahamsson, Lena, Professor in Human Work Science, Luleå University of Technology, Sweden
lena.Abrahamsson@ltu.se

Albin, Maria, Professor of Occupational and Environmental Medicine, Institute of Environmental Medicine, Karolinska Institute, Stockholm, Sweden
maria.albin@ki.se

Anyfantis, Ioannis is Project Manager at the European Agency for Safety and Health at work (EU-OSHA)

Berglund, Martina, Assistant Professor, Division of Logistics and Quality Management, Linköping University, Sweden

Bodin, Theo, Associate Professor of Occupational and Environmental Medicine, Institute of Environmental Medicine, Karolinska Institute, Stockholm, Sweden

Boethius, Susanne, Researcher, Department of Sociology, Lund University, Sweden

Bongers, Pauline, Chair, Perosh, and Director of Science, TNO, Netherlands

Brun, Emmanuelle is senior Project Manager at EU-OSHA, responsible for EU-OSHA's activity on Digitalisation and OSH

Daheim, Cornelia is the founder and head of Future Impacts. Consulting Project for EU-OSHA

Eiffe, Franz F. Research Officer, Work Life, Eurofound
Franz.Eiffe@eurofound.europa.eu

Elg, Matthias, Professor of Quality Technology and Management, Linköping University, and centre director at HELIX Competence Centre, Linköping University, Sweden

Ennals Richard, Emeritus Professor, Kingston University, UK, and Editor in Chief of the *European Journal of Workplace Innovation.*
richard.ennals@gmail.com

Exton, Rosemary, Director, Workplace Innovation Europe CLG, UK

Halvørsen, Bjørn E., retired Director General and Special Advisor, Ministry of Labour and Social Affairs, and Centre for Senior Policy, Norway
bjorn.halvorsen@wemail.no

Harlin, Ulrika, Industrial Researcher, RISE Institutes of Sweden and member of HELIX Competence Centre, Linköping University, Sweden
ulrika.harlin@ri.se

Jeanes, Emma is a senior lecturer at the University of Exeter Business School, UK having previously worked at Lund University, Sweden, and Cardiff University, Wales.

Johansson, Jan, Professor in Human Work Science, Luleå University of Technology, Sweden

Kjellberg, Anders, Professor in Sociology, Lund University, Sweden
anders.kjellberg@soc.lu.se

Lansbury, Russell, D., Emeritus Professor of Work and Industrial Relations in the University of Sydney; former Co-Editor of *The Journal of Industrial Relations* and President Emeritus of the *International Labour and Employment Relations Association* (ILERA), Australia
russell.lansbury@sydney.edu.au

Larsson, Allan, former Director-General of DG Employment, European Commission, and advisor to EU President Jean-Claude Juncker on the European Pillar of Social Rights, Stockholm, Sweden

Laurent, Louis, chair PEROSH Scientific Steering Group, director of studies and research of the National Institute for Occupational Safety and Health, France.
louis.laurent@inrs.fr

Levi, Lennart, Emeritus Professor of Psychosocial Medicine, Karolinska Institute, Stockholm, Sweden
lennart.levi@eurostress.se

Lundqvist, Åsa, Professor, Welfare Sociology, Lund University, Sweden

Mathieu, Chris. Associate Professor of Sociology of Work and Organisation, Department of Sociology, Lund University, Sweden
christopher.mathieu@soc.lu.se

Meeuwsen, Jan M., Manager of International Affairs, Perosh
janmichiel.meeuwsen@perosh.eu

Pot, Frank, Emeritus Professor of Social Innovation of Work and Employment, Ratboud University, Nijmegen, and former director of TNO Work and Employment, Netherlands.
frank.pot@ardan.demon.nl

Prendergast, Jessica, is a senior foresight consultant and project manager at Future Impacts

Raghuraman, Shruti is a Postdoctoral Research Associate in the College of Medicine and Health, University of Exeter, UK

Rampacher, Jörg, is a foresight consultant at Future Impacts, having been a trend and foresight researcher for close to two decades.

Reh, Susan, is a Senior Lecturer in Management at the University of Exeter Business School, UK

Skagert, Katrin, Associate Professor in Education, RISE Research Institutes of Sweden

Starren, Annick, Project Manager, European Agency for Safety and Health at Work (EU-OSHA)
starren@osha.europa.eu

Tischler, Victoria, Associate Professor in Public Health, Sustainability and Environment, University of Exeter, UK
V.Tischler@exeter.ac.uk

Totterdill, Peter,Founding Director, Workplace Innovation Europe CLG, and Visiting Professor at Kingston University, UK
peter.totterdill@workplaceinnovation.eu

Trainor, Mary, Head of Science Quality and Impact, UK Health and Safety Executive, UK
Mary.Trainor@hse.gov.uk

Trigg, Laura is a NIHR pre-doctoral fellow at University of Exeter Medical School, UK

Wadensjö, Eskil, Professor of Economics, Swedish Institute for Social Research, Stockholm University, Sweden

Wallo, Andreas, Associate Professor in Education, Department of Behavioural Sciences and Learning, Linköping University, Sweden

Index

Arbeit, Bildung & Gesellschaft
Labour, Education & Society

Herausgegeben von Prof. Dr. György Széll, Prof. Dr. Heinz Sünker, Dr. Anne Inga Hilsen und Dr. Francesco Garibaldo

Bd. 1 György Széll (ed.): Corporate Social Responsibility in the EU & Japan. 2006.

Bd. 2 Katja Maar: Zum Nutzen und Nichtnutzen der Sozialen Arbeit am exemplarischen Feld der Wohnungslosenhilfe. Eine empirische Studie. 2006.

Bd. 3 Daniela De Ridder: Vom urbanen Sozialraum zur kommunikativen Stadtgesellschaft. 2007.

Bd. 4 Heinz Sünker / Ingrid Miethe (Hrsg.): Bildungspolitik und Bildungsforschung: Herausforderungen und Perspektiven für Gesellschaft und Gewerkschaften in Deutschland. 2007.

Bd. 5 Anja Bastigkeit: Bildungsbiographie und elementarpädagogische Bildungsarbeit. 2007.

Bd. 6 Antônio Inácio Andrioli: Biosoja versus Gensoja. Eine Studie über Technik und Familienlandwirtschaft im nordwestlichen Grenzgebiet des Bundeslandes Rio Grande do Sul (Brasilien). 2007.

Bd. 7 Russell Farnen / Daniel German / Henk Dekker / Christ'l De Landtsheer / Heinz Suenker (eds.): Political Culture, Socialization, Democracy, and Education. Interdisciplinary and Cross-National Perspectives for a New Century. 2008.

Bd. 8 Francesco Garibaldo / Volker Telljohann (eds.): New Forms of Work Organisation and Industrial Relations in Southern Europe. 2007.

Bd. 9 Anne Marie Berg / Olav Eikeland (eds.): Action Research and Organisation Theory. 2008.

Bd. 10 György Széll / Carl-Heinrich Bösling / Ute Széll (eds.): Education, Labour & Science. Perspectives for the 21st Century. 2008.

Bd. 11 Francesco Garibaldo / Philippe Morvannou / Jochen Tholen (eds.): Is China a Risk or an Opportunity for Europe? An Assessment of the Automobile, Steel and Shipbuilding Sectors. 2008.

Bd. 12 Yunus Dauda: Managing Technology Innovation. The Human Resource Management Perspective. 2009.

Bd. 13 Jarmo Lehtonen / Satu Kalliola (eds.): Dialogue in Working Life Research and Development in Finland. 2009.

Bd. 14 György Széll / Werner Kamppeter / Woosik Moon (eds.): European Social Integration – A Model for East Asia? 2009.

Bd. 15 Benedicte Brøgger / Olav Eikeland (eds.): Turning to Practice with Action Research. 2009.

Bd. 16 Till Johannes Hoffmann: Verschwendung. Philosophie, Soziologie und Ökonomie des Überflusses. 2009.

Bd. 17 Denis Harrisson / György Széll / Reynald Bourque (eds.): Social Innovation, the Social Economy and World Economic Development. 2009.

Bd. 18 Werner Weltgen: Total Quality Management als Strukturierungsaufgabe für nachhaltigen Unternehmenswandel. 2009.

Bd. 19 György Széll / Ute Széll (eds.): Quality of Life and Working Life in Comparison. 2009.

Bd. 20 Francesco Garibaldo / Volker Telljohann (eds.): The Ambivalent Character of Participation. New Tendencies in Worker Participation in Europe. 2010.

Bd. 21 Richard Ennals / Robert H. Salomon (eds.): Older Workers in a Sustainable Society. 2011.

Bd. 22 Christoph Sänger: Anna Siemsen – Bildung und Literatur. 2011.

Bd. 23 Nam-Kook Kim: Deliberative Multiculturalism in Britain. A Response to Devolution, European Integration, and Multicultural Challenges. 2011.

Bd. 24 Mirella Baglioni / Bernd Brandl (eds.): Changing Labour Relations. Between Path Dependency and Global Trends. 2011.

Bd. 25 Rüdiger Kühr: Japan`s Transnational Environmental Policies. The Case of Environmental Technology Transfer to Newly Industrializing Countries. 2011.

Bd. 26 Francesco Garibaldo / Dinghong Yi (eds.): Labour and Sustainable Development. North-South Perspectives. 2012.

Bd. 27 Francesco Garibaldo / Mirella Baglioni / Catherine Casey / Volker Telljohann (eds.): Workers, Citizens, Governance. Socio-Cultural Innovation at Work. 2012.

Bd. 28 Simone Selva: Supra-National Integration and Domestic Economic Growth. The United States and Italy in the Western Bloc Rearmament Programs 1945-1955. Translation by Filippo del Lucchese, revision by Simone Selva. 2012.

Bd. 29 György Széll / Roland Czada (Hrsg.): Fukushima. Die Katastrophe und ihre Folgen. 2013.

Bd. 30 Siqi Luo: Collective Bargaining and Changing Industrial Relations in China. Lessons from the U. S. and Germany. 2013.

Bd. 31 Litsa Nicolaou-Smokoviti / Heinz Sünker / Julia Rozanova / Victoria Pekka Economou (eds.): Citizenship and Social Development. Citizen Participation and Community Involvement in Social Welfare and Social Policy. 2013.

Bd. 32 Christ'l De Landtsheer / Russell F. Farnen / Daniel B. German / Henk Dekker / Heinz Sünker / Yingfa Song / Hongna Miao (eds.): E-Political Socialization, the Press and Politics. The Media and Government in the USA, Europe and China. 2014.

Bd. 33 Jukka M. Krisp / Michael Szurawitzki (eds.): Doctoral Experiences in Finland. 2014.

Bd. 34 Dimosthenis Daskalakis: Greek Labour Relations in Transition in a Global Context. 2015.

Bd. 35 Antoanneta Potsi: The Capability Approach and Early Childhood Education Curricula. An Investigation into Teachers' Beliefs and Practices. 2016.

Bd. 36 Juho Kim: Die paradoxe Rolle der Demokratie beim Übergang zum neoliberalen Kapitalismus in Südkorea. Von der Kritik zur Rechtfertigung. 2016.

Bd. 37 György Széll / Dasarath Chetty (eds.): Making Popular Participation Real. African and International Experiences. 2018.

Bd. 38 Kenneth Abrahamsson / Richard Ennals (eds.): Sustainable Work in Europe. Concepts, Conditions, Challenges. 2022.

www.peterlang.com

www.ingramcontent.com/pod-product-compliance
Ingram Content Group UK Ltd.
Pitfield, Milton Keynes, MK11 3LW, UK
UKHW020834290926
15470UKWH00004B/1336

9 783631 873502